£45.00

CW00673887

Handbook of International Film, Television and Video Acronyms

Handbook of International Film, Television and Video Acronyms

Edited by Matthew Stevens

British Library Cataloguing-in-Publication Data

Handbook of International Film, Television and Video Acronyms
I. Stevens, Matthew
791.40148

ISBN 0-948911-23-9

First published in 1993 by

FLICKS BOOKS
29 Bradford Road
Trowbridge
Wiltshire BA14 9AN
England
tel +44 225 767728
fax +44 225 760418

This book is published in the United States and Canada by
Greenwood Press, Westport, CT 06881
an imprint of Greenwood Publishing Group, Inc.
under the title *International Film, Television & Video Acronyms*

Printed and bound in Great Britain

Contents

Acknowledgements

Firstly and most importantly, we would like to thank the very many individuals within organisations and companies worldwide who replied to our persistent questionnaires, letters, faxes and telephone calls. Without this generous response this book would never have seen the light of day.

Others deserve credit, and our grateful thanks. Martine Leroy at the Association des Trois Mondes (ATM) in Paris kindly and quickly provided information on some 50 acronyms of organisations and associations from the African continent. Raissa Fomina of Intercinema Agency in Moscow verified acronyms of Russian organisations. Rafael de España of the Centre for Cinematic Research FILM-HISTÓRIA in Barcelona contributed information on Portuguese and Spanish institutions. Johan Blignaut of Showdata in Cape Town provided valuable entries on South African organisations. John Gainsborough, editor of *Image Technology* at the British Kinematograph Sound and Television Society (BKSTS) in London confirmed various elusive technical terms.

Technical departments of the following manufacturers provided literature as well as help with our queries on specialist terminology: Ace Coin Equipment, Agfa-Gevaert, Aiwa, Akai, Akura, Arri, Bang & Olufson, Blaupunkt, Canon, Dolby, Ferguson, Fuji, Goldstar, Grundig International, Hitachi, JVC, Kodak, Mitsubishi Electric, Nokia Consumer Electronics, Optex, PAG, Panasonic Consumer Electronics, Panavision, Philips, Pioneer Electronic, Samsung, Sanyo, Scala Computer Television, Sharp Electronics, Solid State Logic, Sony Broadcast and Professional, Thomson Broadcast and Toshiba.

Other individuals and companies deserve special mention for their prompt and generous assistance:

Carlos A Arnaldo, Communication Division, UNESCO, Paris
Nicola Baty, Sony Consumer Products Company, UK
Corporation for Public Broadcasting (CPB), Washington
Sue Cullip, BSI, Milton Keynes
Embassy of the Czech Republic, London
Department of Trade and Industry, London
Ann Eliott and Maria Zimmann, A C Nielsen (ACN), New York
Francisco Gaytan, Filmoteca, UNAM, Mexico
Jacques Gibout, MIPCOM, Paris
Philip Hill and Ken Biggins, AGFA-Gevaert, Brentford
Independent Television Commission (ITC), London
Andrea Marcotulli, ANICA, Rome
Mirjam Prenger, SFW-AVA, Amsterdam
Marilyn Sarmiento, BUFVC, London
David Soothill, ABC Radio, Australia
Norshah Thamby, FINAS, Malaysia
Nissi Joanny Traoré, DIPROCI, Ouagadougou
Richard Walsh, Sony Broadcast International, Basingstoke
R M Wasner, AGICOA, Geneva

Much of the research for this book was initiated in libraries and I am grateful for the efficiency and kindness of staff at the following institutions: Bath University Library, Bristol Commercial and Reference Libraries, Bristol University Library, British Film Institute Book Library and Independent Television Commission Book Library.

Matthew Stevens
16 August 1993

Introduction

This book lists over 3400 acronyms and abbreviations in common usage in the broad areas of film, television and video. These comprise two distinct types - organisations, associations, societies and companies (c2000) and technical terms (c1400) - which for ease of reference are grouped together in one alphabetical listing.

Acronyms for organisations/companies are represented on an international basis with 144 countries included. The technical terms - with some obvious exceptions such as SCART and SECAM - cover the English language. Subject categories tend easily to overlap and therefore coverage has been widened to include a substantial number of acronyms originating in the areas of audio, cable, satellite, telecommunications and digital technology, as well as emerging subjects such as laserdisc. Inevitably acronyms also appear from the larger fields of communication and mass media.

The criteria for inclusion are as follows: that the acronym has been created by most, if not all, of the initial letters of the words in the full name. Alternatively, it may have been created by the first two or three initial letters of most of the words; a combination of both is allowed and we have exercised a degree of flexibility in this respect. We have preferred acronyms which are 'autonomous' and therefore almost all companies with names such as "JMA Productions" have been excluded. Similarly the many television stations abbreviated, for example, to "TV1" and "M6", have been overlooked in favour of those without numerals. In addition, examples such as "YLE" (Yleisradio) are considered not to be acronyms, and have been omitted.

The organisations, associations and companies represented include the following:

archives
associations
broadcasting authorities
cable/satellite stations
distributors
educational institutions
festivals/events
finance sources
government bodies and committees

information sources
institutes
libraries
pressure groups
production companies
promotional bodies
societies
television stations

Wherever possible, each entry provides information in the following format:

acronym · country of origin/usage
■ full name(s) or description
address
telephone / fax (numbers are listed with international codes)
telex
founding date □ description of activities/objectives

Acronyms have almost exclusively been capitalised. Head office addresses are included, rather than regional or overseas addresses.

Where identical acronyms exist, they are listed in alphabetical country order, followed by any technical terms.

Where an organisation or company has recently changed its name, merged or been replaced, this is indicated.

Acronyms which appear in other entries are indicated in bold type.

It has been our aim wherever possible to include complete information for each entry and the majority of this book has been compiled by direct questionnaire. However, given the nature of such an enormous task and the difficulties of communication with certain countries, contents of many entries have by necessity been verified with other sources (see **Bibliography**); inevitably certain isolated details remain unknown at the time of going to press.

Additional reference material is provided in the **Indexes**, divided into **Full Name Index**, enabling the reader to locate institutions/companies and technical terms by their complete description; **Country Index**, listing all acronyms from each individual country; and **Subject/Theme Index**, which provides a selective keyword analysis of the activities and interests of the organisations and companies profiled. To our knowledge no previous book has documented in such detail the growing use of acronyms in the moving picture industries. Whilst several books include a glossary of technical terms, none is extensive.   Naturally, we are aware that this book cannot be exhaustive.   We invite additions, revisions and corrections which may be incorporated into further editions.

International
Film, Television and Video
Acronyms

3-D · TECHNICAL TERM
- 3-dimensional

A

A2 · FRANCE
- Société Nationale Antenne 2
22 avenue Montaigne
75008 Paris
tel   +33 1 44 21 42 42
fax +33 1 44 21 51 45
tlx   204068
□ public service television station.

A&E · USA
- Arts and Entertainment Network
9th floor
235 East 45th Street
New York
NY 10017
tel   +1 212 661 4500
fax +1 212 210 9755
1984 □ cable/television station. It
publishes *Arts and Entertainment
Magazine.*

AA · TECHNICAL TERM
- Academy Award®
- audience appreciation
- average audience

AAAA · USA
- Associated Actors and Artistes of
America
Room 500
165 West 46th Street
New York
NY 10036
tel   +1 212 869 0358
fax +1 212 869 1746
1919 □ organisation of 8 performing
arts trade unions: Actors' Equity
Association (**AEA**), American Federation
of Television and Radio Artists (**AFTRA**),
American Guild of Musical Artists
(**AGMA**), American Guild of Variety
Artists (**AGVA**), Hebrew Actors' Union
(**HAU**), Italian Actors Union, Screen
Actors Guild (**SAG**) and Screen Extras
Guild (**SEG**).

AAB · JAPAN

- Akita Asahi Broadcasting Co
233-209 Okawabata
Kawashiri-machi
Akita 010
tel   +81 188 66 5111
□ television station.

AACTO · USA
- American Association of Cable
Television Owners

AAE · TECHNICAL TERM
- automatic assemble editing

AAPTS · USA
- Association of America's Public
Television Stations
see APTS · USA

AAV · BELGIUM
- Assistance Audio-Visuelle
74 Box 2 ave de Woluwé St Lambert
B-1200 Brussels
tel   +32 2 736 5560
fax +32 2 736 5560
1982 □ rental of production, post-
production and reproduction of all
types of audiovisual equipment.

AAV · SWITZERLAND
- Schweizerischer Verband für
Auftragsfilm und Audiovision
- Association Suisse du Film de
Commande et de l'Audiovision (FCA)
Weinbergstr. 31
8006 Zürich
tel   +41 1 262 27 71
fax +41 1 262 29 96
1972 □ group of some 50 leading
Swiss producers of commissioned films
and videos, and commercials. Its main
purpose is to promote high standards
and professionalism in productions. It
organises an annual competition,
supports training efforts, recommends
trade practices and negotiates with
trades unions.

AAVS · FRANCE
- Advanced Audio Visual Systems
220-226 rue de Rosny
93100 Montreuil
tel   +33 1 48 57 21 64
fax +33 1 48 57 33 58

tlx   AVS 233509F
1979 □ specialises in the design and manufacture of analogue and digital equipment, and the engineering and installation of complete fixed and mobile turnkey systems for television and radio.

AB · TECHNICAL TERM
■ announce booth

ABA · AUSTRALIA
■ Australian Broadcasting Authority
PO Box 1308
North Sydney
NSW 2059
tel   +61 2 959 7817
fax   +61 2 954 4328
previously Australian Broadcasting Tribunal (ABT)
1992 □ independent federal statutory authority responsible for the regulation of the Australian broadcasting industry.

ABA · JAPAN
■ Asahi Broadcasting Aomori Co
1 Jusannichi-machi
Hachinohe 031
tel   +81 178 47 2111
□ television station.

ABBS · ANTIGUA AND BARBUDA
■ Antigua and Barbuda Broadcasting Service
PO Box 590
St John's
tel   +1 809 462 0010
fax   +1 809 462 0821
tlx   2090 TELCO AK
1956 □ television and radio station, government-owned and financed by commercial revenue.
also known as ABS

ABC · AUSTRALIA
■ Australian Broadcasting Corporation
GPO Box 9994
Ultimo
NSW 2007
tel   +61 2 333 1500
fax   +61 2 333 5305
tlx   26506
1932 □ radio and television broadcasting regulator, consisting of 4

output divisions - Radio, Television, Radio Australia and Concerts.

ABC · JAPAN
■ Asahi Broadcasting Corporation
2-2-48 Oyodominami
Kita-ku
Osaka 531-01
tel   +81 6 458 5321
□ television station.

ABC · USA
■ American Broadcasting Company
825 Seventh Avenue
New York
NY 1019
tel   +1 212 456 1725
fax   +1 212 456 1708
tlx   234337 ABC WS
1943 □ major television and radio broadcasting company.

ABC · TECHNICAL TERM
■ automatic beam control
■ automatic brightness control

ABCB · AUSTRALIA
■ Australian Broadcasting Control Board

ABE · ITALY
■ Advanced Broadcasting Electronics
ABE Elettronica SpA
Via Galileo Galilei, 1
24043 Caravaggio
tel   +39 363 52550 / 51107
fax   +39 363 50756
tlx   352829 ABETEL I

ABERT · BRAZIL
■ Associção Brasileira de Emissoras de Rádio e Televisão
Mezanino do Hotel Nacional
salas 5 a 8
CP 04280
70322 Brasília, DF
tel   +55 61 224 4600
fax   +55 61 321 7583
tlx   2001
1962 □ broadcasting association operating more than 200 television stations and some 2000 radio stations.

ABEVC · BRAZIL
■ Associação Brasileira das Empresas de

Video Comunicação
□ national association of video companies.

ABL · TECHNICAL TERM
■ automatic black level

ABM · TECHNICAL TERM
■ apogee boost motor

ABMPTP · USA
■ Association of Black Motion Picture and Television Producers

ABN · JAPAN
■ Nagano Asahi Broadcasting Co Ltd
989-1 Kurita
Nagano 380
tel   +81 262 23 1000
□ television station.

ABO · TECHNICAL TERM
■ automatic beam optimiser

ABS · ANTIGUA AND BARBUDA
■ Antigua and Barbuda Broadcasting Service
see **ABBS** · ANTIGUA AND BARBUDA

ABS · ITALY
■ Aquila Broadcasting Sets SpA
Via Colle S Giovanni
67063 Oricola
tel   +39 863 995150 / 995875/7/8
fax   +39 863 995215
tlx   600372 ABSC I
□ designs and manufactures a complete range of transmitter and repeater equipment for television and radio.

ABS · JAPAN
■ Akita Broadcasting System
9-42 Sanno 7-chome
Akita 010
tel   +81 188 24 5151
□ television station.

ABS-TV · NIGERIA
■ Anambra State Television
Enugu
tel   +234 42 337502
□ state-owned television station.

ABT · AUSTRALIA

■ Australian Broadcasting Tribunal
see **ABA** · AUSTRALIA

ABU · MALAYSIA
■ Asia-Pacific Broadcasting Union
PO Box 1164
Pejabat Pos Jalan Pantai Bharu
59700 Kuala Lumpur
tel   +60 3 282 3592
fax   +60 3 282 5292
tlx   MA 32227 (ABU) Kuala Lumpur
1964 □ professional association of broadcasting organisations, established to assist in the development of radio and television in Asia and the Pacific. It is a non-governmental, non-political and non-commercial organisation, with some 83 members in 50 countries. It publishes *ABU News* (6) and *ABU Technical Review* (6).

ABW · UK
■ Association of Black Film and Video Workshops
now incorporated within Black Media UK

AC · TECHNICAL TERM
■ alternating current
■ assistant cameramen

AC-T · TECHNICAL TERM
■ advertising control for television

ACA · FRANCE
■ Association de Créateurs pour l'Audio-Visuel
2 rue Berthe Morisot
78360 Montesson
tel   +33 30 71 10 13
1987 □ association of professionals working in the audiovisual field.

ACATS · USA
■ Advisory Committee on Advanced Television Service
1987 □ committee of the Federal Communications Commission (**FCC**), advising on **HDTV**.

ACBB · USA
■ American Council for Better Broadcasts

ACC · TECHNICAL TERM
- automatic chroma/chrominance/colour/contour/contrast control

ACCFT · AUSTRALIA
- Australian Council for Children's Films and Television
PO Box 129
Daw Park
SA 5041
tel +61 8 374 0260
fax +61 8 374 0453
1957 □ national non-profit community organisation and coordinating body for all affiliated State and Territory Councils for Children's Film and Television. It aims to stimulate and maintain public interest in the provision of quality entertainment film, television and videotape programmes for children and young Australians. It publishes *Small Screen* (12).

ACCO · COLOMBIA
- Asociación de Cinematográficas Colombianas
Calle 77
No 15-09
Bogota
□ association of Colombian cinematography.

ACE · USA
- American Cinema Editors Inc.
1041 N Formosa Avenue
West Hollywood
CA 90046
tel +1 213 850 2900
fax +1 213 850 2922
1950 □ association of professional editors working in the film and television industries.

ACE · USA
- Award for Cablecasting Excellence
National Academy of Cable Programming (NACP)
1724 Massachusetts Avenue NW
Washington
DC 20036
tel +1 202 775 3611
fax +1 202 775 3689
□ annual award presented by NCAP for achievement in the cable industry.

ACE · TECHNICAL TERM
- advanced conversion equipment
- annular control electrode
- attitude control electronics

ACEC · ITALY
- Associazione Cattolica Esercenti Cinema
Via Nomentana 251
00161 Rome
tel +39 6 44 02 280
fax +39 6 44 02 273
□ Catholic association of cinema exhibitors.

ACES · TECHNICAL TERM
- automated camera effects system

ACF · TECHNICAL TERM
- auto chase focus

ACFC · CANADA
- Association of Canadian Film Craftspeople
Suite 105
65 Heward Avenue
Toronto
Ontario M4M 2T5
tel +1 416 462 0211
fax +1 416 462 3248
□ independent union whose members form a resource of film technicians throughout Canada.

ACFEA · FRANCE
- Association pour la Création Française et Européenne dans l'Audiovisuel

ACG · GABON
- Association des Cinéastes Gabonais
BP 1647
Libreville
tel +241 730906
□ professional organisation established to defend its members' interests and to promote African cinema.

ACI · TECHNICAL TERM
- adjacent channel interference

ACIC · FRANCE
- Amicale des Cadres de l'Industrie Cinématographique

9 rue St-Pierre
92200 Neuilly
tel +33 47 45 80 10
□ association of cinematographic
industry personnel.

ACLB · UK
■ Association of Christians in Local
Broadcasting
PO Box 124
Westcliff-on-Sea
Essex SS0 OQU
tel +44 702 348369
fax +44 702 348369
1980 □ association of Christians
interested in local television or radio,
funded by the Churches Advisory
Council for Local Broadcasting
(**CACLB**). It organises an annual
broadcasting conference/exhibition, a
video/cable television consultation, and
the Andrew Cross Awards for local
religious broadcasting. It also publishes
a list of radio training courses and a
special publication on community
radio, and the magazine *Crosstalk* (4).

ACLE · TECHNICAL TERM
■ analogue component link equipment

ACN · USA
■ A C Nielsen Company
1290 Avenue of the Americas
New York
NY 10104
tel +1 212 708 7500
fax +1 212 708 7795
1950 □ provides the industry standard
for buying, selling, planning and
programming national television.
Nielsen provides tools in a
comprehensive form covering every
facet of television audience
measurement continually throughout
the year and with fast availability.

ACN · USA
■ American Cable Network, Inc
□ cable television network.

ACOCINE · COLOMBIA
■ Asociación Colombiana de
Distribudores y Exhibidores de Cine
Calle 56 No 13-36

Bogota
□ association of Colombian film
distributors and exhibitors.

ACON · TECHNICAL TERM
■ auto-convergence alignment system

ACP · TECHNICAL TERM
■ auto channel programming

ACPC · SPAIN
■ Agrupació Catalana de Productors
Cinematogràfics
Castanyer, 31 Baixos
08022 Barcelona
tel +34 3 212 5508
fax +34 3 418 6984
□ group of Catalan film producers.

ACPCA · FRANCE
■ Association Cinématographique
Professionnelle de Conciliation et
d'Arbitrage
43 Boulevard Malesherbes
75008 Paris
tel +33 1 42 66 09 20
fax +33 1 42 66 96 92
1975 □ its members are the Fédération
Internationale des Associations de
Distributeurs de Films (**FIAD**) and the
Fédération Internationale des
Associations de Producteurs de Films
(**FIAPF**). Its aim is to act as a
conciliation service in order to resolve
disputes among parties in the film
industry.

ACPFT · CANADA
■ Association Canadienne de
Production de Film et Télévision
■ Canadian Film and Television
Production Association (CFTPA)
Suite 806
175 Bloor Street E
North Tower
Toronto
Ontario M4W 3R8
tel +1 416 927 8942
fax +1 416 922 4038
□ association representing some 300
companies involved in independent
production in Canada. Membership is
open to any entrepreneurial Canadian
corporation, partnership, association, or

other organisation engaged in film, television, video production, distribution, or in the provision of facilities or services to the independent production industry. It promotes the wider interests of the Canadian independent film and television industry by lobbying government on policy matters, negotiating labour agreements on behalf of independent producers, offering educational programmes and by publishing. It publishes *Action* (4) and *The Guide* (1).

ACR · TECHNICAL TERM
■ audio cassette recorder

ACRIF · FRANCE
■ Association des Cinémas de Recherche de l'Ile-de-France

ACRIRA · SWITZERLAND
■ Association - Française - des Cinémas de Recherche Indépendants de la Région Alpine

ACS · SENEGAL
■ Association des Cinéastes Sénégalais
see **CINESEAS** · SENEGAL

ACS · SWITZERLAND
■ Association Cinématographique Suisse
also known as Association Cinématographique Suisse Romande (ACSR)
see **SKV** · SWITZERLAND

ACS · TECHNICAL TERM
■ active communications satellite
■ advanced charging system
■ attitude control system

ACSN · USA
■ American Community Service Network
Suite 750
1 Thomas Circle
Washington
DC 20005
tel   +1 202 457 5353
fax   +1 202 457 5381
□ provides programmes to cable television networks.

ACSN · USA
■ Appalachian Community Service Network

ACSR · SWITZERLAND
■ Association Cinématographique Suisse Romande
also known as Association Cinématographique Suisse (ACS)
see **SKV** · SWITZERLAND

ACT · ITALY
■ Association of Commercial Television in Europe
■ Association des Télévisions Commerciales Européennes
via Paleocapa, 3
20121 Milan
tel   +39 2 85 41 43 60 / 1
fax   +39 2 85 41 42 72
tlx   320609 FINCOM I
1989 □ promoting cooperation between its members and with the companies active in the field of communication in Europe.

ACT · USA
■ Action for Children's Television
20 University Road
Cambridge
MA 02138
tel   +1 617 876 6620
1971 □ group which is campaigning for quality television for children and for the removal of commercials in children's programming.

ACT · USA
■ American Citizens' Television Committee, Inc

ACT · USA
■ Association for Competitive Television

ACT · TECHNICAL TERM
■ advanced circuit technology
■ anti comet-tail

ACTA · ITALY
■ Attività Cinetelevisive, Audio, Distribuzione Film
Via Monte Zebio 28
00195 Rome

□ television, film, and audio activities and film distribution.

ACTAC · AUSTRALIA
■ Australian Children's Television Action Committee

ACTC · CANADA
■ Association Canadienne de Télévision par Câble
Bureau 1010
360 rue Albert
Ottawa
Ontario K1R 7X7
tel   +1 613 232 2631
fax +1 613 232 2137
□ promotes the distribution of television by cable.

ACTF · AUSTRALIA
■ Australian Children's Television Foundation
199 Grattan Street
Carlton
VIC 3053
tel   +61 3 348 1144
fax +61 3 347 4194
tlx   AA151378 KIDSTV
1982 □ to encourage the development, production and transmission of high quality children's television programmes. It publishes *Care for Kids Television News* (4).

ACTING · PORTUGAL
■ Actors Training to Improve New Generation
c/o Small Countries Improve their Audiovisual Level in Europe (SCALE)
Rua D João V, 8-R/C Dto.
1200 Lisbon
tel   +351 1 386 0630 / 0982
fax +351 1 386 0647
1993 □ an initiative of **MEDIA**, this programme is devoted to the professional training and promotion of actors in "small" EC countries.

ACTRA · CANADA
■ Alliance of Canadian Cinema, Television and Radio Artists
2239 Yonge Street
Toronto
Ontario M4S 2B5

tel   +1 416 489 1311
fax +1 416 489 1435
1963 □ group which represents approximately 10 000 actors, writers and journalists working in the recorded media, maintaining international affiliations with other unions and guilds within the industry. It publishes a *Talent Directory*.

ACTRF · CANADA
■ Association Canadienne de la Radio et de la Télévision de Langue Française Inc
3631 rue Saint-Denis
Montreal
Quebec H2X 3L6
tel   +1 514 923 5455
fax +1 514 499 5283

ACTRS · USA
■ Association of Catholic Television and Radio Syndicators

ACTS · USA
■ All-Channel Television Society

ACTS · USA
■ American Christian Television System

ACTS · USA
■ Association of Cable Television Suppliers

ACTS · TECHNICAL TERM
■ advanced communications technology satellite

ACTT · UK
■ Association of Cinematograph, Television and Allied Technicians
see **BECTU** · UK

ACTV · TECHNICAL TERM
■ advanced compatible television

ACUBS · USA
■ Association of College and University Broadcasting Stations

ACVL · USA
■ Association of Cinema and Video Laboratories, Inc

A/D · TECHNICAL TERM
- analogue to digital

AD · TECHNICAL TERM
- art/assistant/associate director

ADAC · TECHNICAL TERM
- advanced digital adaption converter

ADACOM · FRANCE
- Association pour le Développement de l'Audio-Visuel et du Court Métrage
□ association for the development of the audiovisual and the short film.

ADAM™ · TECHNICAL TERM
- Acrodyne's digital amplitude modulation

ADAPT · UK
- Access for Disabled People to Arts Premises Today
Cameron House
Abbey Park Place
Dunfermline
Fife KY12 7PZ
tel   +44 383 623166
fax   +44 383 622149
1989 □ charity whose aim is to provide matching funds to primary arts venues, not in the commercial or public sector, which are attempting to improve their accessibility for disabled people.

ADC · TECHNICAL TERM
- analogue-to-digital convertor/coding

ADCCP · TECHNICAL TERM
- advanced data communications control

ADETE · FRANCE
- Agence Française pour le Développement de la Télévision en Arabie Séoudite
□ French agency for the development of television in Saudi Arabia.

ADI · TECHNICAL TERM
- area of dominant influence

ADICAN · SPAIN
- Asociación de Distribuidores y Importadores Cinematográficos de

Ambito Nacional
Blanca de Navarra 7
28010 Madrid
tel   +34 1 308 0120
fax   +34 1 319 0036
tlx   48999 ADIC
1977 □ theatrical distributors covering the whole of Spain.

ADICIEL · FRANCE
- Association pour la Diffusion du Cinéma d'Expression Latine
□ promotes screenings of Latin American cinema.

ADISQ · CANADA
- Association Québécoise de l'Industrie du Disque, du Spectacle et de la Vidéo
Bureau 706
3575 Boulevard Saint-Laurent
Montreal
Quebec H2X 2T7
tel   +1 514 842 5147
fax   +1 514 842 7762

ADIVAN · SPAIN
- Asociación de Distribuidores y Importadores Videográficos de Ambito Nacional

ADM · TECHNICAL TERM
- adaptive delta modulation

ADO™ · TECHNICAL TERM
- amplex digital optics

ADPCM · TECHNICAL TERM
- adaptive delta/differential pulse code modulation

ADR · TECHNICAL TERM
- additional/automatic dialogue replacement

ADRC · CANADA
- Association du Droit de Retransmission Canadien
see CRRA · CANADA

ADRC · FRANCE
- Agence pour le Développement Régional du Cinéma
104 rue de Cambrai
59000 Lille

tel +33 20 52 44 34
□ committed to the development of cinema throughout France.

ADS · TECHNICAL TERM
▪ automatic dependent surveillance

ADTV · TECHNICAL TERM
▪ advanced digital television

AE · TECHNICAL TERM
▪ auto(matic) exposure

AEA · USA
▪ Actors' Equity Association
165 West 46th Street
New York
NY 10036
tel +1 212 869 8530
fax +1 212 719 9815
1913 □ union which represents some 30 000 professional actors and actresses.

AEEMA · BELGIUM
▪ Association Européenne pour l'Education aux Médias Audiovisuels
□ educational organisation in the audiovisual media field.

AEEU-EETPU · UK
▪ Amalgamated Engineering and Electrical Union - Electrical and Electronic Telecommunication and Plumbing Union Division
Hayes Court
West Common Road
Bromley
Kent BR2 7AU
tel +44 81 462 7755
fax +44 81 462 4959
1968 □ trade union which represents members, including many employed in the film, television and telecomm-unications industries. It publishes *Contact* (4-6) and a *Yearbook*.

AEF · TECHNICAL TERM
▪ apogee engine firing
▪ automatic editing function

AEFA · BELGIUM
▪ Association Européenne du Film d'Animation

see **EAFF** · BELGIUM

AEG · USA
▪ Atlantic Entertainment Group
□ film distributors.

AEJMC · USA
▪ Association for Education in Journalism and Mass Communications
College of Journalism
1621 College Street
University of South Carolina
Columbia
SC 29208-0251
tel +1 803 777 2005
fax +1 803 777 4728

AERT · USA
▪ Association for Education by Radio-Television

AES · USA
▪ Audio Engineering Society
Room 2520
60 East 42nd Street
New York
NY 10165
tel +1 212 661 8528
fax +1 212 682 0477
1948 □ association of audio engineers, technicians and others who are involved in the design and operation of reproducing and recording equipment for film, television and radio.

AETC · SWITZERLAND
▪ Alliance Europe pour la TV et la Culture
c/o UER
Ancienne Route 17A
Case Postale 67
1218 Geneva
also known as European Alliance for Television and Culture (EATC)

AF · TECHNICAL TERM
▪ audio follow

AFA · USA
▪ Actors' Fund of America

AFBA · USA
▪ Armed Forces Broadcasters Association

AFC · AUSTRALIA
- Australian Film Commission
8 West Street
North Sydney
NSW 2060
tel +61 2 951 6444
fax +61 2 959 5403
tlx AA25157 FICOM
1975 ☐ federal statutory authority
which invests in the development of
Australian film and television
programmes. It also represents and
provides facilities for the Australian
industry at major markets and
coordinates entries to international film
festivals, undertakes research and
information activities, assists various
cultural activities and provides policy
advice to government. It publishes *AFC
News* (12), an Annual National
Production Survey, irregular reports and
information sheets and *Get the Picture*,
bi-annual statistics on film and
television.

AFC · FRANCE
- Association Française des Directeurs
de la Photographie Cinématographique
16 rue Saint-Ferdinand
75017 Paris
tel +33 1 40 68 99 56
fax +33 1 40 68 99 56
1990 ☐ represents its members'
professional interests and aims to
enhance the profession's influence in
the film business and to improve the
working conditions which guarantee
artistic and creative output. It publishes
Les Cahiers de l'AFC (2) and *La Lettre
de l'AFC* (12).

AFC · TECHNICAL TERM
- assistant film cameraman
- automatic (fine) frequency control

AFCA · FRANCE
- Association Française du Cinéma
d'Animation

AFCAB · FRANCE
- Association pour le Festival de
Cinéma d'Animation de Baillargues
49 rue des Ecoles
34670 Baillargues

tel +33 67 87 33 05
fax +33 67 70 84 06
1984 ☐ annual festival of animated
films (short and long) worldwide.

AFCAE · FRANCE
- Association Française des Cinémas
d'Art-et-Essai
22 rue d'Artois
75008 Paris
tel +33 1 45 61 16 15
☐ national group of art-house cinemas.

AFCBS · AUSTRALIA
- Australian Federation of Commercial
Broadcasting Stations

AFCF · USA
- Anthropology Film Center Foundation

AFCI
- Association of Film Commissioners
International

AFDAS · FRANCE
- Fonds d'Assurance Formation des
Activités du Spectacle et de l'Audio-
Visuel
20 rue Fortunay
75858 Paris
tel +33 1 42 27 95 93
1972 ☐ insurance fund for the
formation of theatre and audiovisual
activities.

AFF · GERMANY
- Aktion Funk und Fernsehen
Postfach 96 01 29
51085 Cologne
tel +49 7252 2491
fax +49 7252 80232

AFFC · AUSTRALIA
- Australian Film Finance Commission

AFFC · AUSTRALIA
- Australian Film Finance Corporation
see **FFC** · AUSTRALIA

AFFM · AUSTRALIA
- Australian Film Fund Management

AFI · AUSTRALIA
- Australian Film Institute

Research and Information Centre
49 Eastern Road
South Melbourne
VIC 3205
tel   +61 3 696 1844
fax +61 3 696 7972
□ library, with member access; offers
fee-based research and data collection
services to the public. It publishes
Cinedossier (52), *AFI Newsletter* (4), as
well as a quarterly series of
monographs, *The Moving Image.*

AFI · USA
▪ American Film Institute
2021 N Western Avenue
Los Angeles
CA 90027
tel   +1 213 856 7600
fax +1 213 467 4578
1967 □ national trust dedicated to
preserving the heritage of film and
television; to identifying, developing
and training creative individuals; and to
preserving the moving image as an art
form. It publishes *Dialogue* (4).

AFICCA · FRANCE
▪ Association pour la Fondation
Internationale du Cinéma et de la
Communication Audiovisuelle
1 bis avenue du Roi Albert
06400 Cannes
tel   +33 93 94 07 77
fax +33 93 43 88 95
1987 □ information and library centre
about the cinema and audiovisual
communication. It publishes *Script*
magazine (4).

AFIFF · FRANCE
▪ Association du Festival International
de Films de Femmes
Maison des Arts
Place Salvador Allende
94000 Créteil
tel   +33 49 80 38 98 / 49 80 90 50
fax +33 43 99 04 10
tlx 231211
1978 □ film festival which aims to
discover and promote women directors
worldwide. It is an international
meeting place for women working in
the film industry. Each year some 40

female directors attend the festival to
present their work to an audience of
more than 35 000 and meet
professionals from all over the world.

AFIT · FRANCE
▪ Agence Francophone d'Images et de
Télévision
see **AITV** · FRANCE

AFM · USA
▪ American Film Market
12424 Wilshire Boulevard
Suite 600
Los Angeles
CA 90025
tel   +1 310 447 1555
fax +1 310 447 1666
1981 □ the AFM is held annually in
Los Angeles in late February and is one
of the largest and most successful film
markets in the world, attracting
approximately 10 000 producers,
international and domestic distributors
and film buyers, film commissioners
and government officials from some 65
countries and all 50 states.

AFM · TECHNICAL TERM
▪ assistant floor manager

AFMA · USA
▪ American Film Marketing Association
12424 Wilshire Boulevard
Suite 600
Los Angeles
CA 90025
tel   +1 310 447 1555
fax +1 310 447 1666
1980 □ association which has as its
members 115 independent film
production/distribution companies. It
has 2 important functions: to create
services and lobbying efforts that will
facilitate its members' business
worldwide and to stage the American
Film Market (**AFM**). It publishes a
Newsletter (4).

AFN · THE NETHERLANDS
▪ Audiovisuele Federatie Nederlands

AFN · USA
▪ Armed Forces Network

□ television and radio service mainly for American service men and women.

AFNOR · FRANCE
■ Association Française de Normalisation

AFOMAV · FRANCE
■ Association pour la Formation aux Métiers de l'Audio-Visuel
20 rue de Châtillon
75014 Paris
tel +33 1 45 41 24 42
fax +33 1 45 41 35 06
□ association for instruction in audiovisual professions.

AFP · TECHNICAL TERM
■ anti-flicker processor
■ axial front projection

AFPF · FRANCE
■ Association Française des Producteurs de Films et de Programmes Audiovisuels
50 avenue Marceau
75008 Paris
tel +33 1 47 23 70 30
fax +33 1 47 20 78 17
1972 □ defence and promotion of French film producers.

AFR · TECHNICAL TERM
■ assistant film recordist

AFRHC · FRANCE
■ Association Française de Recherche sur l'Histoire du Cinéma
15 rue Lakanal
75015 Paris
tel +33 1 48 28 60 10
1984 □ to promote and coordinate research into the history of the cinema and to liaise with institutes, libraries, film theatres, universities etc.; to publish information and studies of French research into film history; to establish working relations with similar associations abroad. It publishes the magazine *1895* (2/3).

AFRTS · USA
■ Armed Forces Radio and Television Service

10888 La Tuna Canyon Road
Sun Valley
CA 91352
tel +1 818 504 1208
tlx 6831327
1942 □ television and radio service which aims to entertain and inform US military personnel and their families stationed worldwide. It operates 800 radio and television outlets in 120 countries.
also known as Armed Forces Television Service (AFTS)

AFT · TECHNICAL TERM
■ automatic fine tuning

AFTC · SOUTH AFRICA
■ African Film and Television Collective
PO Box 11065
Johannesburg 2000
tel +27 11 402 4570
1992 □ to promote the development of black film and video production.

AFTRA · USA
■ American Federation of Television and Radio Artists
260 Madison Avenue
New York
NY 10017
tel +1 212 532 0800
fax +1 212 532 2242
1937 □ union which also publishes *AFTRA Magazine* (4).

AFTRS · AUSTRALIA
■ Australian Film, Television and Radio School
Cnr. Epping and Balaclava Roads
PO Box 126
North Ryde
NSW 2113
tel +61 2 805 6611
fax +61 2 887 1030
previously Australian Film and Television School (AFTS)
1973 □ national centre for professional training in film, television and radio production. It publishes *Media Information Australia* (4) and the *AFTRS Student Handbook* (1).

AFTS · AUSTRALIA

- Australian Film and Television School
see AFTRS · AUSTRALIA

AFTS · USA
- Armed Forces Television Service
see AFRTS · USA

AFTS · TECHNICAL TERM
- airborne flight test system

AFV · TECHNICAL TERM
- audio follow(s) video

AFVA · USA
- American Film and Video Association
8050 Milwaukee Avenue
PO Box 48659
Niles
IL 60714
tel   +1 708 698 6440
fax   +1 708 823 1561
1943 □ to encourage and promote the use, production and distribution of films, videos and other visual media of the highest quality to schools, libraries etc. It also organises the annual American Film and Video Festival. It publishes *Sightlines* (6), *AFVA Bulletin* (6) and *AFVA Evaluations* (1).

AFVM · UK
- Amateur Film & Video Maker
33 Gassiot Way
Sutton
Surrey SM1 3AZ
tel   +44 81 644 0839
fax   +44 81 644 0839
1932 □ bi-monthly magazine of the Institute of Amateur Cinematographers (**IAC**), a non-profit making society dedicated to the art of amateur video and film-making.

AFVPA · UK
- Advertising Film and Videotape Producers' Association
26 Noel Street
London W1V 3RD
tel   +44 71 434 2651
fax   +44 71 434 9002
1984 □ represents the interests of advertising film producers and formally represents all the major production companies involved in the making of

television commercials. It provides an advisory service in all matters relating to production, including copyright, legal and employment practices.

AFYVE · SPAIN
- Asociación Fonográfica y Videográfica Española
Pedro Muguruza 8, entreplanta izda
Calle Saturno 10
28036 Madrid
tel   +34 1 345 4154
fax   +34 1 345 6674
□ association which specialises in intellectual property.

AGC · TECHNICAL TERM
- automatic gain control

AGFA-Gevaert · BELGIUM/GERMANY
- Actiengesellschaft für Anilin-Fabrikation-Gevaert
AGFA-Gevaert nv
Septestraat 27
2640 Mortsel
tel   +323 444 2111
fax   +323 444 7094
or AGFA-Gevaert AG
Werk Leverkusen
Postfach 100160
51301 Leverkusen
tel   +49 214 301
fax   +49 214 04990
1867 □ manufacturers of photographic and electronic imaging systems and materials.

AGICOA · SWITZERLAND
- Association de Gestion Internationale Collective des Œuvres Audiovisuelles
26 rue de Saint-Jean
1203 Geneva
tel   +41 22 340 3200
fax   +41 22 340 3432
1981 □ to defend the producers' copyrights whenever collective management of rights is required, in particular as far as simultaneous retransmission by cable is concerned.

AGIS · ITALY
- Associazione Generale Italiana dello Spettacolo
Via di Villa Patrizi 10

00161 Rome
tel   +39 6 4402704
fax   +39 6 4404257
1947 □ general Italian show business
association which publishes *Giornale
dello Spettacolo* and *Notizia di
Spettacolo.*

AGMA · USA
▪ American Guild of Musical Artists
1727 Broadway
New York
NY 10019
tel   +1 212 265 3687
fax   +1 212 262 9088
□ union.

AGS · TECHNICAL TERM
▪ animated graphics system

AGVA · USA
▪ American Guild of Variety Artists
184 Fifth Avenue
New York
NY 10010
tel   +1 212 675 1003
fax   +1 212 633 0097
□ union.

AI · TECHNICAL TERM
▪ appreciation index
▪ artificial intelligence

AIACE · ITALY
▪ Associazione Italiana Amici del
Cinema d'Essai
Via Gaeta 23
00186 Rome
tel   +39 6 474 0905 / 481 4959
□ association of friends of experimental
film-making.

AIBD · MALAYSIA
▪ Asia-Pacific Institute for Broadcasting
Development
PO Box 1137
Jalan Pantai Baru
Kuala Lumpur 59200
tel   +60 3 274 4046
fax   +60 3 274 0761
tlx   APBRO MA30083
1977 □ organisation which aims to
assist members in developing television
and radio broadcasting systems and

personnel. It publishes *Broadcaster* (4).

AIC · ITALY
▪ Associazione Italiana Autori della
Fotografia
Via Tuscolana 1055
00178 Rome
tel   +39 6 7229 3289
fax   +39 6 7222 155
1950 □ promotes the development of
cinematography as a medium of
communication and as a language of
art, and the history of photography in
film, studying the different personalities
of the masters of that art form.

AIC · UK
▪ Association of Independent Cinemas
*now incorporated within Cinema
Exhibitors Association (CEA)*

AICC · ITALY
▪ Associazione Italiana Cultura
Cinematografica
Via Villa Albani 8
00198 Rome
tel   +39 6 84 42 589
□ association for film culture.

AICCA · ITALY
▪ Associazione Internazionale del
Cinema Comico d'Arte
Casella Postale 6306
00195 Rome
tel   +39 6 3700 266
fax   +39 6 3120 68
1959 □ international association of
comic cinema.

AICE · USA
▪ Association of Independent
Commercial Editors

AICP · ITALY
▪ Associazione Italiana Cineoperatori
Professionisti
□ association of professional cinema
operators.

AICP · USA
▪ Association of Independent
Commercial Producers, Inc
5th floor
136 West 21st Street

New York
NY 10011
tel +1 212 675 0125
fax +1 212 675 0370
□ trade association.

AID · BELGIUM
■ Alliance Internationale de la
Distribution par Câble
see **ECCA** · BELGIUM

AIDAA · BELGIUM
■ Association Internationale des Auteurs
de l'Audiovisuel
29 avenue Jeanne
1050 Brussels
tel +32 2 646 3346
fax +32 2 646 3666
□ international association of
audiovisual authors.

AIDAC · ITALY
■ Associazione Italiana Dialoghisti
Adattatori Cinetelevisivi
Via Goito 39
00185 Rome
tel +39 6 447 00191
fax +39 6 447 00208
1976 □ to protect the moral and
economic interests of its members; to
urge new and more adequate forms of
welfare and social security and watch
over their correct application; to
promote and/or support all technical,
juridical, cultural and social enterprises
relevant to its category; to carry out any
other activity necessary to achieve its
aims. It publishes *AIDAC Gazette -
Produzione e Cultura* (4) with the
National Writers Syndicat (SNS).

AIERI · THE NETHERLANDS
■ Association Internationale des Etudes
et Recherches sur l'Information
see **IAMCR** · THE NETHERLANDS

AIFVA · CANADA
■ Atlantic Independent Film and Video
Association
Suite 32
5211 Blowers Street
Halifax
Nova Scotia B3J 1J6
tel +1 902 425 0124

AILS · ITALY
■ Associazione Italiana Lavoratori
Spettacolo
□ association of workers in show
business.

AIM · UK
■ All-Industry Marketing for Cinema
22 Golden Square
London W1R 3PA
tel +44 71 437 4383
fax +44 71 734 0912
□ to promote cinema as the best place
to see a film; to provide a forum for
promotional proposals from inside and
outside the industry; to undertake
specific industry promotional events; to
support film education and awareness
of young future cinema-goers and to
supply educational material in support
of media studies.

AIM · USA
■ Accuracy in Media, Inc
Suite 330
4455 Connecticut Avenue NW
Washington
DC 20008
tel +1 202 364 4401
fax +1 202 364 4098
1969 □ organisation which monitors
news media on a nationwide basis.

AIMC · ITALY
■ Associazione Italiana Maestranze
Cinematografiche
Via Niso 35/37
00181 Rome
tel +39 6 79 43 714
fax +39 6 79 83 550
□ association of show business
employees.

AIMS · USA
■ Association of Independent
Metropolitan Stations

AIPV · SPAIN
■ Asociación Independiente de
Productores Vascos
(Independent Basque Film Producers
Association)
Republica Argentina 2
Teatro Victoria Eugenia

20004 San Sebastián
tel   +34 43 422944
fax +34 43 428782
1984 □ brings together independent
companies with a view to contributing
to the development and consolidation
of film and audiovisual productions in
the Basque country.

AIR · URUGUAY
■ Asociación Internacional de
Radiodifusión
■ Association Internationale de
Radiodiffusion
■ International Association of
Broadcasting (IAB)
Calle Yí
1264 Montevideo
tel   +598 2 488121/9
fax +598 2 488121
tlx   31173
1946 □ organisation with some 100
international members who are mainly
television and radio companies and
organisations. Its primary objective is to
defend the right to freedom of
expression in the broadcasting media. It
produces *La Gaceta de AIR* (6), as well
as other publications.

AISCA · ITALY
■ Associazione Italiana Studi
Cineaudiovisivi
□ association of sound and film studios.

AIT · USA
■ Agency for Instructional Television
1973

AIT · TECHNICAL TERM
■ assembly, integration and test

AITC · ITALY
■ Associazione Italiana
Telecineoperatori
□ association of film and television
operators.

AITS · ITALY
■ Associazione Italiana Tecnici del
Suono
□ association of sound technicians.

AITS · USA

■ Association of Independent Television
Stations, Inc.
Suite 502
1200 18th Street NW
Washington
DC 20036
tel   +1 202 887 1970
fax +1 202 887 0950

AITV · FRANCE
■ Agence Internationale d'Images TV de
RFO
Radio Télévision Française d'Outre-Mer
5 avenue du Recteur Poincaré
75016 Paris
tel   +33 1 45 24 71 00
fax +33 1 42 24 95 96
tlx   648 450
□ RFO's international television picture
agency, whose editorial staff and
satellite links serve some 100 television
stations through 78 African, Asian,
Middle Eastern, Latin American and
Eastern European countries. It offers a
host of material from French channels
as well as material created by its own
production teams.
*also known as Agence Francophone
d'Images et de Télévision (AFIT)*

AIV · TECHNICAL TERM
■ advanced interactive video

AIVAC · SWITZERLAND
■ Association Internationale pour la
Vidéo dans les Arts et la Culture
Via Varenna 45
6600 Locarno
tel   +41 93 312210
tlx   846040
□ international association for the use
of video in arts and culture.

AIVF · USA
■ Association for Independent Video
and Film-Makers
9th floor
625 Broadway
New York
NY 10012
tel   +1 212 473 3400
fax +1 212 677 8732
1974 □ national service organisation
for independent media producers, with

over 5000 members. It creates public awareness of independent media and is a leading advocate for independents' access to public television and cable systems, as well as to theatres, museums, art galleries and community centres across the USA. It publishes *The Independent Film and Video Monthly* (10).

AKM · GERMANY
▪ Arbeitsgruppe Kommunikations-forschung München
Adalbertstr. 104
80798 Munich
tel   +49 89 271 2595

AKM · TECHNICAL TERM
▪ apogee kick motor

AKT · JAPAN
▪ Akita Television Co Ltd
2-14 Yabase-Honcho 3-chome
Akita 010
tel   +81 188 24 4141
▢ television station.

AL-GA-AS · TECHNICAL TERM
▪ Aluminium-Gallium Arsenide

ALAI · FRANCE
▪ Association Littéraire et Artistique Internationale

ALC · TECHNICAL TERM
▪ automatic lamp changer
▪ automatic level control

ALF · TECHNICAL TERM
▪ annual licence fee

ALPA · FRANCE
▪ Association de Lutte Contre la Piraterie Audiovisuelle
9 rue Marignan
75008 Paris
tel   +33 1 42 89 16 65
fax +33 1 42 56 52 64
1985 ▢ association which defends its members against copyright theft.

ALTO · UK
▪ Association of Local TV Operators
13 Bellevue Place

Edinburgh EH7 4BS
tel   +44 31 557 8610
fax +44 31 557 8608
1989 ▢ to provide a forum for small scale local television operators in Scotland, and to link with a similar organisation in Europe.

AM · TECHNICAL TERM
▪ amplitude modulation

AMC · BELGIUM
▪ Artists and Music Consultants
AMC Média Diffusion
412 avenue de Tervuren
1150 Brussels
tel   +32 2 771 6440
fax +32 2 762 4828
▢ producer of television programmes; specialised press; advertising campaign.

AMC · USA
▪ American Movie Classics
150 Crossway Park West
Woodbury
NY 11797
tel   +1 516 364 2222
▢ satellite television broadcaster.

AMC · USA
▪ American Multi Cinema

AME · UK
▪ Association for Media Education in England
Jeannette Ayton
Bretton Hall College
West Bretton
Wakefield
West Yorks WF4 4LG
tel   +44 924 830261
fax +44 924 830521
1991 ▢ to promote media education at all levels; to stimulate links with and between existing media networks; to provide a forum for the dissemination of effective ideas and practice. The association is open to anyone involved or interested in media education across all age groups and including media professionals and cultural workers. It publishes a *Newsletter* (2/3), and distributes *In the Picture* and *Media Education* magazines to members. It

holds an annual conference and administers the Chrisi Bailey Memorial Award for photographic education with younger children.

AMES · UK
- Association for Media Education in Scotland
c/o Scottish Film Council
Dowanhill
74 Victoria Crescent Road
Glasgow G12 9JN
tel   +44 41 334 4445
fax +44 41 334 8132

AMF · TECHNICAL TERM
- apogee motor firing

AMFI · MEXICO
- Asociación Mexicana de Filmadoras
José Ma. Ibarrarán, 31
Col. Sn. José Insurgentes
Mexico, D.F. 03900
tel   +52 5 651 5088

AMFIT · UK
- Association for Media, Film and Television Studies in Further and Higher Education
c/o Phillip Drummond
Dept. of English/Media Studies
University of London
Institute of Education
20 Bedford Way
London WC1H OAL
1989 □ group of some 150 members which aims to serve as a representative and professional association for researchers and teachers in higher and further education.

AMI · FRANCE
- Audiovisuel Multimedia International
116 bis Avenue des Champs-Elysées
75008 Paris
tel   +33 1 42 25 16 45
fax +33 1 42 25 42 26
tlx   648549
□ film and television programme distributors.

AMI · TECHNICAL TERM
- alternate-mark-inversion

AMIA · USA
- Association of Moving Image Archives

AML · TECHNICAL TERM
- amplitude modulated link

AMOL · USA
- Automated Measurement of Line-Up
Nielsen Media Research
1290 Avenue of the Americas
New York
NY 10104
tel   +1 212 708 7500
fax +1 212 708 7795
□ Nielsen-developed technology which allows clients to obtain, on a Special Analysis basis, "as telecast" information on commercials contained within AMOL-encoded programmes or aired as "spins" or "spots" outside the programme environment. On-air promotional announcements can also be encoded for tracking purposes.

AMPAS · USA
- Academy of Motion Picture Arts And Sciences
8949 Wilshire Boulevard
Beverly Hills
CA 90211
tel   +1 310 247 3000
fax +1 310 859 9619
1928 □ organisation of producers, actors and others which is responsible for widely promoting and supporting the film industry, as well as for awarding the annual Oscars®.

AMPDC · CANADA
- Alberta Motion Picture Development Corporation
Suite 690
10020-101A Avenue
Edmonton
Alberta T5J 3G2
tel   +1 403 424 8855
fax +1 403 424 7669
□ focus on the development of viable and substantial Alberta film and/or television companies with emphasis on money spent and job enterprise in the province. It provides financial and consultative services to established

producers and their companies through loans and equity investments, and publishes a *Newsletter* (3/4).

AMPEC · USA
■ American Motion Picture Export Company
Motion Picture Association of America (MPAA)
1600 Eye Street NW
Washington
DC 20006
tel   +1 202 293 1966
fax +1 202 452 9823
1965 □ established by major US film production companies, to distribute members' product material in English-speaking parts of Western Africa.

AMPIA · CANADA
■ Alberta Motion Picture Industries Association
210 MacLeod Building
10136 100th Street
Edmonton
Alberta T5J OP1
tel   +1 403 944 0707 / 429 0578
fax +1 403 426 3057
1973 □ non-profit professional service organisation serving the independent motion picture production community in the province of Alberta. Its primary aim is to further the independent film and video production industry.

AMPPA · INDONESIA
■ Asian Motion Picture Producers Association
Turino Junaidy
Pusat Perfilman H Usmar Ismail
Jalan H R Rasuna Said
Jakarta
□ association of film producers.

AMPS · TECHNICAL TERM
■ automatic music programme search

AMPTP · USA
■ Alliance of Motion Picture & Television Producers
15503 Ventura Boulevard
Encino
CA 91436-3140
tel   +1 818 995 3600

fax +1 818 382 1793
1982 □ provides services to its member companies covering all aspects of employment within the television and theatrical motion picture industry and other issues which affect the industry as a whole. Perhaps the most significant of these functions is its role as the bargaining agent for its member companies in industry-wide bargaining with the industry's unions and guilds. In that capacity it provides ongoing advice to those companies regarding the administration of their industry-wide agreements.

AMS · TECHNICAL TERM
■ auto music scan

AMSS · TECHNICAL TERM
■ aeronautical mobile satellite service

AMST · USA
■ Association for Maximum Service Television
Suite 610
1400 16th Street NW
Washington
DC 20036
tel   +1 202 462 4351
fax +1 202 462 5335
1990 □ organisation whose principal aim is to promote, develop and ensure a nationwide structure of television broadcasting which is based on local stations which provide broadcast services of distinction.
formerly Association of Maximum Service Telecasters (AMST / MST)

AMST · USA
■ Association of Maximum Service Telecasters
also known as MST
see AMST □ USA

AMT · TECHNICAL TERM
■ amplitude modulated transmitter

ANADET · FRANCE
■ Association Nationale pour la Défense de la Télévision
□ group formed to promote television as a medium.

ANALTRARADIO · COLOMBIA
- Asociación Nacional de Trabajadores de Radio y Televisión
Cra 7 No 19-38 / Of 501
Bogota
□ national association of workers in television and radio.

ANB · JAPAN
- Asahi National Broadcasting Co (TV Asahi)
1-1-1 Roppongi
Minato-ku
Tokyo 106
tel   +81 3 3587 5111
fax   +81 3 3505 3539
tlx   22520
1959 □ television station.

ANCCI · ITALY
- Associazione Nazionale Circoli Cinematografici Italiani
Via Nomentana 251
00161 Rome
tel   +39 6 44 02 280
□ association of Italian film clubs.

AND · TECHNICAL TERM
- active nutation damping

ANDEBU · URUGUAY
- Asociación Nacional de Broadcasters Uruguayos
Calle Yí 1264
Montevideo
tel   +2 900053
tlx   843
1933 □ association of some 100 members.

ANDICCA · SPAIN
- Associació Nacional de Distribuidors Cinematogràfics de Catalunya
Rambla de Catalunya, 47 1º
08007 Barcelona
tel   +34 3 317 7370
□ national association of Catalan film distributors.

ANDTA · ITALY
- Associazione Nazionale Distributori Televisivi e Affini
□ national association of television and associated distributors.

ANEC · ITALY
- Associazione Nazionale Esercenti Cinema
Via di Villa Patrizi 10
00161 Rome
tel   +39 6 884731
fax   +39 6 44231838 / 4404255
1947 □ association of Italian exhibitors, representing about 2100 cinemas, whose aims are: to study the problems concerning the general economic and technological development of the sector, and to suggest the most appropriate solutions; to draw up collective labour agreements; to promote and carry out initiatives aiming at the improvement of the professional skills of its associates; to ensure assistance in all fiscal, legal and union matters. It publishes *AGIS Giornale dello Spettacolo* (52).

ANEPA · SPAIN
- Asociación Nacional Empresas Produccion Audiovisual
Sagasta 20 - 2º Izda
28004 Madrid
tel   +34 1 448 22 89
fax   +34 1 593 46 48
□ national association of audiovisual production companies.

ANGIS™ · TECHNICAL TERM
- automated news graphics interface system

ANGOA · FRANCE
- Association Nationale de Gestion des Œuvres Audiovisuelles
5 rue du Cirque
75008 Paris
tel   +33 1 42 25 71 93
fax   +33 1 42 25 94 27
1981 □ represents the interests and manages the rights of producers in the cable retransmission of their audiovisual works.

ANICA · ITALY
- Associazione Nazionale Industrie Cinematografiche e Audiovisive
Viale Regina Margherita 286
00198 Rome
tel   +39 6 884 1271

fax   +39 6 440 4128
tlx   624659 ANICA I
1944 □ trade association for the Italian independent motion picture and television industry, currently representing some 1000 companies, with 11 regional branch offices throughout Italy. Its aims are: to preserve and protect the rights of copyright owners; to represent major producers and distributors of feature films, television programmes and home video; to negotiate agreements on matters relating to members' activities in order to preserve the freedom of the marketplace; to organise meetings, seminars and research projects; to promote Italian participation in international film festivals and markets; to operate the Title Registration Bureau, for the registration of titles of films destined for theatrical release in Italy. It publishes *Cinema d'Oggi* magazine (26) and a *Yearbook.*

ANIPA · ITALY
■ Associazione Nazionale Imprese Pubblicità Audiovisiva
Via Santa Sofia 27
20122 Milan
tel   +39 2 5830 6007 / 5830 5982
fax +39 2 5830 6014
1972 □ the enhancement of the professional standing of producers of advertising films, as well as the promotion of, and participation in, all initiatives which may develop and improve such professional activity, along with the protection on the part of associated firms of the good name, ethics and professional skills of its members.

ANSEOC · ITALY
■ Associazione Nazionale Studi Effetti Ottici Cinetelevisivi
Via Luigi Settembrini 24
Rome
□ national association of film and television optical effects studios.

ANSI · USA
■ American National Standards Institute
11 West 42nd Street

New York
NY 10036
tel   +1 212 642 4900
1982 □ body which lays down standards for communications equipment.
formerly American Standards Association (ASA)

ANT · TECHNICAL TERM
■ antenna noise temperature

ANTC · AUSTRALIA
■ Australian National Television Council

ANTEA · FRANCE
■ Antenne des Téléspectateurs Actifs
10 rue Jean Goujon
75008 Paris
tel   +33 1 45 63 44 74
fax +33 1 45 63 44 74
□ magazine bulletin of Association Nationale des Téléspectateurs et Auditeurs (**ANTEA**).

ANTEA · FRANCE
■ Association Nationale des Téléspectateurs et Auditeurs
10 rue Jean Goujon
75008 Paris
tel   +33 1 45 63 44 74
fax +33 1 45 63 44 74
□ to establish a dialogue between televiewers, audiences and leaders within the audiovisual communication industries; to monitor the quality of broadcasts; to urge the public to react and voice its needs. It publishes the bulletin *ANTEA* (4).

ANTEL · EL SALVADOR
■ Administración Nacional de Telecomunicaciones
Edif. Administrativo ANTEL
Centro de Gobierno
San Salvador
tel   +503 71 7171
tlx   20252
1963 □ national body which administers telecommunications policy and practice.

ANTI · ITALY

■ Associazione Nazionale Teleradio
Indipendenti
via Cantore 14/5
16149 Genoa
tel +39 10 645 7767
fax +39 10 411 679
1974 □ defends the liberty and freedom
of information in broadcasting and
functions in order to guarantee the
survival of local television and radio
stations in Italy. It publishes *Il
Notiziario Anti* (12).

AOC · TECHNICAL TERM
■ ass on curb

AOCI · ITALY
■ Associazione Operatori
Cinematografici Italiani
Via Tuscolana 1055
0173 Rome
tel +39 6 72 293 3289
□ association of Italian
cinematographic operators.

AOCS · TECHNICAL TERM
■ attitude and orbital control system

AOS · TECHNICAL TERM
■ acquisition of signal

AP · TECHNICAL TERM
■ associate producer

APB · USA
■ Associated Press Broadcasters
Suite 710
1825 K Street NW
Washington
DC 20006
tel +1 202 955 7236
fax +1 202 955 7347
1941 □ group of some 50 US
broadcasting stations which aims to
promote journalism through the media
of television and radio.

APC · TECHNICAL TERM
■ automatic phase/picture/power
control

APCEIS · FRANCE
■ Association de Préfiguration du
Centre Européen de l'Image et du Son

Palais de Tokyo
13 Avenue du Président Wilson
75016 Paris
tel +33 1 49 52 05 36
□ association for the preparation of the
Centre Européen de l'Image et du Son
(**CEIS**).

APCM · TECHNICAL TERM
■ asynchronous pulse code modulation

APCQ · CANADA
■ Association des Propriétaires de
Cinémas du Québec, Inc
445 rue Saint-Sulpice
Montreal
Quebec H2Y 2V7
□ group of cinema owners in Quebec.

APD · ITALY
■ Federazione Associazioni Produttori
Distributori
Via Fr. Carrara 24
00196 Rome
tel +39 6 36 10 857
□ Italian federation of associations of
producers and distributors.

APD · TECHNICAL TERM
■ avalanche photodiode

APDS · FRANCE
■ Association Professionnelle du
Spectacle et de l'Audio-Visuel
10 rue de la Chaussée d'Antin
75009 Paris
tel +33 1 47 70 12 56
□ professional association for theatre
and the audiovisual.

APEC · BELGIUM
■ Association des Professeurs pour la
Promotion de l'Education
Cinématographique
73 avenue des Coccinelles
1170 Brussels
tel +32 2 538 5791 / 223 1948

APEC · TECHNICAL TERM
■ Arri precision exposure control

APF · TECHNICAL TERM
■ auto programme find

APFTQ · CANADA
■ Association des Producteurs de Films et de Télévision du Québec
Bureau 201
740 rue Saint-Maurice
Montreal
Quebec H3C 1L5
tel +1 514 397 8600
fax +1 514 392 0232
1971 □ association established to represent and defend the interests of producers.

APFVQ · CANADA
■ Association des Producteurs de Films et de Vidéo du Québec
□ film and video producers' association.

API · FRANCE
■ Association pour la Promotion de l'Image
5 bis rue Jacquemont
75017 Paris

APICE · ITALY
■ Associazione Produttori Indipendenti Cinematografico Elettronici
Via Principessa Clotilde 7
Rome
□ association of independent electronic film producers.

APL · TECHNICAL TERM
■ average picture level

APO · TECHNICAL TERM
■ action print only

APRAC · FRANCE
■ Association Professionnelle des Réalisateurs d'Œuvres Audiovisuelles de Commande
14 rue Val de Grâce
75005 Paris
tel +33 1 44 07 10 49
□ professional association of producers of commissioned audiovisual work.

APRFP · PORTUGAL
■ Associação de Produtores/Realizadores de Filmes Publicitarios
Rua D Pedro V 60 1ª
Sala 13

1200 Lisbon
tel +351 1 347 6073/4
fax +351 1 346 2708
□ association of producers and directors of publicity films.

APRICA · FRANCE
■ Association pour la Promotion des Professionnels de l'Image et de la Communication de la Côte d'Azur
Ecole Supérieure de Réalisation Audiovisuelle (ESRA)
9 quai des Deux Emmanuel
06300 Nice
tel +33 92 00 00 92
□ association for professionals involved in communication and audiovisual in the Côte d'Azur region.

APRS · UK
■ Association of Professional Recording Services Ltd
2 Windsor Square
Silver Street
Reading
Berks RG1 2TH
tel +44 734 756218
fax +44 734 756216
1947 □ trade association for all facets of the professional sound industry. It provides a broad range of services - from technical forums and training to commercial promotion and consultation with government and other industry bodies. It also publishes various books, including an *Annual Yearbook*, and organises the APRS International Exhibition held annually in London in June.

APTPA · USA
■ American Public Television Producers Association

APTS · USA
■ Association of America's Public Television Stations
1350 Connecticut Avenue, NW
Suite 200
Washington
DC 20036-1716
tel +1 202 887 1700
fax +1 202 293 2422
1979 □ non-profit organisation which

provides planning, research, communications services and representation/lobbying on behalf of its members, who are American public television stations. *also known as AAPTS*

APVQ · CANADA
- Association des Professionnel-le-s de la Vidéo du Québec
Bureau 234
6674 Avenue de l'Esplanade
Montreal
Quebec H2V 2L5
tel   +1 514 270 0008
fax +1 514 270 6094

AQCC · CANADA
- Association Québécoise des Critiques de Cinéma
PO Box 1134
Place d'Armes
Montreal
Quebec H2Y 3J6
tel   +1 514 522 0494
fax +1 514 522 0494
1973 □ film critics union which publishes occasional books.

AQEC · CANADA
- Association Québécoise des Etudes Cinématographiques
Secretary
René Beauclair
2123 Laurier Est
Montreal
Quebec H2H 1C1
□ association for the study of cinema in Quebec.

AQH · TECHNICAL TERM
- average quarter hour

AQL · TECHNICAL TERM
- acceptable quality level

AQRRCT · CANADA
- Association Québécoise des Réalisateurs et Réalisatrices de Cinéma et de Télévision
Bureau 122
1600 De Lorimier
Montreal
Quebec H2K 3W5
tel   +1 514 521 1984

fax +1 514 521 7081
1990 □ association of some 150 members who are directors of fiction and documentary films.

AR · TECHNICAL TERM
- aspect ratio
- audience research
- auto ranging

AR&D · USA
- Audience Research & Development
Suite 600
8828 Stemmons
Dallas
TX 75247
tel   +1 214 630 5097
fax +1 214 630 4951
□ research and consultancy service for local television programming.

ARAS · FRANCE
- Association des Responsables et Spécialistes Audiovisuels des Etablissements d'Enseignement Supérieur
Sufco Montpellier
Université Montpellier III
Route de Mende
BP 5043
34032 Montpellier
tel   +33 67 14 23 35
fax +33 67 14 20 52
□ association of audiovisual specialists in higher educational establishments.

ARAV · FRANCE
- Atelier de Recherches Audiovisuelles
Institut d'Etude du Développement Economique et Social (IEDES)
Université de Paris I (Panthéon-Sorbonne)
58 Boulevard Arago
75013 Paris
tel   +33 1 43 36 23 55
□ research and study centre.

ARC · SWITZERLAND
- Association Romande du Cinéma
Côtes-de-Montbenon
1008 Lausanne
tel   +41 21 311 5858
fax +41 21 312 9343
1992 □ association working for the

benefit of film producers and directors
in French-speaking Switzerland.

ARC · TECHNICAL TERM
- advanced robotic control (system)
- aspect ratio controller

ARCH · TECHNICAL TERM
- automatic remote cassette handler

ARD · GERMANY
- Arbeitsgemeinschaft der öffentlich-
rechtlichen Rundfunkanstalten der
Bundesrepublik Deutschland
Appellhofplatz 1
Postfach 101950
50667 Cologne
tel   +49 221 2201
fax +49 221 2204800
tlx   8882575
□ coordinating body and association of
public law broadcasting institutions,
consisting of 13 independent
broadcasting corporations. Their joint
task, by law, is to provide television
and radio services.

ARM · TECHNICAL TERM
- activity release monitor
- automatic reconfiguration mode

ARP · FRANCE
- Association des Auteurs-Réalisateurs-
Producteurs
Palais de Tokyo
2 rue de la Manutention
75116 Paris
tel   +33 1 40 70 15 54
fax +33 1 40 70 19 05
□ association of producers, directors
and authors.

ARRI · GERMANY
- Arnold & Richter Cine Technik
Türkenstraße 89
80799 Munich
tel   +49 89 3809-1
fax +49 89 3809-244
tlx   524317 ARRI
□ manufacturers of motion picture
cameras and lenses, and lighting
equipment.

ART · TURKEY

- Alo Radio and Television Company
PO Box 98
Maltepe-Ankara
tel   +90 4 467 0098
fax +90 4 427 6671
□ television broadcaster.

ART · UK
- Anadolu Radio Television
Corporation
47 Leeward Gardens
London SW19 7QR
tel   +44 81 947 5677
fax +44 81 944 0175
1992 □ cable/satellite station aiming to
provide all-round television
programming to the Turkish-speaking
community, initially in London and
eventually throughout Europe.

ART · USA
- Applied Research and Technology,
Inc
215 Tremont Street
Rochester
NY 14608
tel   +1 716 436 2720
fax +1 716 436 3942
□ manufactures professional mixing
consoles, high definition series
equalizers and a full line of professional
signal processors, including time
delays, digital reverbs, programmable
equalizers, compressors, gates,
expanders and time/pitch compressors.

ARTE · FRANCE
- Association Rélative à la Télévision
Européenne
2a rue de la Fonderie
67080 Strasbourg Cedex
tel   +33 88 52 22 22
fax +33 88 52 22 00
tlx   891009
1992 □ German-French television
channel which aims to act as a forum
for intercultural dialogue for and via the
documentary film and to give film-
makers scope to experiment.

ARTEMIS · TECHNICAL TERM
- advanced systems and technology
mission satellite

ARTER · FRANCE
- Association des Réalisateurs de Télévision Exerçant en Régions
3 rue Schwendi
67000 Strasbourg
tel +33 88 36 54 51
□ group which comprises television directors, working in regional France.

ARTNA · USA
- Association of Radio and Television News Analysts

ARTS · USA
- Alpha Repertory Television Service

AS · TECHNICAL TERM
- angled shot

ASA · USA
- American Standards Association
replaced by American National Standards Institute (ANSI)

ASB · TECHNICAL TERM
- asymmetric sideband

ASBU · EGYPT
- Arab States Broadcasting Union
Secretariat
22a Taha Hussein Street
Zamalek
Cairo
tel +20 2 805825
tlx 347 ASBUUN
1969 □ intergovernmental union made up of Arab television and radio organisations.

ASC · USA
- American Society of Cinematographers
1782 North Orange Drive
Hollywood
CA 90028
tel +1 213 969 4333
fax +1 213 876 4973
1919 □ educational, cultural and professional organisation with membership by invitation to those who are actively engaged as directors of photography and have demonstrated outstanding ability. It publishes *American Cinematographer* (12) and

various books.

ASC · TECHNICAL TERM
- automatic slope control

ASDA · AUSTRALIA
- Australian Screen Directors Association
PO Box 211
Rozelle
NSW 2039
tel +61 2 555 7045
fax +61 2 555 7086
□ association representing Australian film directors.

ASDF · SWITZERLAND
- Association Suisse des Distributeurs de Films
see **SFV** · SWITZERLAND

ASE · FRANCE
- Agence Spatiale Européenne
see **ESA** · FRANCE

ASED · SWITZERLAND
- Association Suisse des Exploitants et Distributeurs de Films
see **SVKF** · SWITZERLAND

ASFA · USA
- American Science Film Association

ASFFHF · USA
- Academy of Science Fiction, Fantasy and Horror Films

ASG · TECHNICAL TERM
- audio test signal generator

ASI · USA
- Audience Studies, Inc
Los Angeles
□ company which operates television advertising testing services.

ASIC · TECHNICAL TERM
- application specified integrated circuit

ASIFA · NORWAY
- Association Internationale du Film d'Animation
Møre og Romsdal distriktshøgskule
PO Box 188

N-6101 Volda
tel   +47 70 075100
fax   +47 70 075051
1960 □ UNESCO-affiliated international
association formed by professional
animators to support the art of
animation. With about 1500 members
in 50 countries, it patronises major
animation festivals and symposia, has
its own archive and supports
collaborations between international
animation film-makers on all levels. It
publishes *ASIFA News* (4), several
national newsletters, as well as other
publications.

ASJC · SWITZERLAND
▪ Association Suisse des Journalistes
Cinématographiques
see **SVFJ** · SWITZERLAND

ASK · TECHNICAL TERM
▪ amplitude shift keying

ASM · TECHNICAL TERM
▪ assistant stage manager

ASO · TECHNICAL TERM
▪ active sideband optimum

ASP · TECHNICAL TERM
▪ acoustic surround processors
▪ augmentation signal package

ASR · TECHNICAL TERM
▪ array shunt regulator
▪ automatic sequence register

ASRF · SWITZERLAND
▪ Association Suisse des
Réalisateurs/trices de Films
see **VSFG** · SWITZERLAND

ASSECCI · SENEGAL
▪ Association Sénégalais des Critiques
de Cinéma
c/o Recidak 93
Villa 2744
Sicap Dieuppeul
Dakar 3
tel   +221 235300
□ professional organisation of
Senegalese film critics.

AST · TECHNICAL TERM
▪ automatic scan tracking

ASTA · USA
▪ Advertiser Syndicated Television
Association

ASTF · SWITZERLAND
▪ Association Suisse des Techniciennes
et Techniciens du Film
see **SFTV** · SWITZERLAND

ASTISA · MEXICO
▪ Asesoramiento y Servicios Técnicos
Industriales, SA
Niños Héroes 15
Mexico 7, D.F.
tel   +52 5 585 333
tlx   1773994
□ commercial television station.

ASTVC · USA
▪ American Society of Television
Cameramen, Inc
PO Box 296
Washington Street
Sparkhill
NY 10976
tel   +1 914 359 5569
1974 □ group of professional television
cameramen which aims to share
experiences and also to further
standards throughout the industry. It
publishes *Zoom Out!* magazine (12)
and a *Newsletter*.

AT&T · USA
▪ American Telephone and Telegraph
Company
900 Route 202/206
PO Box 752
Bedford
NJ 07921-0752
tel   +1 908 234 3409
fax   +1 908 234 3628
tlx   ATT Mail: dthovson
□ telecommunications operating
agency.

ATA · ARGENTINA
▪ Asociación de Teleradiodifusoras
Argentinas
Córdoba 323, 6°
1054 Buenos Aires

tel   +54 1 312 4219
fax   +54 1 312 4208
tlx   17253 ATA AR
1959 □ association of some 20 private television stations.

ATAS · USA
▪ Academy of Television Arts and Sciences
Suite 700
3500 West Olive Avenue
Burbank
CA 91505
tel   +1 818 953 7575

ATC · ARGENTINA
▪ Argentina Televisora Color
Avda Figueroa Alcorta 2977
1425 Buenos Aires
tel   +54 1 802 6001
fax   +54 1 802 9878
□ state-controlled television broadcasting channel.

ATC · USA
▪ American Television & Communications Corporation
160 Inverness Drive West
Englewood
CO 80112
tel   +1 303 799 1200
fax   +1 303 790 7672
□ operator of cable TV systems.

ATC · TECHNICAL TERM
▪ automatic test equipment

ATE · TECHNICAL TERM
▪ automated test equipment

ATEC · CANADA
▪ Association for Tele-Education in Canada
▪ Association de Télévision Educative au Canada
c/o Maître Luc Audet
800 rue Fullum
Montreal
Quebec H2K 3L7
tel   +1 514 521 2424
fax   +1 514 873 7739
1974 □ promotes an exchange of information among members and presents an opportunity for the

discussion on pan-Canadian educational communications matters. Its aims are: to promote and advance interest in mediated educational materials and to establish relations with other organisations with similar interests; to promote cooperation in development, acquisition, production, distribution, exchange, utilisation and evaluation of mediated educational materials; to represent the interests of members in a fair and equitable manner.

ATF · TECHNICAL TERM
▪ automatic track finding/following

ATFP · USA
▪ Alliance of Television Film Producers

ATIC · ITALY
▪ Associazione Tecnica Italiana per la Cinematografia e la Televisione
Viale Regina Margherita 286
00198 Rome
tel   +39 6 884 1271
fax   +39 6 440 4128
1951 □ technical industries association, which publishes *Note di Tecnica Cinematografica* (4).

ATM · FRANCE
▪ Association des Trois Mondes
63, bis rue Cardinal Lemoine
75005 Paris
tel   +33 1 43 54 78 69
fax   +33 1 46 34 70 19
1983 □ audiovisual information centre, specialising in film and video from developing nations. It has 15 000 dossiers, including articles, reviews, photos about films from Africa, Latin America, Asia and about development and north-south relations. It publishes *Images Nord-Sud* magazine (4).

ATM · UK
▪ Advanced Television Markets
23 Boreham Road
Wood Green
London N22 6SL
tel   +44 81 889 2965
fax   +44 81 889 2965
1991 □ monthly industry newsletter for

all those who need to keep pace with the changes and commercial implications for their industry sector and organisation in technology in the international television market, including **HDTV**, **EDTV**, interactive television and video compression.

ATN · INDIA
■ Asia Television Network
□ television station.

ATN · SURINAME
■ Abonnee Televisie Nederland
Adrianusstraat
PO Box 2995
Paramaribo
tel +597 75811
fax +597 79260
tlx 488
1985 □ government-owned television station, broadcasting in Dutch, English, Portuguese and Spanish.

ATOM · AUSTRALIA
■ Australian Teachers of Media
PO Box 222
Carlton South
VIC 3053
tel +61 3 482 2393
fax +61 3 482 5018
□ group of academics and teachers which also publishes *Metro* magazine (4).

ATP · TECHNICAL TERM
■ acquisition, tracking and pointing

ATR · TECHNICAL TERM
■ audio tape recorder

ATS · USA
■ Advanced Television Services
□ study group within the Federal Communications Commission (**FCC**).

ATS · USA
■ American Television Society

ATS · TECHNICAL TERM
■ advanced telecommunications service
■ application(s) technology satellite
■ auto tuning system
■ automatic transmission system

ATSC · USA
■ Advanced Television Systems Committee
Suite 300
1776 K Street NW
Washington
DC 20006
tel +1 202 828 3130
fax +1 202 828 3131
1982

ATTC · USA
■ Advanced Television Test Center

ATTS · TECHNICAL TERM
■ auto tape time select

ATV · HONG KONG
■ Asia Television Ltd
81 Broadcast Drive
Kowloon
tel +852 3 399111
fax +852 3 380438
tlx HX44680
□ television broadcasting service.

ATV · JAPAN
■ Aomori Television Co Ltd
4-8 Matsumori 1-chome
Aomori 030
tel +81 177 41 2233 / 62 1111
tlx 44680
1973 □ television broadcaster, operating two commercial television stations (in Chinese and English), and producing television programmes.

ATV · SURINAME
■ Alternatieve Televisie Verzorging
Adrianusstraat 1
Paramaribo
tel +597 410027
fax +597 470425
1987 □ television broadcasting service.

ATV · TECHNICAL TERM
■ advanced television

ATW · TECHNICAL TERM
■ auto tracing white

AU · TECHNICAL TERM
■ angstrom unit

AUDECAM · FRANCE
- Association Universitaire pour le Développement, l'Education et la Communication en Afrique et dans le Monde
100 rue de l'Université
75007 Paris
tel +33 1 45 51 28 24
fax +33 1 45 56 10 72
1988 □ maintains a library of films on the subjects of Africa, the Caribbean, and Hispanic and Indian peoples.

AUDETEL · TECHNICAL TERM
- audio description of television

AV · TECHNICAL TERM
- audiovisual
- audio/video

AVA · UK
- Audio Visual Arts Ltd
7b Broad Street
Nottingham NG1 3AJ
tel +44 602 483684
1987 □ independent video production company, specialising in work for visual and performing artists, museums and galleries.

AVA · UK
- Audio Visual Association
46 Manor View
London N3 2SR
tel +44 81 349 2429

AVA · USA
- Adult Video Association

AVA · USA
- American Video Association
Suite 140
2885 North Nevada Street
Chandler
AZ 85225-1215
tel +1 602 892 8553

AVC · TECHNICAL TERM
- audio, video, control
- audiovisual communications
- automatic volume control

AVCP · FRANCE
- Association des Vidéo Clubs

Professionnels
1988 □ association of video clubs.

AVDAA · AUSTRALIA
- Audio Visual Distributors Association of Australia
6th floor
157 Liverpool Street
Sydney
NSW 2000
tel +61 2 267 4300
fax +61 2 267 4066

AVE · SPAIN
- Asociación Videográfica Española

AVH · ARGENTINA
- Argentina Video Home
Av. Callao 660
Capital Federal
1022 Buenos Aires
tel +54 1 41 5369 / 42 6640 / 812 8119 / 812 2826 / 812 4583
fax +54 1 953 6090 / 953 6091
1984 □ home video representatives in the Argentine Republic of the following companies: CIC Video (Paramount Pictures-Universal Pictures), Warner HomeVideo (Warner Brothers-MGM-United Artists). It publishes *Contacto en Video* (6).

AVI · TECHNICAL TERM
- audio video interactive

AVIA · ARGENTINA
- Asociación de Videoeditores Independientes de la Argentina

AVID · TECHNICAL TERM
- audio video interactive development

AVLS · UK
- Audio Visual Library Services

AVM · DENMARK
- AudioVisuelle Media
Specialbladsforlaget
Finsensvej 80
2000 Frederiksberg
tel +45 3888 3222
fax +45 3888 3038
1976 □ magazine (11 issues annually) for professional users and producers of

audio, video and broadcasting equipment in Denmark.

AVMZ · GERMANY
- Audiovisuelle Medienzentrum Paderborn

AVRO · THE NETHERLANDS
- Algemene Vereniging Radio-Omroep
PO Box 2
1200 JA Hilversum
tel   +31 35 717911
fax   +31 35 717517
1923 □ television broadcasting company and production company. It publishes *AVRObode* (52) and *Televizier* (52).

AVS · USA
- Aerial Video Systems
712 South Main Street
Burbank
CA 91506
tel   +1 818 954 8842
fax   +1 818 954 9122
1981 □ provides specialised video packages and production services.

AVUP · FRANCE
- Office Audiovisuel de l'Université de Poitiers
95 avenue du Recteur Pineau
86022 Poitiers
tel   +33 49 45 32 26
fax   +33 49 45 32 27
□ regional centre.

AWB · TECHNICAL TERM
- auto(matic) white balance

AWF · GERMANY
- Arbeitskreis Wissenschaftlicher Film
Hans-Holbein-Str. 6
50999 Cologne
tel   +49 221 354608
fax   +49 221 7390044
1983 □ the promotion of scientific and medical films.

AWGN · TECHNICAL TERM
- additive white Gaussian noise

AWIFAV · AFRICAN CONTINENT
- African Women in Film & Video

Association
1991

AWO · TECHNICAL TERM
- analogue write once

AWRT · USA
- American Women in Radio and Television, Inc
1101 Connecticut Avenue NW
Suite 700
Washington
DC 20036
tel   +1 202 429 5102
fax   +1 202 223 4579
1951

AZ/EL · TECHNICAL TERM
- Azimuth/elevation

B

BABEL · SWITZERLAND
- Broadcasting Across the Barriers of European Language
c/o European Broadcasting Union
Ancienne Route 17A
Case Postale 67
CH-1218 Grand-Saconnex/Geneva
tel   +41 22 717 2111
fax   +41 22 798 5897
tlx   415 700 ebu ch
1988 □ an initiative of **MEDIA**, this association attempts to provide an answer to the problem of dubbing and subtitling European audiovisual productions. It aims to facilitate the transmission of productions already made for which international distribution is sought.

BAC TV · UK
- British Action for Children's Television
British Film Institute
21 Stephen Street
London W1P 1PL
tel   +44 71 255 1444
fax   +44 71 436 7950
tlx   27624 BFILDNG
1989 □ organisation aiming to bring together all those interested in children

and television, but especially to support parents' and children's needs. It publishes a quarterly *Newsletter* for members.

BAFC · UK
■ Black Audio Film Collective
Unit 9
Bowmans House
7-12 Greenland Street
London NW1 OND
tel +44 71 267 0845/6
fax +44 71 267 0845
1983 □ film production company working on broadcast commissions and development of original screenplays, with its main areas of production being features and documentaries.

BAFTA · UK
■ British Academy of Film and Television Arts
195 Piccadilly
London W1V 9LG
tel +44 71 734 0022
fax +44 71 734 1792
1946 □ aims to advance the art and technique of film and television and encourage experiment and research. The giving of awards to both industries (craft, production and performance awards) is an annual televised event. It publishes *BAFTA News* (12).

BAPSA · USA
■ Broadcast Advertising Producers Society of America

BAR · USA
■ Broadcast Advertisers Reports
Suite 1202
56 West 45th Street
New York
NY 10036
tel +1 212 719 9471
fax +1 212 768 3081
□ body which observes and reports on commercial activities on network television and radio.

BARB · UK
■ Broadcasters' Audience Research Board Ltd
Glenthorne House

Hammersmith Grove
London W6 OND
replaced Joint Industries' Committee for Television Audience Research (JICTAR)
tel +44 81 741 9110
fax +44 81 741 1943
1980 □ to provide a single system for television audience research in the UK. A subscription-based organisation. *The Weekly Viewing Summary* and *The Monthly Viewing Summary* are available to the general public; however, all other data are confined to subscribers.

BATC · UK
■ British Amateur Television Club
Grenehurst
Pinewood Road
High Wycombe
Herts HP12 4DD
1949 □ non-profit organisation established to inform, instruct, co-ordinate and represent the activities of television enthusiasts in the UK and worldwide. It publishes *CQTV* magazine (4).

BAVA · UK
■ British Amateur Video Awards
WV Publications
57-59 Rochester Place
London NW1 9JU
tel +44 71 485 0011
fax +44 71 482 6269
1989 □ a competition for non-professional movie-makers shooting on any domestic video format, with a maximum running time of 10 minutes.

BAVC · USA
■ Bay Area Video Coalition
1111 17th Street
San Francisco
CA 94107
tel +1 415 861 3282
fax +1 415 861 4316
1976 □ member-supported non-profit video arts centre, providing production and post-production equipment to independent producers, media artists, educators and students. It publishes the magazine *Video Networks* (6).

BB · TECHNICAL TERM
- bayonet base
- black burst

BBB · USA
- Back to the Bible Broadcast
PO Box 82808
Lincoln
NE 68501
tel   +1 402 474 4567
fax   +1 402 474 4519
□ satellite television service,
broadcasting evangelical preaching and
music.

BBC · CANADA
- Border Broadcasters' Collective
c/o WXYZ
PO Box 2469A
Station A
Toronto
Ontario M5W 2S6
tel   +1 313 827 9390
fax   +1 313 827 4454

BBC · JAPAN
- Biwako Broadcasting Co Ltd
16-1 Tsurunosato
Ohtsu 520
tel   +81 775-24 0151
□ television station.

BBC · UK
- British Broadcasting Corporation
BBC Television Centre
Wood Lane
London W12 7RJ
tel   +44 81 743 8000
fax   +44 81 749 7520
tlx   265781
1936 □ national broadcasting service of
the UK, supplying 2 television channels
and 4 radio channels, as well as local
stations. It also operates extensive
educational and publishing services.

BBC-WSTV · UK
- British Broadcasting Corporation -
World Service Television
Woodlands
80 Wood Lane
London W12 OTT
tel   +44 81 576 2783
fax   +44 81 576 2782

tlx   946359 BBC WNG
1991 □ established to provide a global
news and information service dedicated
to an international audience. It draws
on the worldwide news gathering
resources of BBC Television and the
World Service Radio to produce
impartial news and information. It also
broadcasts major BBC current affairs
and documentary series, as well as
lively factual series on science, nature
and lifestyle issues.

BBFC · UK
- British Board of Film Censors
*now British Board of Film Classification
(BBFC)*

BBFC · UK
- British Board of Film Classification
3 Soho Square
London W1V 5DE
tel   +44 71 439 7961
fax   +44 71 287 0141
1912 □ classification of all films shown
in licensed cinemas; classification of all
video works for sale or hire.
*formerly British Board of Film Censors
(BBFC)*

BBI · CHINA
- Beijing Broadcasting Institute

BBM · USA
- Broadcast Bureau of Measurement

BBS · TECHNICAL TERM
- business band service

BBTV · THAILAND
- Bangkok Broadcasting and Television
Company Ltd
998/1 Soi Ruamsirimitr Phaholyothin
Road
Ladyao Jattujak
Bangkok 10900
tel   +66 2 278 1255-60 / 2799280-4
fax   +66 2 270 1975
tlx   82730 BBTV TH
1968 □ television channel which
publishes *TV Magazine* (12).

BC · TECHNICAL TERM
- broadcast

BCB · BAHAMAS
■ Broadcasting Corporation of the
Bahamas
PO Box N-1347
Third Terrace
East Centreville
Nassau
tel   +1 809 322 4623
fax   +1 809 322 3924
tlx   ZNS Nassau 253
1936 □ broadcasting corporation which
runs one television station and 4 radio
stations. Its main role is the preparation
and transmission of educational,
informational and generally cultural
programmes to and for Bahamians.

BCB · BELIZE
■ Broadcasting Corporation of Belize
Albert Catouse Building
PO Box 89
Belize City
tel   +501 2 77246-8
fax   +501 2 75040
1990 □ radio and television
broadcasting service, producing news
and cultural programmes and providing
facilities and trained personnel for the
production of television commercials,
features and documentaries.

BCC · TAIWAN
■ Broadcasting Corporation of China
32 Jen-Ai Road
Section 3
Taipei
tel   +886 2 771 3849
fax   +886 2 751 9277
tlx   27498 BCCROC
□ national broadcasting organisation.

BCC · UK
■ Broadcasting Complaints Commission
Grosvenor Garden House
35-37 Grosvenor Gardens
London SW1W OBS
tel   +44 71 630 1966
fax   +44 71 828 7316
1981 □ considers complaints of unjust
or unfair treatment in radio, television
or cable programmes and complaints of
unwarranted infringement of privacy or
in connection with such programmes.
The complaints have to be made by

participants in the programme
complained of or by individuals or
organisations with a direct interest in
the subject matter of the treatment
complained of. It publishes an Annual
Report to Parliament.

BCCA · USA
■ Broadcast Cable Credit Association

BCD · TECHNICAL TERM
■ binary-coded decimal

BCFM · USA
■ Black Citizens for a Fair Media

BCFMA · USA
■ Broadcast Cable Financial
Management Association

BCH · TECHNICAL TERM
■ Bose-Chaudhuri-Hocquenghem

BCMPA · CANADA
■ British Columbia Motion Picture
Association
Suite 1101
207 West Hastings Street
Vancouver
British Columbia V6B 1H7
tel   +1 604 684 4712
fax   +1 604 684 4979
1965 □ servicing British Columbia's
motion picture industry.

BCN · TECHNICAL TERM
■ broadband communications network

BCOS · NIGERIA
■ Broadcasting Corporation of Oyo
State
Ibadan
□ state-owned television station.

BCS · TECHNICAL TERM
■ big character select

BCSP · TECHNICAL TERM
■ Betacam Standard Play

BCTV · UK
■ Bath Community Television Ltd
7 Barton Buildings
Bath BA1 2JR

tel +44 225 314480
1986 □ to promote the use of film and video, through equipment hire, professional consultancies and a programme of quality training courses.

BCU · TECHNICAL TERM
▪ big close-up

BD · TECHNICAL TERM
▪ block down

BDA · USA
▪ Broadcast Designers Association, Inc
Suite 611
251 Kearney Street
San Francisco
CA 94108
tel +1 415 788 2324
fax +1 415 788 7622
1978 □ organisation of designers, art directors, artists, illustrators, animators and others working in television.

BDF · GERMANY
▪ Bundesverband Deutscher Fernsehproduzenten
Widenmayerstraße 32
80538 Munich
tel +49 89 223535
fax +49 89 2285562
1965 □ represents the independent television production sector in Germany. It aims to lobby for more independent production by convincing politicians that the sector's output is an integral and essential part of movie culture in the country. It publishes an *Annual Yearbook*.
also known as BVDFP

BDFA · GERMANY
▪ Bundes Deutscher Filmamateure
□ amateur film association.

BDT · SWITZERLAND
▪ Bureau de Développement des Télécommunications
International Telecommunications Union (ITU)
Place des Nations
CH-1211 Geneva 20
tel +41 22 730 5111
fax +41 22 733 7256

tlx 421 000 UIT CH
□ committee whose duties consist in principle of discharging, in the field of assistance to developing countries, the ITU's dual responsibility as a UN agency specialised in telecommunications and as an executing agency for implementing projects financed by the United Nations Development Programme (UNDP), and by other sources. It facilitates and enhances telecommunications development by offering, organising and coordinating technical cooperation and assistance activities.

BEA · USA
▪ Broadcast Education Association
1771 N Street, NW
Washington
DC 20036-2891
tel +1 202 429 5354
1955 □ organisation whose members - colleges, universities, broadcast stations and graduate students - offer specific training in television and radio broadcasting. It publishes the *Journal of Broadcasting & Electronic Media* (4) and *Feedback* (4).

BECT · SWITZERLAND
▪ Bureau Européen du Cinéma et de la Télévision
c/o Union Européenne de Radio-Télévision (UER)
Ancienne Route 17A
Case postale 67
CH-1218 Grand Saconnex/Geneva
tel +41 22 717 2111
fax +41 22 798 5897
tlx 415700 ebu ch
□ coordination of common positions among the organisations representative of film and television vis-à-vis the Council of Europe and the European Community.

BECTU · UK
▪ Broadcasting Entertainment Cinematograph and Theatre Union
111 Wardour Street
London W1V 4AY
tel +44 71 437 8506
fax +44 71 437 8268

*formed by the amalgamation of ACTT
and BETA*
1991 □ the main trade union for
technicians and support personnel in all
areas of broadcasting, film, video and
theatre. It publishes *Stage Screen &
Radio* (10).

BER · TECHNICAL TERM
■ bit error rate

BERC · USA
■ Broadcast Equipment Rental
Company

BERT · TECHNICAL TERM
■ bit error rate testing

BEST · USA
■ Black Efforts for Soul in Television

BET · USA
■ Black Entertainment Television
Suite 2200
1700 North Moore Street
Rosslyn
VA 22209
tel   +1 703 875 0430
fax +1 703 875 0441
1979 □ cable television network
showcasing quality black programming
24 hours a day. It is committed to:
providing a national platform which
showcases the creativity and diversity
of the black entertainment industry;
presenting quality black entertainment,
music, sports and public affairs; being
the dominant medium which
advertisers use to effectively reach the
black consumer.

BETA · UK
■ Broadcasting and Entertainment
Trades Alliance
see **BECTU** · UK

BFA · USA
■ Broadcasting Foundation of America

BFB · UK
■ Black Film Bulletin
British Film Institute
21 Stephen Street
London W1P 1PL

tel   +44 71 255 1444
fax +44 71 436 7950
tlx   27624 BFILDNG
1993 □ quarterly magazine which
covers African, Caribbean and Asian
film activity in the UK and a selection
of information from the international
context.

BFBS
■ British Forces Broadcasting Service
□ television and radio broadcasting
service.

BFC · UK
■ British Film Commission
70 Baker Street
London W1M 1DJ
tel   +44 71 224 5000
fax +44 71 224 1013
1992 □ to promote the United
Kingdom as an international production
centre and to encourage the use of
British services, facilities, personnel and
locations.

BFC/NCC · USA
■ Broadcasting and Film
Commission/National Film Council of
the Churches of Christ

BFDG · UK
■ British Film Designs Guild
24 St Anselm's Place
London W1Y 1FG
tel   +44 71 499 4336
1977 □ to promote the interests of
members of film arts departments. It
produces a *Newsletter* (12).

BFF · GERMANY
■ Bund Freischaffender Foto-Designer
Postfach 75 03 47
70603 Stuttgart
tel   +49 40 349151
fax +49 40 34915270
tlx   211642

BFFS · UK
■ British Federation of Film Societies
c/o Film Society Unit
British Film Institute
21 Stephen Street
London W1P 1PL

tel   +44 71 255 1444
fax   +44 71 436 7950
tlx   27624 BFILDNG
1937 □ 280 societies across the UK,
screening films to more than 50 000
members annually. It publishes the bi-
monthly magazine *Film*.

BFI · UK
▪ British Film Institute
21 Stephen Street
London W1P 1PL
tel   +44 71 255 1444
fax   +44 71 436 7950
tlx   27624 BFILDNG
1933 □ works to promote and develop
the 20th century's major new art form,
the moving image. Its work ranges
across many aspects of film, television
and video. Its aims are: to encourage
the development of the art of film in
Great Britain; to promote its use as a
record of contemporary life and
manners; to foster study and
appreciation of it from these points of
view; to foster study and appreciation
of films for television and television
programmes generally; to encourage
the best use of television in Great
Britain. It publishes *Sight and Sound*
(12), *Black Film Bulletin* (4), *BFI
Membership News* (4), the *BFI Film and
Television Handbook* (1), as well as
other book publications.

BFI · USA
▪ Broadcasters' Foundation, Inc
320 West 57th Street
New York
NY 10019
tel   +1 212 830 2581
fax   +1 212 956 2059

BFS · GERMANY
▪ Bundesverband Filmschnitt Cutter
Kaiserstr. 41
80801 Munich
tel   +49 89 336573
fax   +49 89 336573
□ association of film editors.

BFTPA · UK
▪ British Film & Television Producers
Association

BFWS · TECHNICAL TERM
▪ big fat wide shot

BG · TECHNICAL TERM
▪ background (*aka* B/G or BKG)

BGM · TECHNICAL TERM
▪ background music

BGV · TECHNICAL TERM
▪ background video

BH · TECHNICAL TERM
▪ buried heterostructure

BHDTV · GERMANY
▪ Bundesverband HDTV
Eugen-Langen-Str. 20
50968 Cologne
tel   +49 221 372984
fax   +49 221 372241
□ association for HDTV.

BIB · USA
▪ Board for International Broadcasting
1201 Connecticut Avenue NW
Washington
DC 20036
tel   +1 202 254 8040
1973

BIFF · INDIA
▪ Bombay International Film Festival
Films Division
Ministry of Information and
Broadcasting
24 Dr G Deshmukh Marg
Bombay 400 026
tel   +91 22 386 4633 / 385 3655
fax   +91 22 386 0308 / 494 9751
tlx   75463 FD-IN
□ film festival (February, even years
only) showing documentary, short and
animation films.

BILIFA · FRANCE
▪ Bureau International de Liaison des
Instituts du Film d'Animation

BIMA · UK
▪ British Interactive Multimedia
Association
6 Walsingley Road
Folksworth

Peterborough
Cambs PE7 3SY
tel +44 733 242370
fax +44 733 240020
1984 □ representative body for the
interactive multimedia industry. It
provides a platform for the
development, creation and use of
interactive multimedia products in all
markets; for collaboration amongst
members; and for a better
understanding of multimedia.

BINA · USA
■ Broadcast Institute of North America

BISDN · TECHNICAL TERM
■ broadband integrated services digital
network

BISFA · UK
■ British Industrial & Scientific Film
Association

BITC · TECHNICAL TERM
■ built-in time code

BJF · GERMANY
■ Bundesverband Jugend und Film eV
Schweizer Str. 6
6000 Frankfurt/M 70
1992 □ group, with some 1200
members, established to provide
support to work among young people
in the area of film. It runs a
Clubfilmothek, is involved in non-
commercial distribution of films, and
produces *BJF Magazine* and various
other publications.

BKG · TECHNICAL TERM
■ background (*aka* BG or B/G)

BKS · GERMANY
■ Bundesverband Kable und Satellite

BKSTS · UK
■ British Kinematograph Sound and
Television Society
M6-M14 Victoria House
Vernon Place
London WC1B 4DF
tel +44 71 242 8400
fax +44 71 405 3560

1931 □ to disseminate information on
film, television and related industries,
which is achieved through publications,
conferences, exhibitions and training
courses and seminars. It publishes
Image Technology (10), its supplement
Cinema Technology (4) and a
Members' Directory (1).

BLC · TECHNICAL TERM
■ back light compensation

BLEC · FRANCE
■ Bureau de Liaison Européen du
Cinéma
43 Boulevard Malesherbes
75008 Paris
tel +33 1 42 66 05 32
fax +33 1 42 66 96 92
□ European centre for discussion about
the cinema.

BLIC · FRANCE
■ Bureau de Liaison de l'Industrie
Cinématographique
43 Boulevard Malesherbes
75008 Paris
tel +33 1 42 66 05 32
fax +33 1 42 66 96 92
□ centre for discussion about the
cinematographic industry.

BMI · USA
■ Broadcast Music, Inc
320 West 57th Street
New York
NY 10019
tel +1 212 586 2000
fax +1 212 489 2368
tlx 12-7823
1940 □ organisation which comprises
composers, music publishers and
songwriters and whose task is to collect
royalty payments from television
broadcasters, film producers and others
for the broadcast of its members' music.
It publishes *BMI Music World* (4).

BMP · TECHNICAL TERM
■ bit map

BMS · TECHNICAL TERM
■ below minimum standards

BMTT · UK
▪ Black Media Training Trust

BNBA · BANGLADESH
▪ Bangladesh National Broadcasting
Authority
NBA House
Shahbag Avenue
Dhaka 2
tel   +880 2 865294 / 500143-7
tlx   642228 NBA BJ
1939 □ television and radio
broadcasting authority.
*also known as National Broadcasting
Authority of Bangladesh (NBAB) and
National Broadcasting Authority (NBA)*

BNC · TECHNICAL TERM
▪ baby N connector
▪ bayonet connector

BO · TECHNICAL TERM
▪ box office

BOD · TECHNICAL TERM
▪ biochemical oxygen demand

BONAC · SERBIA
▪ Broadcasting Organisations of the
Non-Aligned Countries
c/o Jugoslovenskih Radiotelevizija
Hratigova 70/1
11000 Belgrade
tel   +38 11 434910
tlx   11469 YU JURATE
□ grouping of broadcasters.

BOOS · THE NETHERLANDS
▪ Bart Omroep Organisatie Stichting
Emmastraat 40a
1211 NH Hilversum
tel   +31 35 212564
fax   +31 35 241186
□ children's television programming.

BOT · TECHNICAL TERM
▪ beginning of tape

BP · USA
▪ Broadcast Pioneers
320 West 57th Street
New York
NY 10019
tel   +1 212 830 2581

fax   +1 212 956 2059
1942 □ organisation whose members
are those who have worked for more
than 20 years in the fields of television
or radio broadcasting. It publishes *The
Broadcast Pioneer* (4).

BP · TECHNICAL TERM
▪ back projection

BPCJ · JAPAN
▪ Broadcast Programming Centre of
Japan

BPEF · USA
▪ Broadcast Pioneers Educational Fund,
Inc

BPG · UK
▪ Broadcasting Press Guild
c/o Richard Last
Tiverton
The Ridge
Woking
Surrey GU22 7EQ
tel   +44 483 764895
□ group of journalists working in
television and radio.

BPL · USA
▪ Broadcast Pioneers Library
1771 North Street NW
Washington
DC 20036
tel   +1 202 223 0088
□ established by Broadcast Pioneers
(**BP**) as a library and reference centre
documenting the history of television
and radio broadcasting.

BPME · USA
▪ Broadcast Promotion and Marketing
Executives
6255 Sunset Boulevard
Suite 624
Los Angeles
CA 90028-7426
tel   +1 213 465 3777
fax   +1 213 469 9559
1956 □ international association of
promotion and marketing professionals
in the electronic media, dedicated to
advancing the role and increasing the
effectiveness of promotion and

marketing within the industry, related industries and the academic community. It publishes *BPME Image* (10) and an *Annual Directory*.

BPSK · TECHNICAL TERM
- binary phase-shift keying

BR · GERMANY
- Bayerischer Rundfunk
Rundfunkplatz 1
80335 Munich
tel   +49 89 5900 01
fax   +49 89 5900 2375
tlx   521070
□ regional broadcasting organisation which produces and distributes television and radio programmes.

BR · TECHNICAL TERM
- black range

BRC · USA
- Broadcast Rating Council
see **EMRC** · USA

BREMA · UK
- British Radio and Electronic Equipment Manufacturers Association
19 Charing Cross Road
London WC2H OES
tel   +44 71 930 3206
fax   +44 71 839 4613
□ member organisation which supports the UK radio and electronic manufacturing industries.

BRR · TECHNICAL TERM
- bit-rate reduction

BRT · BELGIUM
- Belgische Radio en Televisie
Omroepcentrum
August Reyerslaan 52
1043 Brussels
tel   +32 2 741 3111
fax   +32 2 735 3662
tlx   22486 BRTBIN B
□ Dutch-language public radio and television broadcasting station.
also known as BRTN

BRTK · CYPRUS
- Bayrak Radio and Television

Corporation
Dr Fazıl Küçük Avenue
Lefkoşa (Nicosia)
Mersin 10
tel   +357 2 520 85555
fax   +357 2 520 81991
tlx   57264
□ independent Turkish-Cypriot radio and television broadcasting corporation.

BRTN · BELGIUM
- Belgische Radio en Televisie
see **BRT** · BELGIUM

BRTV · NIGERIA
- Borno State Radio and Television Corporation
Maiduguri
□ state-owned television station.

BRU · UK
- Broadcasting Research Unit
see **VLV** · UK

BRW · GERMANY
- Bayerische Rundfunkwerbung GmbH
Amulfstraße 42
8000 Munich 2
tel   +49 89 5900 04
fax   +49 89 5900 42 24
□ regional and national sales of television and radio advertising.

BS · TECHNICAL TERM
- broadcast satellite

BSAC · UK
- British Screen Advisory Council
93 Wardour Street
London W1V 3TE
tel   +44 71 413 8009
fax   +44 71 734 5122
1985 □ to advance the prosperity and enhance the prestige, effectiveness and reputation of the moving picture industries of the UK and pursue these objectives through the following: to foster good communication between Government and Parliament, on the one hand, and UK film, television and video industries on the other; to provide and/or bring to the attention of Government information and opinion from a wide range of sources on

matters of national importance relating to film, television and video; to assist the moving picture industries in achieving better or alternative modes of communication with Government; to provide an extremely broad spectrum of knowledge, contacts and experience in the moving picture media; to operate as an objective body placing priority on the collection and presentation of facts and of views which different sectors of the industry may hold.

BSB · UK
▪ British Satellite Broadcasting
see **BSKYB** · UK

BSC · UK
▪ British Society of Cinematographers
11 Croft Road
Chalfont St Peter
Gerrards Cross
Bucks SL9 9AE
tel +44 753 888052
fax +44 753 891486
1949 □ to promote and encourage the pursuit of the highest standards in the craft of motion picture photography. It publishes a *Newsletter* (6) and the *BSC Directory*.

BSC · UK
▪ Broadcasting Standards Council
5-8 The Sanctuary
London SW1P 3JS
tel +44 71 233 0544
fax +44 71 233 0397
1988 □ seeks to act as an independent body on behalf of consumers, considering complaints, conducting research and monitoring, and providing a forum for the discussion of wider issues. It publishes a *Bulletin* (12).

BSC · TECHNICAL TERM
▪ binary synchronous communication

BSD · UK
▪ British Screen Development
c/o British Screen Finance (BSF)
14-17 Wells Mews
London W1P 3FL
tel +44 71 323 9080
fax +44 71 323 0092

1991 □ from 1976 until 1991 the National Film Development Fund (**NFDF**) was the recipient of a government grant through the Department of Trade and Industry (DTI), for the purpose of supporting the writing of screenplays and the development of feature film projects. The DTI ceased funding the NFDF in April 1991 and the yearly grant which it used to receive now forms part of British Screen's grant. BSD, under newly-devised guidelines, continues the work of the NFDF in financing screenwriting and project development and in co-financing (with **C4**) an annual programme of short films. The NFDF now exists purely to administer its own past loans.

BSF · UK
▪ British Screen Finance Ltd
14-17 Wells Mews
London W1P 3FL
tel +44 71 323 9080
fax +44 71 323 0092
1986 □ to provide support for British film-makers seeking to develop and produce films for the cinema. The support takes the form of commercial loans for specific projects. Since its inception it has had at its disposal, after deduction of overhead costs, between £4m and £5m annually to assist the development and production of film projects. It participates in the financing of 10-12 feature films each year, typically providing about 20% of a film's production budget.

BSKYB · UK
▪ British Sky Broadcasting
6 Centaurs Business Park
Grant Way
Syon Lane
Isleworth
Middlesex TW7 5QD
tel +44 71 782 3000
fax +44 71 782 3030
1990 □ 6-channel English language satellite and cable channel.
created by the merger of British Satellite Broadcasting (BSB) and Sky Television

BSN · JAPAN
■ Broadcasting System of Niigata Inc
3-18 Kawagishi-cho
Niigata 951
tel   +81 25 267 4111
□ television station.

BSS · JAPAN
■ Broadcasting System of San-In
423 Nishi-Fukuhara
Yonago 683
tel   +81 859 33 2111
□ television station.

BSS · UK
■ Broadcasting Support Services
252 Western Avenue
London W3 6XJ
tel   +44 81 992 5522
fax   +44 81 993 6281
1975 □ independent educational
charity which runs helplines on topics
ranging across the fields of health,
social welfare, education, the
environment and recreation and
provides follow-up services for viewers
and listeners on **BBC**, Channel 4 (**C4**),
ITV and other media. It also publishes a
range of viewers' and listeners' guides
which extend knowledge and
appreciation of particular programme
topics beyond the actual broadcast.

BSS · TECHNICAL TERM
■ broadcast(ing) satellite service

BT · BULGARIA
■ Bålgarska Televizija
ul. San Stefano 29
1504 Sofia
tel   +359 2 43481
fax   +359 2 871871
tlx   22581
□ national television service, operating
2 channels.
also known as BTV

BT · TECHNICAL TERM
■ block termination

BTA · TECHNICAL TERM
■ best time available

BTL · TECHNICAL TERM

■ behind the lens

BTM · TECHNICAL TERM
■ break tape manager

BTRE · USA
■ Broadcast Television Recording
Engineers
Suite 721
6255 Sunset Boulevard
Hollywood
CA 90028
tel   +1 213 851 5515
fax   +1 213 466 1793
□ union.

BTS · GERMANY
■ Broadcast Television Systems GmbH
Robert-Bosch-Straße 7
64293 Darmstadt
tel   +49 6151 8080
fax   +49 6151 894463
1986 □ development, production, sales
and worldwide service of both mobile
and stationary television systems and
equipment. In addition to consultancy
and planning, the services provided
also include the setting up and
commissioning of television
installations, as well as the training of
operating and maintenance personnel.

BTS · USA
■ Broadcast Technology Society
c/o Institution of Electrical and
Electronics Engineers, Inc
345 East 47th Street
New York
NY 10017-2394
tel   +1 212 705 7900
fax   +1 212 752 4929
□ body which issues information and
guidance in the area of broadcast
transmission systems engineering.

BTSC · USA
■ Broadcast Television Systems
Committee
□ committee within the Electronic
Industries Association (**EIA**)

BTV · BANGLADESH
■ Bangladesh Television
PO Box 456

Rampura
Dhaka 1219
tel   +880 2 400131
tel   +880 2 832927
tlx   675624 BTV BJ
1971 □ television broadcasting service.

BTV · BENIN
▪ Bendel State Television
Benin
□ state-owned television station.

BTV · BULGARIA
▪ Bâlgarska Televizija
see **BT** · BULGARIA

BTV · TECHNICAL TERM
▪ business television

BU · TECHNICAL TERM
▪ build-up

BUFF · SWEDEN
▪ Barn och ungdomsfilmfestivalen i
Malmö
PO Box 6197
S-200 11 Malmö
tel   +46 40 30 53 22
fax +46 40 30 53 22
1984 □ annual international film
festival in January, featuring the latest in
Swedish and Scandinavian children's
and youth films, with an audience of
over 12 000.

BUFVC · UK
▪ British Universities Film & Video
Council
55 Greek Street
London W1V 5LR
tel   +44 71 734 3687
fax +44 71 287 3914
*formerly the British Universities Film
Council*
1948 □ promotes the use, production
and study of audiovisual aids and
techniques in higher education teaching
and research and provides a forum for
the exchange of information and
experience in this field. It publishes
Viewfinder (3) and various book
publications.

BV · TECHNICAL TERM

▪ broadcast video

BVA · UK
▪ British Videogram Association
22 Poland Street
London W1V 3DD
tel   +44 71 437 5722
fax +44 71 437 0477
1980 □ to implement collective
action - lobbying, market research,
public relations - on behalf of UK
publishers of pre-recorded video
cassettes.

BVB · TECHNICAL TERM
▪ black-video-black

BVDFP · GERMANY
see **BDF** · GERMANY

BVE · UK
▪ Broadcast Video Engineering Ltd
64/66 Glentham Road
London SW13 9JJ
tel   +44 81 563 0600
fax +44 81 563 7601
1984 □ design, manufacture and
consultancy of innovative products for
the broadcast television industry.

BVE · TECHNICAL TERM
▪ broadcast video editing

BVHT · UK
▪ British Video History Trust
55 Greek Street
London W1V 5LR
tel   +44 71 734 3687
fax +44 71 287 3914
1987 □ established to meet the need
for videotaped documentation of
everyday British life. It enables
amateurs to record aspects of British life
and culture which might otherwise be
lost.

BVM · TECHNICAL TERM
▪ broadcast video monitor

BVS · TECHNICAL TERM
▪ broadcast video switcher

BVTV · UK
▪ Black Variety Television

33 Shrubbery Road
London N9 OPA
tel   +44 81 884 0966
1992 □ cable television broadcaster.

BVU · TECHNICAL TERM
▪ broadcast video U-matic®

BW · TECHNICAL TERM
▪ black and white (*aka* B/W)

C

C³ · TECHNICAL TERM
▪ clean, clear coat

C4 · UK
▪ Channel Four Television Company
Ltd
60 Charlotte Street
London W1P 2AX
tel   +44 71 631 4444
fax +44 71 637 1495
tlx 892355
1980 □ television station established
with the following objectives: to
provide information, entertainment and
education; to appeal to interests and
tastes not generally catered for by
Channel 3 (**ITV**); to support and
encourage innovation and experiment.

C/I · TECHNICAL TERM
▪ carrier/interference

C/N · TECHNICAL TERM
▪ carrier-to-noise ratio (*aka* CNR)

C-QUAM · TECHNICAL TERM
▪ compatible-quadrature amplitude
modulator

C-SPAN · USA
▪ Cable Satellite Public Affairs Network
Suite 650
400 N Capitol Street NW
Washington
DC 20001
tel   +1 202 737 3220
fax +1 202 737 6226
1979 □ television station.

CA · UK
▪ Cable Authority
*now replaced by Independent
Television Commission (ITC)*

CA · TECHNICAL TERM
▪ commercial announcement

CAA · UK
▪ Cinema Advertising Association
127 Wardour Street
London W1V 4AD
tel   +44 71 439 9531
fax +44 71 439 2395
1953 □ trade association of cinema
advertising contractors operating in the
UK and Éire. Its main purpose is to
promote, monitor and maintain
standards of cinema advertising
exhibition and to commission and
conduct research into cinema itself as
an advertising medium. It commissions
the annual Cinema and Video Industry
Audience Research (**CAVIAR**) studies,
providing unique data on cinema and
video viewers from the age of 5
upwards. It produces *Projections*
magazine (seasonal), as well as annual
guides.

CAA · USA
▪ Creative Artists Agency Inc
Suite 1400
1888 Century Park East
Los Angeles
CA 90067
tel   +1 310 277 4545
fax +1 310 284 3300
tlx 688467 CREATLSA
□ theatrical agency, including
representing artistes from the film and
television industries.

CAAMA · AUSTRALIA
▪ Central Australian Aboriginal Media
Association
PO Box 2924
Alice Springs
Northern Territory
tel   +61 89 523744
fax +61 89 555219
1980 □ maintenance and promotion of
aboriginal culture, languages and way
of life.

CAB · CANADA
■ Canadian Association of Broadcasters
165 Sparkes Street
PO Box 627
Station B
Ottawa K1P 5S2
tel   +1 613 233 4035
fax +1 613 233 6961

CAB · USA
■ Cable Television Advertising Bureau, Inc
757 Third Avenue
New York
NY 10017
tel   +1 212 751 7770
fax +1 212 832 3268
□ body comprising individuals working in cable television sales and advertising which aims to encourage cable television as an effective medium for advertising. It publishes *Ad Tier* (12).
also known as CTAB

CABC · BARBADOS
■ Caribbean Broadcasting Corporation (Barbados)
PO Box 900
Bridgetown
tel   +1 809 429 2041
fax +1 809 429 4795
tlx   2560 CABROCO
1963 □ television and radio broadcasting corporation.
also known as CBC

CAC · GABON
■ Comité Africain de Cinéastes

CACI · VENEZUELA
■ Conferencia de Autoridades Cinematográficas Iberoamericanas
c/o Fondo de Fomento Cinematográfico (FONCINE)
Avde. Diego Cisneros Edif.
Centro Colgate Ala Sur Piso 2
Los Ruices
Caracas 1071
tel   +58 2 381775 / 381622 / 381050 / 381564 / 395973 / 393942
fax +58 2 394786
tlx   25531 FONCI-VC
1991 □ conference on Ibero-American cinema, aiming to develop policies to consolidate film production and distribution throughout Latin America.

CACLB · UK
■ Churches Advisory Council for Local Broadcasting
PO Box 124
Westcliff-on-Sea
Essex SSO OQU
tel   +44 702 348369
fax +44 702 348369
1967 □ council established for the advancement of the Christian religion through broadcasting on radio and television. It carries out the following: acts on behalf of the churches in the field of local broadcasting; monitors local media developments and advises the churches on an appropriate response; liaises with local broadcasting stations; encourages Christian involvement in broadcasting; helps and advises Christian broadcasters and provides continuous fellowship for them in the Association of Christians in Local Broadcasting (**ACLB**).

CAD · TECHNICAL TERM
■ computer-aided/assisted design

CADA · UK
■ Commercial Art Directors Association
Odd Fellows Hall
Fletcher Road
London W4 5AS
tel   +44 81 995 1661
fax +44 81 995 1817
1987 □ association of art directors who work on commercials.

CADAM · TECHNICAL TERM
■ computer-aided/assisted design and manufacture

CAF · USA
■ Cable Arts Foundation, Inc

CAI · TECHNICAL TERM
■ colour aperture/actuance improvement

CAIV · TECHNICAL TERM
■ computer-assisted interactive video

CAM · TECHNICAL TERM
■ conventional amplitude modulation

CAMECO · GERMANY
■ Catholic Media Council
Publizistische Medienplanung für
Entwicklungsländer
Anton-Kurze-Allee 2
Postfach 1912
52074 Aachen
tel +49 241 73081
fax +49 241 73462
tlx 832719 mira d
1969 □ professional research and
advisory office in the field of
communications in developing
countries, whose main objectives are:
to evaluate and coordinate
communication projects from
developing countries submitted to
Church funding agencies in the
Western world - over 650 projects are
received for evaluation each year,
related to film, radio and television,
press and publishing, group media and
new technologies, and others; to advise
communicators from developing
countries on all questions concerning
project planning and execution; to
promote cooperation and coordination
with other Christian media
organisations and funding agencies on
an ecumenical basis, as well as with
international secular media
organisations and funding agencies for
developing countries; to collect and
collate relevant data on communication
and media in developing countries.

CAMIS · TECHNICAL TERM
■ computer-assisted makeup and
imaging system

CAMPP · CANADA
■ Canadian Association of Motion
Picture Producers
□ association representing Canadian
film producers.

CAMR · TECHNICAL TERM
■ conférence administrative mondiale
des radiocommunications

CANAMECC · COSTA RICA
■ Cámara Nacional de Medios de
Comunicación Colectiva
Apdo. 6.574
1000 San José
tel +506 22 4820
1954 □ national body which promotes
means of collective communication.

CAPAC · FRANCE
■ Compagnie Artistique de Productions
et d'Adaptations Cinématographiques
5 rue de Lincoln
75008 Paris
tel +33 1 42 25 51 42 / 42 25 53 54
tlx 643765
□ film school.

CAPRICAS · FRANCE
■ Caisse de Prévoyance et de Retraite
de l'Industrie Cinématographique, des
Activités du Spectacle et de
l'Audiovisuel
7 rue Henri Rochefort
75854 Paris
tel +33 1 44 15 24 24
fax +33 1 44 15 24 20
1943 □ reserve and superannuation
fund of staff of the cinematographic,
theatre and audiovisual industries.

CAR · TECHNICAL TERM
■ central apparatus room

CARA · USA
■ Classification and Rating
Administration

CARCICAS · FRANCE
■ Caisse de Retraite des Cadres de
l'Industrie Cinématographique, des
Activités du Spectacle et de
l'Audiovisuel
7 rue Henri Rochefort
75854 Paris
tel +33 1 44 15 24 24
fax +33 1 44 15 24 20
1947 □ superannuation fund of the staff
of the cinematographic, theatre and
audiovisual industries.

CARIMAC · JAMAICA
■ Caribbean Institute of Mass
Communication
West Indies University

Mona
Kingston 7
tel   +1 809 927 1481
fax   +1 809 927 5353
tlx   2123
□ institution for mass communication education and training.

CARM · UK
▪ Campaign Against Racism in the Media
see **CPBF** · UK

CARS · TECHNICAL TERM
▪ community antenna relay service
▪ cable television relay service

CARTA · USA
▪ Catholic Apostolate of Radio, Television and Advertising

CARTOON · BELGIUM
see **EAFF** · BELGIUM

CATA · USA
▪ Community Antenna Television Association
3950 Chain Bridge Road
Box 1005
Fairfax
VA 22030
tel   +1 703 691 8875
fax +1 703 691 8911
1974 □ organisation of cable television owners and operators which campaigns and advises both nationally and locally. It publishes *Catacable* (12).

CATA · TECHNICAL TERM
▪ computer assisted traditional animation

CATV · TECHNICAL TERM
▪ cable television
▪ central aerial television
▪ community antenna television

CAV · TECHNICAL TERM
▪ constant angular velocity
▪ component analogue video

CAVCO · CANADA
▪ Canadian Audio-Visual Certification Office

Communications Policy
Department of Communications
Room 602
300 Slater Street
Ottawa
Ontario K1A 0C8
tel   +1 613 990 4091
fax +1 613 952 5110
□ administers the Capital Cost Allowance (**CCA**) programme, under which investors in certified Canadian films and television programmes may deduct 30% of their investment from their taxable income on declining balance basis. The CCA also provides an additional allowance allowing investors to claim a deduction on film revenues.

CAVIAR · UK
▪ Cinema and Video Industry Audience Research
see **CAA** · UK

CAWO · THE NETHERLANDS
▪ Contactgroep Audiovisuele Centra Wetenschappelijk Onderwijs
Meibergdreef 15
1105 AZ Amsterdam
tel   +31 20 566 4704
tel   +31 20 566 4656
□ contact group for audiovisual centres of university education.

CB · TECHNICAL TERM
▪ chain break

CBA · BELGIUM
▪ Centre Bruxellois de l'Audiovisuel
18 rue Joseph II
B-1040 Brussels
tel   +32 2 218 4080
fax +32 2 217 9197
1979 □ production centre for documentaries, with the aim to produce and/or coproduce documentary film projects and to help in their distribution.

CBA · UK
▪ Commonwealth Broadcasting Association
BBC White City
201 Wood Lane

London W12 7TS
tel +44 81 752 5022
      +44 81 752 5252 x.25022
fax +44 81 752 4137
tlx 265781
1945 □ association of some 60 national broadcasting organisations in 52 Commonwealth countries whose main objectives are: to improve, through collective study and mutual assistance, all aspects of broadcasting in member countries; to further the concept that public service broadcasting is vital to member countries as an instrument to promote their social, cultural and economic aspirations; to provide a basic information service on broadcasting matters of common interest and concern; to represent and promote internationally the collective interests of Commonwealth public service broadcasting organisations. It publishes *Combroad* (4) and a *Handbook.*

CBA · USA
■ Community Broadcasters Association
PO Box 9556
Panama City Beach
FL 32407
tel +1 904 234 1179

CBC · BARBADOS
■ Caribbean Broadcasting Corporation
see **CABC** · BARBADOS

CBC · CANADA
■ Canadian Broadcasting Corporation
1500 Bronson Avenue
PO Box 8478
Ottawa
Ontario K1G 3J5
tel +1 613 724 1200
fax +1 613 738 6749
tlx 053 4260
1936 □ provides a national broadcasting service in the English language.

CBC · CYPRUS
■ Cyprus Broadcasting Corporation
see **CYBC** · CYPRUS

CBC · JAPAN

■ Chubu-Nippon Broadcasting Co Ltd
2-8 Shin-Sakae 1-chome
Naka-ku
Nagoya 460-05
tel +81 52 241 8111
□ television station.

CBC · USA
■ Completion Bond Company, Inc
2121 Avenue of the Stars
Suite 830
Los Angeles
CA 90067-5017
tel +1 310 553 8300
fax +1 310 553 6610
1980 □ bonding films.

CBFC · PAKISTAN
■ Central Board of Film Censors
St. No. 55
F-6/4
Islamabad
tel +92 42 824939 / 825918
fax +92 42 817323
□ film censorship board.

CBG · TECHNICAL TERM
■ character background generator

CBI · USA
■ CBS Broadcast International
51 West 52 Street
New York
NY 10028
tel +1 212 975 8585
fax +1 212 975 7452
tlx 662101 CBINY
1981 □ television programme distributor.

CBN · USA
■ Christian Broadcasting Network
700 CBN Center
Virginia Beach
VA 23463-0001
tel +1 804 523 7121
fax +1 804 523 7812

CBO · TECHNICAL TERM
■ confirmation of broadcast order

CBP · UK
■ Cable and Broadcast Productions
Riverside Studios

Riverside Estate
Langley Park
Durham DH7 6UA
tel   +44 91 373 0449
fax +44 91 373 0449
1991 □ independent television
programme producers.

CBRA · CANADA
▪ Canadian Broadcasters Rights Agency,
Inc
PO Box 1196, Station B
Suite 1000
280 Albert Street
Ottawa
Ontario K1P 5G8
tel   +1 613 232 4370
fax +1 613 236 9241
□ national collective representing the
copyright interests of private
commercial television and radio
stations in Canada.

CBS · USA
▪ Columbia Broadcasting System, Inc
Floor 35
51 West 52nd Street
New York
NY 10019
tel   +1 212 975 4321
fax +1 212 975 7452
tlx   12435 cbsinc nyk
1927 □ major television and radio
broadcasting network.

CBSK · KOREA
▪ Christian Broadcasting System Korea
917-1 Mok 1-dong
Yangchon-ku
Seoul 158-701
tel   +82 2 650 7000 / 650 7003
fax +82 2 654 2456
1955 □ established as the first
independent broadcasting system on
Korea, it now operates 6 AM radio
stations on a national basis and many
studios, including a television
production studio.

CBU · BARBADOS
▪ Caribbean Broadcasting Union
Wanderers Gap
Dayrells Road
Christ Church

tel   +1 809 429 9146
fax +1 809 429 2171
tlx   2569 CARICAST
□ federation of national broadcasting
companies within the Caribbean and
the Commonwealth which aims to
encourage and facilitate the exchange
of views and experiences between its
members.

CC · UK
▪ The Children's Channel
9-13 Grape Street
London WC2H 8DR
tel   +44 71 240 3422
fax +44 71 937 7817 / 497 9113
1984 □ television channel, delivered by
the **INTELSAT VI** and ASTRA 1b satellite,
devoted to educating as well as
entertaining children between the ages
of 2 and 15 years. It is supported by
subscriptions and advertising and is
watched in over 6 million households.

CC · TECHNICAL TERM
▪ closed captioning
▪ colour compensating
▪ commercial continuity

CCA · CANADA
▪ Capital Cost Allowance
see **CAVCO** · CANADA

CCA · SENEGAL
▪ Consortium de Communication
Audiovisuelle en Afrique
Ville 2744
Diauppeul 111-sicap
BP 10402
Dakar
tel   +221 24 17 17
□ consortium of audiovisual
communication in Africa.

CCA · USA
▪ Citizens for Cable Awareness

CCAVT · CANADA
▪ Canadian Coalition Against Video
Theft
Canadian Motion Picture Distributors
Association
Suite 1603
22 St Clair Avenue East

Toronto
Ontario M4T 2S4
tel +1 416 961 1888
fax +1 416 968 1016
1989 □ established to attract
independent film and video companies
to the anti-piracy campaign. These
members can join for a flat fee, based
on annual revenues and type of
organisation. Members participate in
formulating anti-piracy, legal,
advertising and education strategies.

CCC · CANADA
▪ Copyright Collective of Canada
Canadian Motion Picture Distributors
Association (CMPDA)
Suite 1603
22 St Clair Avenue East
Toronto
Ontario M4T 2S4
tel +1 416 961 1888
fax +1 416 968 1016
1989 □ represents primarily **CMPDA**
member companies and other US
suppliers of entertainment
programming. It collects copyright
royalties from retransmitters and
distributes the proceeds to its claimants
according to a pre-determined formula.

CCC · ITALY
▪ Cerrato Compagnia Cinematografico
Via Riboty 24/26
Rome
□ film production.

CCC · ITALY
▪ Centro Cattolico Cinematografico
Via Giuseppe Palombini 6
Rome
□ centre for Catholic cinema.

CCC · MEXICO
▪ Centro de Capacitación
Cinematográfica
Calzada de Tlalpan, 1670
Col. Country Club
04220 Mexico, D.F.
tel +52 5 544 9717 / 544 8007
□ film school.

CCC/UN · USA
▪ Communications Coordination

Committee for the United Nations
United Nations
New York
NY 10017
tel +1 212 983 3353
1945 □ group of academics, journalists
and others who work or are active in
the media of film, television, radio and
computing. It publishes a *Newsletter*
(6).

CCD · TECHNICAL TERM
▪ charge coupled device

CCDC · TECHNICAL TERM
▪ channel compatible digicypher

CCETT · FRANCE
▪ Centre Commun d'Etudes de
Télédiffusion et de Télécommunications

CCF · TECHNICAL TERM
▪ chroma crawl free

CCFC · USA
▪ Chicago Children's Film Centre
c/o Facets Multimedia, Inc
1517 West Fullerton Avenue
Chicago
IL 60614
tel +1 312 281 9075
fax +1 312 929 5437
tlx 20-6701

CCHP · TECHNICAL TERM
▪ constant conductance heat pipe

CCI · TECHNICAL TERM
▪ co-channel interference

CCIR · SWITZERLAND
▪ Comité Consultatif International de
Radiocommunications
▪ International Radio Consultative
Committee
International Telecommunications
Union (ITU)
Place des Nations
CH-1211 Geneva 20
tel +41 22 730 5111
fax +41 22 733 7256
tlx 421 000 UIT CH
1929 □ committee established to study
radio and operating questions relating

specifically to radiocommunication, without limit of frequency range, and issue recommendations on them. Its Study Groups are concerned with subjects including television broadcasting, fixed satellite service, and television and sound transmission.

CCIS · TECHNICAL TERM
- coaxial cable information system

CCITT · SWITZERLAND
- Comité Consultatif International de Téléphone et de Télégraph
- International Telephone and Telegraph Consultative Committee
International Telecommunications Union (ITU)
Place des Nations
CH-1211 Geneva 20
tel +41 22 730 5111
fax +41 22 733 7256
tlx 421 000 UIT CH
1956 □ committee established to study and issue recommendations on technical, operating and tariff questions relating to telecommunications services other than technical or operating questions relating specifically to radiocommunication (which come within the range of **CCIR**). Its Study Groups are concerned with subjects such as **ISDN**, television and sound transmission and data communication.

CCM · MOROCCO
- Centre Cinématographique Marocain
Rabat

CCP · TECHNICAL TERM
- colour control panel

CCR · ITALY
- Comitato Cinematografia Ragazzi
Via Tribuna Tir di Specchi 18A
00186 Rome
tel +39 6 67 94 268
□ youths' film committee.

CCR · TECHNICAL TERM
- central control room

CCRTV · SPAIN
- Corporació Catalana de Ràdio i Televisió
Avda Diagonal 477
08036 Barcelona
tel +34 3 410 9696
fax +34 3 419 4051
tlx 97012
1983 □ Catalan-language broadcasting station, with 2 television channels and 3 radio stations.

CCS · TECHNICAL TERM
- clear colour screen
- common channel signalling

CCT · USA
- Committee for Competitive Television

CCT · TECHNICAL TERM
- computer controlled (tele)text

CCTA · CANADA
- Canadian Cable Television Association
Suite 1010
360 Albert Street
Ottawa
Ontario K1R 7X7
tel +1 613 232 2631
fax +1 613 232 2137

CCTI · USA
- Committee on Children's Television, Inc

CCTM · USA
- Council for Children's Television and Media

CCTMA · USA
- Closed-Circuit Television Manufacturers Association
2001 Pennsylvania Avenue NW
Washington
DC 20006-1813
tel +1 202 457 4900
fax +1 202 457 4985
1986 □ association affiliated to the Electronic Industries Association (**EIA**). It comprises companies which manufacture components and systems employed in the transmission of closed-circuit television data, information and pictures.

CCTV · CHINA
- China Central Television
Television Building
11 Fuxing Road
Beijing 100859
tel   +86 1 821 5737
fax +86 1 801 3025
tlx   222 300
1958 □ national television broadcasting service, operating 3 channels.

CCTV · ITALY
- Centro Cattolico Televisivo
Via Giuseppe Palombini 6
Rome
□ Catholic television centre.

CCTV · TECHNICAL TERM
- closed-circuit (cable) television

CCU · TECHNICAL TERM
- camera control unit
- central control unit

CD · TECHNICAL TERM
- compact disc

CD-I · TECHNICAL TERM
- compact disc-interactive

CD-ROM · TECHNICAL TERM
- compact disc read-only memory

CD-ROM XA · TECHNICAL TERM
- compact disc read-only memory extended architecture

CD-RTOS · TECHNICAL TERM
- compact disc real-time operating system

CD-V · TECHNICAL TERM
- compact disc-video
- compressed digital video

CDA · ITALY
- Compagnia Distribuzione Audiovisivi
Via Castelbarco 5
20136 Milan
tel   +39 2 58 30 81 01/2
fax +39 2 58 30 81 12
□ film, television and video programme distributors.

CDC · TECHNICAL TERM
- control and data/delay channel

CDFM · GERMANY
- Club Deutscher Film- und Fernseh-Maskenbildner Sektion München
Schlierseestr. 21
81541 Munich
tel   +49 89 691 2116
□ German film and television club.

CDI · ITALY
- Compagnia Distribuzione Internazionale
Largo A Ponichielli, 6
00198 Rome
tel   +39 6 884 8632
fax +39 6 884 5710
tlx   612302
□ film distributors.

CDK · TECHNICAL TERM
- chroma light and dark

CDMA · TECHNICAL TERM
- code division multiple access

CDMM · FRANCE
- Comité Directeur sur les Moyens de Communication de Masse
- Steering Committee for/on the Mass Media
Conseil de l'Europe/Council of Europe
67075 Strasbourg Cedex
tel   +33 88 41 20 00
fax +33 88 41 27 05
1981 □ intergovernmental steering committee of experts in the mass media field. Its aims are: to develop European cooperation between the member states of the Council of Europe on the mass media with a view to further enhancing freedom of expression and information in a pluralistic democratic society; to further the free flow of information and ideas; to foster a plurality of independent media, reflecting a diversity of opinions and cultures.

CDP · TECHNICAL TERM
- control diagnostic panel

CDS · TECHNICAL TERM
- cable diffusion service

- cadmium disulphide
- Cinema Digital Sound®

CDTV · TECHNICAL TERM
- Commodore dynamic total vision

CDW · TECHNICAL TERM
- compact disc write once

CE · TECHNICAL TERM
- chief engineer

CEA · UK
- Cinema Exhibitors Association
22 Golden Square
London W1R 4PA
tel +44 71 734 9551
fax +44 71 734 6147
1912 □ association representing
exhibitors in the UK. Its members
account for over 90% of all the UK's
commercial cinemas, including
independents, regional film theatres and
those under local authority control. It
represents members' interests both
within the industry and to governments
local, national and European. It
publishes a *Newsletter* (4-6).
*incorporating Association of
Independent Cinemas (AIC)*

CECS · ITALY
- Comitato Ecumenico per le
Comunicazioni Sociali
Casella Postale 6306
00195 Rome
tel +39 6 3700 266
fax +39 6 3120 68
1974 □ to unite exponents of various
religious faiths who specialise in the
means of social communication. It
produces several books.

CED · UK
- CETA Electronic Design (UK) Ltd
40 The Ridgeway
London N11 3LJ
tel +44 81 368 9417
fax +44 81 368 8094
1986 □ specialises in the design and
supply of electronic hardware for the
broadcast, professional and industrial
video markets.

CED · TECHNICAL TERM
- capacitance/capacitive electronic disc

CEDIA · USA
- Custom Electronic Design and
Installation Association
10400 Roberts Road
Palos Hills
IL 60464
□ organisation whose members
specialise in designing and installing
home theatres and multi-room
audio/video systems.

CEIS · FRANCE
- Centre Européen de l'Image et du Son
Arles
tel +33 90 93 19 99
□ information, research, production
and teacher-training centre for the
cinema.

CENACI · GABON
- Centre National du Cinéma
BP 2193
Libreville
1975 □ national cinema centre.

CEPI · FRANCE
- Coordination Européenne des
Producteurs Indépendants
59 rue de Châteaudun
75009 Paris
tel +33 1 44 53 03 03
fax +33 1 49 95 99 80
□ European network of associations of
television producers.

CERAV · BURKINO FASO
- Centre d'Enseignement et de
Recherche Audiovisuel

CERC · ARGENTINA
- Centro de Experimentación y
Realización Cinematográfica

CERIS · FRANCE
- Centre d'Etudes et de Recherches de
l'Image et du Son
Château de Montvillargenne
60270 Gouvieux
tel +33 44 58 21 24
□ institution offering courses in video
and film.

CES · UK
■ The Continuing Education Service
Aston University
Aston Triangle
Birmingham B4 7ET
tel +44 21 359 3611
fax +44 21 359 6427
1984 ❑ coordinates the development
and promotion of short courses as well
as being the focus of video-based
distance learning programmes.

CESTI · SENEGAL
■ Centre d'Etudes des Sciences et
Techniques de l'Information
Université Cheikh Anta Diop de Dakar
Dakar
tel +221 230758
fax +221 230366
1965 ❑ research and study centre,
specialising in mass communication,
media and journalism.

CET · UK
■ Continuing Education and Training
BBC Education
BBC White City
201 Wood Lane
London W12 7TS
tel +44 81 752 5252
fax +44 81 752 4398
❑ produces high quality educational
programmes and resources. A varied
portfolio of broadcasts addresses a
diverse range of subjects, with language
learning, training for work, equal
opportunities, information and advice
constituting the main focus of CET
series. Most programmes are
supplemented by support materials:
books, leaflets, helplines, cassettes and
expert advice on courses and further
opportunities for study are part of the
back-up service designed to encourage
learners at every stage.

CEU · TECHNICAL TERM
■ control electronics unit

CEV · SPAIN
■ Centro de Estudios de la Imagen y del
Video
Calle Regueros 3
28004 Madrid

tel +34 1 419 8450
fax +34 1 419 8500
❑ private educational organisation.

CEVMA · UK
■ Christian European Visual Media
Association
235 Shaftesbury Avenue
London WC2H 8EL
tel +44 71 836 2255
fax +44 71 240 0005
1982 ❑ networking organisation of
Christians who are active in both the
mainstream and specialist media -
primarily in film and television. It holds
an annual convention.

CF · TECHNICAL TERM
■ children's feature/film

CFC · USA
■ California Film Commission
6922 Hollywood Boulevard
Suite 600
Hollywood
CA 90028
tel +1 213 736 2465
fax +1 213 736 3159
1985 ❑ the reawakening of
communities statewide to the benefits
of filming in their area; the
reintroduction of the film industry of
the beauty, diversity and simplicity of
shooting in California. It publishes a
Newsletter (6) and other publications,
including *Your Property In a Starring
Role* and *Scouting Handbook*.

CFDA · USA
■ Christian Film Distributors'
Association

CFDC · CANADA
■ Canadian Film-Makers Distribution
Centre
see **CFMDC** · CANADA

CFEJ · FRANCE
■ Centre Nationale Français du Film
pour l'Enfance et la Jeunesse
133 rue du Château
75014 Paris
tel +33 1 43 21 51 60
1962 ❑ national centre of film for

young people.

CFG · FRANCE
▪ Compagnie Française
Cinématographique

CFI · FRANCE
▪ Canal France International
59 Boulevard Exelmans
75016 Paris
tel +33 1 40 71 11 71
fax +33 1 40 71 11 72
tlx 648467 CFINT
1989 □ broadcasting of French
programmes to foreign countries. It
publishes *CFI Avant Première* (12).

CFI · USA
▪ Consolidated Film Industries
□ film processing laboratory.

CFL · UK
▪ CFL Vision
formerly Central Film Library
PO Box 35
Wetherby
Yorks LS23 7EX
tel +44 937 541010
fax +44 937 541083
1948 □ CFL Vision is part of the Films
and Television Division of the Central
Office of Information and provides a
complete marketing service for videos
and films on information, training and
educational subjects, produced by both
the private and public sectors. It
produces the *CFL Vision Video
Directory* (every 2 years).

CFMDC · CANADA
▪ Canadian Film-Makers Distribution
Centre
67a Portland Street
Toronto
Ontario M5V 2M9
tel +1 416 593 1808
fax +1 416 593 8661
1967 □ to promote the distribution of
independent films in Canada and
throughout the world. It is a non-profit
artist-run centre, with a mandate to
service the needs of its film-maker
members by assisting them in
developing markets for their films. The

membership centres on an open-door,
non-exclusive policy.
also known as CFDC

CFMT · CANADA
▪ "Canada's First Multilingual
Television"
Channel Forty Seven Television
545 Lakeshore Boulevard West
Toronto
Ontario M5V 1A3
tel +1 416 260 0047
fax +1 416 260 0509
tlx 06 23643
1979 □ television broadcasting in 15
different languages throughout Ontario.

CFTC · UK
▪ Commonwealth Fund for Technical
Cooperation
Commonwealth Broadcasting
Association Secretariat
BBC White City
201 Wood Lane
London W12 7TS
tel +44 81 752 5022 / 5252
fax +44 81 752 4137
tlx 265781
1971 □ provides technical assistance
for economic and social development
in Commonwealth developing
countries. On-site training courses have
been provided in continuity and
newsreading; current affairs production;
transmitter maintenance; agricultural
and rural broadcasting; drama and
features production; and news
production and presentation.

CFTCA · USA
▪ Children's Film and Television Center

CFTF · UK
▪ The Children's Film and Television
Foundation Ltd
Elstree Studios
Borehamwood
Herts WD6 1JG
tel +44 81 953 0844
fax +44 81 207 0860
tlx 922436 EFILMS G
1951 □ production of quality
entertainment films for children and the
financing of script development for

subjects deemed suitable for children in the age range of 5 to 12 years.

CFTPA · CANADA
- Canadian Film and Television Production Association
- Association Canadienne de Production de Film et Télévision (ACPFT)
Suite 806
175 Bloor Street E
North Tower
Toronto
Ontario M4W 3R8
tel   +1 416 927 8942
fax +1 416 922 4038
□ association representing some 300 companies involved in independent production in Canada. Membership is open to any entrepreneurial Canadian corporation, partnership, association, or other organisation engaged in film, television, video production, distribution, or in the provision of facilities or services to the independent production industry. It promotes the wider interests of the Canadian independent film and television industry by lobbying government on policy matters, negotiating labour agreements on behalf of independent producers, offering educational programmes and by publishing. It publishes *Action* (4) and *The Guide* (1).

CFU · UK
- The Children's Film Unit
9 Hamilton House
66 Upper Richmond Road
London SW15 2RP
tel   +44 81 871 2006
fax +44 81 871 2140
1981 □ unique film production unit which offers any child under 16 years of age the opportunity to learn about all aspects of film-making and to participate in the making of feature films. The unit currently makes at least one feature film each year.

CFVF · MARTINIQUE
- Caribbean Film and Video Foundation

CFVF · SOUTH AFRICA
- Cape Film and Video Foundation
c/o Johan Blignaut
PO Box 15756
Vlaeberg
Cape Town 8018
tel   +27 21 24 5483
fax +27 21 24 5483
□ to facilitate co-productions; to ensure efficient production service for local and foreign film-makers; to develop and promote an indigenous film culture; to provide research and information; to liaise with authorities.

CG · TECHNICAL TERM
- character generator
- completion guarantor
- computer graphics

CGA · TECHNICAL TERM
- colour graphics adaptor

CGGB · UK
- Cine Guild of Great Britain
Pinewood Studios
Pinewood Road
Iver Heath
Bucks SLO ONH
tel   +44 753 651700
fax +44 753 656844
□ association of British film guilds.

CGH · TECHNICAL TERM
- computer-generated holograms

CGI · TECHNICAL TERM
- computer-generated image(ry)

CGO · TECHNICAL TERM
- can go over

CGS · ITALY
- Cinecircoli Giovanili Socio-Culturali
Via Appia Antica 78
00179 Rome
tel   +39 6 74 82 575
□ social and cultural young persons film clubs.

CGVT · FRANCE
- Compagnie Générale de Télécommunication Téléservice

CH · TECHNICAL TERM
- critical hours

CHN · USA
- Cable Health Network

CHU · TECHNICAL TERM
- camera head unit

CHUT · TECHNICAL TERM
- cable households using television

CI · TECHNICAL TERM
- colour index

CIAC · ITALY
- Centro Italiana Addestramento Cinematografico
Via dello Camilluccia 112
00135 Rome
tel   +39 6 34 20 872
□ Italian centre for film training.

CIAVER · BELGIUM
- Centre International Audiovisuel d'Etudes et de Recherches
45 Avenue des Ecoles
7330 Saint-Ghislain
tel   +32 65 785331
□ international audiovisual study and research centre.

CIAVU · FRANCE
- Centro Internacional del Audiovisual Universitario
c/o URTI
Maison de Radio France
116 Avenue du Président-Kennedy
75786 Paris Cedex 16
tel   +33 1 42 30 23 61 / 39 98 / 23 64
fax   +33 1 40 50 89 99
tlx   200 002 F
known as Centre International de l'Audiovisuel Universitaire
1987 □ to provide a link between universities, professional training colleges, institutes, research centres and museums in all countries which would like to pool some of their audiovisual productions and make them more widely known; to create firmer bonds of cooperation between audiovisual media and universities.

CIBC · COOK ISLANDS
- Cook Islands Broadcasting Corporation
PO Box 126
Avarua
Rarotonga
tel   +682 29460
fax   +682 21907
1989 □ television and radio broadcasting service.

CIC · CUBA
- Centro de Información Cinematográfica
Calle 23 no. 1166 e/ 10 y 12
Vedado
Cuidad Havana 10400
tel   +53 7 3 6322 / 30 9067
fax   +53 7 33 3032
tlx   511419 ICAIC CU
1960 □ film institute which also publishes the magazine *Cine Cubano* (4).

CIC · FRANCE
- Centre d'Initiation au Cinéma, aux Communications et aux Moyens Audiovisuels

CIC · USA
- Cinema International Corporation
□ film distributor.

CIC · TECHNICAL TERM
- cross-interleave code

CICA · FRANCE
- Centre International du Cinéma d'Animation
BP 399
74013 Annecy Cedex
tel   +33 50 57 41 72
fax   +33 50 67 81 95
1956 □ holds the largest international animated film festival with an official selection (competition and panorama sections), retrospectives, tributes, exhibitions, together with the Marché International du Film d'Animation pour le Cinéma et la Télévision (**MIFA**): trade fair, seminars and workshops, and project area.

CICAE · FRANCE

■ Confédération Internationale des Cinémas d'Art-et-Essai Européens
22 rue d'Artois
75008 Paris
tel +33 1 45 61 16 15
1955 □ international group of art-house cinemas.

CICCE · FRANCE
■ Comité des Industries Cinématographiques et Audiovisuelles des Communautés Européennes et de l'Europe Extracommunautaire
c/o CSPEFF
5 rue du Cirque
75008 Paris
tel +33 1 42 25 70 63
fax +33 1 42 25 94 27
1979 □ committee whose main function is to represent the European cinematographic and audiovisual industries to European authorities and to the Conseil de l'Europe / Council of Europe, and to stimulate conformity of legislation.

CICFF · USA
■ Chicago International Children's Film Festival
c/o Facets Multimedia, Inc
1517 West Fullerton Avenue
Chicago
IL 60614
tel +1 312 281 9075
fax +1 312 929 5437
tlx 20-6701
1984 □ 10-day international film festival featuring films and videos, both live action and animation for children aged from 6 to 12 years. Emphasis is placed on exhibiting non-violent, non-exploitative, humanistic films which appeal to a multicultural audience. It publishes a *Festival Programme* (1).

CICT · FRANCE
■ Conseil International du Cinéma, de la Télévision et de la Communication Audiovisuelle
UNESCO
1 rue Miollis
75732 Paris Cedex 15
tel +33 1 45 68 25 56
1958 □ group of professional audiovisual organisations in the fields of cinema, television, radio and related subjects.
also known as International Council for Film, Television & Audio Communications (IFTC)
also known as International Film and Television Council (IFTC)

CICT · ITALY
■ Consiglio Internazionale Cinema e TV
Lungotevere dei Vallati 2
00186 Rome
tel +39 6 687 5898
□ international film and television council.

CICV · FRANCE
■ Centre International de Création Video
Château Eugene Peugeot
BP 5
25310 Herimoncourt
tel +33 81 30 90 30
fax +33 81 30 95 25
1990 □ production centre funded by the French Ministry of Culture and local authorities which provides post-production facilities.

CID · TECHNICAL TERM
■ compact iodide, daylight
■ compact iodine/indium discharge

CIDALC · FRANCE
■ Comité International pour la Diffusion des Arts et des Lettres par le Cinéma
24 Boulevard Poissonnière
75009 Paris
tel +33 1 42 46 65 36
1930 □ international committee for the diffusion of arts and literature through the cinema. It publishes a *Bulletin* (6).

CIDC · BELGIUM
■ Centre International de Documentation Cinématographique
29 rue d'Arschot
5660 Mariembourg
□ film documentation centre.

CIDC · SENEGAL
■ Consortium Interafricain de Distribution Cinématographique

1979 □ pan-African organisation covering 14 countries.
replaced Société d'Importation de Distribution et d'Exploitation Cinématographique (SIDEC)

CIDECCA · FRANCE
■ Centre International de Documentation et d'Echanges sur le Cinéma et la Communication Audiovisuelle
1 bis avenue du Roi Albert
06400 Cannes
tel   +33 93 94 07 77
fax +33 93 43 88 95
1989 □ library, documentation centre and museum on cinema and audiovisual media. It publishes *Script* (4).

CIE · FRANCE
■ Commission Internationale d'Eclairage

CIFC · CANADA
■ Canadian Independent Film Caucus
Suite 102
Cinevillage
65 Heward Avenue
Toronto
Ontario M4M 2T5
tel   +1 416 469 2596
fax +1 416 462 3248
1983 □ non-profit professional film and video makers' association devoted to developing, promoting and supporting the production and distribution of independent Canadian films and videos. It publishes *P.O.V. Magazine* (4).

CIFEJ · FRANCE
■ Centre International du Film pour l'Enfance et la Jeunesse
9 rue Bargue
75015 Paris
tel   +33 1 40 56 00 67
□ association represented in more than 60 countries.
also known as International Centre of Films for Children and Young People (ICFCYP)

CIFF · SOUTH AFRICA
■ Cape Independent Film-Makers

Forum
c/o Cas Rasch
PO Box 1317
Stellenbosch
Cape Town 7599
tel   +27 2231 92369
fax +27 2231 92369
□ to address issues which stifle independent film-making; to engage with other forums in order to advance independent film-making.

CIITC · FRANCE
■ Confédération Internationale des Industries Techniques du Cinéma
□ international federation of technical cinematographic industries.

CILECT · BELGIUM
■ Centre International de Liaison des Ecoles de Cinéma et de Télévision
8 rue Thérésienne
1000 Brussels
tel   +32 2 511 9839
fax +32 2 511 0279
1955 □ to promote cooperation among higher teaching and research associations for film and television, as well as among members of teaching staff and students of these institutions. It publishes *CILECT News* (10).

CINE · USA
■ Council on International Non-Theatrical Events
1001 Connecticut Avenue, NW
Suite 1016
Washington
DC 20036
tel   +1 202 785 1136
fax +1 202 785 4114
1957 □ organisation comprising film directors and others interested in short films and documentaries for the non-theatrical markets. It presents the "Golden Eagle" and "CINE Eagle" awards and publishes *Cine News* (4) and the annual directories: *Worldwide Directory of Film and Video Festivals* and *Cine Yearbook of Awards.*

CINESEAS · SENEGAL
■ Les Cinéastes Sénégalaises Associés
c/o Recidak 93

Villa 2744
Sicap Dieuppeul
Dakar 3
tel +221 235300
▢ professional association of film-
makers.
also known as Association des
Cinéastes Sénégalais (ACS)

CINIT · ITALY
▪ Cineforum Italiano
Segreteria Nazionale
CP 289
30170 Mestre-Ve
tel +39 41 988745
fax +39 41 980061
1971 ▢ its quarterly magazine
Ciemme - Ricerca e studio sulla
comunicazione di massa is the
expression of its activity: to deal and
study all the 'signs' which constitute
social communication. Its particular
aim is to educate and urge the onlooker
to become free of all conditioning,
violence, shown or hidden
manipulations; film viewers are
expected to form a critical attitude
towards mass media influences.
Particular stress is put on adult
permanent education.

CIOAPDS · FRANCE
▪ Centre d'Information d'Orientation de
l'Association Professionnelle du
Spectacle et de l'Audiovisuel
10 rue de la Chaussée d'Antin
75009 Paris
tel +33 1 48 24 11 11 / 47 70 37 18
▢ serves as an information source for
all those interested in taking
audiovisual courses in France.

CIRC · TECHNICAL TERM
▪ cross-interleaved Reed-Solomon code

CIRCA · FRANCE
▪ Cinématographie, Representation,
Communication Audiovisuelle
Université de Toulouse II (Le Mirail)
5 Allées Antonio-Machado
31058 Toulouse Cedex
tel +33 61 50 44 46
▢ research and study centre.

CIRCAV · FRANCE
▪ Centre Interdisciplinaire de Recherche
en Communication Audiovisuelle
Département de Filmologie
Université de Lille III, Charles de
Gaulle
BP 149
59653 Villeneuve d'Ascq Cedex
tel +33 20 91 92 02
tel +33 20 91 91 71
▢ research and study centre.

CIRTEF · BELGIUM
▪ Conseil International des Radios-
Télévisions d'Expression Française
c/o RTBF
52 Boulevard Auguste Reyers
B-1044 Brussels
tel +32 2 732 4585
fax +32 2 732 6240
tlx 21437
1978 ▢ to establish a permanent
dialogue throughout the world among
radio and television stations using the
French language, either totally or
partially, as a medium for broadcasting;
to uphold the interests of its members
and promote the role of radio and
television as a main development factor
for the community; to foster
cooperation between its members; to
organise regular seminars in all aspects
of broadcasting for the professional
benefit of staff of its member
organisations. It publishes *Bulletin*
CIRTEF (4).

CIS · CANADA
▪ Canadian International Studios, Inc
Suite 410
1170 Peel Street
Montreal
Quebec H3B 4P2
tel +1 514 871 8606
fax +1 514 871 9189
1985 ▢ film and television producers.

CISA · SWITZERLAND
▪ Conservatorio Internazionale di
Scienze Audiovisive
Via Brentani 5
6900 Lugano
tel +41 91 515161
fax +41 91 510767

□ higher educational institution, offering courses in film and audiovisual.

CISAS · ITALY
■ Centro Italiano Studi sull'Arte dello Spettacolo & TV
Via A Poliziano 51
00184 Rome
tel   +39 6 733092
1965 □ women's film journalists organisation.

CITAC · TECHNICAL TERM
■ computer interface for tuning and analogue control

CLACPI · PERU
■ Comisión Organizadora Festival Americano de Cine de Los Pueblos Indígenas
Avenida Juan de Aliaga 204
Lima 27
tel   +51 14 61 7949
□ film festival, held every 2 years, showing films and videos about the indigenous peoples of North and South America.

CLAV · BELGIUM
■ Confédération Laïque de l'Audiovisuel

CLCF · FRANCE
■ Conservatoire Libre du Cinéma Français
16 rue du Delta
75009 Paris
tel   +33 1 48 74 65 94
□ film school offering courses lasting 2 years.

CLCT · ITALY
■ Cooperativa Lavoratori del Cinema e del Teatro
via Francesco Lo Iacono, 16
90144 Palermo
tel   +39 91 306968
1971 □ to increase the production of documentary films on wildlife and of films of fiction, cooperating with national and international staff.

CLD · TECHNICAL TERM
■ compact laser disc player

■ controlled light diffusion

CLEARTV · USA
■ Christian Leaders for Responsible Television

CLM · TECHNICAL TERM
■ control lens motor

CLT · LUXEMBOURG
■ Compagnie Luxembourgeoise de Télédiffusion
Villa Louvigny
Luxembourg
tel   +352 47661
fax   +352 4766 2730
tlx   0402 3453 tele lu
□ television broadcasting company, operating several channels.

CLUT · TECHNICAL TERM
■ colour look-up table

CLV · TECHNICAL TERM
■ constant linear velocity

CM · TECHNICAL TERM
■ commercial matter
■ communications module

CMCA · FRANCE
■ Centre Méditérranéen de la Communication Audiovisuelle
■ Centro Mediterrãneo da Comunição Audiovisual
c/o URTI
Maison de Radio France
116 Avenue du Président-Kennedy
75786 Paris Cedex 16
tel   +33 1 42 30 23 61 / 42 30 39 98 / 42 30 23 64
fax   +33 1 40 50 89 99
tlx   200 002 F
also known as Mediterranean Centre of Audiovisual Communication (MCAC)
□ organisation which groups together broadcasting organisations in countries bordering the Mediterranean and endeavours to promote Mediterranean cultural activities, including: exchanging programmes; organising coproductions; arranging meetings between officials in the audiovisual field; building up archives concerning

the region.

CMCCR · TECHNICAL TERM
- colour mobile central control room

CMCR · UK
- Centre for Mass Communication Research
University of Leicester
104 Regent Road
Leicester LE1 7LT
tel   +44 533 523863
fax +44 533 523874
1966 □ undertakes a wide range of research projects, with the aim of producing results which will contribute to public debate and inform policy on the major media and communication issues of the day.

CMCR · TECHNICAL TERM
- colour mobile control room

CMOS · TECHNICAL TERM
- complementary metal-oxide semiconductor/silicon

CMP · TECHNICAL TERM
- cross-modulation products

CMPC · TAIWAN
- Central Motion Picture Corporation
6F./116 Hung-Chung Street
Taipei 10817
tel   +886 2 371 5191
fax +886 2 314 6238
1954 □ integrated film-making organisation, with film archive, studio compound, film printing laboratory, and theatres in various locations. It has produced more than 160 feature films and an equal number of documentaries. It also releases and distributes local and foreign films, coproduces films with foreign or local independent film-makers by providing personnel, equipment, location and technical support, and invests in film-related enterprises.

CMPDA · CANADA
- Canadian Motion Picture Distributors Association
Suite 1603

22 St Clair Avenue East
Toronto
Ontario M4T 2S4
tel   +1 416 961 1888
fax +1 416 968 1016
1920 □ film industry trade association which is the Canadian affiliate of the Motion Picture Export Association of America, Inc (**MPEAA**). It serves as a voice and advocate of the major US studios whose distribution divisions market feature films, primetime entertainment programming for television and **PAY TV** and pre-recorded videocassettes in Canada.

CMRR · TECHNICAL TERM
- common mode rejection ratio

CMS · TECHNICAL TERM
- candela-meter-second
- close medium shot

CMT · USA
- Country Music Television
704 18th Avenue South
Hendersonville
TN 37203
tel   +1 615 824 3573
□ cable television network offering country music.

CMV · TECHNICAL TERM
- centimetres visible

CNA · LUXEMBOURG
- Centre National de l'Audiovisuel
5 Route de Zoufftgen
L-3598 Dudelange
tel   +352 51 93 44
fax +352 52 06 55
1988 □ national film fund and archive for all issues about cinema in Luxembourg.

CNA · SENEGAL
- Conseil National de l'Audiovisuel

CNAD · USA
- Cable National Audience Demographics
Nielsen Media Research
1290 Avenue of the Americas
New York

NY 10104
tel +1 212 708 7500
fax +1 212 708 7795
□ provides the user with data to develop competitive sales stories highlighting delivery of specific target audiences as well as to track target audiences over time for programming and sales needs.

CNAP · FRANCE
■ Centre National des Archives de la Publicité
Village de la Communication
44/50 Avenue du Capitaine Glarner
93585 Saint-Ouen
tel +33 49 48 66 00
fax +33 49 48 66 99
1980 □ collects all material referring to advertising, especially film and video; it has over 300 000 commercials dating from the beginning of the century. It is open for both public and professional use, providing services to advertisers, production companies and television channels.

CNBC · USA
■ Consumer News & Business Channel
2200 Fletcher Avenue
Ft. Lee
NJ 07024
tel +1 201 585 2622
fax +1 201 585 6393
1989 □ cable television network.

CNC · BELGIUM
■ Cooperative Nouveau Cinéma
60 Chaussée de Haecht
1000 Brussels
tel +32 2 217 9441
fax +32 2 217 9459
1973 □ film distribution and exhibition

CNC · FRANCE
■ Centre National de la Cinématographie
12 rue de Lübeck
Paris 75016
tel +33 44 34 34 40
fax +33 47 55 04 91
tlx CN CINE 650306
1946 □ administration and legislation of the French cinema industry. It

publishes *CNC Infos* (6) and *Bilan Annuel* (1).

CNC · IVORY COAST
■ Centre National du Cinéma
BP 539
Abidjan
tel +225 21 15 45
□ national film centre.

CNCB · BURKINA FASO
■ Centre National du Cinéma du Burkina Faso
S/Ministère de la Culture
Ouagadougou
tel +226 312551
1991 □ established to coordinate, promote and develop cinema in Burkina Faso.
also known as Centre National du Cinéma Burkinabé

CNCL · FRANCE
■ Commission Nationale de la Communication et des Libertés
formerly Haute Autorité de la Communication Audiovisuelle (HACA)

CNN · USA
■ Cable News Network
1 CNN Network
PO Box 105366
Atlanta
GA 30348-5366
tel +1 404 827 1519
fax +1 404 827 3134
1980 □ 24-hour all-news television network providing in-depth live coverage and analysis of news events. It also offers a wide range of programmes covering the latest in business, entertainment, sports, health, weather, science news and topical interviews.

CNPA · FRANCE
■ Confédération Nationale de la Publicité Audiovisuel
□ national federation for publicity in the audiovisual sphere.

CNPC · MALI
■ Centre National de Production Cinématographique
BP 116

Bamako
tel   +223 225913
1977 □ state service under the
authority of the Ministère de
l'Information.
*previously Service Cinématographique
du Ministére de l'Information du Mali
(SCINFOMA)*

CNR · TECHNICAL TERM
■ carrier-to-noise ratio (*aka* C/N)
■ chrominance noise reducer

CNSAD · FRANCE
■ Conservatoire National Supérieur
d'Art Dramatique
2 bis rue du Conservatoire
75009 Paris
tel   +33 1 42 46 12 91
fax   +33 1 48 24 11 72
1786 □ film school.

CO · TECHNICAL TERM
■ change-over

COBO · THE NETHERLANDS
■ Coproduktiefonds Binnenlandse
Omroep

COFECIC · FRANCE
■ Coordination des Fédérations de
Ciné-Clubs
12 rue des Lyonnais
75005 Paris
tel   +33 1 45 35 35 39
fax   +33 1 47 07 81 20
1981 □ coordinating body for cineclubs.

COFFP · FINLAND
■ Central Organisation of Finnish Film
Producers
■ Suomen Elokuvatuottajien Keskusliitto
Kaisaniemenkatu 3 B 29
00100 Helsinki
tel   +358 0 636 305

COH · TECHNICAL TERM
■ constricted double heterojunction

COL · PORTUGAL
■ Company Overhead Loan
c/o Scale Producers Support System
(SPSS)

Rua D João V, 8-R/C Dto.
1200 Lisbon
tel   +351 1 386 0630 / 0982
fax   +351 1 386 0647
1992 □ loan offered by Scale Producers
Support System (**SPSS**).

COLT · UK
■ Coventry's Own Local Television
London Road
Coventry CV3 4HL
tel   +44 203 505345
fax   +44 203 505445
□ local television broadcasting.

COLTAM · USA
■ Committee on Local Television
Audience Measurement
1964 □ technical advisory and research
subcommittee of **NAB**.

COM · THE NETHERLANDS
■ Centrum voor Omroep en Media

COMEX
■ Consortium of Media Exhibitors

COMMAG · TECHNICAL TERM
■ composite magnetic

COMOPT · TECHNICAL TERM
■ composite optical

COMPACT · USA
■ Committee to Preserve American
Color Television
Suite 400
3050 K Street NW
Washington
DC 20007
tel   +1 202 342 8400
fax   +1 202 338 5534
1976 □ federation of both unions and
companies which are involved in
manufacturing colour television
appliances.

COMPO · USA
■ Council of Motion Picture
Organisations

CONATEL · HAITI
■ Conseil National des
Télécommunications

16 avenue Marie Jeanne
Cité de l'Exposition
Port-au-Prince
tel   +509 220300
fax +509 230579
tlx   0353
1969 □ government authority
established to license communications.

CONTAM · USA
▪ Committee on Nationwide Television
Audience Measurement
1963 □ advisory committee of **NAB**
which appraises network audience
estimates.

COSIP · FRANCE
▪ Compte de Soutien à l'Industrie des
Programmes

COST · BELGIUM
▪ European Cooperation in the Field of
Scientific and Technical Research
Secretariat
Commission of the European
Communities
DG XIII/B
Bu-9 2/69
Rue de la Loi
1049 Brussels
tel   +32 2 299 0240
fax +32 2 296 2981
1971 □ provides a mechanism for
European scientific and technological
collaboration which complements the
EC's research and development
programmes. It operates through a
series of cooperative projects which
enable a variable number of
participants to undertake research in
areas of common interest and to
exchange the results among themselves.
Among the areas the programme covers
are telecommunications and
informatics.

COST · USA
▪ Coalition Opposing Signal Theft
Washington
1986 □ advises on cable signal theft
and supports the National Cable
Television Association's (**NCTA**) work
in this area.

COTSA · MEXICO
▪ Compañía Operadora de Teatros

CP · TECHNICAL TERM
▪ candle power
▪ circularly polarised/circular
polarisation
▪ co-producer
▪ colour print(ing)
▪ construction permit

CPA · SOUTH AFRICA
▪ Commercial Producers Association
PO Box 2299
Midrand
Johannesburg 1685
tel   +27 11 883 4536

CPA · TECHNICAL TERM
▪ colour phase alternation

CPB · USA
▪ Corporation for Public Broadcasting
901 East Street NW
Washington
DC 20004-2037
tel   +1 202 879 9600
fax +1 202 783 1019
tlx   7831019
1967 □ private organisation responsible
to Congress for the success of public
broadcasting in America. Its main
objective is to use the federal
government contribution to fund
national programmes and to foster the
growth and development of public
broadcasting. It publishes *CPB Today*
(12).

CPBC · BELGIUM
▪ Chambre Professionnelle Belge de la
Cinématographie

CPBF · UK
▪ Campaign for Press and Broadcasting
Freedom
96 Dalston Lane
London E8 1NG
tel   +44 71 923 3671
fax +44 71 923 3672
*incorporating Campaign Against Racism
in the Media (CARM) and Television
Users' Group (TUG)*
1979 □ organisation campaigning for

more diverse, democratic and representative media in Britain, with the support of 27 national trade union movement. It acts as a parliamentary lobby group on censorship and media reform. Specialist groups deal with specific issues, such as censorship, disability, sexuality and media racism. It publishes *Free Press* magazine (6).

CPE · TECHNICAL TERM
- customer premises equipment

CPM · TECHNICAL TERM
- cycles per minute

CPS · TECHNICAL TERM
- cassette preparation system
- cathode-potential stabilised-target scanning
- combined propulsion system
- cycles per second

CPSK · TECHNICAL TERM
- coherent phase shift keying

CPT · USA
- Households & Persons Cost Per 1000 Report
Nielsen Media Research
1290 Avenue of the Americas
New York
NY 10104
tel   +1 212 708 7500
fax +1 212 708 7795
□ monthly report which gives buyers and planners data as to which programmes and networks are the most efficient in delivering commercial messages to households and 13 different age/sex categories. From the report special industry cost benchmarks can be created to meet nearly every client need.

CPU · TECHNICAL TERM
- caption projection unit
- central processing unit
- community programmes unit

CRAC · BELGIUM
- Centre de Recherche sur les Arts de la Communication
Arts et Sciences de la Communication

Université de Liège
Allée du Six-Août B11
4000 Liège
tel   +32 41 56 32 86-9
□ research and study centre into communication and the arts.

CRC · CANADA
- Canadian Retransmission Collective
- Société Collective de Retransmission du Canada
175 Bloor Street East
Suite 806
North Tower
Toronto
Ontario M4W 3R8
tel   +1 416 927 9348
fax +1 416 927 8285
1989 □ non-profit corporation collecting a copyright tariff from cable systems in Canada for the carriage, in distant signals, of programmes controlled by certain domestic, US and international rights holders. It specifically represents programmes which comprise independently produced Canadian content, those carried on **PBS** signals, those owned by non-North Americans and those from TVOntario (**TVO**).

CRC · ITALY
- Cinema Romana Cineproduzione
Piazza Galeno 1
00162 Rome
□ film production.

CRC · TECHNICAL TERM
- cyclic redundancy code

CRCC · FRANCE
- Coopérative Régionale du Cinéma Culturel de Strasbourg
12 rue de Rome
67000 Strasbourg
tel   +33 88 60 17 00

CRC(C) · TECHNICAL TERM
- cyclic redundancy check (code)

CRE · TECHNICAL TERM
- colour roving eye

CREATIS · FRANCE

■ Centre de Recherche et d'Etudes sur les Arts du Texte, de l'Image et du Spectacle
Secteur Cinéma et Audiovisuel
Université de Aix-Marseille I
(Université de Provence)
29 Avenue Robert Schuman
13621 Aix-en-Provence
tel   +33 42 59 99 30
□ research and study centre which also publishes the journal *Admiranda*.

CRECA · FRANCE
■ Centre de Recherches d'Esthétique du Cinéma et des Arts Audiovisuels
Université de Paris I (Panthéon-Sorbonne)
162 rue Saint-Charles
75740 Paris Cedex 15
tel   +33 1 45 54 97 24
□ research and study centre.

CRETE · FRANCE
■ Association des Correspondants des Radios et Télévisions Etrangères à Paris
Maison de la Radio
116 Avenue du Président-Kennedy
75970 Paris Cedex 16
tel   +33 1 45 24 03 73
fax +33 1 45 25 86 02
1972 □ organisation of foreign correspondents in the fields of radio and television in France.

CRI · TECHNICAL TERM
■ colour rendering index
■ colour reversal intermediate

CRMC · FRANCE
■ Centre de Recherches Cinéma, Rites et Mythes Contemporains
Ecole Pratique des Hautes Etudes (EPHE)
Section des Sciences Religieuses
45 rue des Ecoles
75005 Paris
tel   +33 1 40 46 31 37
□ educational institution.

CRO · TECHNICAL TERM
■ cathode ray oscilloscope

CRRA · CANADA
■ Canadian Retransmission Right

Association
■ Association du Droit de Retransmission Canadien (ADRC)
c/o CBC
1500 Bronson Avenue
PO Box 8478
Ottawa
Ontario K1G 3J5
tel   +1 613 738 6612
fax +1 613 738 6688
□ collection of cable royalties and management of a collective for broadcasters.

CRT · TECHNICAL TERM
■ cathode ray tube

CRTC · CANADA
■ Canadian Radio-Television and Telecommunications Commission
■ Conseil de la Radiodiffusion et des Télécommunications Canadiennes
Ottawa
Ontario K1A 0N2
tel   +1 819 997 9254
fax +1 819 994 0218
tlx   053 4253
1968 □ regulatory body which licenses Canadian broadcasters and decides to what extent a licensee's schedule must be set aside for programmes of a Canadian content.

CRTG · SPAIN
■ Compañía de Radio Televisión de Galicia
see **TVG** · SPAIN

CRTV · CAMEROON
■ Office de Radiodiffusion-Télévision Camerounaise
BP 1634
Yaoundé
tel   +237 214077
fax +237 204340
tlx   8888 KN
1987 □ government-controlled national television and radio service, broadcasting in English and French.

CRTVG · SPAIN
■ Compañía de Radio Televisión de Galicia
see **TVG** · SPAIN

CRV · TECHNICAL TERM
- compact recording videodisc
- component recorded/recording video(disc)

CS · TECHNICAL TERM
- channel stops
- CinemaScope
- close shot
- close-up shot
- communications satellite

CSA · ALGERIA
- Conseil Supérieur de l'Audiovisuel
Palais de la Culture
Annassers
Algiers
tel +213 267 9420
fax +213 267 8729
tlx 65-668
□ television broadcasting body.

CSA · FRANCE
- Conseil Supérieur de l'Audiovisuel
Tour Mirabeau
39/43 quai André Citroën
75739 Paris Cedex 15
tel +33 1 40 58 38 00
fax +33 1 45 79 00 06
tlx 200365
1989 □ body which regulates and supervises the whole range of French broadcasting, including television, radio and the press, and issues broadcast licences.

CSC · CANADA
- Canadian Society of Cinematographers
89 Pinewood Trail
Mississauga
Ontario L5G 2L2
tel +1 416 271 4684
fax +1 416 271 7360
□ to promote the art and science of cinematography.

CSC · ITALY
- Centro Sperimentale di Cinematografia
Via Tuscolana 1524
00173 Rome
tel +39 6 722941 / 7222369
fax +39 6 7211619

1936 □ film school.

CSC · ITALY
- Centro Studi Cinematografici
Via Gregorio VII, 6
00165 Rome
tel +39 6 63 82 605
□ centre for the study of cinematography.

CSCC · USA
- Centre for the Study of Communication and Culture
321 North Spring Avenue
PO Box 56907
St Louis
MO 63136-0907
tel +1 314 658 8160
fax +1 314 535 5241
1977 □ international service for communication research, established by the Jesuits, which publishes the journal *Communication Research Trends* (4).

CSCTV · ITALY
- Centro Studi Cinetelevisivi
Casella Postale 6104
00100 Rome
tel +39 6 35 80 266
□ centre of cinema and television studios.

CSEA · FRANCE
- Chambre Syndicale de l'Edition Audiovisuelle

CSI · FRANCE
- Centre de Sociologie de l'Innovation
Ecole Nationale Supérieure des Mines
62 Boulevard Saint Michel
75006 Paris
tel +33 1 40 51 91 91
fax +33 1 43 54 56 28
1967 □ educational and research institution, exploring the sociology of science, technology and media.

CSI · TECHNICAL TERM
- compact source iodide

CSL · USA
- Cable Sport and Leisure
□ cable television network.

CSO · TECHNICAL TERM
▪ colour separation overlay

CSP · TECHNICAL TERM
▪ channelled substrate plomar

CSPEFF · FRANCE
▪ Chambre Syndicale des Producteurs
et Exportateurs de Films Français
5 rue de Cirque
75008 Paris
tel   +33 1 42 25 70 63
fax +33 1 42 25 94 27
1945 □ to defend the professional
interests of producers of audiovisual
media, as well as film distributors.

ČST · CZECH REPUBLIC
▪ Česká Televize
Kavčí hory
Na Hřebenech II
140 00 Prague 4
tel   +42 2 410 7111
fax +42 2 425 484
tlx   122747
1953 □ Czecho-Slovak television
service, operating 5 channels: F1
(national), CTV (regional serving Czech
population), **STV** (regional serving
Slovak population), OK3 (satellite for
Czech audience), TA3 (satellite for
Slovak audience).
previously known as Česko &
Slovenske Televize
also known as ČSTV

CST · FRANCE
▪ Commission Supérieure Technique de
l'Image et du Son
11 rue Galilée
75116 Paris
tel   +33 1 47 20 96 39
fax +33 1 47 23 09 94
1944 □ association which brings
together cinema and audiovisual
professionals and whose main objective
is to introduce technical progress
capable of improving the quality of
audiovisual expression. It also acts as
an advisor, gives technical assistance
and organises meetings.

CST · SÃO TOMÉ AND PRINCIPE
▪ Compagnie São-Toméenne de

Télécommunications
1989 □ company set up to allow more
extensive links by telecommunication
and greater television reception by
satellite.

ČSTV · CZECH REPUBLIC
▪ Česko & Slovenske Televize
see **ČST** · CZECH REPUBLIC

CT · RUSSIA
▪ Centralnoje Televidenije
□ television broadcasting service.

CT · UK
▪ Creative Technology
271 Merton Road
London SW18 5JS
tel   +44 81 874 7227
fax +44 81 877 1980
□ provides facilities hardware in
graphics, presentation and outside
broadcast.

CT · TECHNICAL TERM
▪ cartridge tape
▪ colour temperature
▪ control track

CTA · ITALY
▪ Cineteleaudio Cooperativa
Via Pieve di Cadore 29
Rome
□ film, television and sound
cooperative.

CTA · UK
▪ Cable Television Association
5th floor
Artillery House
Artillery Row
London SW1P 1RT
tel   +44 71 222 2900
fax +44 71 799 1471
1985 □ trade body representing the
interests of companies with an interest
in the provision of cable communications in the UK. It takes a leading
role in matters concerning member
companies and the industry as a whole.
It meets the professional needs of those
who work in the cable industry and
supports the continued development of
the business. It also facilitates the

interchange of information between cable operators and their suppliers. The CTA's annual convention, European Cable Communications (**ECC**), makes a positive contribution to the development of cable communications across Europe. It publishes the magazine *Cablegram* (4).

CTA · UK
▪ Cinema Theatre Association
44 Harrowdene Gardens
Teddington
Middlesex TW11 ODJ
tel   +44 81 977 2608
1967 □ to promote serious interest in all aspects of cinema buildings, including architecture, lighting, film projection and stage facilities. Consideration is given to their study, in terms of the history of entertainment, social history and architectural history. Wherever possible, it campaigns for the preservation and continued use of cinemas and theatres for their original purpose. It publishes *Picture House* magazine (1-2) and *CTA Bulletin* (6).

CTAB · USA
▪ Cable Television Advertising Bureau, Inc
see **CAB** · USA

CTAC · USA
▪ Cable Television Technical Advisory Committee
□ committee of the Federal Communications Commission (**FCC**)

CTAM · USA
▪ Cable Television Administration and Marketing Society
Suite 250
635 Slaters Lane
Alexandria
VA 23314
tel   +1 703 549 4200
1975 □ organisation whose members are professionals working in marketing in cable television. It aims to assist communication amongst members, conducts seminars and publishes *CTAM Database.* (4).

CTBF · UK
▪ Cinema and Television Benevolent Fund
Royalty House
22 Golden Square
London W1R 4AD
tel   +44 71 437 6567
fax   +44 71 437 7186
1924 □ to provide positive, financial and caring support for anyone who has worked or is working, in any capacity, in the British cinema, film or independent television industries and their dependants.

CTC · ITALY
▪ Centro Telecinematografica Culturale
Viale Legioni Romane 43
20147 Milan
□ cultural film and television centre.

CTC · JAPAN
▪ Chiba Television Broadcasting Corporation
1-25 Miyako-cho 1-chome
Chuo-ku
Chiba 260
tel   +81 432 313111
□ television station.

CTC · TECHNICAL TERM
▪ colour temperature control

CTCM · TECHNICAL TERM
▪ chroma timer/time compressed multiplex

CTD · SWITZERLAND
▪ Centre for Telecommunications Development
International Telecommunications Union
Place des Nations
CH-1211 Geneva 20
tel   +41 22 730 5111
fax   +41 22 733 7256
tlx   421 000 UIT CH
□ to provide help to developing countries in order to improve their telecommunications networks and to promote improvement of and investment in telecommunications worldwide. The Centre has an advisory board of 21 members.

CTD · TECHNICAL TERM
- component tape drive

CTDM · TECHNICAL TERM
- compressed time division multiple(x)

CTE · UK
- Central Television Enterprises
Hesketh House
43-45 Portman Square
London W1H 9FG
tel   +44 71 486 6688
fax +44 71 486 1707
1988 □ as international sales agents for
Central Television, Carlton Television,
Harlech Television and Meridian
Broadcasting, as well as a growing
number of independent production
companies, CTE is able to offer a full
range of provenly successful
programming in all genres - from
dramas to documentaries, movies to
music, through to light entertainment,
arts, education, children's and family
viewing. CTE's catalogue includes over
1000 hours of quality productions
available for licence worldwide.

CTF · TECHNICAL TERM
- contrast transfer function

CTG · UK
- Comataidh Telebhisein Gàidhlig
- Gaelic Television Committee (GTC)
4 Harbour View
Cromwell Street Quay
Stornoway
Isle of Lewis PA87 2DR
tel   +44 851 705550
fax +44 851 706432
1991 □ independent organisation
which aims to ensure that a broad
range of high-quality programmes are
broadcast in Gaelic for reception in
Scotland.

CTI · TECHNICAL TERM
- colour transient
improvement/improver

CTIC · USA
- Cable Television Information Center

CTM · USA

- Christian Television Mission
1918 South Ingram Mill Road
Springfield
MO 65804
tel   +1 417 881 6303
1956 □ organisation involved in the
production and distribution of Christian
programmes for the television, cable
and closed-circuit broadcasting
markets. It publishes *Christian TV News*
(6).

CTQC · CANADA
- Consortium de Télévision Québec-
Canada

CTR · TECHNICAL TERM
- cassette tape recorder
- current transfer ratio

CTS · TAIWAN
- Chinese Television System
100 Kuang Fu South Road
Taipei 10658
tel   +886 2 7510321
fax +886 2 7775414
tlx   24195
1971 □ educational and cultural
television broadcaster.

CTS · TECHNICAL TERM
- communication technology satellite

CTSDF · CANADA
- Canadian Television Series
Development Foundation
Maclean Hunter Television Fund
(MHTVF)
Suite 412
777 Bay Street
Toronto
Ontario M4W 1A7
tel   +1 416 596 5878
fax +1 416 596 2650
□ private independent foundation
established by Maclean Hunter Ltd to
assist independent production
companies in financing the production
of Canadian television drama series for
broadcasters in the private sector.

CTV · CAMBODIA
- Cambodia Television
19 Road 242

Phnom-Penh
tel   +855 24449
1983 □ television station.

CTV · CANADA
■ Canadian Television
42 Charles Street East
Toronto
Ontario M4Y 1T5
tel   +1 416 928 6000
fax   +1 416 928 0907
tlx   062 2080
□ television station.

CTV · ITALY
■ Centro Televisivo Vaticano
Palazzo Belvedere
00120 Vatican City
tel   +39 6 69 88 54 67
fax   +39 6 69 88 51 92
1983 □ producer and distributor of
religious television programmes.

CTV · JAPAN
■ Chukyo Television Co Ltd
154 Takamine-machi
Showa-ku
Nagoya 466
tel   +81 52 832 3311
□ television station.

CTV · NEW ZEALAND
■ Canterbury Television
196 Gloucester Street
Christchurch
□ television service.

CTV · TAIWAN
■ China Television Company
120 Chung Yang Road
Nan Kang District
Taipei
tel   +886 2 7838308
tlx   25080
1969 □ television broadcasting
company.

CTV · UK
■ Channel Television
The Television Centre
La Pouquelaye
St Helier
Jersey JE2 3ZD
tel   +44 534 68999

fax   +44 534 59446
tlx   4192265 CTV JY G
1962 □ provides an independent
television service for the Channel
Islands.

CTV · TECHNICAL TERM
■ cable television
■ community television

CTVC · UK
■ Churches TV Centre
Hillside Studios
Merry Hill Road
Bushey
Herts WD2 1DR
tel   +44 81 950 4426
fax   +44 81 950 1437
□ television production company
specialising in programmes which focus
on social, religious, educational and
ethical issues in the broadcast sense. It
has its own permanently crewed
production centre, Hillside Studios, and
offers a complete range of studio,
location and post-production facilities.

CTW · USA
■ Children's Television Workshop
One Lincoln Plaza
New York
NY 10023
tel   +1 212 595 3456
fax   +1 212 875 6108
tlx   236168
1968 □ research and development
organisation which investigates new
uses of television and related media for
purposes of education and information.

CU · TECHNICAL TERM
■ close-up (*aka* close shot [CS])
■ control unit

CUEC · MEXICO
■ Centro Universitario de Estudios
Cinematográficos
Adolfo Prieto, 721
Col. de Valle
Mexico, D.F.
tel   +52 5 536 0230 / 687 0696 / 687
0697
□ film school.

CUFC · USA
- Consortium of University Film Centers

CV · UK
- Connoisseur Video
10A Stephen Mews
London W1P OAX
tel   +44 71 957 8957
fax +44 71 957 8968
1990 □ distribution of quality video
cassettes with supporting authoritative
documentation.

CVBS · TECHNICAL TERM
- colour, video, blanking and synchs
- composite video, burst and synchs

CVC · TECHNICAL TERM
- compact video cartridge

CVCCC · USA
- Classics Video Cinema Collector's
Club
□ distributor of videos of silent films.

CVD · TECHNICAL TERM
- compact video disc

CVR · TECHNICAL TERM
- cartridge video recorder

CVS · SOUTH AFRICA
- Community Video School
Film and Allied Workers Organisation
PO Box 16939
Doornfontein 2028
tel   +27 11 402 3660-1
fax +27 11 402 0777
1991 □ a unique, independent
education facility offering students the
opportunity for a visual exploration of
society. It is committed to addressing
the legacy of racial imbalance and
skills acquisition in the South African
film industry. The 2-year course
combines both theoretical and practical
elements.

CVS · TECHNICAL TERM
- computer video synchronizer

CW · TECHNICAL TERM
- continuous wave

CWA · USA
- Communication Workers of America
501 Third Street NW
Washington
DC 20001-2797
tel   +1 202 434 1100
fax +1 202 434 1279
□ union.

CWRT · CANADA
- Canadian Women in Radio and
Television
Suite 104
95 Barber Greene Road
Don Mills
Ontario M3C 3E9
tel   +1 416 446 5353
fax +1 416 446 5354
□ national organisation providing a
range of services.

CYBC · CYPRUS
- Cyprus Broadcasting Corporation
Broadcasting House
PO Box 4824
Nicosia
tel   +357 2 422231
fax +357 2 314050
tlx   2333 CYBC
1953 □ to provide information, culture
and entertainment to the people of
Cyprus. Television and radio
programmes are transmitted on 2 and 3
channels respectively.
also known as CBC

CYT · TECHNICAL TERM
- critical young televiewer

D

D-A · TECHNICAL TERM
- digital-to-analogue

D&AD · UK
- Designers and Art Directors
Association
Graphite Square
85 Vauxhall Walk
London SE11 5HJ
tel   +44 71 582 6487
fax +44 71 582 7784

1963 □ professional association working on behalf of the creative and craft members of the advertising and design communities who service the interests of business. It is a registered charity with a specific remit for education. Its main objectives are: to set standards of creative excellence; to promote the worth of creative excellence to the business community; to inspire the young and make them aware of the career opportunities in the advertising and design industries.

D/N · TECHNICAL TERM
■ day for night

D/S · TECHNICAL TERM
■ double-sided

DA · TECHNICAL TERM
■ directional antenna
■ distribution amplifier
■ double Azimuth

DAB · TECHNICAL TERM
■ digital audio broadcasting

DAC · TECHNICAL TERM
■ dialogue-to-analogue converter/conversion

DAD · TECHNICAL TERM
■ digital audio disc

DAF · TECHNICAL TERM
■ demographic adjustment factor

DAMA · TECHNICAL TERM
■ demand assigned/assignment multiple access

DAMS · TECHNICAL TERM
■ direct access management system

DANDE · TECHNICAL TERM
■ de-spin active nutation damping electronics

DARC · ITALY
■ Distribuzione Angelo Rizzoli Cinematografica
Via Archimede, 164
00197 Rome

tel   +39 6 807 3360
fax +39 6 878 701
□ film distribution.

DASH · TECHNICAL TERM
■ digital audio stationary head

DAT · TECHNICAL TERM
■ digital audio tape

DATE · TECHNICAL TERM
■ digital audio for television

DATV · TECHNICAL TERM
■ digitally assisted television

DAVID · BELGIUM
■ Groupe pour le Développement d'une Identité Audiovisuelle de l'Europe
c/o BRT
Room 9L71
52 Boulevard Auguste Reyers
1043 Brussels
tel   +32 2 737 3676
fax +32 2 734 2925
□ group promoting the development of a European audiovisual identity.

DB · TECHNICAL TERM
■ decibel
■ delayed broadcast

DBA Television · UK
■ David Barker Associates Television Ltd
21 Ormeau Avenue
Belfast
N Ireland BT2 8HD
tel   +44 232 231197
fax +44 232 333302
1982 □ documentary film production company producing exclusively for Channel 4 (**C4**) and **BBC** Network often with coproduction finance.

DBC · UK
■ Deaf Broadcasting Council
70 Blacketts Wood Drive
Chorleywood
Herts WD3 5QQ
tel   +44 923 283127 fax and minicom
1979 □ voluntary consumer organis-ation representing deaf, deafened and hard of hearing viewers. It aims to

ensure that broadcasters are aware of the needs of deaf people and that suitable services are provided to enable those viewers to understand television programmes.

DBC · TECHNICAL TERM
- dynamic beam control

DBF · TECHNICAL TERM
- dynamic beam forming

DBL · TECHNICAL TERM
- dynamic black level

DBM · TECHNICAL TERM
- decibel meter

DBR · TECHNICAL TERM
- distributed Bragg reflector

DBS · TECHNICAL TERM
- direct broadcast(ing) (by/from) satellite

DBSA · USA
- Direct Broadcast Satellite Association
see **SBCA** □ USA

DC · UK
- Dwight Cavendish Developments Ltd
Vincent House
Alington Road
Eynesbury
Cambs PE19 4EA
tel   +44 480 215753
fax +44 480 474525
tlx   32744 DWICAV G
□ manufacturers and sellers of video duplication equipment.

DC · TECHNICAL TERM
- direct current

DCC · TECHNICAL TERM
- digital compact cassette
- distributor control unit
- dynamic contrast control

DCF · TECHNICAL TERM
- dynamic comb filter

DCFP · TECHNICAL TERM
- dynamic crossed field photo multiplier

DCP · TECHNICAL TERM
- digital cartridge player
- display control programme

DCPCM · TECHNICAL TERM
- differentially coherent pulse code modulation

DCRS · TECHNICAL TERM
- data cassette recording system

DCS · TECHNICAL TERM
- digital channel stereo
- dual channel sound

DCT · TECHNICAL TERM
- digital component tape
- discrete cosine transform

DD · TECHNICAL TERM
- direct drive

DDI · INDIA
- Doordarshan (India Television)
Mandi House
New Delhi 110001
tel   +91 11 387786
fax +91 11 386507
tlx   66413 DG DD IN
1976 □ television service.

DDO · TECHNICAL TERM
- direct to disc optical

DDR · TECHNICAL TERM
- digital disc recorder
- direct domestic reception

DEF · TECHNICAL TERM
- daily/delayed electronic feed

DEL · TECHNICAL TERM
- direct exchange line

DELTA · BELGIUM
- Developing European Learning Through Technological Advance
Commission of the European Communities
DG XIII
Rue de la Loi
1049 Brussels
tel   +32 2 296 3406
1988 □ EC programme which originally

sought to examine expected technological advances and harness these to European learning needs, and also to provide tools to help trainers throughout Europe understand and use the new technologies. A new phase has now commenced. Organisations eligible to participate in the flexible and distance learning line of the new Telematics programme include: telecommunications network operators, research establishments, universities and others.

DF · TECHNICAL TERM
- depth of field (aka D/F)
- drop frame

DFA · GERMANY
- Deutsche Fernsehnachrichten Agentur
Bundeskanzlerplatz 2-10
5300 Bonn 1
tel   +49 228 26780
fax +49 228 2678116
□ television and video programme producer.

DFA · USA
- Dance Films Association
Room 507
1133 Broadway
New York
NY 10010
tel   +1 212 727 0764
1956 □ organisation which serves as a link between distributors, producers and viewers of 16mm non-theatrical videos and films on the subject of dance.

DFB · TECHNICAL TERM
- distributed feedback

DFFB · GERMANY
- Deutsche Film- und Fernsehakademie Berlin
Pommernallee 1
14052 Berlin
tel   +49 30 30 7234 / 3071
fax +49 30 30 19875
1966 □ film and television school offering a course lasting 4 years.

DFI · DENMARK

- Danish Film Institute
St. Soendervoldstræde 4
1419 Copenhagen K
tel   +45 3157 6500
fax +45 3157 6700
tlx   31465 (dfilm dk)
1972 □ to subsidise manuscript development and feature film production; to subsidise import, distribution and screening of films of artistic merit as well as films judged to be particularly suitable for children and young people; to present and promote Danish film internationally. It publishes *Danish Films* (1) and *Danish Films - Facts and Figures* (1).

DFI · TECHNICAL TERM
- director's fresh instruction

DG · TECHNICAL TERM
- differential gain

DGA · USA
- Directors' Guild of America
7920 Sunset Boulevard
Los Angeles
CA 90046
tel   +1 310 289 2000
fax +1 310 289 2024
1959 □ professional union of directors working in film and television.

DGC · CANADA
- Directors' Guild of Canada
Suite 401
387 Bloor Street East
Toronto
Ontario M4W 1H7
tel   +1 416 972 0098
fax +1 416 972 6058
□ professional organisation consisting of directors, arts directors, editors, production designers and managers, location managers, and their trainees and assistants. It fosters the craft of film-making across Canada, representing professionals who play a vital role in the development of the industry.

DGGB · UK
- Directors' Guild of Great Britain
Suffolk House
1-8 Whitfield Place

London W1P 5SF
tel +44 71 383 3858
fax +44 71 383 5173
1973 □ trade union and craft guild representing directors in all media.

DGMG · GERMANY
- Deutsche Gesellschaft für Medien und Geschichte
Innstrasse 5
30519 Hannover
□ German society for media and history.

DH · TECHNICAL TERM
- double heterostructure

DI · TECHNICAL TERM
- dolly in

DICE · TECHNICAL TERM
- digital intercontinental conversion equipment

DICINE · MEXICO
- Revista de Difusión e Investigación Cinematográficas
Leonardo da Vinci 161 A
03700 Mexico, D.F.
tel +525 598 6086
fax +525 598 6086
1983 □ magazine (6) concentrating on film and video.

DIFA · THE NETHERLANDS
- Dutch Documentary and Independent Film Association
PO Box 17408
1001 JK Amsterdam
tel +31 20 620 5578

DIFF · GERMANY
- Deutsches Institut für Fernstudien
Universität Tübingen
Wöhrdstr. 8
72072 Tübingen
tel +49 7071 3041
fax +49 7071 37484
□ institute for screen studies.

DIFF · USA
- Denver International Film Festival
999 Eighteenth Street
Suite 1820

Denver
CO 80202
tel +1 303 298 8223
fax +1 303 298 0209
1979 □ brings the world of film to Denver with over 100 films from around the world and over 40 film artists accompanying their films. The festival is scheduled for October and will feature documentaries and independently produced works, classics and retrospectives, children's films and special programmes.

DIFI · ITALY
- Diffusione Internazionale Film Informativi
Viale Parioli 25
Rome
□ international distribution of information films.

DIN · GERMANY
- Deutsche Industrie-Norm

DIP · TECHNICAL TERM
- dual in-line package

DIPROCI · BURKINA FASO
- Direction de la Production Cinématographique
01 BP 647
Ouagadougou 01
tel +226 302305 / 302317
fax +226 303625
1976 □ film production, coproduction, equipment hiring and crew availability.

DIZ · GERMANY
- Deutsche Industriefilm-Zentrale
Gustav-Heinemann-Ufer 84-88
50968 Cologne
tel +49 221 372017
fax +49 221 3708730
tlx 8882768

DLC · TECHNICAL TERM
- dynamic lens correction

DLD · TECHNICAL TERM
- dark line defect

DM · TECHNICAL TERM
- delay modulation

■ delta modulation

DMA · TECHNICAL TERM
■ designated market area
■ direct memory access

DMC · DENMARK
■ Dansk Management Center
Kristianiagade 7
2100 Copenhagen Ø
tel   +45 31 38 97 77
fax +45 31 42 00 56
1971 □ Denmark's largest distributor of
video-based training produced by the
world's leading training companies. It
publishes an annual *Video Catalogue.*

DMC · TECHNICAL TERM
■ dynamic motion control

DME · TECHNICAL TERM
■ dialogue, music and effects
■ digital multi-effects

DMEF · TECHNICAL TERM
■ dialogue music effects and foley

DMS · TECHNICAL TERM
■ dynamic motion stimulator

DNR · TECHNICAL TERM
■ digital noise reducer

DO · TECHNICAL TERM
■ dolly out

DOC · TECHNICAL TERM
■ drop-out compensator

DOD · TECHNICAL TERM
■ depth of discharge

DOP · TECHNICAL TERM
■ director of photography (*aka* DP)

DOR · TECHNICAL TERM
■ digital optical recording

DP · TECHNICAL TERM
■ director of photography (*aka* DOP)
■ double perforated
■ double play

DPCM · TECHNICAL TERM

■ differential pulse code modulation

DPE · TECHNICAL TERM
■ digital production effects

DPM · TECHNICAL TERM
■ digital panel meter

DPO · TECHNICAL TERM
■ dynamic picture optimiser

DPR · TECHNICAL TERM
■ daily production report

DPSS · TECHNICAL TERM
■ digital programme search system

DPT · ITALY
■ Doppiaggio Pubblicità Televisiva
Via R Grazioli Lante 78
Rome
□ television advertising dubbing.

DPX · TECHNICAL TERM
■ digital picture exchange

DQPSK · TECHNICAL TERM
■ differential quadrature phase shift
keying

DR · DENMARK
■ Danmarks Radio
TV-Byen
DK-2860 Søborg
tel   +45 35 203040
fax +45 35 202644
tlx 22695
□ public service television and radio
broadcasting.

DR · TECHNICAL TERM
■ density ratio

DRAM · TECHNICAL TERM
■ dynamic random-access memory

DRAW · TECHNICAL TERM
■ direct-read-after-write

DRCS · TECHNICAL TERM
■ dynamically redefinable character sets

DRI · TECHNICAL TERM
■ dynamic range improvement

DRP · TECHNICAL TERM
■ dual resolution processing

DRS · SWITZERLAND
■ Deutsche und Rätoromanische
Schweiz
Fernsehstraße 1-4
8052 Zürich
tel   +41 1 305 6611
fax   +41 1 305 5711
tlx   823823 TVZ
□ television station, broadcasting in
German.

DS · TECHNICAL TERM
■ dolly shot

DSB · TECHNICAL TERM
■ double sideband

DSC · TECHNICAL TERM
■ digital spectrum compatible

DSCS · TECHNICAL TERM
■ defence service communications
satellite
■ domestic satellite communication
system

DSD · TECHNICAL TERM
■ digital scene detection

DSF · GERMANY
■ Deutsche Sports Fernsehen
Bahnhofstraße 27a
85774 Unterföhring bei München
tel   +49 89 950020
fax   +49 89 95002109
1993 □ satellite television specialising
in sport and leisure.

DSI · TECHNICAL TERM
■ direct serial interfacing

DSIS · TECHNICAL TERM
■ dual sound-in-synch

DSK · TECHNICAL TERM
■ downstream keying/keyer

DSO · TECHNICAL TERM
■ dielectric stabilised oscillator

DSP · TECHNICAL TERM

■ digital signal processing/processor
■ digital surround processor/processing

DSS · TECHNICAL TERM
■ digital scene simulation
■ domestic satellite service
■ dual surface shape

DST · TECHNICAL TERM
■ daylight savings time
■ differential survey treatment

DSTL™ · TECHNICAL TERM
■ digital studio-transmitter link

DSV · TECHNICAL TERM
■ digital sum variation

DT · TECHNICAL TERM
■ dynamic tracking

DTC · TECHNICAL TERM
■ dual time code

DTF · TECHNICAL TERM
■ dynamic track following

DTH · TECHNICAL TERM
■ direct to home

DTL · TECHNICAL TERM
■ diode-transistor logic

DTS · TECHNICAL TERM
■ digital termination service

DTTB · TECHNICAL TERM
■ digital terrestrial television
broadcasting
■ digital television for terrestrial
broadcasting

DTTR · TECHNICAL TERM
■ digital television tape recorder

DTV · TECHNICAL TERM
■ desk top video

DV · TECHNICAL TERM
■ direct voice

DVA · TECHNICAL TERM
■ digital video adaptor

DVE · TECHNICAL TERM
• digital video effects

DVI® · TECHNICAL TERM
• digital video interactive

DVIS · TECHNICAL TERM
• digital image stabiliser

DVPC · TECHNICAL TERM
• digital video processors

DVR · TECHNICAL TERM
• digital video recording

DVTR · TECHNICAL TERM
• digital videotape recorder

DW · GERMANY
• Deutsche Welle
PO Box 100444
50444 Cologne
tel   +49 221 38902
fax +49 221 3893000
tlx   221386 DWK
1965 □ public television and radio
broadcasting corporation.

DWW · USA
• Directing Workshop for Women
American Film Institute
2021 N Western Avenue
Los Angeles
CA 90027
tel   +1 213 856 7600
fax +1 213 467 4578
1974 □ established to provide an
opportunity for women in media arts to
explore their talents in the art and craft
of screen directing.

DXF · TECHNICAL TERM
• drawing exchange file

E

E-E · TECHNICAL TERM
• electronics to electronics

E-FIT · TECHNICAL TERM
• electronic facial identification
technique

EAFA · THE NETHERLANDS
• Eerste Amsterdamse Film Associatie
Leliegracht 25
1016 GR Amsterdam
tel   +31 20 626 5613
fax +31 20 622 8753
□ film production company.

EAFA · UK
• East Anglian Film Archive
Centre of East Anglian Studies
University of East Anglia
Norwich NR4 7TJ
tel   +44 603 592664
fax +44 603 58553
1976 □ to locate and preserve films
and videos showing aspects of life in
Norfolk, Suffolk, Essex and
Cambridgeshire and make them
available for education, research and
enjoyment where copyright allows. It
also offers an MA course in film
archiving/film studies in conjunction
with the School of English and
American Studies at the University of
East Anglia. It publishes an *Annual
Newsletter* as well as various
catalogues.

EAFF · BELGIUM
• European Association of Animation
Film
• Association Européenne du Film
d'Animation (AEFA)
418 Boulevard Lambermont
1030 Brussels
tel   +32 2 245 1200
fax +32 2 245 4689
1988 □ initiative of **MEDIA** which
provides defence, support and
promotion of the European animation
industry. Its main activity is to
consolidate the studios' production
capacities and to ensure that they have
a stable operating environment which
will enable them to assume their
rightful place in the world cartoon film
market. It publishes *CARTOON News*
(4).
also known as CARTOON

EAGC · ITALY
• Ente Autonomo Gestione per Il
Cinema

Via Tuscolana 1055
00173 Rome
tel   +39 6 722 2141
fax   +39 6 722 2362
□ cinema management board.

EAROM · TECHNICAL TERM
▪ electrically alterable read-only
memory

EAV · TECHNICAL TERM
▪ end of active video

EAVE · BELGIUM
▪ Les Entrepreneurs de l'Audiovisuel
Européen
▪ European Audiovisual Entrepreneurs
14 rue de la Presse
1000 Brussels
tel   +32 2 219 0920
fax   +32 2 223 0034
1988 □ initiative of **MEDIA** which
provides for the professional training of
cinema and television producers; the
development of production and
coproduction projects with a distinct
European vocation, and the creation of
a pan-European network of
independent producers striving to be
more creative, more entrepreneurial
and more European; the dissemination
of know-how resulting from these
undertakings.

EBC · JAPAN
▪ Ehime Broadcasting Co Ltd
119 Masago-cho
Matsuyama 790
tel   +81 899 43 1111
□ television station.

EBC · SWITZERLAND
▪ European Business Channel
1989 □ international commercial
television channel.

EBC(NI) · UK
▪ Educational Broadcasting Council for
Northern Ireland
BBC Broadcasting House
Ormeau Avenue
Belfast
N Ireland BT2 8HQ
tel   +44 232 338437

fax   +44 232 338815
1987 □ council whose aim is to advise
the **BBC** within Northern Ireland in its
providing of broadcast programmes in
television and sound to schools and the
continuing education sector.

EBC(UK) · UK
▪ Educational Broadcasting Council for
the United Kingdom
BBC White City
Room 2360
201 Wood Lane
London W12 7TS
tel   +44 81 752 4204
fax   +44 81 752 4441
1987 □ council whose aim is to advise
the **BBC** within the United Kingdom in
its providing of broadcast programmes
in television and sound to schools and
the continuing education sector.

EBCS · UK
▪ Educational Broadcasting Council for
Scotland
c/o John Russell
5 Queen Street
Edinburgh EH2 1JF
tel   +44 31 469 4243
fax   +44 31 469 4220
1987 □ council whose aim is to advise
the **BBC** within Scotland in its
providing of broadcast programmes in
television and sound to schools and the
continuing education sector.

EBCU · TECHNICAL TERM
▪ extra-big close-up

EBR · TECHNICAL TERM
▪ electron beam recording/recorder

EBRL · TECHNICAL TERM
▪ external Bragg reflector

EBS · USA
▪ Emergency Broadcasting System
1964 □ system which gives the
President of the United States and the
federal government a method of
communication with the public when a
national or international emergency
occurs.

EBS · USA
■ Entertainment Business Services
International
Suite 1900
1888 Century Park East
Los Angeles
CA 90067
tel +1 310 284 3210
fax +1 310 284 3235

EBU · SWITZERLAND
■ European Broadcasting Union
Ancienne Route 17A
Case postale 67
CH-1218 Grand Saconnex/Geneva
tel +41 22 717 2111
fax +41 22 798 5897
tlx 415700 ebu ch
1950 □ professional association of
national broadcasters with 114
members in 79 countries. Its main
purposes are: to promote cooperation
between members and broadcasting
organisations; to represent the interests
of members with broadcasting
organisations worldwide; to represent
the interests of members in programme,
legal, technical and other fields. The
activities of the EBU are channelled
through the Television Programme
Committee, the Radio Programme
Committee, the Legal Committee and
the Technical Committee, with their
working parties, sub-groups and ad hoc
groups. It publishes *Diffusion* (4) and
EBU Technical Review (4), both in
separate English and French editions,
and various other publications.
*also known as Union Européenne de
Radio-Télévision (UER)
incorporating Organisation
Internationale de Radio et de Télévision
(OIRT) / International Radio and
Television Organisation (IRTO)*

EC · TECHNICAL TERM
■ earphone commentary
■ electronic cinematography

ECA · GERMANY
■ European Coproduction Association
Secretariat
ZDF Enterprises
Liseweitner Str. 9

55129 Mainz
tel +49 6131 991321
fax +49 6131 991324
□ association comprising public service
television networks devoted to
television coproduction between
European film-producing countries,
particularly in the areas of fiction films.

ECATV · TECHNICAL TERM
■ educational cable television

ECC · UK
■ European Cable Communications
Cable Television Association
5th floor
Artillery House
Artillery Row
London SW1P 1RT
tel +44 71 222 2900
fax +44 71 799 1471
1986 □ annual convention which
provides a positive, industry-led
contribution to the development of
cable communications across Europe
and is designed to meet the needs of all
those involved in the cable industry,
whether operators, equipment suppliers
or programmers.
*previously known as The Cable
Convention*

ECC · TECHNICAL TERM
■ electronic cinematographic camera
■ electronic camera coverage

ECCA · BELGIUM
■ European Cable Communications
Association
Boulevard Anspach 1
Box 28
1000 Brussels
tel +32 2 211 9449
fax +32 2 211 9907
1955 □ encouraging by means of
international contacts the development
of distribution by cable; defending at
the international level the interests of
distribution by cable; participating in
international activities concerned with
distribution by cable; ensuring the
exchange of information among the
various national bodies.
previously Alliance Internationale de la

Distribution par Câble (AID)

ECCO · GERMANY
▪ European Co-Production Conference and Market
c/o Film Fonds Hamburg
Medienhaus
Friedensallee 14-16
22765 Hamburg
tel   +49 40 390 58 83
fax   +49 40 390 44 24
tlx   216 53 55 efdo-d
1990 □ conference which discusses the future of film production in and for Europe.

ECF · UK
▪ European Co-Production Fund Ltd
c/o British Screen Finance
14-17 Wells Mews
London W1P 3FL
tel   +44 71 323 9080
fax   +44 71 323 0092
1991 □ the fund is financed solely by a government grant of £5m through the Department of National Heritage (DNH). The grant is intended to assist British producers in the making of co-productions with partners in other European Community countries. British Screen Finance (**BSF**) administers the grant in accordance with a remit from the DNH and guidelines which British Screen has devised. Loans to film projects are subject to standard terms, the terms being designed to act as an incentive to co-investors and to provide direct support for producers.

ECFLA
▪ European Communities Film Libraries Association

ECG · TECHNICAL TERM
▪ electronic character generator

ECL · TECHNICAL TERM
▪ emitter-coupled logic

ECN · TECHNICAL TERM
▪ Eastman colour negative

ECPA · FRANCE
▪ Establissement Cinématographique et

Photographique des Armées

ECS · TECHNICAL TERM
▪ European Communications Satellite
▪ extended clear scan

ECTO · FRANCE
▪ European Cinema and Television Office
Conseil de l'Europe/Council of Europe
67075 Strasbourg Cedex
1991

ECTVY · FRANCE
▪ European Cinema and Television Year
1988 □ joint venture between the Council of Europe and the EC, bringing together 25 states parties to the European Cultural Convention. The year's activities were co-ordinated and decided upon by a steering committee composed of representatives of European institutions, national committees instituted for the purpose, broadcasting corporations and the major cinema federations. The main objectives were to promote awareness of a strong audiovisual industry and to reflect the European identity in the audiovisual media.

ECU · TECHNICAL TERM
▪ extreme close-up (*aka* XCU)

ED · TECHNICAL TERM
▪ extended definition

EDC · TECHNICAL TERM
▪ error detection code

EDECINE · ANGOLA
▪ Empresa Distribuidora e Exhibidora de Cinema
Rua Dr Américo Boavida, 152
Cx. Postal 1844
Luanda
tel   +244 2 38270 / 38534
tlx   3034 dafrica an
1979 □ film exhibitor.

EDH · TECHNICAL TERM
▪ error detection and handling

EDI · GERMANY

- Europäisches Dokumentarfilminstitut
- European Documentary Film Institute
Leineweberstraße 1
PO Box 100534
45405 Mülheim an der Ruhr
tel   +49 208 471934
fax   +49 208 474113
tlx   8561104 edi d
1988 □ association whose members are documentary film-makers, film theoreticians and others involved in documentary film within Europe. Its main aim is to establish a European network which will facilitate exchanges at various levels between documentary film-makers across Europe. It publishes the *EDI Bulletin* (4).

EDI · USA
- Entertainment Data Inc
331 N Maple Drive
Beverly Hills
CA 90210

EDI · TECHNICAL TERM
- electronic data interchange

EDL · TECHNICAL TERM
- edit decision list

EDT · TECHNICAL TERM
- electronic data transfer

EDTV · TECHNICAL TERM
- educational television
- enhanced/extended/extra definition television

EE · TECHNICAL TERM
- electrical engineer
- electronic editing

EEN · USA
- Eastern Educational Television Network

EEPROM · TECHNICAL TERM
- electrically erasable programmable read-only memory

EETPU · UK
- Electrical and Electronic Telecommunication and Plumbing Union

see **AEEU-EETPU** · UK

EFA · GERMANY
- European Film Academy eV
Katharinenstraße 8
10711 Berlin
tel   +49 30 893 4132-3
fax   +49 30 893 4134
1991 □ an initiative of **MEDIA**, it aims to promote European cinema throughout the world and to strengthen its artistic and commercial position, to improve knowledge and awareness of European cinema and to pass on the substantial experience of its members to the younger generation of film professionals.

EFC · TECHNICAL TERM
- electronic film conforming

EFDO · GERMANY
- European Film Distribution Office
Europaïsches Film Büro
Friedensallee 14-16
22765 Hamburg
tel   +49 40 390 9025
fax   +49 40 390 6249
tlx   216 53 55 EFDO-D
1988 □ an initiative of **MEDIA**, it sponsors the distribution and promotion of European films. It publishes *Press Release* (3).

EFET · FRANCE
- Ecole Française d'Enseignement Technique
10 rue de Picpus
75012 Paris
tel   +33 1 43 46 86 96
fax   +33 1 43 41 03 93
□ film school offering higher education in sound and image editing, and production.

EFFAM · SPAIN
- European Film Finance and Marketing
c/o Media Business School
Torregalindo 10-4°
28016 Madrid
tel   +34 1 359 0247 / 0036
fax   +34 1 345 7606
1991 □ seminars focussing on the EC film industry and exploring the

strengthening of financing and marketing skills as priorities for the European film industry.

EFFIA
■ European Film Finance and Insurers' Association

EFL · TECHNICAL TERM
■ effective focal length

EFLA · USA
■ Educational Film Library Association, Inc

EFM · TECHNICAL TERM
■ eight to fourteen modulation

EFP · TECHNICAL TERM
■ electronic field/film production

EFS · HONG KONG
■ Educational Film Services International
7th floor
Washington Plaza
230 Wan-Chai Road
Wan Chai
tel   +852 5732 661
fax +852 838 2321

EFS · TECHNICAL TERM
■ easy find system

EFT · TECHNICAL TERM
■ electronic funds transfer

EFTSC · UK
■ European Film and Television Studies Conference
Research and Education Division
British Film Institute
21 Stephen Street
London W1P 1PL
tel   +44 71 580 8434
fax +44 71 436 7950
tlx   27624 BFILDNG
1994 □ previously the International Television Studies Conference (**ITSC**), this conference will in 1994 have as its theme "Turbulent Europe: Conflict, Identity and Culture".

EGA · TECHNICAL TERM

■ enhanced graphics adaptor

EGAKU · SWITZERLAND
■ Europäischer Gewerkschaftsausschuss für Kunst, Medien und Unterhaltung Secretariat
15 avenue de Balexert
1219 Châtelaine-Geneva
tel   +41 22 796 2733
fax +41 22 796 5321
□ European committee of trade unions in the fields of entertainment, mass media and the arts.

EGI · TECHNICAL TERM
■ enhanced graphics interface

EGSE · TECHNICAL TERM
■ electrical ground support system

EGT · TECHNICAL TERM
■ electron gun technology

EGTA · BELGIUM
■ European Group of Television Advertising
c/o Pierre-Paul Vander Sande
Régie Media Belge (RMB)
Avenue Louise 479
1050 Brussels
tel   +32 2 648 0245
fax +32 2 648 0387
1971 □ international association established to provide a discussion forum for dealing with practical television advertising issues across Europe.

EHF · TECHNICAL TERM
■ extra high frequency

EHG · TECHNICAL TERM
■ extra high grade

EHS · TECHNICAL TERM
■ extreme high shot (*aka* XHS)

EHT · TECHNICAL TERM
■ extra-high tension

EI · TECHNICAL TERM
■ emulsion in
■ exposure index

EIA · USA
■ Electronic Industries Association
2001 Pennsylvania Avenue NW
Washington
DC 20006-1813
tel +1 202 457 4900
fax +1 202 457 4985
1924 □ association which represents
manufacturers of electronic equipment,
systems, components and parts for
communications and other uses.

EIAJ · JAPAN
■ Electronic Industries Association of
Japan
Tosho Building
No 2-2
Marunouchi
3-chome
Chiyoda-ku
Tokyo 100
tel +81 3 3211 2765
fax +81 3 3287 1712
tlx 072 elindaso j26657

EIAS · TECHNICAL TERM
■ ElectricImage™ Animation System

EIC · USA
■ Exhibitors in Cable
New York

EIC · TECHNICAL TERM
■ engineer in charge

EICTV · CUBA
■ Escuela Internacional de Cine y TV
San Antonio de los Banos
Havana PSF 40/41
tel +53 7 650 3152
fax +53 7 33 5341
tlx 57195 EICTV-CU
□ film and television school.

EIEM · UK
■ European Issues in Educational Media
c/o British Universities Film & Video
Council
55 Greek Street
London W1V 5LR
tel +44 71 734 3687
fax +44 71 287 3914
1992 □ international conference
bringing together European

educationalists to discuss and debate
issues involving the educational uses of
television, film and video.

EIFF · UK
■ Edinburgh International Film Festival
88 Lothian Road
Edinburgh EH3 9BZ
tel +44 31 228 4051
fax +44 31 229 5501
tlx 777582
1946 □ international film festival, with
debate, live events, film premieres and
rare screenings.

EIM · GERMANY
■ European Institute for the Media
Kaistrasse 13
40221 Düsseldorf
tel +49 211 901040
fax +49 211 9010456
tlx 94 011 070 EURO G
1983 □ to undertake research into the
evolving role and structure of the media
on a European scale; to increase the
flow of aid and technical assistance to
the media of developing countries,
especially in Eastern Europe; to provide
a forum for the discussion of media
policies by professionals and
politicians. It publishes *The Bulletin* (4).

EIRP · TECHNICAL TERM
■ equivalent/effective isotropic(ally)
radiated power

EISA · TECHNICAL TERM
■ extended industry standard
architecture

EITB · SPAIN
■ Euskal Irrati Telebista
see **ETB** · SPAIN

EITF · UK
■ Edinburgh International Television
Festival
24 Neal Street
London WC2H 9PS
tel +44 71 379 4519
fax +44 71 836 0702
1976 □ annual television industry
event, taking place during the **EIFF**, and
attracting 1000 programme makers, key

decision makers and young people new to the industry who gather to discuss industry issues and trends. The festival opens with the James MacTaggart Memorial Lecture and includes over 20 sessions.

EJ · TECHNICAL TERM
■ electronic journalism

ELCB · TECHNICAL TERM
■ earth leakage circuit breaker

ELF · TECHNICAL TERM
■ extremely low frequency

ELR · TECHNICAL TERM
■ electronic line replacement

ELS · TECHNICAL TERM
■ extreme long-shot (*aka* XLS)

ELT · UK
■ East London Telecommunications
now incorporated under ENCOM

ELV · TECHNICAL TERM
■ edit-level video
■ expendable launch vehicle

EM · TECHNICAL TERM
■ engineering manager/model

EMEP · TECHNICAL TERM
■ extended mogul end prong

EMFV · UK
■ Educational Media Film & Video Ltd
235a Imperial Drive
Rayners Lane
Harrow
Middlesex HA2 7HE
tel   +44 81 868 1908 / 868 1915
fax +44 81 868 1991
1978 □ distributors of British educational and health video programmes, producing various catalogues.

EMG · FRANCE
■ Euro Media Garanties
66 rue Pierre Charron
75008 Paris
tel   +33 1 43 59 88 03

fax +33 1 45 63 85 58
1991 □ initiative of **MEDIA** which aims to provide financial guarantees across Europe to link the financial sector with the audiovisual production sector. It is intended for European independent producers and the financial institutions providing loans for audiovisual productions.

EMI · TECHNICAL TERM
■ electromagnetic interference

EMMA · UK
■ European MultiMedia Awards Ltd
Rayner House
23 Higher Hillgate
Stockport SK1 3ER
tel   +44 61 429 9448
fax +44 61 429 9568
1992 □ annual awards for products which most successfully exploit the ability of the computer to combine audio, video, text or graphics.

EMR · TECHNICAL TERM
■ electromechanical recorder

EMRC · USA
■ Electronic Media Rating Council
420 Lexington Avenue
Room 308
New York
NY 10017
tel   +1 212 754 3343
fax +1 212 754 6430
1964 □ council of organisations, including mainly cable and broadcast trade bodies, which sets down minimum standards for electronic media ratings surveys.
formerly Broadcast Rating Council (BRC)

EMS · TECHNICAL TERM
■ electronic marker system

EMX · TECHNICAL TERM
■ engineering manual exchange

EN · TECHNICAL TERM
■ edge number(s)

END · TECHNICAL TERM

• equivalent neutral density

ENG · TECHNICAL TERM
• electronic news gathering

ENLL · FRANCE
• Ecole Nationale Louis-Lumière
rue de Vaugirard
BP 22
93161 Noisy-Le-Grand
tel   +33 45 92 23 33
fax +33 43 05 63 44
1926 □ film school.

ENRZ · TECHNICAL TERM
• enhanced non-return to zero

ENS · TECHNICAL TERM
• electronic newsroom system

ENSAD · FRANCE
• Ecole Nationale Supérieure des Arts
Décoratifs
31 rue d'Ulm
Paris 75005
tel   +33 43 29 86 79
1766 □ institution offering courses in
film and video.

ENSAV · BELGIUM
• Ecole Nationale Supérieure des Arts
Visuels de la Cambre
Abbaye de la Cambre, 21
1050 Brussels
tel   +32 2 648 3495 / 9619
1926 □ film school offering courses
lasting 5 years.

ENT · TECHNICAL TERM
• equivalent noise temperature

ENTV · ALGERIA
• Enterprise Nationale de Télévision
21 Boulevard des Martyrs
Algiers
tel   +213 260 2065
fax +213 259 3180
tlx   66-101
□ national television service.

EO · THE NETHERLANDS
• Evangelische Omroep
Postbus 21000
1202 BB Hilversum

tel   +31 35 882411
fax +31 35 882685
tlx   43325 EO NL
1967 □ broadcasting service committed
to spreading the gospel of Jesus Christ
through radio and television. It
publishes *Visie* (52) and *Ronduit* (6).

EO · TECHNICAL TERM
• electro-optical
• emulsion out

EOC · TECHNICAL TERM
• edge of coverage

EOL · TECHNICAL TERM
• end of life

EOR · TECHNICAL TERM
• end of reel

EOT · TECHNICAL TERM
• end of tape
• end of transmission

EP · TECHNICAL TERM
• executive producer
• extended play

EPC · TECHNICAL TERM
• electronic power conditioner

EPP · TECHNICAL TERM
• electronic post-production

EPPG · UK
• European Programme Providers
Group
1983 □ established to protect the
interests of companies/organisations
who are supplying programmes for
cable and satellite television.

EPR · TECHNICAL TERM
• electronic pin registration

EPROD · TECHNICAL TERM
• erasable programmable read-only disc

EPROM · TECHNICAL TERM
• erasable programmable read-only
memory

EPS · CANADA

■ Entertainment Programming Services
720 King Street West
Toronto
Ontario M5V 2T3
tel   +1 416 364 3894
fax +1 416 364 8565
□ film distributor.

EPS · TECHNICAL TERM
■ European Programme on Satellite

ERA · UK
■ The Educational Recording Agency
Ltd
33-34 Alfred Place
London WC1E 7DP
tel   +44 71 436 4883
fax +44 71 323 0486
1990 □ group of organisations joined
together in order to establish a licensing
scheme to apply within the UK. An
ERA licence allows an educational
establishment to record for educational
purposes any radio or television
broadcast and cable output of ERA's
members apart from Open University
(**OU**) programmes which come under a
separate licensing scheme.

ERI · USA
■ Electronics Research, Inc
108 Market Street
Newburgh
IN 47630
tel   +1 812 853 3318
fax +1 812 858 5706
□ manufactures and installs omni and
directional antennae, mounting systems,
towers, filters and combiners for
commercial broadcasting.

ERP · TECHNICAL TERM
■ effective radiated power

ERT · GREECE
■ Elleniki Radiophonia Teleorassi
Messoghion 402
Aghia Paraskevi
15342 Athens
tel   +30 1 639 5970-9
fax +30 1 639 0652
tlx   216066
□ state-controlled national television
broadcasting service.

ERTU · EGYPT
■ Egyptian Radio and Television Union
Radio and TV Building
PO Box 504
Sharia Maspiro
Corniche en-Nil
Cairo
tel   +20 2 749508
fax +20 2 746989
tlx   22609
1928 □ broadcasts television and radio
programmes in a variety of languages.

ESA · FRANCE
■ European Space Agency
■ Agence Spatiale Européenne (ASE)
8-10 rue Mario Nikis
75738 Paris Cedex 15
tel   +33 1 42 73 76 54
fax +33 1 42 73 75 60 / 61 / 62
tlx   042 202746 ESA
1973 □ to promote cooperation among
European states in space research,
technology and applications. Its work is
divided into 6 main programme areas:
satellite telecommunications, space
science, microgravity, Earth
observation, space transportation
systems and the Columbus space
station.

ESAV · SWITZERLAND
■ Ecole Supérieure d'Art Visuel
2 rue Général-Dufour
1204 Geneva
tel   +41 22 311 6706 / 0510
fax +41 22 731 8734
1748 □ higher education institution
offering courses in film and video over
4 or 5 years.

ESCA · FRANCE
■ Ecole Supérieure de Cinéastes et
d'Acteurs
27 avenue Trudaine
75009 Paris
tel   +33 1 48 78 09 61
fax +33 1 42 80 03 71
□ film school, offering courses lasting 2
years.

ESCO · FRANCE
■ European Satellite Consultancy
Organisation

5 rue Louis Lejeune
92128 Montrouge Cedex
tel +33 1 46 57 13 30
tlx 204022
□ international consultants in satellite communications.

ESCOMA · FRANCE
■ Ecole Supérieure Communication Audiovisuelle
23 rue Félix Brun
69007 Lyon
tel +33 78 58 75 63
□ educational institution offering courses in film and audiovisual communication.

ESD · TECHNICAL TERM
■ electrostatic discharge

ESEC · FRANCE
■ Ecole Supérieure d'Etudes Cinématographiques
21 rue de Cîteaux
75012 Paris
tel +33 1 43 42 43 22
fax +33 1 43 41 95 21
1973 □ 2-year professional training in the art and technology of cinema, video and television.

ESF · TECHNICAL TERM
■ expanded sample frame

ESG · TECHNICAL TERM
■ edit sync guide
■ electronic sports gathering

ESP · TECHNICAL TERM
■ executive supervising producer

ESPN · USA
■ Entertainment & Sports Programming Network, Inc
8th floor
605 Third Avenue
New York
NY 10158
tel +1 212 916 9200
fax +1 212 916 9325
□ television network which caters for sports and general entertainment programming.

ESPRIT · BELGIUM
■ European Strategic Programme for Research and Development in Information Technology
Commission of the European Communities
Telecommunications, Information Industries and Innovation
DG XIII
200 rue de la Loi
1049 Brussels
tel +32 2 296 8596
fax +32 2 295 8597
1984 □ programme designed to help provide the European IT industry with the key components of technology it needs to be competitive in world markets. It aims to foster collaboration and pave the way to standards of European origin, while boosting pre-competitive R&D in the key areas of information technology.

ESRA · FRANCE
■ Ecole Supérieure de Réalisation Audiovisuelle
135 avenue Félix Faure
75015 Paris
tel +33 1 44 25 25 25
fax +33 1 44 25 25 26
1972 □ film school offering 3-year study course. The programme includes direction in audiovisual media (16mm and 35mm film, and video) as well as technical training (picture, sound, editing) at a high level.

ESS · TECHNICAL TERM
■ electronic still store

ESTA · BELGIUM
■ European Satellite Television Association
c/o Esselte Pay TV
95 Avenue de la Plage
1940 Brussels
tel +32 2 725 0650
fax +32 2 720 2449

ESTCA · FRANCE
■ Ecole Supérieure des Techniques du Cinéma et de l'Audiovisuel
135 avenue Félix Faure
75015 Paris

tel +33 1 44 25 25 25
fax +33 1 44 25 25 26
1990 □ film school offering 2-year study course in 3 sections: Image, Sound and Production.

ESU · TECHNICAL TERM
- engineering/electronic set-up
- external synchronising unit

ET · GREECE
- Elleniki Tileorassi
Leophoros Messogeion 432
15342 Aghia Paraskevi
tel +30 1 639 5970
fax +30 1 639 2263
tlx 216066
□ public service national television and radio broadcasting station, operating 3 television channels.

ET · TECHNICAL TERM
- educational television (*aka* ETV)

ETA · UK
- Educational Television Association
The King's Manor
Exhibition Square
York YO1 2EP
tel +44 904 433929
fax +44 904 433949
1967 □ aims to bring together institutions and individuals using television and other media for education and training, with over 200 members drawn from educational establishments, television companies and commercial suppliers. It provides a forum for exchange of advice and expertise. There are annual conferences on topical issues, an annual video competition and a schools video competition. It publishes *Journal of Educational Television* (2), *ETA News* (4) and a *Directory* (every 2 years).

ETB · SPAIN
- Euskal Telebista
Barrio Lurreta
48200 Durango
Vizcaya
tel +34 4 681 6600
fax +34 4 681 6416
tlx 34440

1982 □ independent Basque-language broadcasting service, operating 2 television channels and 5 radio stations. *also known as Euskal Irrati Telebista (EITB)*

ETC · PORTUGAL
- Espectaculo & Cultura
Cinema Novo Crl
Rua da Constituição, 311
4200 Porto
tel +351 2 410 8990/1/2
fax +351 2 410 8210
tlx 22367
1993 □ bi-weekly magazine covering film, television, video, cable and satellite, as well as music and theatre.

ETPA · FRANCE
- Ecole Technique Privée de Photographie, de l'Audiovisuel et de Graphisme Publicitaire
1 rue Xavier-Grall
35700 Rennes
tel +33 99 36 64 64
fax +33 99 36 26 40
1974 □ film school offering courses in audiovisual training (3 years), sound (2 years) and photography (2/3 years).

ETRAC · USA
- Educational Radio and Television Center

ETS · USA
- Educational Television Stations

ETV · UK
- Educational and Television Films Ltd
247a Upper Street
London N1 1RU
tel +44 71 226 2298
fax +44 71 226 8016
1961 □ archive film library: materials from Vietnam, China, Eastern Europe and 1930s Labour Movement Britain. It produces a *Catalogue of Films*.

ETV · TECHNICAL TERM
- educational television (*aka* ET)

ETVS · TECHNICAL TERM
- educational television by satellite

EUREKA · BELGIUM
- European Research and Coordination Agency
European Programme for High-Technology Research and Development
Eureka Secretariat
Avenue des Arts 19H, Bte 3
1040 Brussels
tel   +32 2 217 0030
fax +32 2 218 7906
1985 □ framework for industry-led projects aimed at producing high technology goods and services to compete in world markets against the US and Japan. Activities are carried out in a wide variety of advanced technologies, including (tele)communications technology (specifically **HDTV**), **IT**, robotics, lasers and biotechnology.

EUROAIM · BELGIUM
- European Association for an Audiovisual Independent Market
210 avenue Winston Churchill
1180 Brussels
tel   +32 2 346 1500
fax +32 2 346 3842
1988 □ an initiative of **MEDIA**, it is a service and support structure for the promotion and marketing of European independent production. It ensures the presence of independent companies at major markets and also creates new marketing initiatives. In addition, it offers a range of consultancy services and information databases which can facilitate and accelerate contacts between those buying and selling European independent production.

EUROVIP · BELGIUM
- European Video Independent Producers

EUTELSAT · FRANCE
- European Telecommunications Satellite Organisation
Tour Maine-Montparnasse
33 avenue du Maine
75755 Paris Cedex 15
tel   +33 1 45 38 47 47
fax +33 1 45 38 37 00
tlx 203823 EUSAT

1977 □ operates satellites for fixed and mobile communications, with members who are private telecommunications operators in almost 40 countries. Its system currently comprises 8 satellites, used for digital telephony, business communications, land mobile traffic, Eurovision and Euroradio exchanges, satellite news gathering and television distribution to cable and domestic reception systems. It publishes *Eutelsat News* (4).

EUV · TECHNICAL TERM
- extreme ultra-violet

EV · TECHNICAL TERM
- exposure value

EVA · BELGIUM
- European Video Association

EVA · TECHNICAL TERM
- edit video architecture

EVDL · TECHNICAL TERM
- electronically variable delay line

EVE · IRELAND
- Espace Vidéo Européen
c/o Irish Film Institute
6 Eustace Street
Dublin 2
tel   +353 1 679 5744
fax +353 1 679 9657
1990 □ an initiative of the **MEDIA** Programme, founded to promote and support film culture in Europe by providing assistance to European video and laserdisc publishers of feature, documentary and classic films. It also operates a Loan Scheme, with conditionally repayable loans for film publication, and Mediabase, a computerised communication system acting as a comprehensive directory regarding all aspects of the video sector. It publishes *European Video Review* (4).

EVF · TECHNICAL TERM
- electronic viewfinder

EVN · USA

- Eurovision News Exchange

EVR · TECHNICAL TERM
- electronic video recording/recorder

EVS · FRANCE
- European Video Services
6 rue Déserte
67000 Strasbourg
tel +33 88 23 17 41
fax +33 88 32 21 62
1992 □ European network of
organisations representing different
aspects of electronic audiovisual
creation. Its aims are: to promote
electronic audiovisual creation; to
encourage debate on the subject; to
improve the circulation of information;
to create a forum for debate and
exchange; publication of *Scope* (5).

EWTN · USA
- Eternal Word Television Network
5817 Old Leeds Road
Birmingham
AL 35210
tel +1 205 956 9537
□ satellite television network.

EVS · TECHNICAL TERM
- enhanced vertical
definition/resolution system

EZEF · GERMANY
- Evangelisches Zentrum für
Entwicklungsbezogene Filmarbeit
Gänsheidestraße 67
70184 Stuttgart
tel +49 711 240512

F

F/S · TECHNICAL TERM
- frames/feet per second (*aka* FPS)

F/VA · USA
- Film/Video Arts
2nd floor
817 Broadway
New York
NY 10003
tel +1 212 673 9361

fax +1 212 475 3467
1968 □ non-profit media arts centre for
the advancement of emerging and
established media artists of diverse
backgrounds, providing support services
which include low-cost production
equipment and facilities, employment
opportunities, education and training. It
publishes *The Intermediary* (4).

FA · TECHNICAL TERM
- full aperture

FAA · UK
- Film Artistes Association
61 Marloes Road
London W8 6LE
tel +44 71 937 4567
fax +44 71 937 0790
1928 □ to regulate relations between
film artistes and producers, managers,
agents and others, and also between
member and member, to secure unity
of action, by organisation and
otherwise in order to improve the
position and status of film artists.

FAACS · AUSTRALIA
- Federation of Australian Amateur
Cine Societies

FAC · ITALY
- Comitato Nazionale Diffusione Film
d'Arte e Cultura
Via di Villa Patrizi 10
00161 Rome
tel +39 6 884 731
□ national committee for the
publicising of artistic and cultural films.

FACB · AUSTRALIA
- Federation of Australian Commercial
Broadcasters

FACINEB · BELGIUM
- Fédération des Cinéastes Amateurs de
Belgique
□ group of amateur film-makers.

FACS · USA
- Foundation for American
Communications
Suite 409
3800 Barham Boulevard

Los Angeles
CA 90068-1043
tel   +1 213 851 7372
fax   +1 213 851 9186

FACT · UK
▪ Federation Against Copyright Theft
Ltd
7 Victory Business Centre
Worton Road
Isleworth
Middlesex TW7 6ER
tel   +44 81 568 6646
fax   +44 81 560 6364
1982 □ to protect the interests of
members against piracy of their
copyright.

FACTS · AUSTRALIA
▪ Federation of Australian Commercial
Television Stations
44 Avenue Road
Mosman
NSW 2008
tel   +61 2 960 2622
fax   +61 2 969 3520
tlx   121542
1960 □ to represent the interests of
Australian commercial television
stations in the areas of government
relations, technical planning, industrial
issues, codes and standards compliance
and industry promotion.

FAME · UK
▪ Film Archive Management and
Entertainment
18-20 St Dunstan's Road
London SE25 6DU
tel   +44 81 771 6522
fax   +44 81 653 9773
1985 □ management of film and video
collections on behalf of their owners. A
full range of preservation, storage,
cataloguing and library services are
available. A stock shot library service
and out-of-copyright music library are
also operated. It publishes a *Newsletter*.

FAMU · CZECH REPUBLIC
▪ Filmová Akademie Muzických Umění
Smetanovo nábř. 2
116 65 Prague 1
tel   +42 2 266451 / 266262

fax   +42 2 268735
1946 □ academy of arts with a faculty
of film and television.

FAMW · SENEGAL
▪ Federation of African Media Women

FAP · SPAIN
▪ Federación Antipiratería
c/ Alfonso XII, 8
28014 Madrid
tel   +34 1 522 4642 345
fax   +34 1 521 3742
1984 □ protection of motion pictures
copyright. It issues various catalogues.

FAP · TECHNICAL TERM
▪ front axial projection

FAPAV · ITALY
▪ Federazione anti-Pirateria Audiovisiva
Viale Regina Margherita 286
00198 Rome
tel   +39 6 884 1271
fax   +39 6 440 4128
□ organisation which is fighting piracy
in the audiovisual sector.
also known as FAVAV

FAR · TECHNICAL TERM
▪ false alarm rate

FAS · TECHNICAL TERM
▪ frequency of audio sampling
▪ full auto shooting

FAST · TECHNICAL TERM
▪ focus, aperture, shutter, tachometer

FAVA · CANADA
▪ Film and Video Arts Society - Alberta
2nd floor
9722 102nd Street
Edmonton
Alberta T5K 0X4
tel   +1 403 429 1671
fax   +1 403 424 0194
□ non-profit organisation committed to
encouraging and facilitating
independent artist-driven media arts.

FAVAV · ITALY
▪ Federazione anti-Pirateria Audiovisiva
see FAPAV

FAWO · SOUTH AFRICA
▪ Film and Allied Workers Organisation
PO Box 16939
Doornfontein 2028
tel +27 11 402 4570
fax +27 11 402 0777
1987 □ engages in all areas of film and television production, promotes film-making and film literacy among disenfranchised communities and promotes film festivals and training schemes.

FB · TECHNICAL TERM
▪ feedback

FBC · JAPAN
▪ Fukui Broadcasting Co Ltd
5-105 Itagaki
Fukui 910
tel +81 776 34 2800
□ television station.

FBS · JAPAN
▪ Fukuoka Broadcasting System
1-1 Watanabe-dori 1-chome
Chuo-ku
Fukuoka 810
tel +81 92 713 5321
□ television station.

FBU · UK
▪ Federation of Broadcasting Unions
see **FEU** · UK

FBW · GERMANY
▪ Filmbewertungsstelle Wiesbaden
Rheingaustr. 140
65203 Wiesbaden
tel +49 611 670 44
fax +49 611 677 46
1951 □ assessment and classification of films, and the promotion of quality films in cinemas and film theatres.

FC · TECHNICAL TERM
▪ firm contact
▪ foot candle

FCA · SWITZERLAND
▪ Association Suisse du Film de Commande et de l'Audiovision
see **AAV** · SWITZERLAND

FCB · BRAZIL
▪ Fundacão do Cinema Brasileiro
Rua Mayrink Viega 28
20090 Rio de Janeiro
1988 □ film foundation which supports Brazilian cinema.

FCC · USA
▪ Federal Communications Commission
1919 M Street, NW
Washington
DC 20554
tel +202 632 7000
fax +202 653 5402
tlx 7108220160
1934 □ government agency and regulatory body for inter-state and overseas broadcasting.

FCC · TECHNICAL TERM
▪ frame count cueing

FCF · IRAN
▪ Farabi Cinema Foundation
55 Sie-Tir Street
Tehran 11358
tel +98 21 671010 / 678156 / 678545
fax +98 21 678155
tlx 214283 FCF IR
1982 □ to carry out the cultural and artistic policies and directives of the cinematographic affairs of the country and to act as cultural coordinator of Iranian cinema. It has been active in film production and distribution, both domestically and internationally, and also provides professional and vocational guidance regarding film-making. It publishes *Farabi Quarterly* (4) and an annual *Selection of Iranian Cinema*.

FCFC · FRANCE
▪ Fédération des Clubs Français des Cinéastes
□ federation of film-makers' clubs.

FCI · USA
▪ Family Communications, Inc

FCR · FRANCE
▪ France Câbles et Radio
124 rue Réaumur
75091 Paris Cedex 02

tel +33 1 42 21 71 71
tlx 042 fcr x 220731 f
□ telecommunications operating
agency.

FCT · JAPAN
■ Fukushima Central Television Co Ltd
13-23 Ikenodai
Koriyama 963
tel +81 249 23 3300
□ television station.

FD · TECHNICAL TERM
■ film developer
■ frequency demodulator

FDA · DENMARK
■ Fællesforeningen af Danske
Antenneforeninger
PO Box 151
4500 Nykøbing Sjælland
tel +45 53 41 28 95
fax +45 53 41 28 43
1983 □ association of cable TV systems,
representing 250 000 households,
whose aims are: to serve the local
associations with information of any
kind responding to the activities in their
communities; to negotiate any common
interests with authorities and
programme providers (ie. contracts,
juridical and technical matters). It
publishes *FDA Orientering* (5).

FDM · TECHNICAL TERM
■ frequency division multiplex(ing)

FDMA · TECHNICAL TERM
■ frequency-division multiple access

FDP · TECHNICAL TERM
■ fluorescent display panel

FDS · DENMARK
■ Foreningen af Danske
Spillefilmproducenter
c/o Johan Schlüter
Bredgade 6
DK-1260 Copenhagen K
tel +45 3314 3333
fax +45 3332 4333
1991 □ association which represents
Danish feature film producers to the
government, the Danish Film Institute,

collecting societies, unions,
broadcasters and other organisations
and institutions, Danish or foreign, who
directly or indirectly are involved in
production and/or distribution of
feature films.

FDU · TECHNICAL TERM
■ fade down/up

FEC · TECHNICAL TERM
■ forward error correction/control

FEDIC · ITALY
■ Federazione Italiana Cineclub
Via Ugo Ojetti 427
00137 Rome
tel +39 6 88 95 307
□ federation of Italian cinema clubs.

FEITIS · FRANCE
■ Fédération Européenne des Industries
Techniques de l'Image et du Son
50 avenue Marceau
75008 Paris
tel +33 1 47 23 75 76
fax +33 1 47 23 07 45
□ European federation of technical
industries of image and sound.

FEMI · BELGIUM
■ Flemish European Media Institute

FEMIS · FRANCE
■ Institut de Formation et
d'Enseignement pour les Métiers de
l'Image et du Son
Palais de Tokyo
13 Avenue du Président Wilson
75116 Paris
tel +33 1 47 23 36 53
fax +33 1 40 70 17 03
tlx 648208 F PATOIS
1901 □ film school.

FEPACI · BURKINA FASO
■ Fédération Panafricaine des Cinéastes
01 BP 2524
Ouagadougou 01
tel +226 310258
fax +226 311859
1970 □ federation of film-makers and
national associations throughout Africa
which promotes indigenous film

production and ensures the films a visibility on their own screens. It also is initiating a new project for training film-makers at Ouagadougou.

FERA · BELGIUM
- Fédération Européenne des Réalisateurs de l'Audiovisuel
avenue Everærd 55
1190 Brussels
tel +32 2 345 7473
fax +32 2 344 5780
□ European federation of audiovisual directors.

FES · GERMANY
- Friedrich Ebert Stiftung
Godesberger Allee 149
53175 Bonn

FESPACO · BURKINA FASO
- Festival Panafricain du Cinéma de Ouagadougou
01 BP 2505
Ouagadougou 01
tel +226 307538
fax +226 312509
1969 □ film festival and archive which aims to provide distribution of all works by African film-makers, thus allowing them to establish contacts and exchange ideas, and to contribute to the progress and development of African cinema for expression, education and the creation of awareness.

FET · BELGIUM
- Fédération Européenne des Associations de Téléspectateurs
□ European federation of screen viewers' associations.

FET · TECHNICAL TERM
- field effect(s) transmitter/transistor

FEU · UK
- Federation of Entertainment Unions
79 Redhill Wood
New Ash Green
Longfield
Kent DA3 8QP
fax +44 474 874606
incorporating Federation of

Broadcasting Unions (FBU)
1960 □ provides liaison and coordination in some matters between the following trade unions in the entertainment sector: British Actors Equity Association, Broadcasting Entertainment Cinematograph and Theatre Union (**BECTU**), Film Artistes Association (**FAA**), Musicians Union, National Union of Journalists (NUJ) and the Writer's Guild of Great Britain.

FF · TECHNICAL TERM
- fast forward
- follow focus

FFA · GERMANY
- Filmförderungsanstalt Bundesanstalt des öffentlichen Rechts
Budapester Straße 41
10787 Berlin
tel +49 30 254 0900
fax +49 30 262 8976
1968 □ federal film funding institute whose mandate is the overall raising of standards of quality in German film and cinema and the improvement of the economic structure of the industry.

FFC · AUSTRALIA
- Australian Film Finance Corporation
Level 12
130 Elizabeth Street
GPO Box 3886
Sydney
NSW 2001
tel +61 2 956 2555
fax +61 2 954 4253
1988 □ primary vehicle for government assistance in commercial film financing. It invests in certain Australian film and television projects which have demonstrated commercial potential (40% private sector potential).
also known as AFFC

FFD · SWITZERLAND
- Association Suisse des Producteurs de Films de Fiction et de Documentaires
see **SDF** · SWITZERLAND

FFD · UK
- Future Film Developments
11 The Green

Brill
Aylesbury HP18 9RU
tel +44 844 238444
fax +44 844 238106
tlx 837896 BRILL G
□ specialist broadcast and recording studio interconnection and installation equipment supplier.

FFF · FINLAND
■ Finnish Film Foundation
Suomen Elokuvasäätiö/Finlands Filmstiftelse
K13, Kanavakatu 12
SF-00160 Helsinki
tel +358 0 177 727
fax +358 0 177 937
tlx 125032 SESFI SF
□ promotion of Finnish films. It publishes *Films from Finland* (1).

FFI · UK
■ Film Four International
Channel 4 Television
60 Charlotte Street
London W1P 2AX
tel +44 71 631 4444
fax +44 71 580 2622
1984 □ to sell films funded or partially funded by Channel 4 (**C4**) to distributors for theatrical release worldwide.

FG · TECHNICAL TERM
■ fine grain
■ foreground

FI · TECHNICAL TERM
■ fade in

FIA · UK
■ Fédération Internationale des Acteurs
31a Thayer Street
London W1M 5LH
tel +44 71 487 4699
fax +44 71 487 5809
1952 □ service organisation for unions of actors, representing performers at international forums. It also publishes standard and model contracts, promotes international solidarity during national industrial disputes and assists union formation and development. It also publishes *FIA Focus* (2).

FIAD · FRANCE
■ Fédération Internationale des Associations de Distributeurs de Films
43 Boulevard Malesherbes
75008 Paris
tel +33 1 42 66 05 32
fax +33 1 42 66 96 92
1953 □ to represent the interests of film distributors.

FIAF · BELGIUM
■ Fédération Internationale des Archives du Film
190 rue Franz Merjay
1180 Brussels
tel +32 2 343 0691
fax +32 2 343 7622
1938 □ federation which brings together some 93 institutions in 58 countries which are dedicated to the collection and preservation of films. Its aims are: to promote the preservation of film as art and historical document throughout the world and to bring together all organisations devoted to this end; to facilitate the collection and international exchange of films and documents relating to cinematographic history and art for the purpose of making them as widely accessible as possible; to develop cooperation between its members; to promote the development of cinema art and culture. It publishes *FIAF Bulletin* (2), *International Index to Film Periodicals* (1) and various other publications. *also known as International Federation of Film Archives (IFFA)*

FIAIS · ITALY
■ Federazione Internazionale degli Archivi delle Immagini e dei Suoni
Casella Postale 6104
00195 Rome
tel +39 6 3700266
fax +39 6 312068
1991 □ international federation of film and sound libraries whose aim is to affiliate public and private collections and to safeguard their work. It publishes *Bollettini* magazine (2).

FIAPF · FRANCE
■ Fédération Internationale des

Associations de Producteurs de Films
33 avenue des Champs Elysées
75008 Paris
tel +33 1 42 25 62 14
fax +33 1 42 56 23 86
□ international film producers'
association.
*also known as International Federation
of Film Producers' Associations (IFFPA)*

FIAT · SPAIN
▪ Fédération Internationale des Archives
de Télévision
Saturno 10
28223 Madrid
tel +34 1 581 7327
fax +34 1 581 7474
1977 □ organisation of archives within
television stations who aim to preserve
and catalogue televised material.
*also known as International Federation
of Television Archives (IFTA)*

FIC · ITALY
▪ Federazione Italiana Cineforum
Via Pascoli, 3
24121 Bergamo
tel +39 35 244703
fax +39 35 233129
1959 □ organisation of cultural cinema
clubs; diffusion of d'Essai movies;
publication of *Cineforum* magazine. It
publishes *Cineforum* (12).

FICC · ITALY
▪ Federazione Italiana Circoli del
Cinema
Piazza Caprettari 70
00186 Rome
tel +39 6 68 79 307
□ Italian federation of cinema clubs.

FICC · SWITZERLAND
▪ Fédération Internationale des Ciné-
Clubs
Case 825
CH-2301 La Chaux-de-Fonds
1947
*also known as International Federation
of Film Societies (IFFS)*

FICCS · JAPAN
▪ Film Festival of International Cinema
Students

c/o Tokyo Agency Inc
4-8-18 Akasaka
Minato-ku
Tokyo 107
tel +81 3 3475 3855
fax +81 3 5411 0382
1991 □ annual film festival, dedicated
to cultivating new directors.

FICE · ITALY
▪ Federazione Italiana Cinema d'Essai
Via di Villa Patrizi 10
00161 Rome
tel +39 6 884 731
□ federation of art-house cinema.

FICTS · ITALY
▪ Fédération Internationale du Cinéma
et de la Télévision Sportifs
c/o CONI SICILIA
Via Emanuele Notarbartolo, 1/g
Palermo
tel +39 91 625 1858
fax +39 91 625 6256
tlx 911006 CONSICI
1982 □ international federation whose
main aims are: to promote the
exhibition of sports, particularly in the
field of cinema and television but also
in photography and to create a mutual
knowledge of it through all available
media; to act as coordinator by
circulating information relating to
various film and television sports
festivals, by monitoring the transmission
and distribution of sport films and sport
audiovisual programmes, by facilitating
contacts between festivals and other
bodies and representatives of
government and non-government film
and sport organisations, and by other
activities.

FIDES · FRANCE
▪ Fiduciaire d'Editions de Films

FIF · TECHNICAL TERM
▪ fractal image format file

FIFA · FRANCE
▪ Festival International du Film d'Art
Bureau 108
UNESCO
7 Place Fontenoy

75700 Paris
tel   +33 1 42 65 08 88
fax +33 1 49 24 98 45
□ annual film festival (November) showing short films in the following categories: historical documentaries; architectural information; and artists' lives.

FIFAL · SWITZERLAND
■ Festival International du Film d'Architecture et d'Urbanisme de Lausanne
Case postale 2756
CH-1002 Lausanne
tel   +41 21 312 1735 / 237 972
fax +41 21 237842
tlx   454199 TXC CH
□ film festival (odd years only) of films on the subjects of architecture and town planning.

FIFARC · FRANCE
■ Festival International des Films sur l'Architecture
17 Quai de la Monnaie
33800 Bordeaux
tel   +33 56 94 79 05
fax +33 56 91 48 04
□ film festival (February, even years only) showing films and videos about architecture, city planning, urban environment, heritage and design.

FIFART · SWITZERLAND
■ Festival International du Film sur l'Art
Case postale 2783
CH-1002 Lausanne
tel   +41 21 321 1735 / 237 972
fax +41 21 237 842
tlx   454199 TXC CH
□ film festival (even years only) of films on art, including sculpture, painting, design and architecture.

FIFEJ · FRANCE
■ Festival du Film et de la Jeunesse de Paris
35 rue d'Alsace
Courcellor II
92531 Levallois Perret
tel   +33 1 47 54 11 00
fax +33 1 47 54 13 42
□ annual film festival (June) devoted to features produced for children and youth.

FIFEL · SWITZERLAND
■ Festival International du Film sur l'Energie
Case postale 88 - Chauderon
CH-1000 Lausanne 9
tel   +41 21 312 9069
fax +41 21 320 1019
□ annual film festival of films on the subjects of energy, including nuclear power, fossil fuels, solar power, hydraulic installation and hydro-electric plants.

FIFI · FRANCE
■ Fédération Internationale des Festivals Indépendants

FIFO · TECHNICAL TERM
■ first-in first-out

FIFREC · FRANCE
■ Festival International du Film et des Réalisateurs des Ecoles de Cinéma
BP 7144
30913 Nîmes Cedex
tel   +33 66 84 47 40
fax +33 72 02 20 36
1988 □ to confirm Nîmes as the annual meeting place for the best film schools from all over the world to experience and spread a common passion: to support contemporary film-making; to develop and encourage exchanges between film schools; to help to distribute these films; to encourage contacts with professionals who attend the festival.

FIFS · IRELAND
■ Federation of Irish Film Societies Ltd
Irish Film Centre
1-2 Eustace Street
Dublin 2
tel   +353 1 679 4420
fax +353 1 679 4166
1977 □ to protect and promote the interests of member film societies; to handle negotiations with the film trade; to coordinate transport of films; to encourage the formation of new societies; to give technical and

procedural advice to film societies.

FII · IRELAND
- Film Institute of Ireland
6 Eustace Street
Temple Bar
Dublin 2
tel   +353 1 679 5744
fax +353 1 679 9657
1993 □ national body which promotes film culture in Ireland through its activities in exhibition, film and media education, training, production, related activities and the Irish Film Archive.
incorporating Irish Film Centre (IFC) and Irish Film Institute (IFI)

FILIS · ITALY
- Federazione Italiana Lavoratori Informazione e Spettacolo
Piazza Sallustio 24
00187 Rome
tel   +39 6 4814 177
fax +39 6 4824 325
1981 □ national trades union organisation which is the largest for workers in the sectors of television, film and related media, with some 70 000 members. Its objectives are to defend and safeguard the rights of workers in those sectors regarding collective bargaining, pay and working conditions, and their social and legislative status. It is a member of the Confederazione Generale Italiana del Lavoro (CGIL; General Italian Confederation of Labour).

FIM · USA
- Fairness in Media

FINAS · MALAYSIA
- Perbadanan Kemajuan Filem Nasional Malaysia
Kompleks Studio Merdeka
Hulu Klang
68000 Ampang
Selangor Darul Ehsan
tel   +60 3 408 5722
fax +60 3 407 5216
□ national film development corporation.

FIPA · FRANCE

- Festival International de Programmes Audiovisuels
215 rue du Faubourg St-Honoré
75008 Paris
tel   +33 1 45 61 01 66
fax +33 1 40 74 07 96
□ annual international film festival held in Cannes, showing films and videos in 6 categories: fiction; series and serials; documentaries; reportings; image and music; and short programmes.

FIPFI · FRANCE
- Fédération Internationale des Producteurs de Films Indépendants
50 avenue Marceau
75008 Paris
tel   +33 1 47 23 70 30
fax +33 1 47 20 78 17
1974 □ defence and promotion of French film producers.
also known as Independent Film Producers International Association (IFPIA)

FIPRESCI · GERMANY
- Fédération Internationale de la Presse Cinématographique
c/o Klaus Eder, General Secretary
Schliessheimer Str. 83
80797 Munich
tel   +49 89 182303
fax +49 89 184766
tlx   214674
1932 □ to defend the interests and rights of professional film critics and to improve the conditions in which they work. At various film festivals every year it gives FIPRESCI prizes, the criterion for which is to promote film art and to encourage new and young cinema.

FIR · TECHNICAL TERM
- finite impulse response

FISTAV · FRANCE
- Fédération Internationale des Syndicats des Travailleurs de l'Audiovisuel
1 rue Jansens
75019 Paris
tel   +33 1 42 45 72 14
fax +33 1 42 40 90 20

▫ international organisation of trades unions in the audiovisual field.

FIT · USA
▪ Foundation To Improve Television

FIT · TECHNICAL TERM
▪ frame interline/inline transfer

FITCA · FRANCE
▪ Fédération Nationale des Industries Techniques du Cinéma et de l'Audiovisuel
50 avenue Marceau
75008 Paris
tel +33 1 47 23 75 76
fax +33 1 47 23 70 47
1947 ▫ professional organisation for facilities and services to companies involved in production and post-production cinema, television and video.
also known as FNITCA

FITES · CZECH REPUBLIC
▪ Filmový a Televizni Svaz
Pod Nuselskými schody, 3
12000 Prague
tel +42 2 691 0310
fax +42 2 691 1375
tlx 122879
▫ association of Czech film directors and actors.

FIVF · USA
▪ Foundation for Independent Video and Film
9th floor
625 Broadway
New York
NY 10012
tel +1 212 473 3400
fax +1 212 677 8732
▫ non-profit organisation which supports the educational activities of the Association for Independent Video and Film-Makers (**AIVF**).

FK · TECHNICAL TERM
▪ five kilowatt

FKTG · GERMANY
▪ Fernseh- und Kinotechnische Gesellschaft

Veilchenweg 3
6500 Mainz 21
tel +49 6131 471043
1972 ▫ association comprising broadcasting associations, educational institutions and companies, which aims to promote advances in television and film technology, and publishes *Fernseh-und Kinotechnik* (12).

FL · TECHNICAL TERM
▪ focal length
▪ footlambert

FLAPF · BRAZIL
▪ Federação Latinoamericana de Productores de Fonogramas y Videogramas
▫ Latin-American association of producers of videos and records.

FLEC · FRANCE
▪ Fédération Loisirs et Culture
24 Boulevard Poissonnière
75009 Paris
tel +33 1 47 70 31 97
fax +33 1 45 23 23 63
1946 ▫ cine-club group.

FLLA · TECHNICAL TERM
▪ fusible link logic array

FLOF · TECHNICAL TERM
▪ full level one feature

FLOL · TECHNICAL TERM
▪ film library on line

FLS · TECHNICAL TERM
▪ full-length shot

FM · TECHNICAL TERM
▪ flight model
▪ floor manager
▪ frequency modulation/modulated

FMA · SOUTH AFRICA
▪ Film-Makers Association
tel +27 11 726 2395

FMI · FRANCE
▪ France Media International
78 avenue Raymond Poincaré
75116 Paris

tel   +33 1 45 01 55 90
fax   +33 1 45 01 28 39
tlx   614186
1983 □ distribution and merchandising
of television programmes, both within
France and abroad.

FMI · TECHNICAL TERM
▪ FM improvement

FMPP · USA
▪ Foundation of Motion Picture
Pioneers

FMV · TECHNICAL TERM
▪ full-motion video

FNC · ITALY
▪ Federazione Nazionale
Cinevideoautori
Via Giove Tonante 10
Casella Postale 368
47100 Forli
tel   +39 543 25678
fax   +39 543 25678
1958 □ it organises the yearly II
fotogramma d'Oro/Golden Frame Film
and Video Festival with the sponsorship
of the Terme di Castrocaro. It is open to
non-professional works on any subject.

FNDF · FRANCE
▪ Fédération Nationale des
Distributeurs de Films
43 Boulevard Malesherbes
75008 Paris
tel   +33 1 42 66 05 32
fax   +33 1 42 66 96 92
1944 □ to represent the professional
interests of film distributors in France.

FNITCA · FRANCE
▪ Fédération Nationale des Industries
Techniques du Cinéma et de
l'Audiovisuel
also known as **FITCA** · FRANCE

FNN · USA
▪ Financial News Network

FNN · USA
▪ Florida News Network
□ satellite television broadcaster.

FNVC · FUJI
▪ Fuji National Video Centre
c/o Ministry of Information
Government Buildings
Suva
□ video library and production unit,
also involved in educational
programmes.

FO · TECHNICAL TERM
▪ fade out
▪ fibre optic

FOA · TECHNICAL TERM
▪ fan-out amplifier

FOC · TECHNICAL TERM
▪ fibre optic cable

FOCAL · SWITZERLAND
▪ Fondation de Formation Continue
pour le Cinéma et l'Audiovisuel
33 rue St-Laurent
1003 Lausanne
tel   +41 21 312 6817
fax   +41 21 23 59 45
1990 □ national institute, created by
Swiss professional cinema and
audiovisual associations, to organise
specialised on-going education and
training courses. It proposes thematic
seminars, exploratory workshops,
conferences and debates, round-table
meetings, and extended training
courses. These activities cover all
aspects of producing an audiovisual
work, from scriptwriting to the actual
screening in a cinema or on television.

FOCAL · UK
▪ Federation of Commercial
Audiovisual Libraries Ltd
PO Box 422
Harrow
Middlesex HA1 3YN
tel   +44 81 423 5853
fax   +44 81 423 5853
1985 □ international non-profit-making
professional trade association
representing commercial and non-
commercial film/audiovisual libraries,
film and videotape researchers,
technical facilities, storage and
distribution services and interested

individuals. It publishes *Focal International* (2), an *International Directory* (1), *Where On Earth* (technical data; 1) and a *Members Guide* (6).

FOCINE · COLOMBIA
- Compañía de Fomento Cinematográfico
Calle 35, No. 4-89
Bogota
tel +57 1 288 4661 / 288 4575 / 288 4712
fax +57 1 285 5749
1978 □ production and promotion of Colombian cinema.

FODIC · CAMEROON
- Fonds de l'Industrie Cinématographique
□ film fund.

FOM · TECHNICAL TERM
- film operations manager

FONCINE · VENEZUELA
- Fondo de Fomento Cinematográfico
Avde. Diego Cisneros Edif.
Centro Colgate Ala Sur Piso 2
Los Ruices
Caracas 1071
tel +58 2 381775 / 381622 / 381050 / 381564 / 395973 / 393942
fax +58 2 394786
tlx 25531 FONCI-VC
1982 □ contributes to the diffusion and promotion of Venezuelan films; makes possible for national films to participate in international markets and festivals, and also works together with the Venezuelan Foreign Office in order to present weekly shows of Venezuelan films in several foreign countries. It publishes *Foncine-Edicine* (2).

FORTA · SPAIN
- Federación de Organismos de Radio y Televisión Autonómicos
28001 Madrid
tel +34 1 576 1727
fax +34 1 576 5300
1989 □ association of independent radio and television organisations.

FOT · TECHNICAL TERM
- field of travel

FOV · TECHNICAL TERM
- field of view

FP · TECHNICAL TERM
- focal plane
- front projection

FPCA · PORTUGAL
- Federação Portuguesa de Cinema e Audio-Visuals
Rua Domingos Jardo 4
1900 Lisbon
tel +351 1 301 9584
□ national federation for cinema and the audiovisual.

FPF · FRANCE
- Film Parlant Français

FPF · TECHNICAL TERM
- frames per foot

FPM · TECHNICAL TERM
- frames/feet per minute

FPS · TECHNICAL TERM
- frames/feet per second (*aka* F/S)

FPU · TECHNICAL TERM
- floating point unit

FR3 · FRANCE
- France Regions 3
Société Nationale FR3
116 Quai Kennedy
75782 Paris Cedex 16
tel +33 1 42 30 22 22
fax +33 1 46 47 92 94
tlx 630 720
□ national public service television station.

FRC · FRANCE
- Formation de Recherche Cinématographique
Département de Sociologie
Université de Paris X (Paris-Nanterre)
200 Avenue de la République
92001 Nanterre Cedex
tel +33 40 97 75 09
□ research and study centre.

FRT · ITALY
▪ Federazione Radio Televisioni
Viale Regina Margherita 286
00198 Rome
tel +39 6 884 1271
fax +39 6 440 4128
1984 □ private television and radio
association.

FS · TECHNICAL TERM
▪ field synchronisation
▪ film strip
▪ fit and sealed
▪ follow shot
▪ full shot

FSAC · CANADA
▪ Film Studies Association of Canada
▪ Association Canadienne d'Etudes
Cinématographiques
Secretary/Treasurer
Jody Baker
Department of Film Studies
Queen's University
160 Stuart Street
Kingston
Ontario K7L 3N6
tel +1 616 545 2178
□ film studies association which also
publishes *Canadian Journal of Film
Studies* (4).

FSAPO · TECHNICAL TERM
▪ fade sound and picture out

FSFM · TECHNICAL TERM
▪ full screen full motion

FSFMV · TECHNICAL TERM
▪ full screen full motion video

FSK · GERMANY
▪ Freiwillige Selbstkontrolle der
Filmwirtschaft
Kreuzberger Ring 56
65205 Wiesbaden-Erbenheim
tel +49 611 77891-0
fax +49 611 723317
1949 □ classifies films and videos with
regard to their suitability for children
and young people, and in doing so
works closely with national youth
authorities. It publishes *Film & Fakten*
(4).

FSK · TECHNICAL TERM
▪ frequency shift keying

FSM · TECHNICAL TERM
▪ field strength meter

FSS · TECHNICAL TERM
▪ fixed service satellite
▪ fixed satellite service
▪ flying spot scan
▪ frame store synchroniser

FST · TECHNICAL TERM
▪ flat(ter) square(r) tube

FSU · UK
▪ Film Society Unit
c/o British Film Institute
21 Stephen Street
London W1P 1PL
tel +44 71 255 1444
fax +44 71 436 7950
tlx 27624 BFILDNG
□ exists to serve the British Federation
of Film Societies (**BFFS**) and publishes
Films on Offer (1).

FT · TECHNICAL TERM
▪ frame transfer

FTB · JAPAN
▪ Fukui Television Broadcasting
Corporation
3-410 Toiya-cho
Fukui 910
tel +81 776 21 2233
□ television station.

FTB · SWITZERLAND
▪ Schweizerischer Verband
Filmtechnischer Betriebe
▪ Association Suisse des Industries
Techniques Cinématographiques (ITC)
Schwarz-Filmtechnik AG
Breiteweg 36
3072 Ostermundigen
tel +41 31 932 11 11
fax +41 31 932 11 10
□ association of motion picture
technical industries.

FTII · INDIA
▪ Film and Television Institute of India
Law College Road

Poona 411 004
tel   +91 212 330 855
□ national institute.

FTM · TECHNICAL TERM
■ flat tension mark

FTT · UK
■ Film and TV Technician
□ magazine, now *Stage Screen and Radio*, published by the Broadcasting Entertainment Cinematograph and Theatre Union (**BECTU**).

FTT · TECHNICAL TERM
■ film and television technician

FTTI · INDIA
■ Film and Television Technology Institute
DBS Corporate Club
1st floor
World Trade Tower
New Barakhamba Lane
New Delhi 110001
tel   +91 11 312 851 / 331 4668
fax +91 11 331 2830
tlx 63421 DBS D IN
□ professional training in all skills involved in film, television and video production; consultancy in planning, designing and installation; export of films and videos; talent bank of film and television artists; equipment hire; liaison, management and co-ordination of international co-productions.

FTTV · UK
■ Financial Times Television
Number One
Southwark Bridge
London SE1
tel   +44 71 873 4098
fax +44 71 873 3081
1989 □ leading producers of business programmes.

FTV · JAPAN
■ Fukushima Telecasting Co Ltd
2-5 Oyama-cho
Fukushima 960
tel   +81 245 36 8000
□ television station.

FUND · CANADA
■ Foundation to Underwrite New Drama for Pay TV
BCE Place
PO Box 787
Toronto
Ontario M5J 2T3
tel   +1 416 956 5431
fax +1 416 956 2087
tlx 06 22715
1986 □ foundation which advances script development loans and which has 3 components in its programme: script development, senior projects and equity investment. The programme is available to Canadian production companies with a track record in the production of long-form drama.

FV · TECHNICAL TERM
■ family viewing

FVL · TECHNICAL TERM
■ film and video library

FVSO · CANADA
■ Film and Video Security Office
PO Box 29
Châteauguay
Montreal
Quebec J6J 4Z4
tel   +1 514 692 0701
fax +1 514 692 6974
□ protects the interest of **CMPDA** members by combatting all forms of film and video piracy and signal theft.

FWHM · TECHNICAL TERM
■ full width half maximum

FWU · GERMANY
■ Institut für Film und Bild in Wissenschaft und Unterricht
Bavariafilmplatz 3
Postfach 260
82031 Grünwald
tel   +49 89 64971
tlx 5218598
1950 □ institute for media in science and education which publishes *FWU Mitteilungen* (10).

FX · TECHNICAL TERM
■ effects

- sound effects
- special effects (*aka* SFX, SPEFX, SPFX)

G

G/T · TECHNICAL TERM
- gain/temperature

G/V · TECHNICAL TERM
- general view

GA-AS · TECHNICAL TERM
- Gallium Arsenide

GAA · TECHNICAL TERM
- gross average audience

GAASFET · TECHNICAL TERM
- Gallium Arsenide field effect transistor

GACC · USA
- Great American Communications Company

GACSO · FRANCE
- Groupement de Ciné-Clubs et d'Associations Culturelles du Sud-Ouest de la France
47 rue Rosa Bonheur
33000 Bordeaux
tel   +33 56 44 38 94
1987 □ distribution of films and the maintenance of relations with other film societies in Europe.

GAZE · TECHNICAL TERM
- gauged Angenieux zoom equipment

GB · TECHNICAL TERM
- gigabytes

GBA · UK
- Guild of British Animation
26 Noel Street
London W1V 3RD
tel   +44 71 434 2651
fax +44 71 434 9002
1988 □ represents the interests of British animators, providing an advisory service in all matters relating to production, including copyright, legal

and employment practices.

GBC · GHANA
- Ghana Broadcasting Corporation
PO Box 1633
Accra
tel   +233 21 772 341 / 221 161
fax +233 21 773 227
tlx   2114 GBC GH
1935 □ public broadcasting service whose objectives are: to undertake sound, commercial and television broadcasts, to prepare in the fields of culture, education, information and entertainment, programmes reflecting national progress and aspirations; to carry an external service of sound broadcasting.

GBC · GUYANA
- Guyana Broadcasting Corporation
see **GUYBC** · GUYANA

GBCT · UK
- Guild of British Camera Technicians
5-11 Taunton Road
Metropolitan Centre
Greenford
Middlesex UB6 8UQ
tel   +44 81 578 9243
fax +44 81 575 5972
1978 □ to ensure that the value of camera technicians is recognised not only by members of the motion picture industry but also by members of the general public. To promote and provide means whereby members may meet socially and professionally other members of the guild and other bodies and individuals whose interests are allied to that of motion picture photography; to further the standards of professional conduct and achievement by members of the guild and thereby inspire and encourage non-members to aspire to members. It publishes *Eyepiece* (6) and an annual *Crew Directory*.

GBFE · UK
- Guild of British Film Editors
"Travair"
Spurlands End Road
Great Kingshill

High Wycombe
Bucks HP15 6HY
tel +44 494 712313
fax +44 2406 3563
1966 □ to ensure that the true value of film sound editing is recognised not only by those engaged in it but also by the whole of the film industry, as an important part of the creative and artistic aspects of film production; to ensure that members receive due recognition from other professional associations; to seek cooperation with other professional bodies in the industry and to exchange views in order to further the artistic and technical aims of film and sound editing and thereby encourage non-members to aspire to membership.

GBG · THE NETHERLANDS
▪ Vereniging Geschiedenis, Beeld en Geluid
Zeeburgerkade 8
1019 HA Amsterdam
tel +31 20 665 2966
fax +31 20 665 9086
1986 □ the preservation of relevant historical audiovisual sources in The Netherlands; the access to audiovisual sources for all users, whether researchers or programme makers; the academic study and use of (historical) audiovisual sources; the responsible use of audiovisual sources for educational purposes. It publishes *GBG Nieuws* (4).

GBS · JAPAN
▪ Gifu Broadcasting System
9 Imako-machi
Gifu 500
tel +81 582 64 1181
□ television station.

GC/S · TECHNICAL TERM
▪ gigacycles per second

GCR · TECHNICAL TERM
▪ ghost cancellation/cancelling reference
▪ group coded recording

GEAR
▪ Group of European Audience

Researchers

GEECT · FRANCE
▪ Groupement Européen des Ecoles de Cinéma et de Télévision
rue de la Manutention
75116 Paris
tel +33 1 47 20 71 94
fax +33 1 40 70 17 00
□ European federation of film and television schools.

GEEMAC · FRANCE
▪ Groupe Européen d'Enseignement des Métiers de l'Audiovisuel et de la Communication
135 avenue Félix Faure
75015 Paris
tel +33 1 44 25 25 25
fax +33 1 44 25 25 26
□ group comprising the films schools ESRA, ESTCA, IDHECOM and ISEC.

GEFCA · FRANCE
▪ Groupement Européen des Financiers du Cinéma et de l'Audiovisuel

GEHRA · FRANCE
▪ Groupe d'Etudes Historiques sur la Radiotélévision
F214
20 rue Mouchotte
75014 Paris
tel +33 1 40 51 91 89
fax +33 1 43 54 56 28
1982 □ research and meetings on the history of broadcasting. It publishes *Actes des Journées du GEHRA* (every 2 years).

GEO · TECHNICAL TERM
▪ geosynchronous equatorial orbit
▪ geostationary earth orbit

GER · PORTUGAL
▪ Grupo de Estudos e Realizações Lda
Avenida E U da América 51, 5º DTo
1700 Lisbon
tel +351 1 80 46 77
fax +351 1 848 9801
1988

GFC · GREECE
▪ Greek Film Centre

10 Panepistimiou Avenue
10671 Athens
tel   +30 1 363 1733 / 4586
fax +30 1 361 4336
tlx   222614 GFC
1970 ▢ production and promotion of
Greek cinema.

GFPAFA · UK
▪ Guild of Film Production Accountants
and Financial Administrators
Twickenham Film Studios
St Margarets
Twickenham
Middlesex TW1 2AW
tel   +44 81 892 4477
fax +44 81 891 5574
tlx   884497 TWIKSTG
1967 ▢ to promote, maintain and
protect the highest standards of film
production accounting, costing and
financial administration; to safeguard
the interests of the guild and its
members and to promote their
recognition and acceptance within the
film production industry and other
professional associations; to arrange
such functions and disseminate such
information as will enable members to
keep abreast of modern methods,
practice, innovation and legislation; to
promote and provide social, cultural
and professional exchange among and
between its members and those of other
associations or bodies.

GFPE · UK
▪ Guild of Film Production Executives
Pinewood Studios
Pinewood Road
Iver Heath
Bucks SLO ONH
tel   +44 753 651700
fax +44 753 656844

GFVL · UK
▪ German Film and Video Library
Education Distribution Service
Unit 2, Drywall Estate
Castle Road
Sittingbourne
Kent ME10 3RL
tel   +44 795 427614
fax +44 795 474871

▢ distributes a wide range of film and
video programmes about Germany.

GHZ · TECHNICAL TERM
▪ gigahertz

GI · TECHNICAL TERM
▪ gross impression

GIA · FRANCE
▪ Groupement Informatique de
l'Audiovisuel

GIBBC · GIBRALTAR
▪ Gibraltar Broadcasting Corporation
Broadcasting House
18 South Barrack Road
Gibraltar
tel   +350 79760
fax +350 78673
tlx   2229 GBCEE GK
1963 ▢ public television and radio
service broadcaster whose objective is
to inform, educate and entertain.

GLT · UK
▪ Guild of Local Television
see **GOLT** · UK

GMTV · UK
▪ Good Morning Television
London Television Centre
Upper Ground
London SE1 9LT
tel   +44 71 827 7000
fax +44 71 827 7001
1993 ▢ **ITV**'s national breakfast
television station, broadcasting 7 days a
week, from 0600 to 0925 am.

GNS · THE NETHERLANDS
▪ Genootschap van Nederlandse
Speelfilmmakers
PO Box 581
1000 AN Amsterdam
tel   +31 20 676 5088
fax +31 20 676 5837
1981 ▢ to promote the films and
interests of its film-maker members.

GOLT · UK
▪ Guild of Local Television
16 Fountain Road
Edgbaston

Birmingham B17 8NL
tel   +44 21 429 3706
fax +44 21 429 3706
1991 □ national organisation created to offer support, guidance and networking to all those involved in the production or broadcast of locally originated programming to ensure that local television develops as a high quality, locally relevant media. Its aims are: to promote local television and the interests of those engaged in its provision; to gather and make available the pool of experience and knowledge of best practice in local television; to encourage individuals and groups in the community to find an outlet via local television; to represent the interests of those engaged in local television.
also known as GLT

GPD · TECHNICAL TERM
■ gallium photo diode

GPI · TECHNICAL TERM
■ general porte instruction
■ general purpose interface

GPIB · TECHNICAL TERM
■ general purpose interface bus

GPNITL · USA
▣ Great Plains National Instructional Television Library

GPSMVAV · FRANCE
■ Groupement Professionnel des Supports Magnétiques Vierges Audio et Vidéo
5 bis rue Jacquemont
75017 Paris

GRAD · BELGIUM
■ Groupe Européen de Réalisations Audiovisuelles pour le Développement

GREC · FRANCE
■ Groupe de Recherche Enterprise et Communication
Institut des Sciences de l'Information et de la Communication
Université de Bordeaux III
Domaine Université

Esplanade M de Montaigne
33405 Talence
tel   +33 56 84 50 58
fax +33 56 84 50 90
□ research and study centre.

GREC · FRANCE
■ Groupe de Recherches et d'Essais Cinématographiques
215 rue du Faubourg St-Honoré
75008 Paris
tel   +33 1 45 63 72 87 / 45 63 73 09
fax +33 1 40 74 07 96
1969 □ association which aims to help the production of first-time short films (fiction, documentary or animation).

GRECO · GERMANY
■ Groupement Européen pour la Circulation des Œuvres
Bahnhofstraße 33
85774 Unterföhring bei München
tel   +49 89 950 83290
fax +49 89 950 83292
1991 □ an initiative of **MEDIA**, created to favour the worldwide circulation of high quality television fiction. It allows producers better to face development, distribution and marketing costs. By focussing on the independent producer, GRECO is intended to be a strengthening factor for producers and independent broadcasters by allowing them to secure the creation of a catalogue of lasting distribution rights.

GRESEC · FRANCE
■ Groupe de Recherches Sur les Enjeux de la Communication
Université de Grenoble III (Université Stendhal)
BP 25 X
38040 Grenoble Cedex
tel   +33 76 82 43 21
fax +33 76 82 43 84
□ research centre.

GRIN · TECHNICAL TERM
■ graded index

GRISS · FRANCE
■ Groupement des Institutions Sociales du Spectacle au Service des Enterprises, des Salariés et des Retraites du

Spectacle et de l'Audiovisuel
7 rue Henri Rochefort
75017 Paris
tel +33 1 44 15 24 24
fax +33 1 44 15 24 20
□ organisation for those involved in performance in the audiovisual media.

GRP · TECHNICAL TERM
▪ gross rating points

GSE · UK
▪ General Screen Enterprises
Highbridge Estate
Oxford Road
Uxbridge
Middlesex UB8 1LX
tel +44 895 231931
fax +44 895 235335
1966 □ leading optical, title, trailer and post-production house fully equipped and staffed to service international film and television production.

GSFA · SWITZERLAND
▪ Groupement Suisse du Film d'Animation
see **STFG** · SWITZERLAND

GSO · TECHNICAL TERM
▪ geostationary satellite orbit

GSS · TECHNICAL TERM
▪ geostationary satellite

GTC · UK
▪ Gaelic Television Committee
see **CTG** · UK

GTP · TECHNICAL TERM
▪ geostationary transfer orbit

GTS · TECHNICAL TERM
▪ geostationary technology satellite

GTV · JAPAN
▪ Gunma Television Co Ltd
38-2 Kamikoide-machi 3-chome
Maebashi 371
tel +81 272 32 1181
□ television station.

GÜFA · GERMANY
▪ Gesellschaft zur Übernahme und

Wahrnehmung von Filmaufführungsrechten mbH
Vautierstr. 72
Postfach 14 02 63
40235 Düsseldorf
tel +49 211 686 026
fax +49 211 679 8887
1976 □ company which takes care of copyright and copyright-related matters for film producers whose films have a mainly erotic or pornographic content.

GUI · TECHNICAL TERM
▪ graphic user interface

GUYBC · GUYANA
▪ Guyana Broadcasting Corporation
PO Box 10760
Georgetown
tel +592 2 58584
tel +592 2 58756
1979 □ to ensure the provision in Guyana of services by broadcasting and television stations; to ensure that adequate and comprehensive programmes are provided by the corporation to serve the best interests of the public generally.
also known as GBC

GV · TECHNICAL TERM
▪ general view.

GVG · UK
▪ Grass Valley Group
Unit 3, Cherrywood
Chineham Business Park
Basingstoke
Hampshire RG24 OWF
tel +44 256 817817
fax +44 256 817803
tlx 858399
□ specialises in the design and manufacture of production and post-production equipment.

GW · TECHNICAL TERM
▪ gigawatt

GWFF · GERMANY
▪ Gesellschaft zur Wahrnehmung von Film- und Fernsehrechten
Barerstraße 9
80333 Munich

tel +49 89 565612
fax +49 89 555696
1982 □ collecting society whose duty is to look after royalties belonging to authors and producers of films according to copyright law. It safeguards claimants' interests and administrates royalties for them.

H

H&D · TECHNICAL TERM
▪ Hurter & Driffield

H/D · TECHNICAL TERM
▪ height/distance

HA · FRANCE
▪ Haute Autorité de la Communication Audiovisuelle
see **HACA** · FRANCE

HAAT · TECHNICAL TERM
▪ height above average terrain

HAB · JAPAN
▪ Hokuriku Asahi Broadcasting Co
1-32-2 Matsushima
Kanazawa 920-03
tel +81 762 69 8800
□ television station.

HACA · FRANCE
▪ Haute Autorité de la Communication Audiovisuelle
also known as HA
replaced by Commission Nationale de la Communication et des Libertés (CNCL)

HACBSS · AUSTRALIA
▪ Homestead and Community Broadcasting Satellite Service
1985 □ broadcasts 1 television and 3 radio channels in 5 separate geographic zones of Australia; programmes are produced by the Australian Broadcasting Corporation (**ABC**). It was established to bring these programmes to isolated communities and homesteads outside the coverage area of terrestrial national transmission

facilities.
also known as HACBUS

HACBUS · AUSTRALIA
▪ Homestead and Community Broadcasting Satellite Service
see **HACBSS** · AUSTRALIA

HAD · TECHNICAL TERM
▪ half amplitude modulation
▪ hole accumulated diode

HAU · USA
▪ Hebrew Actors' Union
31 East Seventh Street
New York
NY 10003
tel +1 212 674 1923
1900 □ actors' union.

HBC · JAPAN
▪ Hokkaido Broadcasting Co Ltd
Kita Ichijo
Nishi 5-2
Chuoko-ku
Sapporo 060-01
tel +81 11 232 5800
□ television station.

HBF · JAPAN
▪ Hoso Bunka Foundation
5th floor, Kyodo Building
41-1 Udagawa-cho
Shibuya-ku
Tokyo 150
tel +81 3 3464 3131
fax +81 3 3770 7239
1974 □ to assist in the cultural and technological development and progress of radio, television and new telecommunications media. It aims to provide financial assistance to research/projects/events considered useful in promoting the social and cultural aspects of broadcasting and towards the advancement of new technologies. It publishes *HBF Report* (1/2).

HBI · GERMANY
▪ Hans Bredow Institut für Rundfunk und Fernsehen
Universität Hamburg
Heimhuder Str. 21

20148 Hamburg
tel   +49 40 44 703131
fax +49 40 41 7870
1950 □ scientific institution established
to conduct empirical and theoretical
research in the field of telecommunications, radio, television and the
new electronic media. It aims to
cultivate and intensify relationships
between media research and media
practice, and to provide services to
those involved in practical media work,
political decision-makers, the University
of Hamburg and other interested
persons. It publishes the journal
Rundfunk und Fernsehen (4) and other
book publications.

HBO · USA
■ Home Box Office, Inc
1100 Avenue of the Americas
New York
NY 10036
tel   +1 212 512 1000
fax +1 212 512 5517
□ pay-cable network and producer of
film, television and video programmes.

HBST · TECHNICAL TERM
■ high band saticon trinicon

HCMOS · TECHNICAL TERM
■ high speed complementary metal-
oxide-gate semiconductor

HD · TECHNICAL TERM
■ high definition

HDDF · TECHNICAL TERM
■ high definition digital framestore

HDDR · TECHNICAL TERM
■ high density digital recording

HDEP · TECHNICAL TERM
■ high definition electronic production

HDF · GERMANY
■ Hauptverband Deutscher Filmtheater
eV
Kreuzberger Ring 56
65205 Wiesbaden
tel   +49 611 723427
fax +49 611 723403

□ cinema owners' association of
Germany, with some 3200 screen
members. It publishes various
publications.

HDLC · TECHNICAL TERM
■ high-level data link control

HDM · TECHNICAL TERM
■ high density modulation

HDP · TECHNICAL TERM
■ high-definition progressive

HDQ · TECHNICAL TERM
■ high-definition progressive scanning
and quincunx sampling

HDR · TECHNICAL TERM
■ horizontal drive

HDTP · FRANCE
■ High Definition Training Programme
Media Investment Club
4 avenue de l'Europe
94366 Bry-sur-Marne Cedex
tel   +33 1 49 83 28 63 / 32 72
fax +33 1 49 83 25 82
1992 □ an initiative of **MEDIA**, this is a
series of training courses on audiovisual
production in the **HDTV** European
standard.

HDTV · TECHNICAL TERM
■ high definition television

HDVS® · TECHNICAL TERM
■ high definition video system

HE · TECHNICAL TERM
■ heatable eyecup
■ high efficiency

HEFVL · UK
■ Higher Education Film & Video
Library
55 Greek Street
London W1V 5LR
tel   +44 71 734 3687
fax +44 71 287 3914
■ *formerly the Higher Education Film
Library*
1971 □ provides an outlet for visual
materials for degree-level use and

which would not normally be available from other sources. The library's material, which is concerned primarily with the sciences and humanities, is appraised by subject specialists in institutes of higher education.

HEMT · TECHNICAL TERM
- high electron mobility transistor

HF · TECHNICAL TERM
- high frequency

HFF · GERMANY
- Hamburg Film Fonds
Film Fonds Hamburg
Medienhaus
Friedensallee 14-16
22765 Hamburg
tel   +49 40 390 58 83
fax   +49 40 390 44 24
tlx   216 53 55 efdo-d
1982 □ provides commercial film support and development, the aim of which is to facilitate the diversity and quality of film-making in Hamburg and to safeguard employment in the Hamburg film and media industry.

HFF · GERMANY
- Hochschule für Film und Fernsehen
Frankenthaler Str. 23
81539 Munich
tel   +49 89 680 00450
fax   +49 89 680 00436
1954 □ film school offering courses lasting 3 or 4 years.

HFFS · USA
- Horror and Fantasy Film Society
c/o Gary J Svehla, President
PO Box 175
Perry Hall
MD 21128-0175
tel   +1 410 665 1198

HFMDK · AUSTRIA
- Hochschule für Musik und Darstellende Kunst in Wien
Metternichgasse 12
1030 Vienna
tel   +43 1 713 52120 / 52140
fax   +43 1 713 521423
1812 □ higher educational institution

offering courses in film.

HFR · TECHNICAL TERM
- hold for release

HG · TECHNICAL TERM
- high grade

HH · TECHNICAL TERM
- households

HI · TECHNICAL TERM
- high intensity

HID · TECHNICAL TERM
- high-intensity discharge(r)

HIS · TECHNICAL TERM
- hearing-impaired subtitles

HITCS · BELGIUM
- Hoger Rijksinstituut voor Toneel en Cultuurspreiding
see **HRITCS** · BELGIUM

HJT · USA
- Hughes-JVC Technology (Corporation)
2310 Camino Vida Roble
Carlsbad
CA 92009-1416
tel   +1 619 931 6339
fax   +1 619 931 3708
1992 □ supplier of advanced technology high-brightness, high-resolution large screen projection systems for the professional market.
formerly Light Valve Products Inc (LVPI)

HLO-PAL · TECHNICAL TERM
- half-line offset PAL

HMF · TECHNICAL TERM
- high mid frequency

HMI · TECHNICAL TERM
- halogen-metal-iodide
- hydragyrum medium iodide

HOP · TECHNICAL TERM
- highlight overload protection

HPA · TECHNICAL TERM
- high-power amplifier

HPBW · TECHNICAL TERM
▪ half-power beam width

HPF · TECHNICAL TERM
▪ highest possible frequency

HQ · TECHNICAL TERM
▪ high quality

HQTV · TECHNICAL TERM
▪ high quality television

HR · GERMANY
▪ Hessischer Rundfunk
Bertramstraße 8
60320 Frankfurt am Main
tel +49 69 1551
fax +49 69 155 2900
tlx 411-127
□ regional television broadcasting channel.

HR · TECHNICAL TERM
▪ high resolution

HRC · TECHNICAL TERM
▪ harmonic-related carrier
▪ hypothetical reference circuit

HRITCS · BELGIUM
▪ Hoger Rijksinstituut voor Toneel en Cultuurspreiding
Theresienstraat 8
1000 Brussels
tel +32 2 511 9382
fax +32 2 772 0385
1962 □ film school offering courses lasting 2-4 years.
also known as HITCS and RITCS

HRP · TECHNICAL TERM
▪ horizontal radiation pattern

HRT · CROATIA
▪ Hrvatska Radio-Televizija
see **HRTV** · CROATIA

HRTS · USA
▪ Hollywood Radio and Television Society
Suite 202
5315 Laurel Canyon Boulevard
North Hollywood
CA 91607

tel +1 818 769 4313
fax +1 818 509 1262
1947 □ organisation comprising a wide range of professionals working in broadcasting which aims to promote and foster the industry generally. It publishes *Spike* magazine (4).

HRTV · CROATIA
▪ Hrvatska Radio-Televizija
Dežmanova 6
41000 Zagreb
tel +38 41 537 251
fax +38 41 537 921
tlx 21326 HRT CRO
□ television and radio broadcasting.
also known as HRT and HTV

HRTV · TECHNICAL TERM
▪ high resolution television

HSD · TECHNICAL TERM
▪ home satellite dish

HSN · USA
▪ Home Shopping Network
2501 118th Avenue N
Saint Petersburg
FL 33716
tel +1 813 572 8585
□ cable television network.

HT · TECHNICAL TERM
▪ high tension

HTB · JAPAN
▪ Hokkaido Television Broadcasting Ltd
Hiragishi Yojo 13-10-17
Toyohira-ku
Sapporo 062
tel +81 11 821 4411
□ television station.

HTN · USA
▪ Home Theatre Network

HTR · USA
▪ Household Tracking Report
Nielsen Media Research
1290 Avenue of the Americas
New York
NY 10104
tel +1 212 708 7500
fax +1 212 708 7795

□ NTI supplementary report, updated monthly, which is available for an extra charge and tracks programme performance by an individual network within ½ hour time periods. Monthly and quarterly household audiences and shares are reported for all regularly scheduled sponsored network programmes.

HTS · ST LUCIA
■ Helen Television System
PO Box 621
Castries
tel   +1 809 22693
fax   +1 809 41737
tlx   6254
1967 □ national television broadcasting service.

HTV · CROATIA
■ Hrvatska Radio-Televizija
see **HRTV** · CROATIA

HTV · JAPAN
■ Hiroshima Telecasting Co Ltd
6-6 Naka-machi
Naka-ku
Hiroshima 730
tel   +81 82 249 1212
□ television station.

HUT · USA
■ Households Using Television
Nielsen Media Research
1290 Avenue of the Americas
New York
NY 10104
tel   +1 212 708 7500
fax   +1 212 708 7795
□ quarterly summary which provides individual weekly estimates of total US television household usage for each ½ hour time period by week, and day of the week, as well as for Mon-Fri and Mon-Sun. Each report also includes TV usage averages by ½ hours for the most recent 12 months, individually for the most recent 4 quarters and as an annual average.

HV · TECHNICAL TERM
■ high voltage
■ home video

HVC · UK
■ Home Video Channel
Unit 023
Canalot Production Studios
222 Kensal Road
London W10 5BN
tel   +44 81 964 1141
fax   +44 81 964 5934
1986 □ film and entertainment channel carried on cable systems throughout the UK. The programming consists mainly of "B" and second-run movies, primarily from the action, horror, comedy, drama and erotic genres.

HVR · TECHNICAL TERM
■ home video recorder

HZ · TECHNICAL TERM
■ hertz

I

I/O · TECHNICAL TERM
■ input/output

I/P · TECHNICAL TERM
■ input

I-PAL · TECHNICAL TERM
■ improved PAL

I-PAL-M · TECHNICAL TERM
■ improved PAL modified

I/V · TECHNICAL TERM
■ in vision

IA · USA
■ International Alliance of Theatrical Stage Employees & Moving Picture Machine Operators of the United States and Canada
see **IATSE** · USA

IA · TECHNICAL TERM
■ image enhancer

IAAB · USA
■ Inter-American Association of Broadcasting
1948

IAB · URUGUAY
■ International Association of
Broadcasting
see **AIR** · URUGUAY

IABM · UK
■ International Association of
Broadcasting Manufacturers
4-B High Street
Burnham
Slough SL1 7JH
tel   +44 628 667633
fax +44 628 665882
1976 □ non-profit making organisation
founded to foster and co-ordinate the
wide common interests of
manufacturers of sound and television
broadcasting equipment and associated
products worldwide, with a
membership of over 90 companies
from 10 countries.

IABM · USA
■ International Association of Broadcast
Monitors

IAC · ANGOLA
■ Instituto Angolana de Cinema
Rua Dr Américo Boavida 152
Caixa Postal 1844
Luanda
tel   +244 2 38 270 / 38 534
tlx   3034 DAFRICA-AN
1979 □ national film institute.

IAC · ARGENTINA
■ Instituto Arte de Cinematografía
San Martin 797
1870 Avellaneda
Buenos Aires
□ film institute.

IAC · UK
■ Industrial Acoustics Company
Walton House
Central Trading Estate
Staines
Middlesex TW18 4XB
tel   +44 784 456251
fax +44 784 463303
□ specialists in studio design and
construction, providing studio facilities
for leading television, radio, post-
production and recording organisations

worldwide.

IAC · UK
■ Institute of Amateur
Cinematographers
24c West Street
Epsom
Surrey KT18 7RJ
tel   +44 372 739672
1932 □ promotion of amateur video
movie-making, video or cine:
promotion of audiovisual production. It
publishes *Amateur Film and Video
Maker (**AFVM**)* (6).

IAD · BELGIUM
■ Institut des Arts de Diffusion
77 rue des Wallons
1348 Louvain-la-Neuve
tel   +32 10 450685
fax +32 10 451174
1959 □ it has an educational
programme oriented both technically
and artistically, with degrees in film,
video, television, radio, sound and
theatre. Studies for directors take 4
years to complete, whilst the different
degrees in camera, sound and editing
take 3 years. It gives students a
complete theoretical base along with a
thorough technical expertise in each of
the different aspects.

IAFF · NEW ZEALAND
■ International Association of Amateur
Film Festivals

IAFS · USA
■ International Animated Film Society

IAIP · USA
■ International Association of
Independent Producers
Washington
1954 □ organisation of producers
involved in film and the recording
industries internationally. It publishes
Communication Arts International (4), a
Newsletter (8) and other publications.

IAMCR · THE NETHERLANDS
■ International Association for Mass
Communication Research
109-111 Baden Powellweg

1069 LD Amsterdam
tel +31 20 610 1581
fax +31 20 610 4821
1957 □ international organisation with some 1800 members in 65 countries, devoted to research in the field of mass communication.
also known as Association Internationale des Etudes et Recherches sur l'Information (AIERI)

IAMHIST · USA
▪ International Association for Media and History
David Culbert, Secretary General
Department of History
Louisiana State University
Baton Rouge
LA 70803-3601
tel +1 504 388 4471
fax +1 504 388 6400
formerly the International Association for Audio-Visual Media in Historical Research and Education
1977 □ association aiming to further the study of history of the audiovisual media, as well as the use of audiovisual media for teaching and research in history. It publishes the *Historical Journal of Film, Radio and Television* (3) and *IAMHIST Newsletter* (4).

IAMS · THE NETHERLANDS
▪ International Association for Media in Science
PO Box 80125
Heidelberglaan 6
3508 TC Utrecht
tel +31 30 531314
fax +31 30 515463
formerly International Scientific Film Association (ISFA)
1992 □ to promote the production, documentation, preservation, distribution and use of audiovisual media and material for the growth and communication of knowledge in the natural and human sciences, technology and medicine. It publishes *IAMS Newsletter* (2).

IAS · TECHNICAL TERM
▪ integrated authoring system

IAS · USA
▪ International Audiovisual Society

IASUS · USA
▪ International Association of Satellite Users and Suppliers
PO Box DD
McLean
VA 22101
tel +1 703 759 2094
fax +1 703 759 5094
1980 □ body which aims to promote awareness of developments in the field of satellite communications.

IATSE · USA
▪ International Alliance of Theatrical Stage Employees & Moving Picture Machine Operators of the United States and Canada
Suite 601
515 Broadway
New York
NY 10036
tel +1 212 730 1770
fax +1 212 921 7699
1893 □ union whose 60 000 members are technicians from the theatre and film industries.
also abbreviated to IA

IAV · USA
▪ International Association of Video
Suite 601
1440 North Street, NW
Washington
DC 20005
tel +1 202 328 9346
fax +1 202 347 5829
1984 □ organisation for all those involved in video and related industries.

IAVS · BELGIUM
▪ International Audio-Visual Services
74 Box 2 ave de Woluwé St Lambert
B-1200 Brussels
tel +32 2 736 5560
fax +32 2 736 5560
1982 □ low-budget scaled production company, working on film, video etc, and post-production. Also an information centre dealing with the choices in hardware and software for

the whole audiovisual field.

IAWRT · SWEDEN
- International Association of Women in Radio and Television
c/o Christina Ruhnbro
Sveriges Radio
S-105 10 Stockholm
tel +46 8 784 0000
fax +46 8 663 4786
1951 □ organisation of television and radio journalists from over 30 countries, which brings together women broadcasters to share professional experiences and to extend the influence of women in media. It also operates Network, an index of professional women available for women-oriented media projects. It publishes a *Bulletin* (2) and *Newsletter* (3-4), as well as other publications.

IB · TECHNICAL TERM
- international broadcast(ing)

IBA · ISRAEL
- Israel Broadcasting Authority
Torah Metzion
PO Box 7139
Romema
Jerusalem 91071
tel +972 2 301333
fax +972 2 301345
tlx 25301
1968 □ television broadcasting in Arabic, English and Hebrew.

IBA · UK
- Independent Broadcasting Authority
see **ITC** · UK

IBC · CANADA
- Inuit Broadcasting Corporation
Suite 703
251 Laurier Avenue West
Ottawa
Ontario K1P 5J6
tel +1 613 235 1892
fax +1 613 230 8824
1981 □ producing and broadcasting Inuit-language television programmes for the Inuit population living in the Eastern and Central Arctic.

IBC · JAPAN
- Iwate Broadcasting Co Ltd
6-1 Shike-cho
Morioka 020
tel +81 196 23 3111
□ television station.

IBC · THAILAND
- International Broadcasting Corporation Ltd
1376/1 Nakornchaisri Road
Dusit
Bangkok 10310
tel +66 2 243 5981-6 / 241 1118 / 241 2879
fax +66 2 243 5987 / 243 5820
tlx 72195 SHINCOM TH
1985 □ Thailand's first and largest subscription television station, operating multiple channels featuring a wide range of locally produced and international programmes in Thai and English. It uses **MMDS** technology to serve more than 70 000 subscribers throughout Greater Bangkok. It publishes *Spectrum* magazine (12).

IBC · UK
- International Broadcasting Convention
c/o Institution of Electrical Engineers
Savoy Place
London WC2R OBL
tel +44 71 240 3839
fax +44 71 497 3633
tlx 261176 IEE LDN G
1967 □ exhibition and congress, held every 2 years, which covers radio, television, satellite and cable.

IBC · TECHNICAL TERM
- integrated broadband communications

IBE · UK
- International Broadcast Engineer
International Trade Publications Ltd
Queensway House
2 Queensway
Redhill
Surrey RH1 1QS
tel +44 737 768611
fax +44 737 760564
tlx 948669 TOPJNL G
1964 □ magazine published 7 times

annually which is devoted to the design, manufacture and operation of professional television and radio broadcast, and video, equipment.

IBEW · USA
■ International Brotherhood of Electrical Workers
1125 15th Street NW
Washington
DC 20005
tel   +1 202 833 7000
fax   +1 202 467 6316
□ union with some 1 million members.

IBF · FRANCE
■ International Bank Films

IBFG · FRANCE
■ International Broadcast Film Group
Villa Serena
1288 Chemin des Brusquets
06600 Antibes
tel   +33 93 61 76 88
fax   +33 93 67 81 85
□ film, television and video programme producer and distributor.

IBFM · USA
■ Institute of Broadcasting Financial Management
1961

IBFPA · SPAIN
■ Independent Basque Film Producers Association
see **AIPV** · SPAIN

IBO · TECHNICAL TERM
■ integrated broadcast operation

IBS · KOREA
■ International Broadcasting Society
c/o Korean Broadcasting System (KBS)
18 Yoido-dong
Yongdungpo-Gu
Seoul 150
tel   +82 2 781 2424
tlx   KBSKB 24599
1985 □ organisation which aims to change the imbalance in the information flow between developed and developing countries, and in doing so to encourage mutual collaboration

and understanding between broadcasting companies and organisations.

IBS · UK
■ Institute of Broadcast Sound
27 Old Gloucester Street
London WC1N 3XX
tel   +44 753 646404
fax   +44 81 887 0167
1977 □ to promote a better interchange of ideas between practitioners in the various areas of broadcast sound. It keeps members aware of new developments in equipment design and operational techniques, and encourages them to observe the highest technical standards through both its meetings and its journal *Line Up* (6).

IBS · USA
■ Intercollegiate Broadcasting System, Inc

IBT · UK
■ International Broadcasting Trust
2 Ferdinand Place
London NW1 8EE
tel   +44 71 482 2847
fax   +44 71 284 3374
1982 □ charity committed to the fight against world poverty, this partnership of voluntary organisations works with television and radio professionals and provides a full back-up service for television users and learners of all ages. It publishes *Fast Forward* magazine (3) and various publications.

IBTE · IRAQ
■ Iraqi Broadcasting and Television Establishment
□ radio and television broadcasting service.

IBTO · CZECH REPUBLIC
■ International Broadcasting and Television Organisation
now incorporated under European Broadcasting Union (EBU)

IC · TECHNICAL TERM
■ incue
■ input circuit

• integrated circuit

ICAA · SPAIN
• Instituto de la Cinematografía y de las Artes Audiovisuales
Ministerio de Cultura
Plaza del Rey nº1
28071 Madrid
tel +34 1 532 2084
fax +34 1 531 9212 / 522 9377
tlx 27 286 CULTU E
1985 □ the promotion, protection and circulation of film and audiovisual activities in the areas of production, distribution and exhibition; the projection of Spanish films and audiovisual arts abroad; the cultural communication amongst autonomous communities in relation to cinematography and audiovisual arts. It publishes *Spanish Films* (1).

ICAF · FRANCE
• Institut de Coopération Audiovisuelle Francophone

ICAIC · CUBA
• Instituto Cubano de Arte e Industria Cinematográfica
Calle 23 no. 1155
Havana 4
tel +53 7 30 9067 / 3 6322
fax +53 7 33 3032
tlx 511419 ICAIC CU
□ film institute.

ICDB · IRAN
• Iranian Cinema Data Bank
PO Box 11365-5875
Tehran
tel +98 21 679373-4
fax +98 21 6459971
□ information source on Iranian cinema.

ICE · TECHNICAL TERM
• insertion communication equipment

ICEA · USA
• Insulated Cable Engineers Association

ICEC · ITALY
• Iniziative Cinematografiche Editoriali e Commerciali

Viale Regina Margherita 290
Rome
□ publishing and commercial film enterprises.

ICFCYP · FRANCE
• International Centre of Films for Children and Young People
see **CIFEJ** · FRANCE

ICIA · USA
• International Communications Industries Association
3150 Spring Street
Fairfax
VA 22031-2399
tel +1 703 273 7200
fax +1 703 278 8082
1939 □ association of manufacturers, producers, dealers and suppliers of products in the fields of video, audiovisuals and microcomputers. It publishes *Communications Industries Report* (12).

ICM · USA
• International Creative Management
8942 Wilshire Boulevard
Beverly Hills
Los Angeles
CA 90211
tel +1 310 550 4000
fax +1 310 550 4108
1975 □ theatrical agency, including representing artistes from the whole range of film and television industries.

ICN · USA
• International Channel Network
12401 West Olympic
Los Angeles
CA 90064
tel +1 310 478 1818
fax +1 310 479 8118
□ television broadcaster.

ICNATVAS · USA
• International Council of the National Academy of Television Arts and Sciences
Suite 1020
111 West 57th Street
New York
NY 10019

tel   +1 212 586 8424
fax +1 212 246 8129

ICPM · TECHNICAL TERM
■ incidental carrier phase modulation
(*aka* IPM)

ICS · FRANCE
■ Institut de Cinématographie
Scientifique
143 Boulevard Lefebvre
75015 Paris
tel   +33 1 42 50 35 51
1930 ❑ to promote the use of
audiovisual images (essentially on film)
for research, teaching and
popularisation of scientific and
technical knowledge.

ICS · UK
■ International Cinerama Society
15 Dystelegh Road
Disley
Cheshire SK12 2BQ
tel   +44 663 762672
1985 ❑ society devoted to preserving
the original Cinerama process.

ICSADFF · UK
■ International Conference of Short
Animation & Documentary Film
Festivals

ICTV · ISRAEL
■ Israel Commercial Television Ltd
Shmveli Building
4 Shatner Center
Kanfei Nesharim
Givat Shaul
Jerusalem 95464
tel   +972 2 514121
fax +972 2 535441
tlx   26453 ICTV IL
1982 ❑ production of television
programme broadcasting on a
commercial basis, and provision of
studio facilities for foreign companies.

ICW · TECHNICAL TERM
■ interrupted continuous wave

IDA · FRANCE
■ Institut de l'Audiovisuel
30 rue Henri Barbusse

75005 Paris
tel   +33 1 43 25 72 79
❑ film educational institution.

IDA · USA
■ International Documentary
Association
Suite 201
1551 South Robertson Boulevard
Los Angeles
CA 9035
tel   +1 310 284 8422
fax +1 310 785 9334
1982 ❑ organisation which encourages
and promotes non-fiction film and
video internationally. It provides an
arena for discussion and exchange
between film-makers and other
members of the industries and
publishes *International Documentary*
magazine (12).

IDA · TECHNICAL TERM
■ identification data accessory

IDATE · FRANCE
■ Institut de l'Audiovisuel et des
Télécommunications en Europe
BP 4167
34092 Montpellier Cedex 5
tel   +33 67 14 44 44
fax +33 67 14 44 00
tlx   490290
1977 ❑ European study and research
centre, a leader in the field of socio-
economic analysis of information and
communication industries.

IDC · TECHNICAL TERM
■ insulation displacement connector

IDEA · FRANCE
■ International Directory of Electronic
Arts
Chaos
57 rue Falguière
75015 Paris
tel   +33 1 43 20 92 23
fax +33 1 43 20 97 72
❑ annual directory covering video and
electronic art worldwide.

IDERA (Film & Video) · CANADA
■ International Development Education

Resource Association
2678 West Broadway Avenue
Suite 201
Vancouver
British Columbia V6K 2G3
tel   +1 604 738 8815
fax   +1 604 738 8400
1974 □ film and video distribution
centre of IDERA, a non-profit
educational society established to
provide educational resources to
Canadians on international issues and
concerns. IDERA Film & Video
maintains an extensive collection of
films and videos on international
development.

IDFA · THE NETHERLANDS
▪ International Documentary
Filmfestival Amsterdam
Kleine-Gartmanplantsoen 10
1017 RR Amsterdam
tel   +31 20 627 3329
fax   +31 20 638 5388
tlx   20010 PMS NL
1988 □ yearly (December) film festival,
showing over 120 international
documentaries, and organising other
events such as workshops, seminars
and lectures.

IDHECOM · FRANCE
▪ Institut des Hautes Etudes de la
Communication
135 avenue Félix Faure
75015 Paris
tel   +33 1 44 25 25 25
fax   +33 1 44 25 25 26
1984 □ film school.

IDM · FRANCE
▪ International Development Media
37-39 rue du Bois de Bologne
92200 Neuilly-sur-Seine
tel   +33 1 47 47 25 09
fax   +33 1 47 45 36 32
□ film, television and video programme
producers and distributors.

IDT · TECHNICAL TERM
▪ improved definition television (*aka*
IDTV)

IDTV · TECHNICAL TERM

▪ improved definition television (*aka*
IDT)

IEE · BELGIUM
▪ Institut Européen d'Ecriture
Audiovisuelle et Créative

IEE · UK
▪ Institution of Electrical Engineers
Savoy Place
London WC2R OBL
tel   +44 71 240 1871
fax   +44 71 240 7735
tlx   261176 IEE LDN G
1871 □ association with over 130 000
members worldwide, involving all
aspects of electrical, electronics,
software and manufacturing
engineering. It publishes extensively,
both in journals (including *IEE Review*
[6]) and books.

IEEE · USA
▪ Institution of Electrical and Electronics
Engineers, Inc
345 East 47th Street
New York
NY 10017-2394
tel   +1 212 705 7900
fax   +1 212 752 4929
1962 □ engineering society with a
membership of over 320 000. Its
technical objectives centre on
advancing the theory and practice of
electrical, electronic and computer
engineering and computer science. It
sponsors conferences and meetings,
publishes a wide range of professional
papers and provides educational
programmes. It publishes numerous
journals and books, including *IEEE
Spectrum* (12).

IERT · USA
▪ Institute for Education by Radio-
Television

IETEL · ECUADOR
▪ Instituto Ecuatoriano de
Telecomunicaciones
Casilla 3036
Quito
tlx   2202
□ national body which regulates

telecommunications policy and
practice.

IETV · ISRAEL
■ Israel Educational Television
Ministry of Education and Culture
14 Klausner Street
Ramat Aviv
Tel Aviv 69011
tel   +972 3 6466666
fax +972 3 6427091
tlx   342325
1966 □ educational and instructional
television broadcasting.

IF · TECHNICAL TERM
■ instructional television, fixed
■ intermediate frequency

IFA · TURKEY
■ Istanbul Film Ajansı
Gazeteci Erol Dernek Sok
Hanif Han
II/5 Beyoğlu
Istanbul
tel   +90 1 245 5602
fax +90 1 245 5417
□ film organisation.

IFAVA · CANADA
■ Independent Film and Video Alliance

IFB · TECHNICAL TERM
■ interrupted feedback

IFC · IRELAND
■ Irish Film Centre
□ national centre for film in Ireland.
Housing 10 film organisations, each
involved in complimentary film and
video-related activities, the film centre
provides a synergy and central focus for
film in Ireland.
*now incorporated under Film Institute
of Ireland (FII)*

IFCA · FRANCE
■ Institut de Formation aux Métiers du
Cinéma
9 rue Cadet
75009 Paris
tel   +33 1 42 46 42 84
□ film school.

IFCG · FRANCE
■ International Film Conciliation Group

IFCIC · FRANCE
■ Institut pour le Financement du
Cinéma et des Industries Culturelles
66 rue Pierre Charron
75008 Paris
tel   +33 1 43 59 88 03
tel   +33 1 43 63 85 58

IFCO · CANADA
■ Independent Filmmakers Cooperative
of Ottawa, Inc
Arts Court
2 Daly Avenue
Ottawa
Ontario K1N 6E2
tel   +1 613 569 1789 / 1790
fax +1 613 233 0698
1992 □ to nurture and support up-and-
coming film-makers by providing
training, facilities and funds for
production. Among its activities are:
Hands On Film Workshop Series,
covering basic technical steps in film-
making, and the IFCO Production Fund,
accessed by active members. In 1992 it
funded 6 short films.

IFDA · UK
■ Independent Film Distributors'
Association
10A Stephen Mews
London W1P OAX
tel   +44 71 957 8957
fax +44 71 957 8968
1973 □ looks after the interests of
British independent film distributors,
particularly to non-theatrical markets.

IFE · USA
■ International Family Entertainment Inc
1000 Centerville Turnpike
Virginia Beach
VA 23463
tel   +1 804 523 7201
fax +1 804 523 7880
□ television broadcaster.

IFEX · USA
■ International Film Exchange Ltd
210 West 52nd Street
New York

NY 10019
tel +1 212 582 4318
fax +1 212 956 2257
tlx 420748 RAPP UI
□ specialised distributor catering for
independent producers worldwide in
the fields of non-theatrical, theatrical,
television and video material.

IFF · ICELAND
■ Icelandic Film Fund
Laugavegur 24
101 Reykjavík
tel +354 1 623580
fax +354 1 627171
1979 □ the fund is run by the state
which is responsible for the amount of
money the fund raises from one year to
the next. A selection committee
distributes the money as grants to
applicants. It also acts as a media
centre for Icelandic producers and
festivals. It also has an archive, growing
in importance, with hundreds of
Icelandic films made before and after
the war being brought in for
preservation. It publishes various
catalogues.

IFFA · BELGIUM
■ International Federation of Film
Archives
see **FIAF** · BELGIUM

IFFI · INDIA
■ International Film Festival of India
Ministry of Information and
Broadcasting
Government of India
4th floor, Lok Nayak Bhavan
Khan Market
New Delhi 110003
tel +91 11 615953
fax +91 11 694920
tlx 31 62741 FEST IN
□ annual film festival.

IFFM · USA
■ Independent Feature Film Market
Independent Feature Project
132 West 21st Street
New York
NY 10011
tel +1 212 243 7777

fax +1 212 243 3882
1979 □ market, organised by
Independent Feature Project (**IFP**),
devoted to emerging independent film
from America.

IFFPA · FRANCE
■ International Federation of Film
Producers' Associations
see **FIAPF** · FRANCE

IFFS · SWITZERLAND
■ International Federation of Film
Societies
see **FICC** · SWITZERLAND

IFG · UK
■ International Film Guide
c/o Variety
34-35 Newman Street
London W1P 3PD
tel +44 71 637 3663
fax +44 71 580 5559
1963 □ annual yearbook offering an
international survey of cinema and film-
making in some 70 countries.

IFI · IRELAND
■ Irish Film Institute
*now incorporated under Film Institute
of Ireland (FII)*

IFIDA · USA
■ International Film Importers and
Distributors of America

IFM · USA
■ International Film Marketing
□ film distributors.

IFP · USA
■ Independent Feature Project
132 West 21st Street
New York
NY 10011
tel +1 212 243 7777
fax +1 212 243 3882
1979 □ non-profit organisation
committed to serving independent film-
makers and also to the nationwide
promotion of independent films. Its
2000 members include independent
writers, directors, producers, actors,
agents, attorneys and executives who

encourage independent film. It
publishes *Filmmaker* (4).
see also IFP/West

IFP · TECHNICAL TERM
■ independent facilitator and packager

IFP/West · USA
■ Independent Feature Project/West
Suite 204
5550 Wilshire Boulevard
Los Angeles
CA 90036-3888
tel +1 213 937 4379
fax +1 213 937 4038
□ non-profit organisation committed to
serving independent film-makers in
Southern California and also to the
nationwide promotion of independent
films. Its 2000 members include
independent writers, directors,
producers, actors, agents, attorneys and
executives who encourage independent
film. It publishes *Filmmaker* (4).
see also IFP

IFPA · UK
■ Independent Film Production
Associates

IFPA · USA
■ Independent Film Producers of
America

IFPA · USA
■ Information Film Producers of
America

IFPI · UK
■ International Federation of the
Phonographic Industry
54 Regent Street
London W1R 5PJ
tel +44 71 434 3521
fax +44 71 439 9166
tlx 919044 IFPI G
□ organisation representing producers
and distributors of sound and music
video recordings with over 1000
members in 70 countries. Its primary
responsibility is to promote and defend
the rights of those members. Therefore
its work incorporates the promotion of
new and improved copyright legislation

and the organisation takes an active
role in anti-piracy intelligence gathering
and in the direct enforcement of rights
on a global scale. It publishes *For the
Record* (4).

IFPIA · FRANCE
■ Independent Film Producers
International Association
see **FIPFI** · FRANCE

IFRB · SWITZERLAND
■ International Frequency Radio Board
International Telecommunications
Union
Place des Nations
CH-1211 Geneva 20
tel +41 22 730 5111
fax +41 22 733 7256
tlx 421 000 UIT CH
1982 □ committee which is responsible
for managing the radio frequency
spectrum and the geostationary-satellite
orbit (**GSO**) in accordance with
international regulations.

IFTA · SPAIN
■ International Federation of Television
Archives
see **FIAT** · SPAIN

IFTC · FRANCE
■ International Film and Television
Council
■ International Council for Film,
Television & Audio Communications
see **CICT** · FRANCE

IGFET · TECHNICAL TERM
■ insulated gate field effect transistor

IHECS · BELGIUM
■ Institut des Hautes Etudes des
Communications Sociales
58-60 rue de l'Etuve
1000 Brussels
tel +32 2 512 9093
1958 □ film school offering a course
lasting 4 years.

IIC · UK
■ International Institute of
Communications
Tavistock House South

Tavistock Square
London WC1H 9LF
tel +44 71 388 0671
fax +44 71 380 0623
tlx 24578 IICLDN G
1967 □ worldwide membership
association of organisations and
professional people active in or
concerned with one or more fields of
communication. Its aims are: to identify
and explore key issues in communications both present and future; to
promote a climate of enquiry which is
global, interdisciplinary, strategic,
independent and humanitarian; to
provide appropriate opportunities for
debate and the exchange of information; to maintain a global network
within which individuals working at
every level in the communications field
can come together in a non-competitive
environment; to achieve the highest
possible standard of excellence in
intellectual leadership and analytical
studies. It publishes *InterMedia*
magazine (6) and various other book
publications.

IIIS · FRANCE
■ Institut International de l'Image et du
Son
Parc de Pissaloup
78190 Trappes
tel +33 30 69 00 17
fax +33 30 50 43 63
tlx 699800
1988 □ further education institution
offering courses in image and sound
training.

IIR · TECHNICAL TERM
■ infinite impulse response

IKJ · INDONESIA
■ Institut Kesenian Jakarta
Jalan Cikini Raya 73
Jakarta Pusat
tel +62 21 323603
□ institute of arts which teaches film
and television.

IKON · THE NETHERLANDS
■ Interkerkelijke Omroep Nederland
PO Box 10009

1201 DA Hilversum
tel +31 35 233841
fax +31 35 215100
tlx 43974
1946 □ programming on radio and
television on behalf of eight churches
for the whole of The Netherlands. It
publishes *Ikon-Krant* (4) and a
Yearbook (every 2 years).

IKS · TECHNICAL TERM
■ interactive knowledge system

ILV · TECHNICAL TERM
■ interactive laser video

IM · TECHNICAL TERM
■ intermodulation

IMAC · FRANCE
■ Institut Image, Médias, Informatique
de la Communication
Université Paris II
8 Place du 8-Mai 1945
92306 Saint-Denis Cedex 01
tel +33 42 35 44 71
□ educational institution.

IMART · BELGIUM
■ International Medical Association for
Radio and Television
c/o RTBF
52 Boulevard Auguste Reyers
1044 Brussels
tel +32 2 737 4177
fax +32 2 736 9566
tlx 63132
1980 □ group of broadcasting
organisations and others in the
television and radio sectors, whose aim
is to improve the health of those
working in the television and radio
media across some 20 countries.

IMC · TECHNICAL TERM
■ interactive menu control

IMCINE · MEXICO
■ Instituto Mexicano de
Cinematográfica
Atletas 2
Col. Country Club
Mexico, D.F. 04220
tel +52 5 689 7100

fax +52 5 689 1989 / 549 0931
1983 □ government agency promoting Mexican quality film production. It coordinates activities in the fields of production, distribution, sales and production services.

IMD · GERMANY
■ Internationales Institut für Medien und Entwicklung
c/o Prof R Kabel
Bergengruenstr. 60
14129 Berlin
tel +49 30 8012121
□ international institute for media and development.

IMD · TECHNICAL TERM
■ intermodulation distortion

IMEVISION · MEXICO
■ Instituto Mexicano de Televisión
Avda. Periférico Sur 4121
Col. Fuentes del Pedregal
14140 Mexico
tel +52 5 652 0973
tlx 1773878
1968 □ commercial television station.

IMM · GERMANY
■ Institut für Mediengestaltung und Medientechnologie
Weissliliengasse 1-3
6500 Mainz
tel +49 6131 23 14 39
fax +49 6131 23 85 11
□ media design and technology centre whose areas of interest are issues concerning the new media technologies and their audiovisual content.

IMM · TECHNICAL TERM
■ interactive multimedia

IMO · TECHNICAL TERM
■ independent main output

IMPALA · USA
■ International Motion Picture and Lecturers Association

IMPATT · TECHNICAL TERM
■ impact avalanche and transit time

IMUX · TECHNICAL TERM
■ input multiplexer

IN · TECHNICAL TERM
■ internegative (*aka* ITN)

INA · FRANCE
■ Institut National de l'Audiovisuel
4 avenue de l'Europe
94366 Bry-sur-Marne Cedex
tel +33 1 49 83 20 00
fax +33 1 49 83 25 84
1974 □ conserving the television and radio archives of France and putting them to the best use; classifying, marketing and making available a national heritage to the greatest number of people; research into broadcasting and communications; training in image and sound technology for professionals from France and other countries; the encouragement of new creative talent in INA productions. It publishes *INA Mag* (11).

INC · MOZAMBIQUE
■ Instituto Nacional de Cinema
CP 679
Maputo
tel +258 1 29912
1976 □ established to promote a national cinema and to oversee cinematic distribution and exploitation within the country.

INFRAME · UK
■ International Filmographic Reference and Motion-Picture Encyclopedia
29 Bradford Road
Trowbridge
Wilts BA14 9AI
tel +44 225 767728
fax +44 225 760418
1992 □ international moving picture database primarily covering films and their credits, but also including organisations, associations, societies, institutions, magazines, film festivals and other industry data.

INM · GERMANY
■ Interessengemeinschaft Neue Medien
Widenmayerstraße 32
80538 Munich

tel +49 89 223535
tlx 529070
□ association for new media.

INPUT · USA
■ International Public Television

INRACI · BELGIUM
■ Institut National de Radioélectricité et
de Cinématographie
75 avenue Victor-Rousseau
1190 Brussels
tel +32 2 512 9093
1939 □ film school offering a course
lasting 3 years.

INRAVISION · COLOMBIA
■ Instituto Nacional de Radio y
Televisión
Centro Administrativo Nacional (CAN)
Avda El Dorado
Santa Fe de Bogotá, DC
tel +57 1 222 0700
fax +57 1 222 0080
tlx 43311
1954 □ government-operated radio and
television broadcasting network,
involved in both commercial and
educational broadcasting.

INSAS · BELGIUM
■ Institut National Supérieur des Arts du
Spectacle et Techniques de Diffusion
Theresienstraat 8
1000 Brussels
tel +32 2 511 9286
fax +32 2 511 0279
1962 □ film school offering courses
lasting 3 or 4 years.

INSET · IVORY COAST
■ Institut National Supérieur de
l'Enseignement Technique
BP V79
Abidjan
1975 □ educational establishment
offering instruction in film.

INTELSAT · USA
■ International Telecommunications
Satellite Organization
3400 International Drive NW
Washington
DC 20008

tel +1 202 944 7500
fax +1 202 944 7890
1964 □ international commercial
cooperative of 124 member nations
which owns and operates the global
communications satellite system used
worldwide by 180 member and non-
member countries, territories and
dependencies for their international
and, in many instances, domestic
communications. It also offers via its
29-satellite global system such services
as international video, teleconferencing,
facsimile, data and telex. It publishes 2
magazines: *INTELSAT News* (4) and *Via
INTELSAT* (4).

INTV · USA
■ Independent Television Station
Association
Suite 300
1320 19th Street
Washington
DC 20036
tel +1 202 887 1970
fax +1 202 887 0950
1972 □ group of independent,
commercial television broadcasters and
other related organisations whose
objective is to be the voice of
independents and to provide a forum
for discussion. It publishes *INTV
Journal* (6) and *Newsletter* (26).

IO · TECHNICAL TERM
■ image orthicon

IOA · TECHNICAL TERM
■ image optics assembly

IOL · TECHNICAL TERM
■ inter-orbit link

IORTV · SPAIN
■ Instituto Oficial de Radiodifusión y
Televisión
Carretera de la Dehesa de la Vila s/n
28040 Madrid
tel +34 1 549 2250
□ institute for radio and television
broadcasting.

IOS · TECHNICAL TERM
■ internal optical system

IOT · TECHNICAL TERM
- inductive output tube

IP · TECHNICAL TERM
- intelligent picture
- interpositive

IP/IN · TECHNICAL TERM
- interpositive/internegative

IPA · TECHNICAL TERM
- intermediate power amplifier

IPC · PORTUGAL
- Instituto Português de Cinema
Rua S. Pedro de Alcântara 45-1°
1200 Lisbon
tel   +351 1 346 6634
fax +351 1 347 2777
tlx   14068 IPC P
1973 □ government department
providing finance for film projects
selected by a jury and support for the
entering of Portuguese films in national
and international film festivals. It also
helps provide financial aid for the
improvement and restoration of
cinemas. It publishes a yearly
catalogue.

IPDC · FRANCE
- International Programme for the
Development of Communication
UNESCO
1 rue Miollis
75732 Paris Cedex 15
tel   +33 1 45 68 25 56
□ provides support to media and
communication development projects
in the developing world.

IPG · FRANCE
- Independent Producers Group
69 rue de la Croix Nivert
75015 Paris
tel   +33 1 48 42 23 22
fax +33 1 48 56 08 39
tlx   203309
□ group of international film, television
and video programme producers and
distributors.

IPL · TECHNICAL TERM
- interprocessor link

IPM · TECHNICAL TERM
- incidental carrier phase modulation
(*aka* ICPM)

IPMPI · USA
- International Photographers Guild of
the Motion Pictures and Television
Industries
Suite 300
7715 Sunset Boulevard
Los Angeles
CA 90046
tel   +1 213 876 0160
fax +1 213 876 6383
□ union.

IPPA · UK
- Independent Programme Producers
Association
*now incorporated within Producers
Alliance for Cinema and Television
(PACT)*

IPR · TECHNICAL TERM
- interactive photorealistic rendering

IPS · TECHNICAL TERM
- inches per second

IPTAR · MALAYSIA
- Tun Abdul Razak Broadcasting
Training Institute
1976 □ to train staff to be proficient in
their trade so that the Department of
Broadcasting can make full use of their
capabilities. It also helps to provide
courses for broadcasters in the Asian
region in cooperation with UNESCO, the
Asia-Pacific Broadcasting Union (**ABU**)
and the Asia-Pacific Institute for
Broadcasting Development (**AIBD**).

IPTM · TECHNICAL TERM
- interval pulse time modulation

IQ · USA
- International Quorum of Film and
Video Producers

IQ · TECHNICAL TERM
- intelligent quest

IR · TECHNICAL TERM
- infra red

IRC · TECHNICAL TERM
- interval-related carrier

IRCAV · FRANCE
- Institut de Recherche en Cinéma et Audiovisuel
Université Sorbonne Nouvelle, Paris III
13 rue de Santeuil
75005 Paris
tel +33 1 45 87 42 38
□ research institute.

IRD · TECHNICAL TERM
- integrated receiver and decoder

IRIB · IRAN
- Islamic Republic of Iran Broadcasting
Jam-e Jam Street
Mossadegh Avenue
Tehran 1774
tel +98 21 294024
tlx 213910
□ semi-autonomous government broadcasting service, operating 2 television and 3 radio channels.

IRIS · TECHNICAL TERM
- instant recording image system

IRT · GERMANY
- Institut für Rundfunktechnik
Floriansmühlstraße 60
80939 Munich
tel +49 89 323 991
fax +49 89 323 99351
tlx 5215605 irtmd
1957 □ carries out research and development in the field of audio engineering in radio and television, television engineering, broadcasting coverage and transmitter engineering. It publishes *Rundfunktechnische Mitteilungen (RTM)* (6).

IRT · TECHNICAL TERM
- instant record timer

IRTC · IRELAND
- Independent Radio and Television Commission
Marine House
Clanwilliam Court
Dublin 2
tel +353 1 676 0966

fax +353 1 676 0948
1988 □ body established to ensure the creation, development and monitoring of independent broadcasting within Ireland.

IRTF · USA
- International Radio and Television Foundation

IRTO · CZECH REPUBLIC
- International Radio and Television Organisation
see **EBU** · SWITZERLAND

IRTS · USA
- International Radio and Television Society
420 Lexington Avenue
New York
NY 10017
tel +1 212 867 6650
fax +1 212 867 6653
1952 □ organisation of some 2000 individuals involved in the television, cable and radio industries. It publishes *IRTS News* (4).

IRTU · FRANCE
- International Radio and Television University
see **URTI** · FRANCE

ISBA · UK
- Incorporated Society of British Advertisers
44 Hertford Street
London W1Y 8AE
tel +44 71 499 7502
fax +44 71 629 5355
1900 □ association which seeks to promote and protect the advertising interests of its members.

ISBO · SAUDI ARABIA
- Islamic States Broadcasting Services Organisation
PO Box 6351
Jeddah 21442
tel +966 2 672 1121 / 2269
fax +966 2 672 2600
tlx 601442 ISBO SJ
1975 □ association of some 45 countries whose objectives are: to

propagate Islamic teaching; to promote Islamic solidarity; to protect Islamic heritage; to strengthen fraternal relations among Muslim peoples; to defend Islamic causes; to further cooperative relations with regional and international information and cultural organisations. The means to achieve these objectives are as follows: production of television and radio programmes; programme exchange between broadcasting companies of member states; teaching the Arabic language by audiovisual means; training personnel for broadcasting corporations in member states.

ISCA · ITALY
■ Istituto per lo Studio e la diffusione del Cinema di Animazione
P.za Luigi di Savoia 24
Milan
□ institute for the study and publicising of animation for the cinema.

ISCA · TECHNICAL TERM
■ image synthesis and computer animation

ISDN · TECHNICAL TERM
■ integrated services digital network

ISEC · FRANCE
■ Institut Supérieur d'Etudes Cinématographiques
135 avenue Félix Faure
75015 Paris
tel   +33 1 44 25 25 25
fax +33 1 44 25 25 26
1983 □ film school.

ISETU · SWITZERLAND
■ International Secretariat of Arts, Mass Media and Entertainment Trade Unions
■ Secrétariat International des Syndicats des Arts, des Moyens de Communication et du Spectacle
15 Avenue de Balexert
1219 Geneva
tel   +41 22 962 733
fax +41 22 796 5321
1963 □ international organisation representing some 100 000 members who belong to unions of professional performing arts employees. It publishes a *Newsletter.*

ISFA · FRANCE
■ International Scientific Film Association
see **IAMS** · THE NETHERLANDS

ISI · TECHNICAL TERM
■ intersymbol interference

ISIC · FRANCE
■ Institut des Sciences de l'Information et de la Communication
Université Bordeaux III
Domaine Université
Esplanade M de Montaigne
33405 Talence
tel   +33 56 84 50 58
□ institution offering courses in communication and the audiovisual.

ISL · TECHNICAL TERM
■ inter-satellite link

ISO · SWITZERLAND
■ International Standards Organisation
1-3 rue Varembé
Case Postale 56
CH-1211 Geneva 20
tel   +41 22 749 0111
fax +41 22 733 3430
tlx   045 412205 iso ch
□ international body which coordinates standards for, amongst others, film and television.

ISS · TECHNICAL TERM
■ inter-satellite service

ISV · USA
■ International Society of Videographers

IT · TECHNICAL TERM
■ information technology
■ interline/inline transfer

ITA · USA
■ International Tape Association
505 Eighth Avenue
Floor 12-A
New York
NY 10018
tel   +1 212 643 0620

fax +1 212 643 0624
1970 □ international association
dedicated to the exchange of
management-orientated information on
global trends and innovations which
impact the magnetic and optical media
and related industries. It publishes the
ITA Membership Newsletter and
International Source Directory, as well
as various other publications.

ITBC · USA
■ Instructional Television Funding
Cooperative

ITC · JAPAN
■ Ishikawa Television Broadcasting
Corporation
Chi 18
Kannondo-cho
Kanazawa 920-03
tel +81 762 67 2141
□ television station.

ITC · SWITZERLAND
■ Association Suisse des Industries
Techniques Cinématographiques
see **FTB** · SWITZERLAND

ITC · UK
■ Independent Television Commission
33 Foley Street
London W1P 7LB
tel +44 71 255 3000
fax +44 71 306 7800
*formerly the Independent Broadcasting
Authority (IBA) and replacing the Cable
Authority (CA)*
1991 □ public body responsible for
licensing and regulating non-**BBC**
television services including channels 3
(**ITV**) and 4, the proposed Channel 5,
cable, satellite and 'additional services'.
It has a duty: to ensure that a wide
range of television services is available
throughout the UK and that, taken as a
whole, they are of high quality and
appeal to a variety of tastes and
interests; to ensure fair and effective
competition in the provision of these
services; to publish various codes
relating to the standards and content of
licensed services. It publishes *Spectrum*
(4).

ITC · USA
■ International Television Center

ITC · USA
■ International Television Committee
1947

ITEL · UK
■ International Television Enterprises
London
48 Leicester Square
London WC2H 7FB
tel +44 71 491 1441
fax +44 71 493 7677
tlx 25353
1982 □ international television sales
and distribution company owned by
Anglia Television and Time Warner Inc
through its television subsidiary, **HBO.**
It represents Survival, Anglia Television
Entertainment, HBO factual catalogue,
National Geographic Television,
Grampian Television and programming
from Showtime, Time Life, Channel 4
(**C4**), the **BBC** and Roadshow, Coote &
Carroll.

ITFS · TECHNICAL TERM
■ instructional television fixed service

ITN · UK
■ Independent Television News
200 Gray's Inn Road
London WC1 8XZ
tel +44 71 833 3000
fax +44 71 430 4228
tlx 22101
1958 □ organisation which has been
'nominated' by the Independent
Television Commission (**ITC**) to provide
a high quality national and
international news service to Channel
3. The programmes supplied by ITN
must be transmitted live and
simultaneously by the regional Channel
3 companies.

ITN · TECHNICAL TERM
■ internegative (*aka* IN)

ITNA · USA
■ Independent Television News
Association

ITO · USA
■ Independent Television Organisation

ITS · SWITZERLAND
■ International Television Symposium
Montreux

ITS · USA
■ International Teleproduction Society
Suite 2400
350 Fifth Avenue
New York
NY 10018
tel +1 212 629 3266
fax +1 212 629 3265
1986 □ organisation whose members
are suppliers of video and film
equipment, services and systems. It
publishes *ITS News* (4) and organises
an annual forum.

ITS · TECHNICAL TERM
■ insertion test signals
■ international test signal

ITSC · UK
■ International Television Studies
Conference
see **EFTSC** · UK

ITU · SWITZERLAND
■ International Telecommunications
Union
■ Union Internationale des
Télécommunications (UIT)
■ Unión Internacional de
Telecomunicaciones (UIT)
Place des Nations
CH-1211 Geneva 20
tel +41 22 730 5111
fax +41 22 733 7256
tlx 421 000 UIT CH
1865 □ broadcasting association of
over 160 members whose aims are: to
maintain and extend international
cooperation among all members for the
improvement and rational use of
telecommunications of all kinds, as
well as to promote and offer technical
assistance to developing countries in
the field of telecommunications; to
promote the development of technical
facilities and their most efficient
operation with a view to improving the

efficiency of telecommunications
services, increasing their usefulness and
making them, as far as possible,
generally available to the public; to
harmonise the actions of nations in the
attainment of these ends. It publishes
various magazines.

ITV · JAPAN
■ Iyo Television Inc
5 Takewara-machi 1-chome
Matsuyama 790
tel +81 899 21 2121
□ television station.

ITV · UK
■ Independent Television
200 Gray's Inn Road
London WC1X 8HF
tel +44 71 843 8000
fax +44 71 843 8158
tlx 262988
1958 □ federation of 16 companies
who hold the franchises to provide
independent television services in the
UK. They are members of the ITV
Network Centre, formerly known as the
Independent Television Association
(**ITVA**).

ITV · TECHNICAL TERM
■ industrial television
■ instructional television

ITVA · UK
■ Independent Television Association
see **ITV** · UK

ITVA · USA
■ International Television Association
Suite 230
6311 North O'Connor Road, LB 51
Irving
TX 75039
tel +1 214 869 1112
fax +1 214 869 2980
1973 □ organisation which aims to
further the art and science of non-
broadcasting industrial television as it
applies to corporate training and
communications.
*formerly International Industrial
Television Association*

ITVS · USA
■ Independent Television Service
Suite 200
333 Sibley Street
St Paul
MN 55101
tel +1 612 225 9035
□ television station.

IUHFC · UK
■ Inter-University History Film
Consortium
55 Greek Street
London W1V 5LR
tel +44 71 734 3687
fax +44 71 287 3914
1968 □ enables historians to make
films for their own and each other's
use. It encourages the study of film as
visual evidence, arranging conferences
and publications to this end. Its films
fall into 2 series: "British Universities
Historical Studies in Film" and "The
Archive Series". The first deals mainly
with international affairs in the 1930s
and 1940s but also considers the
influence of film and its value as
evidence. The second uses uncut items
from newsreels, using only the original
narration and music (if any).
Accompanying booklets analyse the
extracts in context. It produces various
publications.

IUS · TECHNICAL TERM
■ interim upper stage

IV · TECHNICAL TERM
■ interactive video

IVCA · UK
■ International Visual Communication
Association
Bolsover House
5/6 Clipstone Street
London W1P 7EB
tel   +44 71 580 0962
fax +44 71 436 2606
1987 □ represents all sectors of the
visual communication industry,
including suppliers to the industry such
as writers, production companies and
facilities houses, and the users of visual
and business communication such as

commissioning client and intermediary
organisations. It represents the visual
communications industry through the
promotion of the benefits and uses of
effective visual communication, and the
provision of a wide range of
membership benefits and services,
including conventions, seminars, and
legal and insurance services. It
publishes *IVCA Update* (12),
Professional Communicator (6) the
IVCA Production Handbook (1) and
various other publications.

IVD · TECHNICAL TERM
■ interactive video disc

IVENS · DENMARK
■ Innovation of the European Short and
Documentary
now DOCUMENTARY, an initiative of
MEDIA

IVF · THE NETHERLANDS
■ International Video Federation
see **NVPI** · THE NETHERLANDS

IVIA · LUXEMBOURG
■ International Videotex Industry
Association
now incorporated under European
Information Industry Association (EIIA)

IVIFE · TECHNICAL TERM
■ interactive video in further education

IWF · GERMANY
■ Institut für den Wissenschaftlichen
Film
Nonnenstieg 72
37075 Göttingen
tel   +49 551 2020
fax +49 551 202 2000
tlx 96691
1956 □ the application of audiovisual
media to biology, ecology, engineering,
medicine and psychology.

IWM · UK
■ Imperial War Museum
Department of Film
Lambeth Road
London SE1 6HX
tel   +44 71 416 5000

fax +44 71 416 5379
1919 □ the Department of Film
collects, preserves and makes available
actuality film and video material from
Britain and other countries that relates
to conflict in the 20th century. Core
collections are those transferred to the
Museum by British Government
departments, including the official
service film records or participation in
both World Wars (originally filmed on
35mm nitrate stock). Substantial
collections of allied and former enemy
material are also held, as is a growing
volume of television/video material. It
offers screenings in the Museum
Cinema, as well as viewing and
research facilities which are extensively
used by historians and by film and
television companies. It publishes *A
Working Guide to the Film Archive* and
Film and Video Loans (both
occasional).

IZI · GERMANY
■ Internationales Zentralinstitut für das
Jugend- und Bildungsfernsehen
Bayerischer Rundfunk
Rundfunkplatz 1
80335 Munich
tel   +49 89 5900 2140
fax +49 89 5900 2379
tlx   521070 brm d
□ international institute for youth and
educational television which publishes
TelevIZIon (2).

J

JAMCO · JAPAN
■ Japan Media Communication Center
Chiyoda Media Plaza 1-1
Kioi-cho
Chiyoda-ku
Tokyo 102
tel   +81 3 3238 7410
fax +81 3 3238 7414
1991 □ public service foundation with
funds from the Japanese government,
broadcasters and the private sector. It
helps broadcasters around the world to
obtain Japanese-made programmes and

aims to help resolve the linguistic,
cultural, technical and financial
difficulties involved in sending out
Japanese-made television programmes
for broadcast in other countries. It also
operates a Programme Library of
Japanese television programmes and
holds international conferences,
bringing together broadcasters from
around the world.

JBC · JAMAICA
■ Jamaica Broadcasting Corporation
5 South Odeon Avenue
PO Box 100
Kingston 10
tel   +1 809 926 5620-9
fax +1 809 929 1029
tlx   2218 BRADCORPJA
1958 □ television and radio service.

JCC · ISRAEL
■ Jerusalem Communications Centre
Jerusalem

JCC · TUNISIA
■ Journées Cinématographiques de
Carthage
48 rue du Niger
1002 Tunis Belvedere
tel   +216 1 795272
fax +216 1 795285
1966 □ international film festival.

JCFC · USA
■ Judaica Captioned Film Center
PO Box 21439
Baltimore
MD 21208-0439
tel   +1 410 655 6767
1983 □ organisation which finds and
helps distribute captioned films on
Jewish topics for the deaf and hearing-
impaired.

JCP · TECHNICAL TERM
■ joystick control panel

JESSI · TECHNICAL TERM
■ joint European submicron silicon

JFET · TECHNICAL TERM
■ junction field-effect transistor

JFF · GERMANY
- Institut Jugend Film Fernsehen
Pfälzer-Wald-Str. 64
81539 Munich
tel +49 89 689890
fax +49 89 68989111
□ institute of film and television for
young people.

JFF · UK
- Jewish Film Festival/Foundation
46a Minster Road
London NW2 3RD
fax +44 71 633 0786
1986 □ to promote the production,
distribution and exhibition of films and
television programmes of Jewish
interest, and to organise an annual film
festival.

JICTAR · UK
- Joint Industries' Committee for
Television Audience Research
***see* BARB** · UK

JPEG · TECHNICAL TERM
- Joint Photographics Experts Group

JPM · TECHNICAL TERM
- jolts per minute

JRT · JAPAN
- Shikoku Broadcasting Co Ltd
5-2 Nakatokushima-cho 2-chome
Tokushima 770
tel +81 886 55 7510
□ television station.

JRT · SERBIA
- Jugoslovenskih Radiotelevizija
Hratigova 70/1
11000 Belgrade
tel +38 11 434910
fax +38 11 434023
tlx 11469 YU JURATE
1952 □ television and radio station.

JRTV · JORDAN
- Jordan Radio & Television
Corporation
PO Box 1041
Amman
tel +962 6 638760
fax +962 6 788115

tlx 24213 RTVENG JO
1968 □ government television station,
broadcasting in both Arabic and
English.

JSB · JAPAN
- Japan Satellite Broadcasting Inc
1-19-10 Toranomon
Minato-ku
Tokyo 105
tel +81 3 3501 5311
fax +81 3 3501 5317
□ satellite broadcaster.

JSTV · UK
- Japan Satellite Television Ltd
17 King's Exchange
Tileyard Road
London N7 9AH
tel +44 71 607 7677
fax +44 71 607 7442
1989 □ provides Japanese television by
satellite to the European market,
broadcasting daily between 19.00 and
06.00 UK time. A wide variety of
programme types are selected from
Japan's public service broadcaster,
Nippon Hoso Kyokai (**NHK**), as well as
from the highest quality programmes of
the Japanese commercial network.

JSV · JAPAN
- Japan Sports Vision
Daikyo Shibuya Building
1-13-5 Shibuya
Shibuya-ku
Tokyo 150
tel +81 3 3407 6620
fax +81 3 3797 4188
□ developing Japanese markets for new
sports programmes.

JVC · JAPAN
- Japanese Victor Corporation
- Victor Company of Japan
8-14 Nihonbashi
Honcho-4-chome
Chuo-ku
Tokyo 103
tel +81 3 3246 1091
fax +81 3 3245 1614
□ video and television equipment
manufacturer.

K

KAB · JAPAN
- Kumamoto Asahi Broadcasting Co
12-32 Hanabata-cho
Kumamoto 860
tel +81 96 359 1111
□ television station.

KBC · JAPAN
- Kyushu Asahi Broadcasting
Corporation
1-1 Nagahama 1-chome
Chuo-ku
Fukuoka 810
tel +81 92 721 1234
□ television station.

KBC · KENYA
- Kenya Broadcasting Corporation
Harry Thuku Road
PO Box 30456
Nairobi
tel +254 2 334567
fax +254 2 220675
tlx 25361 KBC KE
1989 □ to entertain, educate and
inform by television (2 languages) and
radio (18 languages).

KBI · KOREA
- Korean Broadcasting Institute

KBP · THE PHILIPPINES
- Kapisanan ng mga Brodkaster sa
Pilipinas
6th floor, LTA Building
118 Perea Street
Legaspi Village
Makati
Metro Manila
tel +63 2 8151990
fax +63 2 8151989
□ association of broadcasters.

KBS · JAPAN
- Kinki Broadcasting System Co Ltd
Kamichojamachi
Karasumadori
Kamigyo-ku
Kyoto 602
tel +81 75 431 1115
□ television station.

KBS · KOREA
- Korean Broadcasting System
(Hanguk Pangsong Kongsa)
18 Yoido-dong
Youngdeungpo-gu
Seoul 150-790
tel +82 2 781 3710
fax +82 2 781 3799
tlx KBSKB K24599
1973 □ television and radio
broadcasting. It publishes *KBS
Newsletter.*

KEA · GREECE
- Kallitehniki Etairia Athinon
□ film school.

KET · USA
- Kentucky Educational Television

KETV · UK
- Kent Educational Television
Fred Martin Studio
Barton Road
Dover
Kent CT16 2ND
tel +44 304 202827
fax +44 304 213824
1971 □ Consultants, Producers and
Distributors of CD-ROM and video-
based learning/information resources.
More than 200 titles to date have been
produced for children and adults in the
education and public sectors. Most
recent productions include: the "Pilote"
series, a 3-part French course for young
beginners (videos, teachers' books,
worksheets, flashcards and software);
the "Design and Technology Starters"
series - 9 videos with teachers' notes
(including INSET and classroom
materials); and "Let's Make News" - 8
videos with teachers' notes and
software, on all facets of newspaper
production.

KF · CZECH REPUBLIC
- Krátký Film Ltd
Jindřišská, 34
110 00 Prague 1
tel +42 2 220452
fax +42 2 220325
tlx 122059
□ production of films, including

animation.

KFM · UK
- Kathy Fairbairn Media
The Courtyard
44 Gloucester Avenue
London NW1 8JD
tel +44 71 916 9242
fax +44 71 916 9243
□ sells footage for broadcast and in-flight programmes.

KHZ · TECHNICAL TERM
- kilohertz

KIIFF · JAPAN
- Kobe International Independent Film Festival
4th floor
Golden Sun Building
4-3-6 Nakayamate Dori
Chuo-ku
Kobe 650
tel +81 78 252 1691
fax +81 78 252 1691
□ annual film festival showing independent short films in any genre.

KIMC · KENYA
- Kenya Institute of Mass Communication
PO Box 42422
Nairobi 42422
tel +254 2 540820 x260
tlx 22244
1965 □ to create a suitable professional centre where personnel in various sections of mass media can train and acquire additional knowledge, skills and information.

KIWI · RUSSIA
- Kino Women International Film-Makers Union
Vasiljevskaya str. 13
Moscow
1989 □ association of women working in the film industry.

KJF · GERMANY
- Kinder- und Jugendfilmzentrum
Postfach 3004
Deutschhausplatz LFD-Haus
55020 Mainz

tel +49 6131 287880
□ centre for children's cinema.

KKB · JAPAN
- Kagoshima Broadcasting Corporation
5-12 Yojiro 2-chome
Kagoshima 890
tel +81 992 51 5111
□ television station.

KKL · NORWAY
- Kommunale Kinematografers Landsforbund
Stortingsgt. 16
0161 Oslo 1
tel +47 22 33 05 30
fax +47 22 42 89 49
also known as National Association of Municipal Cinemas (NAMC)
1917 □ professional, economical and juridical service body for Norwegian communities in film and cinema matters; representing all Norwegian cinemas in matters concerning film rental and music rights. It publishes *Film og Kino* (9).

KKT · JAPAN
- Kumamoto Kenmin Television Corporation
7 Yoyasu-cho
Kumamoto 860
tel +81 96 363 6111
□ television station.

KNB · JAPAN
- Kita-Nihon Broadcasting Co Ltd
10-18 Ushijima-machi
Toyama 930
tel +81 764 32 5555
□ television station.

KNF · THE NETHERLANDS
- Kring van Nederlandse Filmjournalisten
Snelliuslaan 78
1222 TG Hilversum
tel +31 35 856115
1982 □ association which looks after the interests of professional Dutch film journalists.

KNR TV · GREENLAND
- Kalaallit Nunaata Radioa

POB 1007
3900 Nuuk
tel +299 25333
fax +299 25042
tlx 90606
□ commercial television broadcaster.

KRO · THE NETHERLANDS
▪ Katholieke Radio Omroep
Emmastraat 52
1213 AL Hilversum
tel +31 35 713911
fax +31 35 210864
tlx 42223
1925 □ Dutch Catholic broadcasting
organisation, broadcasting television
programmes on Nederland 1, as well as
radio programmes. It is responsible for
broadcasts on behalf of the Roman
Catholic Church (RKK) and its
community. It publishes *Studio* and
Mikro Gids.

KRY · JAPAN
▪ Yamaguchi Broadcasting Co Ltd
Koen-ku
Tokuyama 745
tel +81 834 32 1111
□ television station.

KS · TECHNICAL TERM
▪ Kodak standard

KSB · JAPAN
▪ Kabushiki Kaisha Setonaikai
Broadcasting
5-20 Saiho-cho 1-chome
Takamatsu 760
tel +81 878 62 1111
□ television station.

KSFDC · INDIA
▪ Kerala State Film Development
Corporation Ltd
Chalachitra Kalabhavan
Trivandrum 695 014
tel +91 471 65080 / 62325 / 67041
tlx 0435-365
□ to support Malayalam cinema by
providing state of the art facilities for
film-making at its studio complex
Chithranjali, by conducting film
festivals and screening of world classics
at its theatres and by popularising

cinema as an art form.

KTN · JAPAN
▪ Television Nagasaki Co Ltd
1-7 Kanaya-machi
Nagasaki 850
tel +81 958 27 2111
□ television station.

KTS · JAPAN
▪ Kagoshima Television Station
15-8 Murasakihara 6-chome
Kagoshima 890
tel +81 992 58 1111
□ television station.

KTV · JAPAN
▪ Kansai Telecasting Corporation
5-17 Nishitenma 6-chome
Kita-ku
Osaka 530-08
tel +81 6 315 2121
□ television station.

KTV · KUWAIT
▪ Kuwait Television
PO Box 621
13007 Safat / Kuwait City
tel +965 242 3774
fax +965 245 6660
tlx 496 KTV 22169 KT
1961 □ national television and radio
broadcasting service.

KUTV · JAPAN
▪ Kochi Television Co Ltd
4-27 Kita-honmachi 3-chome
Kochi 780
tel +81 888 83 3311
□ television station.

KV · TECHNICAL TERM
▪ kilovolt

KVA · TECHNICAL TERM
▪ kilo-voltampere(s)

KW · TECHNICAL TERM
▪ kilowatts

KWM · UK
▪ Kagan World Media Ltd
524 Fulham Road
London SW6 5NR

tel   +44 71 371 8880
fax +44 71 371 8716/5
part of Paul Kagan Associates, USA
1988 □ research, consulting and
publishing firm specialising in European
entertainment and communications
media and producing 11 newsletters
and reference books covering
television, home video, television and
film coproductions, cable television,
sports franchise and media rights, radio,
cellular telephony and media regulation
in Europe. It publishes various
newsletters.

L

L/FQ · USA
■ Literature/Film Quarterly
English Department
Salisbury State University
Salisbury
MA 21801
tel   +1 410 543 6446
fax +1 410 543 6068
1973 □ quarterly journal which
focusses upon the problems of adapting
and transforming fiction and drama into
film. It also covers film genre, theory
and criticism and features interviews
with screenwriters and directors.

L/L · TECHNICAL TERM
■ liplock

L-SAT · TECHNICAL TERM
■ large satellite

LA · TECHNICAL TERM
■ low angle
■ live action

LAC · TECHNICAL TERM
■ live action camera

LAD · TECHNICAL TERM
■ laboratory aim density

LAE · TECHNICAL TERM
■ liquid apogee engine

LAIFA · UK

■ Latin American Independent Film and
Video Association
Latin American House
Kinsgate Place
London NW6 4TA
tel   +44 71 372 6442

LAN · TECHNICAL TERM
■ local area network

LASER · TECHNICAL TERM
■ light amplification by the stimulated
emission of radiation

LBC · TECHNICAL TERM
■ lowband colour

LBM · TECHNICAL TERM
■ lowband monochrome

LC² · TECHNICAL TERM
■ liquid coupling and cooling

LCD · TECHNICAL TERM
■ liquid-crystal display

LCL · TECHNICAL TERM
■ light centre length

LCLV · TECHNICAL TERM
■ liquid crystal light valve

LCM · UK
■ Lancier Cabling & Monitoring
Systems Ltd
12 Driberg Way
Braintree
Essex CM7 7NB
tel   +44 376 551059
fax +44 376 321077
□ specialists in cable laying and
monitoring.

LCRS · TECHNICAL TERM
■ left centre right surround

LCS · TECHNICAL TERM
■ lens-control-system

LCT · TECHNICAL TERM
■ low-colour temperature

LCTV · LAOS
■ Laos Central Television

BP 310
Vientiane
tel   +856 21 5609
1983 □ national television broadcasting service.

LCU · TECHNICAL TERM
■ large closeup

LD · TECHNICAL TERM
■ laser diode
■ laserdisc
■ lighting designer/director
■ longitudinal difference

LD-ROM · TECHNICAL TERM
■ laserdisc read-only memory

LDE · TECHNICAL TERM
■ lighting director engineer

LDP · TECHNICAL TERM
■ laserdisc player

LDS · TECHNICAL TERM
■ local delivery/distribution service

LDT · TECHNICAL TERM
■ local delivery service (transitional)

LE · TECHNICAL TERM
■ light entertainment

LED · TECHNICAL TERM
■ light-emitting diode

LEG · USA
■ Landmark Entertainment Group

LENTIC · BELGIUM
■ Laboratoire d'Etudes sur les Nouvelles Technologies et les Industries Culturelles
Arts et Sciences de la Communication
Université de Liège
Allée du Six-Août B11
4000 Liège
tel   +32 41 56 32 86-9
□ research and study centre into cultural and new technology industries.

LEO · TECHNICAL TERM
■ low earth orbit

LF · TECHNICAL TERM
■ low frequency

LFF · UK
■ London Film Festival
South Bank
Waterloo
London SE1 8XT
tel   +44 71 928 3535
fax +44 71 633 0786
1956 □ internationally recognised as a major non-competitive festival of cinema, with screenings of over 250 films to approximately 70 000 people every November at central London venues.

LFM · GERMANY
■ Lokal-Fernsehen-München
Rotenhanstr. 6
81476 Munich
□ local television service.

LFMC · UK
■ London Film-Makers Cooperative
42 Gloucester Avenue
London NW1 8JD
tel   +44 71 586 4806 / 586 8516 / 722 1728
fax +44 71 486 0068
1966 □ to be an international centre for experimental and independent film; to offer support, encouragement and promotion to experimental and independent film and film-makers, to be achieved through a policy of integrated practice encompassing production, distribution, exhibition and education. It is committed to open-access, equal opportunities, cooperative working practices, training and broadening the awareness of the sector through education.

LFOA · TECHNICAL TERM
■ last frame of action

LFVDA · UK
■ London Film and Video Development Agency
25 Gosfield Street
London W1P 7HB
tel   +44 71 637 3577
fax +44 71 637 3578

1992 □ to strengthen and promote all aspects of independent media activity (particularly productions, exhibition and training) in the Greater London region.

LHCP · TECHNICAL TERM
■ left-hand circular polarisation

LIFS · UK
■ London International Film School
24 Shelton Street
London WC2H 9HP
tel　+44 71 836 9642
fax　+44 71 497 3718
□ offers a practical, 2-year diploma course to professional level; approximately half of each term is devoted to film production and half to practical and theoretical tuition. All students work on one or more films each term and are encouraged to interchange unit roles termly to experience different skills areas.

LIFT · CANADA
■ Liaison of Independent Filmmakers of Toronto
Suite 505
345 Adelaide Street West
Toronto
Ontario M5V 1R5

LIKI · RUSSIA
■ Leningradsky Institut Kinoinzhenerov
Pravda oul. 13
191126 Saint-Petersburg
tel　+7 812 3150172
1919 □ institute of film technicians.

LJB · LIBYA
■ Libyan Arab Jamahiriya Broadcasting
Great Socialist People's Libyan Arab Jamahiriya Broadcasting Corporation
PO Box 3731
Tripoli
El-Beida
tel　+218 21 32451
tlx　20010
1957 □ radio and television broadcasting, operating mainly in Arabic and English.

LLL · TECHNICAL TERM
■ low light level

LLTV · UK
■ London Live Television
tel　+44 71 822 3681
□ television project.

LLTV · TECHNICAL TERM
■ low light television

LMCR · TECHNICAL TERM
■ lightweight mobile control room

LMF · TECHNICAL TERM
■ low mid frequency

LMS · TECHNICAL TERM
■ library management system

LMW · UK
■ London Media Workshops
101 King's Drive
Gravesend
Kent DA12 5BQ
tel　+44 474 564676
fax　+44 474 564676
1978 □ training agency which runs a range of short, intensive courses in all forms of scriptwriting for broadcast and non-broadcast television, video and film - including drama for adults and children, dramatised documentaries, documentaries and comedy; plus training, corporate, industrial and business programmes. Audio writing, production and presentation are also included. It also runs a mail order service specialising in media books.

LNA · TECHNICAL TERM
■ low-noise amplifier

LNB · TECHNICAL TERM
■ low-noise block

LNBF · TECHNICAL TERM
■ low noise block filter

LNBS · LESOTHO
■ Lesotho National Broadcasting Service
PO Box 552
Maseru 100
tel　+266 323561
fax　+266 310003
tlx　4340 CLO

1966 □ television and radio broadcasting service, whose primary aim is to educate, inform and entertain.

LNC · TECHNICAL TERM
- low-noise convertor

LO · TECHNICAL TERM
- local origination
- local oscillator

LOC · TECHNICAL TERM
- large optical cavity

LOP · TECHNICAL TERM
- least objectionable programme

LOR · TECHNICAL TERM
- laser optical reflection

LOS · TECHNICAL TERM
- line of sight
- loss of signal

LOT · TECHNICAL TERM
- laser optical transmission

LPC · TECHNICAL TERM
- linear predictive coding

LPF · TECHNICAL TERM
- low pass filter

LPS · TECHNICAL TERM
- licensable programme service

LPTV · TECHNICAL TERM
- low-power television

LPW · TECHNICAL TERM
- lumens per watt

LRC · TECHNICAL TERM
- longitudinal redundancy check

LS · TECHNICAL TERM
- long shot

LSB · TECHNICAL TERM
- least significant bit

LSI · TECHNICAL TERM
- large-scale integration

LSPS · TECHNICAL TERM
- licensable sound programme service

LSW · UK
- London Screenwriters' Workshop
84 Wardour Street
London W1V 3LF
tel   +44 71 434 0942
1983 □ established as a forum for contact, discussion and practical criticism. It is an organisation aimed at those seriously intending to make a career out of writing for the screen. It issues the magazines *Screenwriter* and a *Bulletin* (6).

LTC · TECHNICAL TERM
- last telecast
- linear/longitudinal time-code

LTI · TECHNICAL TERM
- luminance transient improvement/improver

LTV · LATVIA
- Latvijas Televizija
3 Zakusala
Riga 1018
tel   +371 2 200314
tlx   161188
□ television broadcasting service.

LTV · LESOTHO
- Lesotho Television
PO Box 36
Maseru
tel   +266 323561
fax   +266 310003
tlx   4340
1988 □ national television broadcasting service, putting out a daily news magazine supplemented by occasional programmes of national interest.

LTV · NIGERIA
- Lagos Television
PMB 12036
Lagos
□ state-owned television service.

LV · TECHNICAL TERM
- LaserVision

LV-ROM · TECHNICAL TERM

■ LaserVision-Read Only Memory

LVA · UK
■ London Video Access
3rd floor
5-7 Buck Street
London NW1 8NJ
tel   +44 71 284 4588 / 284 4323
fax +44 71 267 6078
1976 □ charity and limited company
which is a national centre for video and
new media art. It aims to provide
practical support for creative video and
television production and offers a
comprehensive range of services
including training, consultancy, facility
hire, distribution, education and
exhibition. It publishes a catalogue of
video art for hire and sale.

LVI · TECHNICAL TERM
■ laser video interactive

LVPI · USA
■ Light Valve Products Inc
see **HJT** · USA

LVR · TECHNICAL TERM
■ longitudinal videotape
recorder/recording

LW · TECHNICAL TERM
■ long wave

LWT · UK
■ London Weekend Television plc
The London Television Centre
Upper Ground
London SE1 9LT
tel   +44 71 620 1620
fax +44 71 928 6948
tlx   918123
1968 □ holds the independent
television licence for London and the
south-east at weekends.

M

M&D · TECHNICAL TERM
■ masters and dupes

MABC · MAURITIUS

■ Mauritius Broadcasting Corporation
Broadcasting House
Louis Pasteur Street
Forest Side
tel   +230 675 5001-2
fax +230 675 7332
tlx   4230 MAUBROD IW
1964 □ broadcasting authority whose
main objectives are: to provide
independent and impartial broadcasting
services of information, education,
culture and entertainment in Bhojpuri,
Creole, English, French, Hindustani and
other such languages spoken or taught
in Mauritius; to provide broadcasting
services which cater for the aspirations,
needs and tastes of the population in
matters of information, education,
culture and entertainment; to provide
external broadcasting services as and
when required.

MAC · UK
■ Movie Acquisition Corporation
now Lumiere Pictures

MAC · TECHNICAL TERM
■ motion analysis camera
■ multiplex(ed) analogue component

MADC · USA
■ Matsushita Avionics Development
Corporation
16269 Laguna Kayon Road
Irvine
CA 92718
tel   +1 714 753 0172
fax +1 714 753 0299
□ designs and develops audio and
video products for aircraft use.

MAP · USA
■ Media Access Project
4th floor
2000 M Street, NW
Washington
DC 20036
tel   +1 202 232 4300
fax +1 202 223 5302
1971 □ organisation working in the
public interest to ensure that television
and other media fully and impartially
keep the public informed on key issues
such as the environment, civil rights,

consumer matters and the political process.

MAP TV · FRANCE
■ Memory-Archives-Programmes TV
c/o France 3
1 Place de Bordeaux
67005 Strasbourg
tel   +33 88 56 68 46
fax +33 88 56 68 49
1989 □ an initiative of **MEDIA**, which aims to help European coproductions of archive-based programmes. It contains an important network of members - producers, broadcasters and archive holders who may participate in archive-based coproductions. It also attributes loans of up to 40 000 ECU for the development period of these coproductions.

MAR · TECHNICAL TERM
■ multiple access receiver

MAS · USA
■ Matsushita Avionics Systems

MATV · TECHNICAL TERM
■ master antenna television

MAZ · SWITZERLAND
■ Medienausbildungszentrum
Krämerstein
6047 Lucerne
tel   +41 41 473636
fax +41 41 473659
□ media centre.

MBA · MALTA
■ Malta Broadcasting Authority
National Road
Blata L-Bajda
tel   +356 221281
fax +356 247908
tlx 1100
1961 □ ensuring the preservation of due impartiality in respect of matters of political or industrial controversy or relating to current public policy. In addition, the Broadcasting Act 1991 provides for the Broadcasting Authority's powers to select and appoint broadcasting licensees and contractors who will operate radio and

television services throughout Malta and to monitor the performance of the stations in terms of constitutional requirements, the provision of the law and of the relevant broadcasting licences and contracts.

MBC · JAPAN
■ Minaminihon Broadcasting Co Ltd
5-25 Korai-cho
Kagoshima 890
tel   +81 992 54 7111
□ television station.

MBC · KOREA
■ Munhwa Broadcasting Corporation
31 Yoido-dong
Yongdeungpo-Gu
Seoul 150728
tel   +82 2 784 2000
fax +82 2 784 0880
tlx 22203
1961 □ national television broadcasting service, operating 19 networks.

MBC · MAURITIUS
■ Mauritius Broadcasting Corporation
1 rue Louis Pasteur
Forest Side
tel   +230 675 5001/2
fax +230 675 7332
tlx 4230 maubroad iw
1962 □ to provide independent and impartial broadcasting services of information, education, culture and entertainment. It has to ensure that its broadcasting programmes maintain a high general standard both in respect of content and quality and also that they do not offend against decency, good taste or public morality. It refrains from expressing its own opinion and observes neutrality and impartiality on current affairs, matters of public policy or matters of controversy relating to culture, politics or religion. It also refrains from giving publicity to any person, product or services other than in a commercial broadcasting advertisement. It ensures that its broadcasting services help towards the development of the knowledge, sense of initiative, civic rights, duties and responsibilities of the population. It also

provides advisory, consultancy or technical facilities.

MBC · UK
- Middle East Broadcasting Centre
10 Heathmans Road
London SW6 4TJ
tel +44 71 371 9597
fax +44 71 371 9601
1991 □ Arabic language satellite television service provides news and entertainment throughout the Middle East, North Africa and Europe.

MBS · JAPAN
- Mainichi Broadcasting System Inc
17-1 Chayamachi
Kita-ku
Osaka 530-04
tel +81 6 359 1123
□ television station.

MBS · SPAIN
- Media Business School
Torregalindo 4, 4°
28016 Madrid
tel +34 1 359 0247 / 0036
fax +34 1 345 7606
1990 □ training, research and development arm of **MEDIA**. It operates through the establishment of training and development structures, the organisation of seminar cycles and the publication of reports, which are designed to take full advantage of the new opportunities offered by the Single European Market. It produces various publications.

MBS · TECHNICAL TERM
- media broadband service

MC · TECHNICAL TERM
- master control
- master of ceremonies

MCA · USA
- Music Corporation of America
MCA Universal Inc
100 Universal City Plaza
Universal City
CA 91608
tel +1 818 777 1000
fax +1 818 777 6276

1924 □ producer and distributor of film, television and video programmes.

MCAC · FRANCE
- Mediterranean Centre of Audiovisual Communication
see **CMCA** · FRANCE

MCB · TECHNICAL TERM
- miniature circuit breaker

MCFB · BELGIUM
- Mediathèque de la Communauté Française de Belgique
Place Eugène Flagey 18
1050 Brussels
tel +32 2 640 3815
fax +32 2 640 0291
1956 □ non-profit making association in charge of the cultural dissemination of video tapes (**VHS**) and music records - both fiction and documentary films - and operates through its own network of 16 branches. It publishes documentary and television programme catalogues.

MCI · TECHNICAL TERM
- multiple controller interface

MCL · TECHNICAL TERM
- master clock .

MCP · TECHNICAL TERM
- master control panel

MCPC · TECHNICAL TERM
- multiple channel per carrier

MCPS · UK
- Mechanical Copyright Protection Society Ltd
Elgar House
41 Streatham High Road
London SW16 1ER
tel +44 81 769 4400
fax +44 81 769 8792
tlx 946792 MCPS G
1924 □ organisation of music publishers and composers which collects and distributes 'mechanical' royalties due from the recording of their copyright musical works. These royalties accrue from the recording of

music onto videos, audiovisual and broadcast productions, advertising, CDS, discs and cassettes.

MCR · TECHNICAL TERM
- mobile/master control room
- multiple camera remotes

MCS · BELGIUM
- Media and Communication Services
Hoedenmakerstraat 11
B-8000 Bruges
tel +32 50 338503
fax +32 50 344208
1985 □ audiovisual production, pre-production and facilities, working in industrial films, commercials, television productions, ENG, videoconferences, video facilities and interactive media.

MCS · TECHNICAL TERM
- machine control system
- medium close shot
- microcell communications simulator

MCTV · CANADA
- Mid-Canada Television Funds
CHRO Television
10 Kimway Avenue
Nepean
Ontario K2E 6Z6
tel +1 613 228 2476
fax +1 613 228 3299
□ fund which provides film development loans.

MCU · TECHNICAL TERM
- master control unit
- medium close-up

MCW · TECHNICAL TERM
- modulated continuous wave

MD · TECHNICAL TERM
- match dissolve
- mini disc
- musical director

MDAC · TECHNICAL TERM
- multiplying digital-analogue convertor

MDR · GERMANY
- Mitteldeutsche Rundfunkwerbung GmbH

Zweigniederlassung Leipzig
Springerstraße 22-24
7022 Leipzig
tel +49 341 2115762
fax +49 341 592421
□ regional sales of television and radio advertising.

MDS · TECHNICAL TERM
- microwave distribution system
- minimum discernible signal
- multipoint distribution system/service

M&E · TECHNICAL TERM
- music and (sound) effects

M/E · TECHNICAL TERM
- mix/effects

MEAL · UK
- Media Expenditure Analysis Ltd
see **Register-MEAL** · UK

MECL · TECHNICAL TERM
- multi emitter coupled logic

MEDIA · BELGIUM
- Measures to Encourage the Development of the Industry of Audiovisual Production
- Mesures pour Encourager le Développement de l'Industrie Audiovisuelle
Commission of the European Communities
Directorate General Audiovisual, Information, Communication, Culture
120 rue de Trèves
1049 Brussels
tel +32 2 299 9436
fax +32 2 299 9214
1991 □ EC initiative which encourages a European audiovisual industry. It provides financial support to: develop programmes for the European market; establish European co-production infrastructures; internationally promote European independent productions; distribute European productions; exhibit European films; restore, preserve and use European archive material; develop new technology; train producers, writers and other audiovisual professionals; create financing

mechanisms for European projects.

MEFW · UK
▪ Media Education Forum for Wales
c/o Media Education Wales
Cardiff Institute of Higher Education
Cyncoed Centre
Cyncoed Road
Cardiff CF2 6XD
tel   +44 222 551111
□ promotes and supports media
education and media studies in Wales,
by running an annual national
conference and regional teachers'
groups and by publishing the bi-lingual
magazine *FForum* (3) to support media
education in the classroom.

MEMO · THE NETHERLANDS
▪ Media Marketing Organisatie
PO Box 9822
Hengeveldstraat 29
3506 GV Utrecht
tel   +31 30 736 400
fax   +31 30 734 774
1986 □ handles the distribution and
marketing of educational and scientific
audiovisual programmes. Programmes
are distributed both nationally and
internationally for and to universities,
institutions of higher education, other
vocational institutes, and companies in
trade and industry.

MENU · UK
▪ Media Education News Update
BFI Education
21 Stephen Street
London W1P 1PL
tel   +44 71 255 1444
fax   +44 71 436 7950
tlx   27624 BFILDNG
1992 □ magazine/newsletter for
audiovisual media educators and
teachers.

MESECAM · TECHNICAL TERM
▪ Middle East Séquence Couleur à
Mémoire

META · USA
▪ Metropolitan Educational Television
Association

MF · TECHNICAL TERM
▪ medium frequency
▪ mixed field
▪ multi function

MFB · SWITZERLAND
▪ Mobile Facilities Basle Ltd
Grellingerstraße 77
4052 Basle
tel   +41 61 312 5528
fax   +41 61 312 5526
tlx   964 898 tvbs
1977 □ high end production and post-
production facilities 4:2:2.

MFD · TECHNICAL TERM
▪ minimum focussing distance

MFM · TECHNICAL TERM
▪ modified frequency modulation

MFSK · TECHNICAL TERM
▪ multiple frequency shift keying

MFU · TECHNICAL TERM
▪ mobile film unit

MFVPA · UK
▪ Music Film and Video Producers'
Association
26 Noel Street
London W1V 3RD
tel   +44 71 434 2651
fax   +44 71 434 9002
1988 □ represents the interests of music
film producers and formally represents
all the major production companies,
providing an advisory service in all
matters relating to production,
including copyright, legal and
employment practices.

MGC · TECHNICAL TERM
▪ manual gain control

MGM · USA
▪ Metro-Goldwyn-Mayer, Inc
640 South San Vicente Boulevard
Los Angeles
CA 90048
tel   +1 310 444 1500
fax   +1 310 658 2111
1924 □ film production and
distribution.

MHE · TECHNICAL TERM
- micro headend

MHFB · USA
- Mental Health Film Board

MHI · USA
- Media Holdings International

MHMC · UK
- Mental Health Media Council
380-384 Harrow Road
London W9 2HU
tel   +44 71 286 2346
fax +44 71 266 2922
1965 □ offers advice and consultancy on video use and production relevant to health, mental health, physical disability, learning difficulty, stress and stress management, women and well-being and most aspects of social welfare. It publishes *Mediawise* (4).

MHTVF · CANADA
- Maclean Hunter Television Fund
Suite 412
777 Bay Street
Toronto
Ontario M4W 1A7
tel   +1 416 596 5878
fax +1 416 596 2650
□ fund established by Canadian Television Series Development Foundation (**CTSDF**) to provide loans or equity investments to qualified independent production companies which have the majority of their financing confirmed and a broadcast licence from a private Canadian broadcaster.

MHZ · TECHNICAL TERM
- megahertz

MI · TECHNICAL TERM
- move in

MIA · AUSTRALIA
- Media Information Australia
Australian Film, Television and Radio School
North Ryde
NSW 2113
tel   +61 2 805 6611

fax +61 2 805 0963
□ quarterly journal.

MIBC · RUSSIA
- Moscow Independent Broadcasting Corporation
□ serves to take PAY TV to the district of Moscow.

MIC · TECHNICAL TERM
- microwave integrated circuit

MICO · JAPAN
- Media International Corporation
2-14-5 Akasaka
Minato-ku
Tokyo 107
tel   +81 3 5561 9588
fax +81 3 5561 9550
tlx 2423313 KMEDIA
□ sales and distribution of **NHK** programmes and films.

MICS · ITALY
- Museo Internazionale del Cinema e dello Spettacolo
Casella Postale 6104
00195 Rome
tel   +39 6 37 00 266
fax +39 6 39 73 32 97
1959 □ international museum of cinema and entertainment whose task is the preservation and publicising of film and show business with particular attention to the European tradition. It produces various publications.

MIDEM · FRANCE
- Marché International du Disque, de l'Edition Musicale et de la Vidéo Musique
Reed Midem Organisation
179 avenue Victor Hugo
75116 Paris
tel   +33 1 44 34 44 44
fax +33 1 44 34 44 00
tlx 269346
1967 □ annual (January) international market of video music, music publishing and records, representing more than 2000 companies.

MIFA · FRANCE
- Marché International du Film

d'Animation pour le Cinéma et la Télévision
see CICA · FRANCE

MIFED · ITALY
■ Indian Summer Cinema and Television Multimedia Market
■ Mercato Internazionale Film e Documentario
E A Fiera Milano
Largo Domodossola, 1
CP 1270
20145 Milan
tel   +39 2 4801 2912 / 4801 2920
fax   +39 2 4997 7020
tlx   331360 EAFM
1960 □ annual international market for selling and buying cinema and television products.

MIP · FRANCE
■ Mars International Productions
1 rue Lord Byron
75008 Paris
tel   +33 1 45 63 49 01
fax   +33 1 42 25 93 22
tlx   648445 F
□ television programme producers.

MIP-TV · FRANCE
■ Marché International des Programmes de Télévision
Reed Midem Organisation
179 avenue Victor Hugo
75116 Paris
tel   +33 1 44 34 44 44
fax   +33 1 44 34 44 00
tlx   630547
1963 □ annual (April) international television programme market, representing nearly 2000 companies.

MIPCOM · FRANCE
■ Marché International des Films et des Programmes pour la TV, la Vidéo, le Câble et le Satellite
Reed-Midem Organisation
179 avenue Victor Hugo
75116 Paris
tel   +33 1 44 34 44 44
fax   +33 1 44 34 44 00
tlx   630547
1985 □ international film and programme market for television, video, cable and satellite, held annually (October) in Cannes and representing nearly 2000 companies.

MISA · CANADA
■ Moving Images and Sound Archives

MIT · HUNGARY
■ Mozgókép Innovációs Társulás & Alapítvány
Mészáros utca 18
1016 Budapest
tel   +36 1 251 4749
fax   +36 1 251 7369
□ film production company.

MIT · JAPAN
■ Iwate Menkoi Television Co Ltd
7-1 Ushirono
Sakurakawa
Mizusawa 023
tel   +81 197 24 3300
□ television station.

MITES · UK
■ Moving Image Touring & Exhibition Service
Moviola
Bluecoat Chambers
School Lane
Liverpool L1 3BX
tel   +44 51 707 2881
fax   +44 51 707 2150
1992 □ developed by Moviola to provide an efficient support service for exhibitors working with moving image artworks. It is the first British organisation established specifically to provide a service combining artistic experience with technical expertise. With subsidised resources, training schemes, and free advice and on-line support, it aims to be a flexible and practical support mechanism assisting in the development of a thriving culture of moving image art.

MITV · GERMANY
■ Management Information Television GmbH
Hans-Stießbergerstr. 2b
85540 Haar
tel   +49 89 45 60 42 12
fax   +49 89 45 60 42 23

◻ European service and production base for interactive and multimedia television programmes.

MLO · TECHNICAL TERM
■ multi-linear orientation

MLS · TECHNICAL TERM
■ medium long shot

MM · TECHNICAL TERM
■ multimedia

MMD · TECHNICAL TERM
■ microwave modules and devices

MMDS · TECHNICAL TERM
■ multi-channel microwave/multipoint distribution system/service

MMG · USA
■ Movie Makers Guild

MMPIA · CANADA
■ Manitoba Motion Picture Industries Association
145 Sherbrook Street
Winnipeg
Manitoba R3C 2B5
tel +1 204 783 5228
fax +1 204 775 1184
◻ non-profit, member-based association whose prime objectives are: to promote and preserve the common interest of those engaged in the industry in Manitoba; to provide leadership and foster cooperation throughout the industry by providing a forum for discussion, decision-making and policy development; to gather and disseminate information relevant to the industry through a newsletter and to promote public awareness of the benefits and values of the industry; to foster a favourable image of the industry in Manitoba and help create a favourable economic and artistic climate by communicating with government, corporations and other organisations and agencies; to promote rational legislation affecting the industry; to stimulate the development of educational opportunities in Manitoba related to the industry.

MNA · TECHNICAL TERM
■ multi-network area

MNOS · TECHNICAL TERM
■ metal-nitride-oxide semiconductor

MO · TECHNICAL TERM
■ magneto-optical
■ move out

MOCVD · TECHNICAL TERM
■ metal-oxide chemical vapour deposition

MOD · TECHNICAL TERM
■ minimum operating distance

MOGPAAFIS · SOMALIA
■ Mogadiscio Pan-African Film Symposium
Mogadiscio
1981 ◻ film festival and symposium.
also known as MOGPAFIS

MOGPAFIS · SOMALIA
■ Mogadiscio Pan-African Film Symposium
see **MOGPAAFIS** · SOMALIA

MOL · TECHNICAL TERM
■ maximum output level

MOMI · UK
■ Museum of the Moving Image
South Bank
Waterloo
London SE1 8XT
tel +44 71 928 3535
fax +44 71 633 9323
1988 ◻ explores the unique and magical history of cinema and television. It is a story told chronologically, from the earliest pre-cinema experiments to the technical wizardry of a modern television studio. There are many interactive exhibits, original costumes and designs, stills and posters.

MOP · TECHNICAL TERM
■ minute of programme

MOS · TECHNICAL TERM
■ metal-oxide semiconductor/surface

- "mit out sound"

MOSFET · TECHNICAL TERM
- metal-oxide field-effect transistor

MOVI · HUNGARY
- Magyar Mozi és Videófilmagyar
Könyves K. krt 13-15
1098 Budapest
tel   +36 1 133 7550

MOW · TECHNICAL TERM
- movie of the week

MP · TECHNICAL TERM
- motion picture

MPAA · USA
- Motion Picture Association of
America
1600 Eye Street NW
Washington
DC 20006
tel   +1 202 293 1966
fax   +1 202 452 9823
1922 □ organisation of major US film
producers and distributors.

MPEA · USA
- Motion Picture Export Association of
America
see **MPEAA** · USA

MPEAA · USA
- Motion Picture Export Association of
America
15503 Ventura Boulevard
Encino
CA 91436
tel   +1 818 995 6600
fax   +1 818 382 1784
1945 □ association which seeks to
defend the export interests of the US
motion picture industry.
also known as MPEA

MPEG · TECHNICAL TERM
- motion picture(s) expert group

MPFC · CANADA
- Motion Picture Foundation of Canada
Canadian Motion Picture Distributors
Association (CMPDA)
Suite 1603

22 St Clair Avenue East
Toronto
Ontario M4T 2S4
tel   +1 416 961 1888
fax   +1 416 968 1016
1989 □ to initiate and execute fund-
raising projects by means of specialised
marketing and merchandising of the
resources of the motion picture, home
video and television industries in order
to achieve the financial goal of the
foundation; to distribute funds to
industry education organisations and
children's charities across Canada; to
facilitate and increase industry
donations and funding to registered
charities; to solicit and enlist a broad
membership of the foundation, with
strong representation from the motion
picture, home video and television
sectors of the industry; to achieve these
objectives while promoting the motion
picture, home video and television
industries.

MPMO · USA
- Motion Picture Machine Operators

MPO · TECHNICAL TERM
- musical power output

MPRF · USA
- Motion Picture Relief Fund

MPTCA · USA
- Motion Picture and Television Credit
Association

MPU · TECHNICAL TERM
- mobile production unit

MQW · TECHNICAL TERM
- multiple quantum well

MRL · TECHNICAL TERM
- multi-role lens

MRS · TECHNICAL TERM
- minimum reporting standards

MRT · JAPAN
- Miyazaki Broadcasting Co Ltd
6-7 Nishi 4-chome
Tachibana-dori

Miyazaki 880
tel +81 985 25 3111
□ television station.

MRTV · MACEDONIA
■ Makedonska Radiotelevizija
Goce Delčev
91000 Skopje
tel +38 91 228410
fax +38 91 236856
□ television and radio service.

MRTV · MONGOLIA
■ Mongol Radio and Television
□ radio and television broadcasting
service.

MS · TECHNICAL TERM
■ master shot
■ medium shot
■ mid shot
■ miniature screw
■ mixed scan

MSB · TECHNICAL TERM
■ most significant bit

MSDS · TECHNICAL TERM
■ multi studio digital system

MSE · TECHNICAL TERM
■ molecular beam epitaxy

MSI · TECHNICAL TERM
■ medium scale integration

MSK · TECHNICAL TERM
■ minimum shift keying

MSN · USA
■ Modern Satellite Network

MSO · TECHNICAL TERM
■ multiple (cable) system operator

MSS · TECHNICAL TERM
■ mobile satellite service

MST · USA
■ Association of Maximum Service
Telecasters
see AMST □ USA

MSU · TECHNICAL TERM

■ main switching unit
■ master set-up unit

MT · TECHNICAL TERM
■ magnetic tape
■ miniature tube

MTBF · TECHNICAL TERM
■ mean time between failures

MTC · GERMANY
■ Media Technology Centre GmbH
Bavariaplatz 7
82031 Geiselgasteig/Munich
tel +49 89 64 99 29 53
fax +49 89 64 99 29 52
□ provides film, video and multimedia
presentations.

MTF · TECHNICAL TERM
■ modular/modulation transfer function

MTM · USA
■ Mary Tyler Moore Enterprises, Inc
4024 Radford Avenue
Studio City
CA 91604
tel +1 818 760 5000
fax +1 818 760 5250
1970 □ producer and distributor of
major US television network dramas
and programmes.

MTS · TECHNICAL TERM
■ multi-channel television sound
■ multi-standard television system

MTT · FRANCE
■ Media Télévision et Téléspectateurs
24 rue d'Aumale
75009 Paris
tel +33 1 42 82 12 25
fax +33 1 42 82 97 66
□ to bring together users of media and
of television; to collect and make
known their aspirations and opinions;
to share their experience and ensure
their full representation at national and
international level. It publishes *La Lettre
des Téléspectateurs* (12) and
L'Observatoire-Critique MTT (1).

MTTF · TECHNICAL TERM
■ mean time to failure

MTTR · TECHNICAL TERM
- mean time to repair

MTV · FINLAND
- Mainos-Televisio
Ilmalantori 2
00240 Helsinki
tel +358 0 15001
fax +358 0 1500721
tlx 125144
1957 □ independent commercial
television company.

MTV · HUNGARY
- Magyar Televízió
Szabadság tér 17
1810 Budapest
tel +36 1 114059
fax +36 1 1574979
tlx 225 568
1957 □ national television broadcasting
service.

MTV · JAPAN
- Mie Television Broadcasting Co Ltd
693-1 Kotani
Shibumi-cho
Tsu 514
tel +81 592 26 1133
□ television station.

MTV · USA
- Music Television
MTV Networks
1515 Broadway
New York
NY 10036
tel +1 212 258 8000
fax +1 212 258 8515
□ cable television network, offering a
programme of music video material.

MTV · TECHNICAL TERM
- music television

MTVRD · MYANMAR
- Myanma Television and Radio
Department
GPO Box 1432
Yangon Taing
Yangon
tel +95 1 31355
tlx 21360
1946 □ radio and television

broadcasting in Arakanese, Burmese,
Chin, English, Kachin, Karen, Kayah,
Mon and Shan.

MUF · TECHNICAL TERM
- maximum usable frequency

MUSE · TECHNICAL TERM
- multiple sub-nyquist sampling
encoder/encoding

MUTV · UK
- Manchester University Television
Productions
University of Manchester
Oxford Road
Manchester M13 9PL
tel +44 61 275 2535
fax +44 61 275 2529
1982 □ acts as a producer of videos in
the fields of training, education and
information for within the university
and for outside groups.

MV · TECHNICAL TERM
- megavolt
- millivolt

MVC · TECHNICAL TERM
- manual volume control

MVDS · TECHNICAL TERM
- microwave video distribution system

MVTR · TECHNICAL TERM
- mobile videotape recorders

MW · TECHNICAL TERM
- medium wave
- megawatt
- microwave
- milliwatt

N

NA · TECHNICAL TERM
- numerical aperture

NAATA · USA
- National Asian American
Telecommunications Association

NAB · JAPAN
- National Association of Commercial Broadcasters in Japan
Bungei-Shunju Building
3-23 Kioi-cho
Chiyoda-ku
Tokyo 102
tel   +81 3 3265 7481
fax   +81 3 3261 2860
tlx   2325163 NABTYO J
1951 □ to strive for the enhancement of broadcast ethics; to promote public welfare through the broadcasting service; to solve problems common to the member commercial broadcasters. It publishes 2 magazines - *Commercial Broadcasting* (34) and *Commercial Broadcasting Monthly* - as well as the books *Japan Commercial Broadcasting Yearbook, Commercial Broadcasting Handbook* (1) and *Japan NAB Handbook* (1).

NAB · USA
- National Association of Broadcasters
1771 N Street NW
Washington
DC 20036
tel   +1 202 429 5300
fax   +1 202 429 5406
1923 □ association of some 8000 members, including representatives from television and radio broadcasting stations and networks, whose aim is to further and promote television and radio broadcasting, at both state and national level. It publishes *TV Today* (52).

NABB · USA
- National Association for Better Broadcasting
Washington
1949 □ organisation which studies television and radio programmes from the point of view of the consumer and with regard to broadcasting regulations. It publishes *Better Radio and Television* (4), as well as various other publications.

NABET · USA
- National Association of Broadcast Employees and Technicians

Suite 800
7101 Wisconsin Avenue
Bethesda
MD 20814
tel   +1 301 657 8420
fax   +1 301 657 9478
1933

NABOB · USA
- National Association of Black Owned Broadcasters
Suite 412
1730 M Street NW
Washington
DC 20036
tel   +1 202 463 8970
fax   +1 202 429 0657
1976 □ organisation comprising black television and radio broadcasting station owners and other interested individuals which defends the interests of black television and radio stations. It produces *NABOB News* (4) and a *Newsletter.*

NABTFP · USA
- National Association of Black Television and Film Producers

NABUG · USA
- National Association of Broadcast Unions and Guilds

NAC · USA
- National Audio-Visual Centre

NAC · TECHNICAL TERM
- national audience composition

NACB · USA
- National Association of College Broadcasters
71 George Street
Providence
RI 02912-1824
tel   +1 401 863 2225
fax   +1 401 863 2221

NACMA · USA
- National Armored Cable Manufacturers Association

NACP · USA
- National Academy of Cable

Programming
1724 Massachusetts Avenue NW
Washington
DC 20036
tel   +1 202 775 3611
fax +1 202 775 3689

NAD · USA
■ National Audience Demographics
Nielsen Media Research
1290 Avenue of the Americas
New York
NY 10104
tel   +1 212 708 7500
fax +1 212 708 7795
□ 2-volume report produced 12 times
each year which provides estimates of
US television usage and sponsored
network programme audiences for both
households and persons. In addition,
person shares are reported.

NAEB · USA
■ National Association of Educational
Broadcasters

NAET · USA
■ National Association for Educational
Television

NAFA · DENMARK
■ Nordic Anthropological Film
Association

NAFB · USA
■ National Association of Farm
Broadcasters
Suite 307
26 E Exchange Street
St Paul
MN 55101
tel   +1 612 224 0508
fax +1 612 224 1956
1944 □ group of television and radio
farm directors involved in broadcasting.

NAFDEC · PAKISTAN
■ National Film Development
Corporation
56-F, Blue Area
PO Box 1204
Islamabad 44000
tel   +92 51 821154 / 823148
fax +92 51 817323

□ national body which promotes and
regulates film in Pakistan.

NAHBO · UK
■ National Association of Hospital
Broadcasting Organisations Ltd
PO Box 2481
London W2 1JR
tel   +44 71 402 8815
1969 □ association which aims to
extend and improve the relief of
sickness, infirmity and old age through
hospital broadcasting. Its main
objectives are: to encourage the
formation of hospital broadcasting
services; to assist in the formation of
such organisations by providing
administrative and technical advice; to
provide a meeting-place and platform
for persons and organisations engaged
in the service; to encourage the
freedom of exchange of ideas and
information; to enable groups of
members to negotiate at national and
regional levels where appropriate. It
publishes *On-Air* magazine (6).

NAHEFV · UK
■ National Association for Higher
Education in Film and Video
c/o London International Film School
24 Shelton Street
London WC2H 9HP
tel   +44 71 836 9642
fax +44 71 497 3718
1983 □ established to represent all
courses in the UK which offer a major
practical study in film, video or
television at the higher education level.
It aims to act as a forum for debate on
all aspects of film, video and television
education and to foster links with
industry, the professions and
government bodies.

NAITPD · USA
■ National Association of Independent
Television Producers and Distributors

NAM · TECHNICAL TERM
■ non-absorbing mirror
■ non-additive mixing

NAMBC · NAMIBIA

■ Namibian Broadcasting Corporation
see **NBC** · NAMIBIA

NAMC · NORWAY
■ National Association of Municipal
Cinemas
see **KKL** · NORWAY

NAMW · USA
■ National Association of Media
Women

NANBA · CANADA
■ North American National
Broadcasters' Association
1500 Bronson Avenue
Ottawa
Ontario K1G 3J5
tel   +1 613 738 6553
fax +1 613 738 6887
tlx   065-28046
1978 □ group of North American
broadcasters who are preoccupied with
issues relevant to international
broadcasting. It produces *NANBA
Bulletin*, and other publications.

NAPA · USA
■ National Association of Performing
Artists

NAPLPS · USA
■ North American Presentation Level
Protocol Syntax

NAPTS · USA
■ National Association of Public
Television Stations

NAR · USA
■ North American Releasing

NAR · TECHNICAL TERM
■ narration
■ net advertising revenue

NARAFI · BELGIUM
■ Nationaal Radio en Filmtechnisch
Instituut
Victor Rousseaulaan, 75
1190 Brussels
tel   +32 2 344 5213
□ film school.

NARBA · USA
■ North American Regional Broadcast
Agreement
1937

NARUC · USA
■ National Association of Regulatory
Utilities Commissioners
□ regulates cable television.

NASCA · USA
■ National Association of State Cable
Agencies

NATAS · USA
■ National Academy of Television Arts
and Sciences
Suite 1020
111 West 57th Street
New York
NY 10019
tel   +1 212 586 8424
fax +1 212 246 8129
1947 □ dedicated to the advancement
of the arts and sciences of television, it
recognises excellence through the
presentation of the Emmy® award. It
publishes the magazine *Television
Quarterly*.
also known as NATVAS

NATESA · USA
■ National Association of Television
and Electronic Servicers of America

NATO · USA
■ National Association of Theatre
Owners
116 North Robertson Boulevard
Plaza Suite F
Los Angeles
CA 90048
tel   +1 310 657 7724
fax +1 310 657 4758
1975 □ it organises NATO/ShoWest,
the annual international convention and
trade fair for the motion picture
industry. It publishes a *Monthly News
Bulletin* (12), as well as the *Annual
NATO/ShoWest Program Journal*.

NATOA · USA
■ National Association of
Telecommunications Officers

NATPE · USA
■ National Association of Television Program Executives
Suite 550E
2425 West Olympic Boulevard
Santa Monica
CA 90404
tel   +1 310 453 5258
tlx   276674 NATP UR

NATRA · USA
■ National Association of Television and Radio Announcers

NATVAS · USA
■ National Academy of Television Arts and Sciences
see **NATAS** · USA

NAVD · USA
■ National Association of Video Distributors
1255 23rd Street NW
Washington
DC 20037
tel   +1 202 872 8545
fax   +1 202 833 3636
1981 □ organisation comprising distributors of home video products, which aims to advance the industry in general.

NAVL · UK
■ National Audio Visual Library
The Arts Building
Normal College (Top Site)
Siliwen Road
Bangor
Gwynedd LL57 2DZ
tel   +44 248 370144
fax   +44 248 351415
1948 □ serves as a single source from which teachers, LEAs and other users can obtain audiovisual materials. It distributes titles from a wide variety of sources and holds for distribution a wide range of 16mm films, videotapes, 35mm filmstrips, 2"x2" slides, overhead projection transparencies, computer software and multimedia kits. It publishes the *Educational Video Catalogue* (1) and a *Teacher In-Service Training Catalogue* (1).

NB · TECHNICAL TERM
■ narrowband
■ noise bandwidth

NBA · BANGLADESH
■ National Broadcasting Authority
see **BNBA** · BANGLADESH

NBAB · BANGLADESH
■ National Broadcasting Authority of Bangladesh
see **BNBA** · BANGLADESH

NBB · THE NETHERLANDS
■ Nederlandse Bond van Bioscopen- en Filmondernemingen
PO Box 5048
Jan Luykenstraat 2
1071 CM Amsterdam
tel   +31 20 679 9261
fax   +31 20 675 0398
□ union of cinema and film companies.

NBC · JAPAN
■ Nagasaki Broadcasting Co Ltd
1-35 Uwa-machi
Nagasaki 850
tel   +81 958 24 3111
□ television station.

NBC · NAMIBIA
■ Namibian Broadcasting Corporation
PO Box 321
Windhoek 9000
tel   +264 61 215811
fax   +264 61 216209
tlx   50908 708
incorporating South West African Broadcasting Corporation (SWABC)
1990 □ autonomous public broadcasting service with a role to inform, educate and entertain by means of television and radio programmes the people of Namibia in order to promote national unity and development.
also known as NAMBC

NBC · USA
■ National Broadcasting Company, Inc
30 Rockefeller Plaza
New York
NY 10112
tel   +1 212 664 6606
fax   +1 212 333 7546

1939 □ television and radio broadcasting network.

NBF · THE NETHERLANDS
■ Beroepvereniging van Film- en Televisiemakers
Jan Luykenstraat 2
1071 CM Amsterdam
tel +31 20 664 6588
fax +31 20 664 3707
1952 □ association of directors working in film and television which publishes *Film en TV Maker* (11), *Intern Bulletin* (4) and *NBF Adressengids* (1).

NBFM · TECHNICAL TERM
■ narrowband frequency modulation

NBMC · USA
■ National Black Media Coalition
38 New York Avenue NE
Washington
DC 20002
tel +1 202 387 8155
fax +1 202 462 4469
1973 □ group which promotes and campaigns for the maximum possible access for blacks throughout the communications media.

NBN · JAPAN
■ Nagoya Broadcasting Networks
9-18 Tachibana 2-chome
Naka-ku
Nagoya 460-77
tel +81 52 331 8111
□ television station.

NBP · TECHNICAL TERM
■ no baseband processing

NBS · JAPAN
■ Nagano Broadcasting System
131-7 Okada-cho
Nagano 380
tel +81 262 27 3000
□ television station.

NC · TECHNICAL TERM
■ noise cancellor
■ noiseless camera

NCAR · USA
■ Nielsen Cable Activity Report

Nielsen Media Research
1290 Avenue of the Americas
New York
NY 10104
tel +1 212 708 7500
fax +1 212 708 7795
□ this quarterly report provides household viewing data in 24 dayparts for all national Nielsen metered viewing options. Ratings, shares and cumulative audiences are reported for specific cable and broadcast network affiliates for total US cable and pay cable households.

NCATA · CANADA
■ National Cable Antenna Television Association of Canada

NCC · JAPAN
■ Nagasaki Culture Telecasting Corporation
3-2 Mori-machi
Nagasaki 852
tel +81 958 43 1000
□ television station.

NCCB · USA
■ National Citizens Committee for Broadcasting

NCFDITFS · USA
■ National Committee for the Full Development of Instructional Television Fixed Services

NCFT · USA
■ National Council for Families and Television

NCI · USA
■ National Captioning Institute
Suite 1500
5203 Leesburg Pike
Falls Church
VA 22041
tel +1 703 998 2400
fax +1 703 998 2458

NCN · USA
■ National Christian Network
1150 West King Street
Cocoa
FL 32922-8686

tel +1 407 632 1000
□ cable television network.

NCORT · USA
▪ National Catholic Office for Radio and Television

NCRV · THE NETHERLANDS
▪ Nederlandse Christelijke Radio Vereniging
Bergweg 30
PO Box 121
1200 JE Hilversum
tel +31 35 719911
fax +31 35 719285
tlx 43249
1924 □ Protestant television and radio station.

NCSCT · USA
▪ National Center for School and College Television

NCT · USA
▪ National College Television
□ cable television network.

NCTA · USA
▪ National Cable Television Association Inc
1724 Massachusetts Avenue NW
Washington
DC 20036-1969
tel +1 202 775 3550
fax +1 202 775 3604
1952 □ association of **CATV** operators, working to limit the regulatory powers of government over cable operations.

NCTI · CANADA
▪ Nation's Capital Television Incorporated
PO Box 5813
Merivale Depot
Nepean
Ontario K2C 3G6
tel +1 613 224 1313
fax +1 613 224 7998

NCTI · USA
▪ National Cable Television Institute
801 West Mineral Avenue
Littleton
CO 80120-4501

tel +1 303 761 8554
fax +1 303 797 9394
1968 □ provides training for those working in cable television.

NCTV · USA
▪ National Council on Television Violence

ND · TECHNICAL TERM
▪ neutral density
▪ non-directional

NDF · TECHNICAL TERM
▪ non-drop frame

NDR · GERMANY
▪ Norddeutscher Rundfunk
Rothenbaumchaussee 132-134
20149 Hamburg
tel +49 40 41560
fax +49 40 447602
tlx 2198910
1956 □ regional broadcasting organisation.

NDS · TECHNICAL TERM
▪ non-domestic satellite service

NECCTA
▪ National Educational Closed-Circuit Television Association

NEF · FRANCE
▪ Nouvelles Editions de Films

NEFVF · USA
▪ National Educational Film & Video Festival
655 Thirteenth Street
Oakland
CA 94611
tel +1 510 465 6885
fax +1 510 465 2835
1970 □ one of the largest and most important annual US competitions for educational media, NEFVF Gold Apple winners qualify for entry into the Academy of Motion Picture Arts and Sciences' (**AMPAS**) Oscar® competition. Over 1400 entries worldwide compete in 180 subject categories and are judged by subject specialists and media professionals,

users and buyers. NEFVF also sponsors an annual Media Market, a unique marketplace which showcases independent productions for non-theatrical distributors seeking new acquisitions. A NEFVF-sponsored conference is held each spring, bringing together film/video producers, distributors, buyers and users of educational media. The 6-day conference features screenings of over 45 documentaries in 2 venues, numerous seminars and workshops, a variety of social events and the Media Market. The organisation also sponsors a variety of media literacy and production programmes which involve nearly 2000 local students per year.

NEM · TECHNICAL TERM
■ new electronic media

NEMA · USA
■ National Electrical Manufacturers Association
Suite 300
2101 L Street NW
Washington
DC 20037
tel   +1 202 457 8400
fax +1 202 457 8411

NEMTC · UK
■ North East Media Training Centre
Stonehills
Shields Road
Gateshead
Tyne and Wear NE10 OHW
tel   +44 91 438 4044
fax +44 91 438 5508
1986 □ non-profit making group established by a local group of independent television production companies, freelance technicians and individuals interested in creating opportunities for film and television training in north-east England. Its main aims are: to provide truly professional training for new entrants; to reskill and retrain redundant and existing televisual workers; to develop international links.

NEP · TECHNICAL TERM
■ noise equivalent power

NETFA · UK
■ North East Television and Film Archive
Library and Media Services Unit
University of Teeside
Borough Road
Middlesborough
Cleveland TS1 3BA
tel   +44 642 342115
fax +44 642 244140
1986 □ regional archive which contains some 100 000' of **BBC** North Eastern news film and some 400 000' of footage from programmes produced by Tyne Tees Television (**TTTV**).

NF · TECHNICAL TERM
■ noise figure
■ normal frequency

NFA · UK
■ National Film Archive
see **NFTVA** · UK

NFB · CANADA
■ National Film Board of Canada
■ Office National du Film du Canada (ONF)
PO Box 1600
Station A
Montreal
Quebec H3C 3H5
tel   +1 514 283 9439
fax +1 514 496 1895
1939 □ to initiate and promote the production and distribution of films in the national interest, with the primary object of interpreting Canada to Canadians and to other nations. The International Program of NFB is responsible for all foreign sales and marketing of NFB products and through its 4 offices sells and licenses films and videos to television, theatrical and non-theatrical and home video markets worldwide.
also known as NFBC

NFBC · CANADA
■ National Film Board of Canada
see **NFB/ONF** · CANADA

NFC · THE NETHERLANDS
■ Nederlandse Federatie voor de

Cinematografie
Jan Luykenstraat 2
1071 CM Amsterdam
tel   +31 20 679 9261
fax +31 20 675 0398
1928 □ Dutch cinematographic
association which takes care of the
mutual interest of cinema exhibitors,
film distributors and feature film
producers. It publishes *Film* (8).

NFC · SRI LANKA
▪ National Film Corporation
1972 □ national body responsible for
promoting and administering cinema.

NFD · TECHNICAL TERM
▪ narrow field acquisition detector

NFDC · INDIA
▪ National Film Development
Corporation
6th floor, Discovery of India
Nehru Centre
Dr Annie Besant Road
Worli
Bombay 400 018
tel   +91 22 494 9855 / 494 9971
fax +91 22 494 9751
tlx   011 73489 NFDC IN
1980 □ financing and production of
low budget and quality films; financing
construction of cinemas; import of
foreign films and export of Indian films;
distribution and exhibition of films;
international film coproduction;
marketing of legal video cassettes; fight
against video piracy. It publishes
Cinema in India (12).

NFDF · UK
▪ National Film Development Fund
see **BSD** · UK

NFF · NORWAY
▪ Norsk Filmforbund
Storengveien 8 B
N-1342 Jar
tel   +47 67 59 10 00
fax +47 67 12 48 65
1946 □ association representing its film
worker members which also strives to
strengthen the position of Norwegian
cinema both at home and abroad. It

publishes *Rush Print* (8).

NFFC · UK
▪ National Film Finance Corporation
see **NFTC** · UK

NFK · NORWAY
▪ Norsk Filmklubbforbund
Teatergata 3
N-0180 Oslo 1
tel   +47 22 11 42 17
fax +47 22 20 79 81
1968 □ federation of film societies,
whose aim is the promotion of film art.
It publishes *Z* magazine (4) and various
booklets.

NFLCP · USA
▪ National Federation of Local Cable
Programmers
*now called The Alliance for
Community Media*

NFSA · AUSTRALIA
▪ National Film and Sound Archive
McCoy Circuit
Acton
ACT 2601
tel   +61 6 267 1711
fax +61 6 267 4651
tlx   AA 61930
□ archive holding over 50 000 film and
video titles, as well as stills, scripts,
posters and other material.

NFT · UK
▪ National Film Theatre
South Bank
Waterloo
London SE1 8XT
tel   +44 71 928 3535
       +41 71 928 3232 *(box office)*
fax +44 71 623 9323
1952 □ to bring audiences the widest
possible range of film and television
from all over the world, screened in the
best possible conditions and supported
by background, notes, lectures and
other activities designed to stimulate
debate, inform and entertain.

NFTC · UK
▪ National Film Trustee Company
c/o British Screen Finance

14-17 Wells Mews
London W1P 3FL
tel +44 71 323 9080
fax +44 71 323 0092
1971 □ independent revenue collection
agency which monitors, collects and
disburses revenues generated by the
exploitation of most films which British
Screen (**BSD**) has helped to finance,
together with many films previously
backed by the National Film Finance
Corporation (**NFFC**). It also handles a
number of films in which neither the
NFFC nor British Screen is involved,
since the service which the NFTC
provides is regarded by some
independent producers as an efficient
and economical form of insurance.

NFTS · UK
▪ National Film and Television School
Beaconsfield Studios
Station Road
Beaconsfield
Bucks HP9 1LG
tel +44 494 671234
fax +44 494 674042
1971 □ to provide training in the art of
film and television programme making
through a range of courses, lasting up
to 3 years.

NFTVA · THE NETHERLANDS
▪ Nederlandse Film en Televisie
Academie
Ite Boeremastraat 1
1054 PP Amsterdam
tel +31 20 683 0206
fax +31 20 612 6266
1958 □ provides a 4-year full-time
course for makers of film, television
and audiovisual programmes. Specialist
courses are offered after the first year's
study. It also offers a 4-year full-time
teachers training for audiovisual
education.

NFTVA · UK
▪ National Film and Television Archive
21 Stephen Street
London W1P 1PL
tel +44 71 255 1444
fax +44 71 580 7503
tlx 27624 BFILDNG

1935 □ to acquire, preserve and make
permanently available a national
collection of moving images which
have lasting value as examples of the
art and history of cinema and
television, or as a documentary record
of the 20th century. It now holds
approximately 280 000 titles dating
from 1895 to the present day. The
collection includes newsreels, features
and short films, animation, documentaries, television programmes and
amateur films.
formerly National Film Archive (NFA)

NFU · NEW ZEALAND
▪ National Film Unit
PO Box 31444
Lower Hutt
Wellington
tel +64 4 619 0759
fax +64 4 567 4411

NFV · GERMANY
▪ Norddeutscher Filmhersteller Verband
Jenfelder Allee 80
22039 Hamburg
tel +49 40 66 885381
fax +49 40 66 885369
□ North German film-makers
association.

NFVPF · NORWAY
▪ Norske Film- og Videoprodusenters
Forening
Storengveien 8 B
N-1342 Jar
tel +47 67 53 74 98
fax +47 67 12 48 65
□ Norwegian film and video producers
association.

NG · TECHNICAL TERM
▪ no good (*aka* N/G)

NHI · USA
▪ Nelson Holdings International

NHK · JAPAN
▪ Nippon Hoso Kyokai
NHK Hoso Centre
2-2-1 Jinnan
Shibuya-ku
Tokyo 150

tel   +81 3 465 1111
fax   +81 3 481 1576
tlx   22377
1925 □ public broadcasting
corporation, operating 5 networks (2
television, 3 radio) and 2 **DBS** television
services.

NHTI · USA
▪ Nielsen Hispanic Television Index
Nielsen Media Research
1290 Avenue of the Americas
New York
NY 10104
tel   +1 212 708 7500
fax   +1 212 708 7795
1992 □ report which allows customers
to evaluate Spanish language television
more effectively using the same
research methodology as other national
television. It provides a wealth of
information about the TV viewing habits
of the fastest growing segment of the
United States. The data reported will be
based on viewing information from the
Nielsen People Meter from a separate
sample of randomly selected Hispanic
households.

NI · TECHNICAL TERM
▪ network identification

NIAM · THE NETHERLANDS
▪ Nederlands Instituut voor
Audiovisuele Media
Neuhurnyskade 94
Postbus 97734
2509 GK The Hague
tel   +31 70 314 3500
tel   +31 70 314 3588
□ Dutch institute for audiovisual media.

NIB · JAPAN
▪ Nagasaki International Television
Broadcasting Inc
11-1 Dejima-machi
Nagasaki
tel   +81 958 20 3000
□ television station.

NIC · TECHNICAL TERM
▪ nearly instantaneous companding

NICAM · TECHNICAL TERM

▪ near instantaneously companded
audio multiplex

NIKFI · RUSSIA
▪ Vsesojuzny Nauchno-Issledovateljsky
Kinophotoinstitut
Leningrad prospect 47
125167 Moscow
tel   +7 095 157 2923
tlx   7508
1929 □ cinematographic and
photographic scientific and research
institute.

NIMC · BANGLADESH
▪ National Institute of Mass
Communication
59/A Shatsmasjid Road
Dhanmondi
Dhaka 1209
tel   +880 2 811668 / 325051-5
fax   +880 2 832927
tlx   675624 BTV BJ
1980 □ apex training centre for the
development of mass communication,
whose main objective is to develop
professional skills and increase
technical knowledge of broadcasting
personnel working in television, film,
radio and other media.
also known as NIMCO

NIMCO · BANGLADESH
▪ National Institute of Mass
Communication
see **NIMC** · BANGLADESH

NIS · THE NETHERLANDS
▪ Netherlands Information Service
Anna Paulownastraat 76
2518 BJ Den Haag
tel   +31 70 356 4205
fax   +31 70 356 4681
tlx   33159
□ in charge of the international
distribution of audiovisual media, with
some 300 titles on film and video. The
NIS audiovisual archive also holds
considerable footage concerning
historic films.

NITA · USA
▪ National Instructional Television
Association

NITC · USA
■ National Instructional Television Center

NKFF · NORWAY
■ Norsk Kino- og Filmfond
Stortingsgt. 16
0161 Oslo 1
tel +47 22 33 05 30
fax +47 22 42 89 49
1970 □ foundation to support the import, distribution and screening of quality and children's films; to support and manage film programming of the Norwegian Film Festival in Haugesund; to organise courses for cinema-managers and projectionists; to offer technical guidance; to launch commercial films; to develop film-study material for schools. It publishes *Film som kommer* (7-10).

NKT · JAPAN
■ Nihon-Kai Telecasting Co Ltd
3-102 Hon-machi
Tottori 680
tel +81 857 24 7111
□ television station.

NMFE · UK
■ New Media for Europe
Stephen Rance, Secretary
6 Redwood Mount
Beech Road
Reigate
Surrey RH2 9NR
□ academic research group comprising individuals interested in the future of new media and communications technology within the EC.

NMM · UK
■ New Media Markets
Financial Times Newsletters
30/31 Great Sutton Street
London SE1 9HL
tel +44 71 873 3000
fax +44 71 873 3195
1983 □ newsletter published every 2 weeks providing detailed coverage of new developments in media, including cable and satellite.

NMOS · TECHNICAL TERM

■ N-channel metal-oxide semiconductor

NOB · THE NETHERLANDS
■ Nederlandse Omroepproductie Bedrijf
PO Box 10
1200 JB Hilversum
tel +31 35 775445
fax +31 35 775444
tlx 73015
□ audiovisual production centre which provides technical services for the Dutch public broadcasting organisations, and also works for foreign television and radio stations, independent producers, industry and government. It is also responsible for the daily transmissions on national Dutch television and radio channels.

NOMIC · TECHNICAL TERM
■ nouvel ordre mondial de l'information et de la communication

NOS · THE NETHERLANDS
■ Nederlandse Omroepprogramma Stichting
Postbus 26444
1202 JJ Hilversum
tel +31 35 779222
fax +31 35 772649
tlx 43312
1969 □ broadcasting of television and radio programmes; umbrella organisation for Dutch national public broadcasting. It publishes *HilverSummary* (4).

NOT · THE NETHERLANDS
■ Stichting Nederlandse Onderwijs-Televisie
Noordse Bosje 18
1211 BG Hilversum
tel +31 35 723611
fax +31 35 210143
□ educational television channel.

NOW · UK
■ Network of Workshops
Video in Pilton
30 Ferry Road Avenue
Edinburgh EH4 4BA
tel +44 31 343 1151
fax +44 31 343 2820

□ network of independent film and video workshops in England, Northern Ireland, Scotland and Wales.

NPA · TECHNICAL TERM
■ network programme analysis

NPACT · USA
■ National Public Affairs Center for Television

NPC · TECHNICAL TERM
■ non-phased colour

NPITI · USA
■ National Project for the Improvement of Televised Instruction

NPPAG · USA
■ National Program Production and Acquisition Grant

NPR · TECHNICAL TERM
■ noise power ratio

NPS · USA
■ National Program Service
Public Broadcasting Service
1320 Braddock Place
Alexandria
VA 22314
tel   +1 703 739 5000
fax +1 703 739 0775
1969 □ operated by **PBS**, public television's general-audience NPS provides quality children's, cultural, educational, news and public affairs, science and nature, fund-raising and skills programmes to 346 non-commercial television stations serving all 50 states, Puerto Rico, the Virgin Islands, Guam and American Samoa.

NR · TECHNICAL TERM
■ noise reduction

NRB · USA
■ National Religious Broadcasters
7839 Ashton Avenue
Manassas
VA 22110
tel   +1 703 330 7000
fax +1 703 330 7100
1944 □ international organisation

comprising television and radio programme producers and broadcasters whose aim is to provide and promote religious programming in the television and radio formats. It publishes *Religious Broadcasting Magazine* (12) and *Directory of Religious Broadcasting* (1).

NRK · NORWAY
■ Norsk Rikskringkasting
Bjørnstjerne Bjørnsons Plass
0340 Oslo 1
tel   +47 22 45 90 50
fax +47 22 45 96 45
tlx 76820
□ public service broadcasting corporation.

NRP · TECHNICAL TERM
■ net rating points

NRZ · TECHNICAL TERM
■ non-return to zero

NRZ-L · TECHNICAL TERM
■ non-return to zero-level

NRZ-M · TECHNICAL TERM
■ non-return to zero-mask

NRZ-S · TECHNICAL TERM
■ non-return to zero-space

NS · TECHNICAL TERM
■ nanosecond
■ no sound

NSC · CANADA
■ New Studio City
Vancouver
□ production company.

NSC · UK
■ Northern Screen Commission
Stonehills
Shields Road
Gateshead
Tyne and Wear NE10 OHW
tel   +44 91 469 1000
fax +44 91 469 7000
1992 □ will assist production companies using the North of England. It carries out preliminary research on locations, can organise recces of

locations, gives advice and support when dealing with public agencies. It has extensive knowledge, through its database and local networks, about facilities, services and talent. By using its services, production companies are spared the trouble of finding their way through bureaucracy. They benefit from local knowledge and, by dealing with people who understand their needs, save time and money.

NSC · TECHNICAL TERM
■ network switching centre

NSFDC · CANADA
■ Nova Scotia Film Development Corporation
1724 Granville Street
Halifax
Nova Scotia B3J 1X5
tel   +1 902 424 7177
fax +1 902 424 0617
1990 □ to fund the development and production of motion picture and video projects which contribute to the cultural life and economic health of the province of Nova Scotia. Projects must have a significant Canadian technical, artistic and creative content.

NSFTV · UK
■ Northern School of Film and Television
Leeds Metropolitan University
Caverley Street
Leeds LS1 3HE
tel   +44 532 832600
fax +44 532 833112
1989 □ to provide an advanced level practical training and education in professional film and television. The emphasis of the course is the achievement of professional standards under pressure, yet still retaining creative control. There are intensive programmes of scriptwriting and production and the school benefits from substantial industry sponsorship.

NSI · USA
■ Nielsen Station Index
Nielsen Media Research
1290 Avenue of the Americas

New York
NY 10104
tel   +1 212 708 7500
fax +1 212 708 7795
□ measures television audiences and provides season-to-season trend reports and time period viewing estimates in all local markets in the Continental United States, Hawaii and Alaska. Data provided include ¼ hour/½ hour audiences for programme and time period evaluation by households and a wide range of demographic breaks. This audience research serves as the basis for buying and selling television time in local markets; the information is also used to evaluate an advertiser's investment in both spot and network television in those markets.

NSS · USA
■ Nielsen Syndication Service
Nielsen Media Research
1290 Avenue of the Americas
New York
NY 10104
tel   +1 212 708 7500
fax +1 212 708 7795
□ the weekly *NSS Pocketpiece™* report provides household and persons audience estimates on programmes distributed by subscribing syndicators and producers for which ratings information was ordered. The report also contains total audience, station counts, programme coverage and gross average audience.

NSS · TECHNICAL TERM
■ non-synchronous switch

NST · JAPAN
■ Niigata Sogo Television Co Ltd
11-31 Kamitokoro 1-chome
Niigata 950
tel   +81 25 245 8181
□ television station.

NSTP · USA
■ National Society of Television Producers

NSWFTO · AUSTRALIA
■ New South Wales Film and

Television Office
Level 6
1 Francis Street
East Sydney
NSW 2010
tel   +61 2 380 5599
fax +61 2 380 1095
□ state government film body.

NT · TECHNICAL TERM
■ noise temperature

NT-21 · JAPAN
■ Niigata Television Network 21 Inc
2230-19 Rokunocho
Shimo-okawa Maedori
Niigata 950
tel   +81 25 223 0021
□ television station.

NTA · NIGERIA
■ Nigerian Television Authority
Television House
Ahmadu Bello Way
Victoria Island
PO Box 12036
Lagos
tel   +234 1 614966 / 615154 / 612529
fax +234 1 610289 / 619485
tlx   22536 NTA HQ / 21245 NTV NG
1977 □ to ensure the establishment and
maintenance of standards and to
promote the efficient operation of the
broadcasting system in accordance with
national policy.

NTA · TECHNICAL TERM
■ news transmission assistant

NTC · USA
■ Network Transmission Committee

NTFC · USA
■ National Television Film Council

NTFDC · USA
■ National Video and Film Distributors
Council
c/o International Communications
Industries Association (ICIA)
3150 Spring Street
Fairfax
VA 22031
tel   +1 703 273 7200

fax +1 703 278 8082
1945 □ organisation comprising film
and video distributors and companies
which aims to circulate educational
videos and film productions to schools,
libraries and other markets.

NTI® · USA
■ Nielsen Television Index
Nielsen Media Research
1290 Avenue of the Americas
New York
NY 10104
tel   +1 212 708 7500
fax +1 212 708 7795
□ the weekly *NTI Pocketpiece™* reports
the level of audience during the ¼ hour
in which a commercial is aired. It
contains information about national
television including: household and
persons audience estimates for all
sponsored network programmes;
demographics matched to specific
daypart target audiences; quarter-to-
date programme averages; premiere-to-
date programme averages; programme
type averages; household and persons
TV usage by time period; household
ratings and shares by half-hour for 4
different station groups; **VCR**
contribution by programme.
The annual *NTI Planners' Report*
provides convenient trends of television
audience and cost data needed in the
planning of network television buys.
The quarterly *Up-Front-Buying Guide*
(UFBG) provides estimates of household
and persons television usage and
network audiences by daypart and by
half-hour time periods. The quarterly
Households Using Television (HUT)
summary provides individual week
estimates of total US television
household usage for each ½ hour time
period by week, and day of the week,
as well as for Mon-Fri and Mon-Sun.
Each report also includes TV usage
averages by ½ hours for the most
recent 12 months, individually for the
most recent 4 quarters and as an
annual average. NTI also publishes
numerous special releases and
supplementary reports.

NTL · UK
- National Transcommunications Ltd
Crawley Court
Winchester
Hampshire SO21 2QA
tel +44 962 822243
fax +44 962 822374
1991 □ the provision of transmission
and broadcast services, transmitting the
programmes of **ITV**, **C4**, **S4C** in Wales
and independent radio stations in
Britain. It is also developing a range of
products and services for a growing
international customer base, including
system design and project management
from small-scale to total turnkey
contracts.

NTSC · TECHNICAL TERM
- National Television System
Committee

NTV · JAPAN
- Nippon Television Network
Corporation
14 Niban-cho
Chiyoda-ku
Tokyo 102-40
tel +81 3 5275 4139
fax +81 3 5275 4008
tlx J24566
□ television station.

NTVA · SOUTH AFRICA
- National Television and Video
Association
PO Box 84707
Greenside 2034
tel +27 11 888 6035
fax +27 11 885 6036
□ is dedicated to keeping its members
informed of advances in technology
and systems, and promotes high
standards for the below-the-line video
production industry.

NV · TECHNICAL TERM
- nanovolt

NVALA · UK
- National Viewers' and Listeners'
Association
Ardleigh
Colchester

Essex CO7 7RH
tel +44 206 230123
also known as NVLA
1964 □ monitors television and radio
programme content and stimulates
public and parliamentary concern
about moral standards in the media,
especially regarding the cumulative
effects of violent entertainment upon
society. It publishes *The Viewer and
Listener* (3).

NVASP · UK
- National Video Archive of Stage
Performance
The Theatre Museum
1E Tavistock Street
London WC2E 7PA
tel +44 71 836 7891
fax +44 71 836 5148
1991 □ to create a record of stage
performances which will provide
theatre professionals, researchers,
students and academics with a wealth
of usable material and which will
become a collection for posterity.

NVC · USA
- National Video Corporation

NVLA · UK
- National Viewers' and Listeners'
Association
see **NVALA** · UK

NVPI · THE NETHERLANDS
- Nederlandse Vereniging van
Producenten en Importeurs van Beeld-
en Geluiddragers
Albertus Perkstraat 36
1217 NT Hilversum
tel +31 35 240951
fax +31 35 241954
tlx 73564 nvpi nl
1972 □ represents audio and video
producers and distributors, giving
objective information about
developments in both markets and
negotiates with users concerning
released material of its members. NVPI
is the national group of the
International Federation of the
Phonographic Industry (**IFPI**) and the
International Video Federation (IVF). It

publishes a *Yearbook, Newsletter Audio and Video* and *Statistics Audio and Video*.

NVR · USA
■ National Video Resources
Suite 606
73 Spring Street
New York
NY 10012
tel +1 212 274 8080
fax +1 212 274 8081
1990 □ to increase the public's awareness of, and access to, a wide range of high quality, independent work including narrative films, documentaries, video art and performing arts on videocassette. It works to identify the problems facing independent media and to design and implement a long-term strategy that addresses those issues. It publishes *Library Video Review* (4).

NVRAM · TECHNICAL TERM
■ non-volatile random-access memory

NWFA · UK
■ North West Film Archive
Manchester Metropolitan University
Minshull House
47-49 Chorlton Street
Manchester M1 3EU
tel +44 61 247 3097/8
fax +44 61 247 3098
1977 □ the recognised public home for moving images (film, videotape and television programmes) relating to Greater Manchester, Lancashire and Cheshire. Its main responsibilities are the custodianship and development of its collection (acquisition; preservation; documentation and storage) in order to secure this exciting record of 20th century life for future generations. In addition, public and commercial access services are provided. It produces a *Newsletter* (1).

NWIO · TECHNICAL TERM
■ new world information order

NZFC · NEW ZEALAND
■ New Zealand Film Commission

■ Te Tumu Whakaata Tonga
PO Box 11-546
Wellington
tel +64 4 385 9754
fax +64 4 384 9719
tlx NZ30386 FILMCOM
1978 □ development, production, exhibition and promotion of New Zealand cinema.

O

O&O · TECHNICAL TERM
■ owned and operated

O/P · TECHNICAL TERM
■ output

OAR · TECHNICAL TERM
■ open architecture receiver

OAT · TECHNICAL TERM
■ on-air test

OB · TECHNICAL TERM
■ outside broadcast

OBS · JAPAN
■ Oita Broadcasting System
1-1 Imazuru 3-chome
Oita 870
tel +81 975 58 1111
□ television station.

OBT · TECHNICAL TERM
■ orbital test satellite (*aka* OTS)

OC · TECHNICAL TERM
■ on camera

OCB · TECHNICAL TERM
■ octal coded binary

OCIC · BELGIUM
■ Organisation Catholique Internationale du Cinéma et de l'Audiovisuel
■ Organización Católica Internacionale del Cine y del Audiovisual
8 rue de l'Orme
B-1040 Brussels
tel +32 2 734 4294

fax +32 2 734 3207
tlx via Geonet-Luxembourg-0402
6105905
1928 □ non-governmental organisation with over 100 members specialising in cinema and audiovisuals. Its activities include aid in the production and distribution of quality films and audiovisuals; the development of media infrastructures to serve the promotion of man and understanding between peoples; training professionals in the communication professions; and educating the public to exercise their critical faculties. It also contributes to the development of the media in the field of the Catholic Church's education and evangelical tasks, and publishes *Cine & Media* (6), a *Yearbook* and various other publications.

OCINAM · MALI
■ Office Cinématographique National du Mali
□ organisation for the distribution and promotion of films.

OCL · TECHNICAL TERM
■ on-chip lens

OCP · TECHNICAL TERM
■ operational control panel

OCS · TECHNICAL TERM
■ oscillating colour sequence

OCST · USA
■ Office of Cable Signal Theft
c/o National Cable Television Association Inc (NCTA)
1724 Massachusetts Avenue NW
Washington
DC 20036
tel +1 202 775 3550
fax +1 202 775 3604

ODC · USA
■ Optical Disc Corporation
12150 Mora Drive
Santa Fe Springs
CA 90670
tel +1 310 946 3050
fax +1 310 946 6030
□ manufactures laserdisc recording

systems and recordable laser videodiscs (**RLV**) which are compatible with standard laservision or laserdisc format consumer and industrial players.

ODP™ · TECHNICAL TERM
■ over discharge protection

ODTV · NIGERIA
■ Ondo State Television
see **OSTV** · NIGERIA

OEC · USA
■ Office of Emergency Communications
□ office within the Federal Communications Commission (**FCC**)

OEM · TECHNICAL TERM
■ original equipment manufacturer

OFA · CANADA
■ Ontario Film Association
Suite 1341
3-1750 The Queensway
Etobicoke
Ontario M9C 5H5

OFCG · TECHNICAL TERM
■ Overflow Control Gate

OFDC · CANADA
■ Ontario Film Development Corporation
■ Société de Développement de l'Industrie Cinématographique Ontarienne
Suite 300
175 Bloor Street E
North Tower
Toronto
Ontario M4W 3R8
tel +1 416 314 6858
fax +1 416 314 6876
tlx 06 219728
□ provincial government agency which helps finance film productions, from both domestic and foreign producers, which are filmed in Ontario.

OFDM · TECHNICAL TERM
■ orthogonal frequency division multiplex(ing)

ÖFF · AUSTRIA

■ Österreichischer Filmförderungsfonds

OFF · SWEDEN
■ Oberoende Filmares Förbund
Tantogatan 49
S-118 42 Stockholm
tel +46 8 720 6628
fax +46 8 658 5265
1984 □ association of some 270
independent producers and film-makers
in Sweden, active primarily in the
matters of media policy and rights.

OFRT · FRANCE
■ Organismes Français de
Radiodiffusion et de Télévision

OFS · TECHNICAL TERM
■ operational fixed service

OGFKM · AUSTRIA
■ Österreichische Gesellschaft für
Filmwissenschaft, Kommunications- und
Medienforschung
Rauhensteingasse 5/3
1010 Vienna 1
tel +43 1 512 9936
fax +43 1 513 5330
1952 □ institute, archive and library
which promotes cooperation between
all those involved in scientific research
into television and film. It publishes the
journals *Filmkunst* (4) and *Mitteilungen*
(8/10).

OGTV · NIGERIA
■ Ogun State Television
Abeokuta
□ state-owned television station.

OHK · JAPAN
■ Okayama Broadcasting Co Ltd
2-1 Gakunan-cho 3-chome
Okayama 700
tel +81 862 52 3211
□ television station.

OIRT · CZECH REPUBLIC
■ Organisation Internationale de Radio
et de Télévision
*now incorporated under European
Broadcasting Union (EBU)*

OIT · MEXICO

■ Organisation Ibéroamericaine de
Télévision
see **OTI** · MEXICO

OIV · UK
■ Oxford Independent Video
Pegasus Theatre
Magdalen Road
Oxford OX4 1RE
tel +44 865 250150
fax +44 865 204976
1986 □ specialist arts producer,
distributor and trainer, working in
collaboration with innovative artists and
performers from across the world,
carefully selecting and commissioning a
broad range of high quality work. Its
tapes are distributed internationally.

OJD · SPAIN
■ Oficina de Justificación de la Difusión
Sainz de Baranda 35
28009 Madrid
tel +34 1 574 7002
fax +34 1 574 3650

OK · RUSSIA
■ Ostankino Kanal
ul. Akademika Korol'ova 19
Moscow 127427
tel +7 095 217 9666
fax +7 095 215 9868
1992 □ television channel.

OLON · THE NETHERLANDS
■ Organisatie van Lokale Omroepen
Nederland
Postbus 441
6500 AK Nijmegen
tel +31 80 601222
fax +31 80 601656
□ organisation of local radio and
television broadcasting companies.

OM · TECHNICAL TERM
■ operations manager

OMI · THE NETHERLANDS
■ Onderwijs Media Instituut
PO Box 80125
3508 TC Utrecht
tel +31 30 531314
fax +31 30 515463
1993 □ production of video,

photography, digital printing, CD-I, CD photo and offset printing.

OMT · TECHNICAL TERM
- orthogonal mode transducer
- orthomodal transducer

OMUX · TECHNICAL TERM
- output multiplexer

ONACI · CONGO
- Office National du Cinéma
BP 1068
Brazzaville
1979 □ official organisation with responsibility for cinema.

ONF · CANADA
- Office National du Film du Canada
- National Film Board of Canada (NFB)
3155 Chemin de la Côte de Liesse
CP 1600, succ. A
Montreal
Quebec H3C 3H5
tel   +1 514 283 9247
fax   +1 514 496 1895
1939 □ to initiate and promote the production and distribution of films in the national interest, with the primary object of interpreting Canada to Canadians and to other nations. The International Program of ONF is responsible for all foreign sales and marketing of ONF products and through its 4 offices sells and licenses films and videos to television, theatrical and non-theatrical and home video markets worldwide.
also known as NFBC

ONI · UK
- Optical Networks International
Unit 4
Chailey Estate
Pump Lane
Hayes
Middlesex UB3 3NU
tel   +44 81 569 3724
fax   +44 81 813 6063
□ optical transportation systems.

OOK · TECHNICAL TERM
- on-off keying

OOV · TECHNICAL TERM
- out-of-vision

OPP · TECHNICAL TERM
- optimal pivot point

OPT · USA
- Operation Prime Time

OQPSK · TECHNICAL TERM
- offset quadrature phase shift keying

OR · TECHNICAL TERM
- optical receiver
- outside rehearsals

ORF · AUSTRIA
- Österreichischer Rundfunk
ORF Zentrum
Würzburggasse 30
1136 Vienna
tel   +43 1 222 87 8780
fax   +43 1 222 87 878 2250
tlx   133601 orfz a
1974 □ national television and radio network, established as an independent public-law institution. Its objectives are: unbiased reporting on current affairs relating to the most prominent areas of social and political interests; to provide information, science, economy, sports, education and culture; to transmit feature films, recreation, light entertainment and practical help; to offer comprehensive and independent information in reports on global politics and domestic affairs; to transmit local radio and television programmes produced and disseminated in the Austrian provinces or lands.

ORTB · BENIN
- Office de Radiodiffusion et Télévision de Benin
PO Box 366
Cotonou
tel   +229 301 0628
□ government-controlled television and radio broadcasting service.

ORTM · MAURITANIA
- Office de Radiodiffusion et Télévision de Mauritanie
BP 200

Nouakchott
tel +222 52164
tlx 515
1958 □ state radio and television broadcasting service.

ORTN · NIGER
▪ Office de Radiodiffusion et Télévision du Niger
BP 309
Niamey
tel +227 723163
fax +227 723548
tlx 5229 NI
1979 □ television service.

ORTS · SENEGAL
▪ Office de Radiodiffusion et Télévision Sénégalais
▪ Office de Radio-Télévision du Sénégal
58 Avenue de la République
BP 1765
Dakar
tel +221 211472
fax +221 212545
tlx 51-634
□ national television broadcasting service.

OS · TECHNICAL TERM
▪ off-screen
▪ off-stage
▪ over-the-shoulder shot (*aka* OSS)

OSD · TECHNICAL TERM
▪ on-screen display

OSF · UK
▪ Oxford Scientific Films Ltd
Lower Road
Long Hanborough
Oxon OX8 8LL
tel +44 993 881881
fax +44 993 882808
1968 □ independent wildlife production company with an international reputation for the production of award-winning natural history films and science-based programmes, television commercials and corporate films. It also operates extensive photo and film footage libraries specialising in wildlife and special effects.

OSP · TECHNICAL TERM
▪ on-screen programming

OSR · TECHNICAL TERM
▪ optical solar reflector

OSRC · NIGERIA
▪ Ondo State Radiovision Corporation
Akure
□ state-owned radio/television service.

OSS · TECHNICAL TERM
▪ over-the-shoulder shot (*aka* OS)

OSTV · NIGERIA
▪ Ondo State Television
PMB 709
Akure
□ state-owned television service
also known as ODTV

OT · TECHNICAL TERM
▪ optical transmitter

OTA · TECHNICAL TERM
▪ over-the-air

OTF · TECHNICAL TERM
▪ optical transfer function

OTI · MEXICO
▪ Organización de la Televisión Iberoamericana
1971 □ Ibero-American television organisation.
also known as Organisation Ibéroamericaine de Télévision (OIT)

OTO · TECHNICAL TERM
▪ one-time only

OTP · THE NETHERLANDS
▪ Onafhankelijke Televisie Producenten
Tielweg 6
PO Box 2174
2800 BH Gouda
tel +31 1820 71422
fax +31 1820 71533
1988 □ association of Dutch independent television producers. It produces a *Yearbook*.

OTR · TECHNICAL TERM
- one-touch (timer) record(ing)

OTS · TECHNICAL TERM
- orbital test satellite (*aka* OBT)

OTT · TECHNICAL TERM
- over the top

OTV · CROATIA
- Omladinska Televizija
Teslina 7
41000 Zagreb
tel   +38 41 424 124
fax +38 41 424 124
□ television station.

OTV · JAPAN
- Okinawa Television Broadcasting Co
Ltd
2-20 Kumoji 1-chome
Naha 900
tel   +81 98 863 2111
fax +81 98 861 0193
1959 □ television station.

OTV · TECHNICAL TERM
- orbital transfer vehicle

OU · UK
- Open University
Walton Hall
Milton Keynes
Bucks MK7 6AA
tel   +44 908 274066
fax +44 908 653744
1979 □ has led the world in making
higher education accessible to ordinary
people throughout the UK and in
Europe, through distance-learning. The
University has 127 000 registered
students on its undergraduate, graduate
and postgraduate and associate courses,
making it the largest single teaching
institution in the UK. Approximately 47
television and 16 radio programmes are
transmitted each week to in excess of 7
million viewers and listeners.

OUPC · UK
- Open University Production Centre
BBC Education
BBC White City
201 Wood Lane

London W12 7TS
tel   +44 81 752 5252
fax +44 81 752 4398
□ is responsible for producing the
television and radio programmes and
also the video and audio cassettes
associated with Open University (**OU**)
courses. The centre brings together
producers, academics, state-of-the-art
production and post-production
facilities.

OXTV · UK
- Oxford Television
University of Manchester
59 George Street
Oxford OX1 2BH
tel   +44 865 278800
fax +44 865 278834
□ acts as a production unit and
audiovisual service, and is involved in
the areas of development, production
and research in multimedia.

OZACI · ZAÏRE
- Organisation Zaïroise des Cinéastes
1972 □ organisation of Zaïrean film-
makers established to fight against
monopoly created by foreign film-
makers.

OZRT · ZAÏRE
- Office Zaïrois de Radiodiffusion et
Télévision
BP 3167
Kinshasa
□ national television service.

P

P-AS-B · TECHNICAL TERM
- programme-as-broadcast

P-AS-C · TECHNICAL TERM
- programme-as-completed

P-AS-T · TECHNICAL TERM
- programme as televised

P/L · TECHNICAL TERM
- payload

P-P · TECHNICAL TERM
- peak to peak

PA · TECHNICAL TERM
- power amplifier
- production assistant
- production associate
- programme assistant
- public address
- pulse addition

PAC · ITALY
- Produzione Atlas Cinematografica
Rome
□ film production.

PAC · ITALY
- Produzioni Atlas Consorziate
Viale Regina Margherita 279
00198 Rome
tel   +39 6 440 3797
fax +39 6 844 3356
tlx   612426
□ film production.

PACCT · USA
- Political Action Committee for Cable Television

PACT · UK
- Producers Alliance for Cinema and Television
Gordon House
Greencoat Place
London SW1P 1PH
tel   +44 71 233 6000
fax +44 71 233 8935
1991 □ trade association of the UK independent television and feature film production sector and UK contact point for coproduction, co-finance partners and distributors. It works for producers in the industry at every level and operates a members' regional network throughout the UK. It lobbies actively with broadcasters, financiers and governments to ensure that the producer's voice is heard and understood in Britain and Europe on all matters affecting the film and television industry. It publishes *Fact* (12) and *Impact*, and various other publications. *incorporating Independent Programme Producers Association (IPPA) and The*

Producers Association (TPA)

PACT · USA
- Protective Action for Children's Television

PAF · USA
- Program for Art on Film
980 Madison Avenue
New York
NY 10021
tel   +1 212 988 4876
fax +1 212 628 8963

PAHT · TECHNICAL TERM
- power-augmented hydrazine transfer

PAL · LUXEMBOURG
- Producteurs Associés Luxembourgeois
18 rue de l'Eau
1449 Luxembourg
tel   +352 27955
tel   +352 27956
□ organisation of film producers working in Luxembourg.

PAL · TECHNICAL TERM
- programmable array logic
- phase alternation by line/phase alternate line

PAL-S · TECHNICAL TERM
- PAL-simple

PAM · TECHNICAL TERM
- payload assist module
- pulse amplitude modulation

PAM-A · TECHNICAL TERM
- payload assist module-Atlas

PAM-D · TECHNICAL TERM
- payload assist module-Delta

PAR · TECHNICAL TERM
- parabolic aluminized reflector

PARA · USA
- Professional Audiovideo Retailers Association
52 Kilsyth Road
Brookline
MA 02146
tel   +1 617 739 9877

PAV · TECHNICAL TERM
▪ public access videotex

PAWE · SOUTH AFRICA
▪ Performing Arts Workers Equity
PO Box 34
Newtown
Johannesburg 2113
tel   +27 11 836 4425
fax +27 11 836 4501
1990 □ union which aims to protect
and improve the position, status and
interest of performing arts workers, and
to regulate relations between members
and their employers and agents.

PBA · JAPAN
▪ Pacific Broadcasting Association
see **THK** · JAPAN

PBAA · AUSTRALIA
▪ Public Broadcasting Association of
Australia

PBIS · TECHNICAL TERM
▪ pan bar imitator/input system

PBME · UK
▪ Public Broadcasting for a
Multicultural Europe
c/o Surinder Sharma
Room C202
British Broadcasting Corporation
Centre House
Television Centre
56 Wood Lane
London W12 7RJ
tel   +44 81 576 1208 / 7220
fax +44 81 742 9066
1991 □ conference held in The
Netherlands in October 1992 which
addressed the issues of employment
and representation of ethnic minorities
on television; networking throughout
and beyond Europe; the educational
role of broadcasting; and specialist
programming.

PBS · USA
▪ Public Broadcasting Service
1320 Braddock Place
Alexandria

VA 22314-1698
tel   +1 703 739 5000
fax +1 703 739 0775
tlx   9103501854
1969 □ provides quality children's,
cultural, educational, news and public
affairs, science and nature, fund-raising
and skills programmes to 346 non-
commercial television stations serving
the United States, Puerto Rico, the
Virgin Islands, Guam and Samoa. Its
varied activities include programme
acquisitions and scheduling, educational services, video marketing,
advertising and promotion, audience
research, broadcast and technical
operations, fund-raising development,
engineering and technology development and revenue-producing
enterprises.

PBU · TECHNICAL TERM
▪ photo blow-up

PC · TECHNICAL TERM
▪ personal computer
▪ phano-convex
▪ printed circuit
▪ provisional cut

PCB · TECHNICAL TERM
▪ printed circuit board

PCC · TECHNICAL TERM
▪ picture clear circuit

PCM · TECHNICAL TERM
▪ pulse-code modulation

PCP · UK
▪ Producers Creative Partnership
Ramillies House
1-2 Ramillies Street
London W1V 1DF
tel   +44 71 439 1966
fax +44 71 439 1977
1990 □ established as an umbrella
company for the talents of a group of
distinguished programme makers from a
wide range of programme disciplines,
including 5 former heads of department
at major broadcasters. It also aims to
assist smaller independents and
encourage talented younger programme

makers.

PCR · UK
- Professional Casting Report
PO Box 11
London SW15 6AY
tel   +44 81 789 0408
fax +44 81 780 1977
1968 □ magazine.

PCS · TECHNICAL TERM
- programme correspondence section

PCU · TECHNICAL TERM
- power control unit

PD · TECHNICAL TERM
- path distance
- production director
- professional digital
- programme director

PDA · TECHNICAL TERM
- post-deflection acceleration
- pulse distribution amplifier

PDC · TECHNICAL TERM
- Philips depressed collector
- programme delivery control

PDF · TECHNICAL TERM
- probability density function

PDI · TECHNICAL TERM
- picture description instruction
- public domain interface

PDM · TECHNICAL TERM
- pulse duration modulation

PDO · UK
- Philips and Du Pont Optical
Company
Philips Road
Blackburn
Lancs BB1 5RZ
tel   +44 254 52448
fax +44 254 54729
□ manufacturing and marketing of
optical discs in a range of formats,
including videodiscs **CD-I** and **CD-ROM**.

PDSL · TECHNICAL TERM
- prescribed diffusion service

PDWM · TECHNICAL TERM
- pulse duration width modulation

PE · TECHNICAL TERM
- poly-ethylene

PEB · TECHNICAL TERM
- party election broadcast

PEM · TECHNICAL TERM
- pulse edge modulation

PERITEL · TECHNICAL TERM
- peripheral television connector

PES · TECHNICAL TERM
- private earth station

PETAR · UK
- Pan-European Television Audience
Research
c/o RSL - Research Services Ltd
Elmgrove Road
Harrow
Middlesex HA1 2QG
tel   +44 81 861 6000
fax +44 81 861 5515
1987 □ annual audience research
survey which uses a 4-week diary
method to measure viewing of all
channels available in households
connected to a cable network or an
individual dish, including national
broadcasters, overspill from other
countries and cable/satellite delivered
channels. 6 countries were surveyed in
the 1993 survey: Germany, The
Netherlands, Belgium (Flanders only),
Sweden, Denmark and Norway, with a
total sample of 2308 individuals aged 4
or over. The latest survey represents a
universe of 58 million individuals in 25
million homes.

PFD · TECHNICAL TERM
- power flux density

PFL · TECHNICAL TERM
- pre-fade listen

PFM · TECHNICAL TERM
- pulse frequency modulation

PFPA · PAKISTAN

■ Pakistan Film Producers Association
Regal Cinema Building
Sharah-e-Quaid-Azam
Lahore
tel   +92 42 322904
□ association of film producers.

PFVEA · USA
■ Professional Film and Video
Equipment Association
PO Box 9436
Silver Spring
MD 20916
tel   +1 301 460 8084
1973 □ association of manufacturers,
dealers, distributors and servicing
agents for video and film equipment.

PFWC · USA
■ Philadelphia Festival of World
Cinema
International House
3701 Chestnut Street
Philadelphia
PA 19104
tel   +1 215 895 6593
fax +1 215 895 6562
□ film festival.

PG · TECHNICAL TERM
■ parental guidance

PGA · USA
■ Producers Guild of America
400 South Beverly Drive
Beverly Hills
CA 90212
tel   +1 310 557 0807
1950 □ group of producers working in
film and television.

PGBM · TECHNICAL TERM
■ pulse-gated binary modulation

PGSE · TECHNICAL TERM
■ payload ground support equipment

PHC · TECHNICAL TERM
■ phase correlation (motion estimation)

PI · TECHNICAL TERM
■ parallel input
■ programme interrupt

PIBA · VANUATU
■ Pacific Islands Broadcasting
Association
PO Box 116
Port Vila
tel   +678 24250
fax +678 24252
1987 □ association of broadcasters
which aims to further the development
of broadcasting throughout the region,
as well as to train personnel, maintain a
structure for news and programme
exchange and provide technical
cooperation.

PIL · TECHNICAL TERM
■ precision in line

PILOTS · SPAIN
■ Programme for the International
Launch of Television Series
c/o Media Business School
Torregalindo 10-4°
28016 Madrid
tel   +34 1 359 0247 / 0036
fax +34 1 345 7606
□ research and analysis project of the
market and practice of writing and
producing long-running series for
television.

PIM · TECHNICAL TERM
■ pulse internal modulation

PIN · TECHNICAL TERM
■ positive intrinsically negative

PIP · TECHNICAL TERM
■ picture in picture

PIVN · USA
■ Public Interest Video Network

PJTV · TECHNICAL TERM
■ projection television

PKA · USA
■ Paul Kagan Associates, Inc
126 Clock Tower Place
Carmel
CA 93923
tel   +1 408 624 1536
fax +1 408 624 3105
1969 □ company specialising in the

worldwide financial analysis of the media and communication industries. It publishes many newsletters in the subjects of broadcast banking, broking and investment, cable, pay and satellite television and SMATV, and organises seminars.

PKM · TECHNICAL TERM
- pedigree kick motor

PL · TECHNICAL TERM
- party line
- private line

PLA · TECHNICAL TERM
- programmable logic array

PLC · TECHNICAL TERM
- programme length commercial

PLD · TECHNICAL TERM
- programme logic device

PLL · TECHNICAL TERM
- phase-lock(ed) loop

PLM · TECHNICAL TERM
- pulse length modulation

PLUGE · TECHNICAL TERM
- picture line-up generating equipment

PLV · TECHNICAL TERM
- production-level video

PM · TECHNICAL TERM
- phase modulation
- production manager

PMMA · TECHNICAL TERM
- polymethyl methacrylate

PMOS · TECHNICAL TERM
- p-channel metal-oxide semiconductor

PMPEA · USA
- Professional Motion Picture Equipment Association

PN · TECHNICAL TERM
- pseudo-noise

PNR · TECHNICAL TERM
- producer's net receipts

POP · TECHNICAL TERM
- picture-outside-picture

POT · TECHNICAL TERM
- potential out-take

POV · CANADA
- Point-of-View
Suite 102
65 Heward Avenue
Toronto
Ontario M4M 2T5
tel   +1 416 469 2596
fax +1 416 462 3248
1991 □ quarterly magazine published on behalf of the Canadian Independent Film Caucus (**CIFC**) and covering film, television, video, cable and satellite.

POV · TECHNICAL TERM
- point of view

PPB · TECHNICAL TERM
- party political broadcast

PPBM · TECHNICAL TERM
- pulse polarisation binary modulation

PPC · TECHNICAL TERM
- pay per channel

PPDN · TECHNICAL TERM
- presentation protocol data unit

PPFM · MALAYSIA
- Persatuan Pengeluar Filem Malaysia
Studio Panca Delima
Lot 1045, 7½ miles
Jalan
Hulu Kelang
68000 Ampang
Selangor D.E.
tel   +60 3 408 1522
□ film producers' association of Malaysia.

PPM · TECHNICAL TERM
- peak programme meter
- pictures per minute
- pulse phase modulation
- pulse position modulation

PPS · TECHNICAL TERM
- pictures per second

PPV · TECHNICAL TERM
- pay-per-view

PQM · TECHNICAL TERM
- pulse quaterny modulation

PRBC · LIBYA
- People's Revolutionary Broadcasting Corporation
PO Box 333
Tripoli
☐ television broadcasting corporation.

PRBS · TECHNICAL TERM
- pseudo-random binary sequence

PRC · USA
- Plastic Reel Corporation of America
Brisbin Avenue
Lyndhurst
NJ 07071
tel +1 201 933 5100
fax +1 201 933 9468
1958 ☐ manufacturer of plastic storage and shipping reels and canisters for audio and video tape as well as motion picture film; of microfilm reels and canisters for audio and video tape and motion picture film; of microfilm spools and flame retardant archival film, audio and video canisters for long-term preservation.

PRF · TECHNICAL TERM
- pulse repetition frequency

PRIME · TECHNICAL TERM
- prediction and retrospective ionospheric modelling over Europe

PRISM · TECHNICAL TERM
- precision digital decoding system

PROD · TECHNICAL TERM
- programmable read-only disc

PROGEFI · FRANCE
- Production Générale de Films

PROM · TECHNICAL TERM
- programmable read-only memory

PROTEC · TECHNICAL TERM
- programmable technical equipment control

PRT · POLAND
- Polskie Radio i Telewizja
PO Box 35
ul. J P Woronicza, 17
00-950 Warsaw
tel +48 22 478501
fax +48 22 437408
tlx 815331
☐ state broadcaster, operating 2 national television channels.

PSA · TECHNICAL TERM
- public service announcement

PSB · TECHNICAL TERM
- public service broadcaster

PSC · TECHNICAL TERM
- portable single camera
- programme sequence control
- programme switching centre

PSFN · POLAND
- Polskie Stowarzyszenie Filmu Naukowego
ul. Mokotowska 58
00534 Warsaw
tel +48 22 290832
1959 ☐ association established to promote the production and use of scientific films.

PSG · USA
- Producer Services Group, Inc
7461 Beverly Boulevard
Los Angeles
CA 90036
tel +1 213 937 5020
fax +1 213 937 5027
☐ distributors of television programmes.

PSI · TECHNICAL TERM
- para-social interaction

PSK · TECHNICAL TERM
- phase shift keying

PSM · TECHNICAL TERM
- production services manager

PSN · TECHNICAL TERM
- public switched network

PSNI · USA
- Professional Systems Network

PSRA · TECHNICAL TERM
- pre-sunrise service authorisation

PSSA · TECHNICAL TERM
- post-sunset service authorisation

PSSC · USA
- Public Service Satellite Consortium
Washington
1975

PSU · TECHNICAL TERM
- power supply unit

PT · TECHNICAL TERM
- packet type

PTAR · TECHNICAL TERM
- prime time access rule

PTC · TECHNICAL TERM
- positive temperature coefficient

PTI · USA
- Public Television International
1790 Broadway
16th floor
New York
NY 10019
tel   +1 212 708 3048
fax +1 212 708 3045
□ distributor of US public television
programming to overseas broadcasters,
with over 500 hours in subject areas
such as documentary series,
science/environment, art/music and
how-to.

PTL · USA
- Public Television Library

PTOA · USA
- Public Television Outreach Alliance

PTR · USA
- Persons Tracking Report
Nielsen Media Research
1290 Avenue of the Americas

New York
NY 10104
tel   +1 212 708 7500
fax +1 212 708 7795
□ **NTI** supplementary report, updated
monthly, which is available for an
additional charge and tracks
programme performance in terms of
household audiences and Viewers-Per-
1000 Viewing Households (**VPVH**) (by
20 age/sex categories) for all sponsored
network programmes, including
specials.

PTR · TECHNICAL TERM
- particle transfer roller

PTV · PAKISTAN
- Pakistan Television Corporation
Constitution Avenue
Shalimar F-5/1
PO Box 1221
Islamabad
tel   +92 51 828651-5 / 822194-5
fax +92 51 823406
tlx   PK 5833 (PTVRP PK)
1967 □ television service established to
promote Pakistan's own heritage,
awareness of world affairs and
guidance for progress and prosperity.

PTV · TECHNICAL TERM
- Philips TV
- public television

PU · TECHNICAL TERM
- pick-up

PUMA · TECHNICAL TERM
- periscope unit and mirror attachment

PUT · TECHNICAL TERM
- persons using television

PV · TECHNICAL TERM
- preview (*aka* PVW)

PVA · TECHNICAL TERM
- polyvinyl acetate

PVC · TECHNICAL TERM
- polyvinyl chloride

PVT · TECHNICAL TERM

■ persons viewing television

PVW · <small>TECHNICAL TERM</small>
■ preview (*aka* PV)

PWM · <small>TECHNICAL TERM</small>
■ pulse-width modulation

PWSFTVIT · <small>POLAND</small>
■ Państwowa Wyższa Szkoła Filmowa
Telewizyjna i Teatralna im. Leona
Schillera w Łódź
Ul. Targowa 61/63
90-323 Łódź
tel   +48 42 743943
fax   +48 42 748139
1948 ▢ higher educational institution
offering courses in film and television
direction and cinematography, acting,
production, stage management,
screenwriting and editing.

PZM · <small>TECHNICAL TERM</small>
■ pressure zone microphone

PZT · <small>TECHNICAL TERM</small>
■ piezoelectric transducer unit

Q

Q&A · <small>TECHNICAL TERM</small>
■ question(s) and answer(s)

Q-PAL · <small>TECHNICAL TERM</small>
■ quality PAL

QA · <small>TECHNICAL TERM</small>
■ quality assurance

QAM · <small>TECHNICAL TERM</small>
■ quadrature amplitude modulator

QDBS · <small>TECHNICAL TERM</small>
■ quasi-direct broadcasting by satellite

QFT · <small>UK</small>
■ Queen's Film Theatre
Festival House
25 College Gardens
Belfast
N Ireland BT9 6BS
tel   +44 232 667687

fax   +44 232 663733
1968 ▢ film theatre.

QI · <small>TECHNICAL TERM</small>
■ quartz iodine

QK · <small>TECHNICAL TERM</small>
■ quick kinescope

QM · <small>TECHNICAL TERM</small>
■ quadrature modulation

QP · <small>TECHNICAL TERM</small>
■ quadruple play

QPSK · <small>TECHNICAL TERM</small>
■ quadrature phase shift keying

QRFV · <small>USA</small>
■ Quarterly Review of Film and Video
University of Southern California
School of Cinema-Television
University Park
Los Angeles
CA 90089-2211
tel   +1 213 740 3334
fax   +1 213 740 9471
1976 ▢ journal which publishes
critical, theoretical and historical essays
and extended book reviews on film,
television and video, exploring these
media in their technological,
institutional and cultural contexts. Its
scope is international and features
articles and special issues assessing
developments in theory and practice
from around the world, as well as
translations of foreign-language texts.

QTV · <small>QATAR</small>
■ Qatar Television Service
Ministry of Information
PO Box 1944
Doha
tel   +974 894444
fax   +974 864511
tlx   4040 TV DH
1970 ▢ television service, operating 8
channels.

QUME · <small>TECHNICAL TERM</small>
■ quadrature modulation of the picture
carrier

QW · TECHNICAL TERM
- quarter wave

R

R&F · TECHNICAL TERM
- reach and frequency

RA · TECHNICAL TERM
- reduced aperture

RACE · BELGIUM
- Research and Development in Advanced Communications Technologies in Europe
Commission of the European Communities
Information Technologies and Telecommunications
DG XIIIB
Bu9 4/4b
200 rue de la Loi
1049 Brussels
tel   +32 2 296 3443 / 3410
fax +32 2 295 0654
1985 □ programme to establish a strong community manufacturing industry in broadband communications and to accelerate the emergence of a competitive community market for telecommunications equipment and services, at the same time working towards uniform standards throughout Europe.

RACE · TECHNICAL TERM
- rapid action cutting equipment

RACK · TECHNICAL TERM
- read address clock

RAI · ITALY
- Radiotelevisione Italiana
Viale Mazzini 14
00195 Rome
tel   +39 6 3878
fax +39 6 372 5680
tlx   614432
1924 □ public service television broadcaster, offering entertainment, news and cultural programmes.

RAM · TECHNICAL TERM
- random-access memory

RAS · ITALY
- Rundfunk Anstalt Südtirol
Europaallee 164A
39100 Bozen
tel   +39 471 932 933
□ public organisation of the autonomous region of Southern Tyrol, whose objective is to broadcast radio and television from Austria, Germany and Switzerland to the German-speaking audience.

RAW · TECHNICAL TERM
- read after write

RB · GERMANY
- Radio Bremen
Bürgermeister-Spitta-Allee 45
28329 Bremen
tel   +49 421 2460
fax +49 421 1010
tlx   245181
1945 □ regional television and radio broadcasting organisation.

RB · TECHNICAL TERM
- return to bias

RBC · JAPAN
- Ryukyu Broadcasting Co Ltd
3-1 Kumoji 2-chome
Naha 900
Okinawa
tel   +81 98 867 2151
tlx   5247
1954 □ television station.

RBL · TECHNICAL TERM
- re-broadcast link

RBR · TECHNICAL TERM
- re-broadcast reception

RC · TECHNICAL TERM
- remote control
- resistor/capacitor

RCA · USA
- Radio Corporation of America
RCA Global Communications, Inc.
2 International Drive

Rye Brook
NY 10573
tel +1 914 934 6303
fax +1 914 934 6912
tlx 023 6502 188984
1919

RCC · JAPAN
▪ Chugoku Broadcasting Co Ltd
21-3 Moto-machi
Naka-ku
Hiroshima 730
tel +81 82 222 1112
◻ television station.

RCCB · TECHNICAL TERM
▪ residual current circuit breaker

RCD · TECHNICAL TERM
▪ remote control degauss

RCP · TECHNICAL TERM
▪ remote control panel

RCS · TECHNICAL TERM
▪ reaction control system

RCTC · TECHNICAL TERM
▪ rewritable consumer time code

RCTI · INDONESIA
▪ Rajawali Citra Televisi Indonesia
Jalan Raya Perjuangan
Kebun Jeruk
Jakarta 11530
tel +62 21 530 3540
fax +62 21 549 3852
1989 ◻ Indonesia's first privately
owned television station.

RCTS · AUSTRALIA
▪ Remote Commercial Television
Service
c/o Australian Broadcasting Authority
PO Box 34
Belconnen 2616
◻ commercial television satellite
service, serving the remoter parts of
Australia.

RCTV · VENEZUELA
▪ Radio Caracas Televisión
2a Transversal
Apdo. 70734

Los Cortijos de Lourdes
Caracas
tel +58 2 256 1665
fax +58 2 256 2672
tlx 21507
1953 ◻ national radio and television
broadcasting station.

RCU · TECHNICAL TERM
▪ remote control unit

RDAT · TECHNICAL TERM
▪ rotary-head/rotating digital audio tape

RDS · CANADA
▪ Réseau des Sports
Bureau 300
1755 Boulevard René-Lévesque Est
Montreal
Quebec H2K 4P6
tel +1 514 599 2244
fax +1 514 599 2299
◻ public television broadcaster.

RDS · TECHNICAL TERM
▪ radio data system

RDTVQ · CANADA
▪ Regroupement des Distributeurs
Télévision du Québec
872 rue Charles-Guimond
Boucherville
Quebec J4B 3Z5
tel +1 514 641 4691
fax +1 514 449 2651

RDU · TECHNICAL TERM
▪ remote detection unit

Register-MEAL · UK
▪ Register Media Expenditure Analysis
Ltd
2 Fisher Street
London WC1R 4QA
tel +44 71 833 1212
fax +44 71 831 7686
1968 ◻ Register-MEAL data provide the
industry standard for advertising
expenditure and volume measurement
in the UK. Its comprehensive service
covers all of the key advertising media:
press, television, cinema, radio,
outdoor.

RETRA · UK
- Radio, Electrical and Television Retailers' Association
Retra House
St John's Terrace
1 Ampthill Street
Bedford MK42 9EY
tel   +44 234 269110
fax +44 234 269609
1942 □ membership organisation consisting of over 6000 nationwide electrical retail outlets in the retailing, rental and servicing of consumer electronics and the small appliance market. It represents the interests of its members to those making the decisions likely to affect the servicing and selling of electronic products, such as government, official and institutional organisations, and manufacturers. It also provides its members with many time and cost-saving services. It publishes *Alert* (12), as well as a *Yearbook*.

RF · TECHNICAL TERM
- radio frequency

RFI · FRANCE
- Radio France Internationale
116 Avenue du Président-Kennedy
75016 Paris
tel   +33 1 42 30 22 22
fax +33 1 45 24 39 13
tlx   200 002
□ broadcasting company.

RFI · TECHNICAL TERM
- radio frequency interference

RFO · FRANCE
- Radio Télévision Française d'Outre-Mer
5 avenue du Recteur Poincaré
75016 Paris
tel   +33 1 45 24 71 00
fax +33 1 42 24 95 96
tlx   648450
1983 □ radio and television broadcaster serving French overseas territories throughout the world.

RFP · TECHNICAL TERM
- request for proposals

RFT · TECHNICAL TERM
- regional film theatre

RGB · TECHNICAL TERM
- red-orange, green, blue-violet

RGTRK · RUSSIA
- Rossijskaja Gosudarstvennaja Teleradioveschateljnaja Kompanija Ostankino
Moscow
1991 □ produces the television channels Ostankino Kanal (**OK**) and Radiotelevidenie Ostankino (**RTO**) which broadcast throughout Russia.

RH · TECHNICAL TERM
- room humidity

RHCP · TECHNICAL TERM
- right-hand circular polarisation

RI · TECHNICAL TERM
- reaction index

RIPTA · UK
- Richard Price Television Associates
RPTA · UK

RIRECA · BELGIUM
- Réseau Interuniversitaire de Recherche et d'Enseignement du Cinéma
Arts et Sciences de la Communication
Université de Liège
Allée du Six-Août B11
4000 Liège
tel   +32 41 56 32 86-9
□ research and study centre into cinema.

RISC · TECHNICAL TERM
- reduced instruction set computer

RITCS · BELGIUM
- Hoger Rijksinstituut voor Toneel en Cultuurspreiding
see **HRITCS** · BELGIUM

RITE · UK
- Resources In Training & Education Ltd
Cadbury House
Cadbury Lane

Weston-in-Gordano
Portishead BS20 8PT
tel +44 275 844925
fax +44 275 845168
1991 □ non-theatrical video
distribution to education, business,
industry and government departments
in Europe, the Middle East and Africa.

RKB · JAPAN
■ RKB Mainichi Broadcasting
Corporation
1-10 Watanabe-dori 4-chome
Chuo-ku
Fukuoka 810
tel +81 92 713 2111
□ television station.

RKC · JAPAN
■ Kochi Broadcasting Co Ltd
2-15 Hon-machi 3-chome
Kochi 780
tel +81 888 22 2111
□ television station.

RKK · JAPAN
■ Kumamoto Broadcasting Co Ltd
30 Yamasaki-machi
Kumamoto 860
tel +81 96 328 5511
□ television station.

RKO · USA
■ Radio-Keith-Orpheum
Suite 448
1801 Avenue of the Stars
Los Angeles
CA 90067
tel +1 310 277 0707
fax +1 310 284 8574
1928 □ film production, distribution
and exhibition.

RLC · TECHNICAL TERM
■ real-time lens error correction

RLE · TECHNICAL TERM
■ run length encoding

RLV · TECHNICAL TERM
■ recordable laser videodisc

RMB · BELGIUM
■ Régie Media Belge

Avenue Louise 479
1050 Brussels
tel +32 2 648 0245
fax +32 2 648 0387
□ responsible for selling advertising on
Radio-Télévision Belge de la
Communauté Française (**RTBF**).

RMS · TECHNICAL TERM
■ remote manipulator system
■ root mean square(d)

RMTK · RUSSIA
■ Rossijskaya Moskovskaja
Teleradioveschateljnaya Kompanija
Moskva
1992

RMW · TECHNICAL TERM
■ read modify write

RNB · JAPAN
■ Nankai Broadcasting Co Ltd
6-24 Dogohimata
Matsuyama 790
tel +81 899 23 1111
□ television station.

RNC · JAPAN
■ Nishi-Nippon Broadcasting Co Ltd
8-15 Marunouchi
Takamatsu 760
tel +81 878 39 3811
□ television station.

RNTC · THE NETHERLANDS
■ Radio Netherland Training Centrum
PO Box 222
1200 JG Hilversum
tel +31 35 47779
□ institution which offers training in
radio and television.

RNTV · THE NETHERLANDS
■ Radio Netherlands Television
PO Box 222
1200 JG Hilversum
tel +31 35 724486
fax +31 35 724489
tlx 43336 WOMR NL
□ television and video programme
producers and distributors.

ROC · TECHNICAL TERM

• regional operational centre

ROES · TECHNICAL TERM
• receive-only earth satellite

ROG · TECHNICAL TERM
• read out gate

ROM · TECHNICAL TERM
• read-only memory

ROOS · THE NETHERLANDS
• Regionale Omroep Overleg en Samenwerking

ROS · TECHNICAL TERM
• run of schedule/station

RP · TECHNICAL TERM
• rear projection
• remote pick-up (*aka* RPU)

RPM · TECHNICAL TERM
• revolutions per minute

RPN · TECHNICAL TERM
• residual point noise

RPTA · UK
• Richard Price Television Associates
Seymour Mews House
Seymour Mews
Wigmore Street
London W1H 9PE
tel +44 71 935 9000
fax +44 71 935 1992
1968 □ film distributor.
also known as RIPTA

RPU · TECHNICAL TERM
• remote pick-up (*aka* RP)

RRO · TECHNICAL TERM
• radio receive only

RS · TECHNICAL TERM
• remote sensor/switch
• reverse shot

RSC · TECHNICAL TERM
• recessed single contact

RSK · JAPAN
• Sanyo Broadcasting Co Ltd

1-3 Marunouchi 2-chome
Okayama 700
tel +81 862 255531
□ television station.

RSS · TECHNICAL TERM
• remote subscriber stage
• root sum square

RT · TECHNICAL TERM
• reverberation time

RTA · AFGHANISTAN
• Radio-Television Afghanistan
□ radio and television broadcasting service.

RTA · ALGERIA
• Radiodiffusion Télévision Algérienne
Immeuble RTA
21 Boulevard des Martyrs
Algiers
tel +213 2 602300
tlx 52042
1970 □ television and radio broadcasting service.

RTA · BELGIUM
• Radio-Télévision Animation

RTB · BRUNEI DARUSSALAM
• Radio Television Brunei
Jalan Elizabeth Kedua
Bandar Seri Begawan 2042
tel +673 2 243111
fax +673 2 241882
tlx BU2311
1957 □ television and radio service, broadcasting programmes in English and Malay.

RTB · SERBIA
• Radiotelevizija Beograd
see **RTVB** · SERBIA

RTBF · BELGIUM
• Radio-Télévision Belge de la Communauté Française
52 Boulevard Auguste Reyers
1044 Brussels
tel +32 2 737 2111
fax +32 2 737 3032
tlx 63132
□ French language television and radio

broadcasting service.

RTC · PORTUGAL
- Radiotelevisão Comercial, LDA
Avenida Fontes Pereira de Melo 19-2
1000 Lisbon
tel +351 1 352 8835
fax +351 1 335 7076
tlx 64630 RTC / 65352 RTC
□ owner of the concession for
commercial advertising on
Radiotelevisão Portuguesa (**RTP**).

RTCA · USA
- Radio and Television Correspondents
Association

RTD · DJIBOUTI
- Radiodiffusion-Télévision de Djibouti
BP 97
Djibouti
tel +253 352294
tlx 5863
1957 □ radio and television station,
broadcasting programmes in Afar,
Arabic, French and Somali.

RTDG · USA
- Radio and Television Directors Guild

RTE · IRELAND
- Radio Telefís Éireann
Donnybrook
Dublin 4
tel +353 1 643111
fax +353 1 643080
tlx 93700
1960 □ national public service
broadcasting channels on television (2)
and radio (3).

RTEA · FRANCE
- René Thévenet et Associés
50 avenue Marceau
75008 Paris
tel +33 1 47 23 70 30
fax +33 1 47 20 78 17
1980 □ consultancy and expert
guidance on judicial, economic,
institutional and practical questions
regarding motion picture production
and distribution.

RTES · USA

- Radio and Television Executives
Society

RTG · GABON
- Radiodiffusion-Télévision Gabonaise
BP 150
Libreville
tel +241 732025
fax +241 732153
tlx 5342
1959 □ state-controlled television
broadcasting service.

RTG · GUINEA
- Radiodiffusion-Télévision Guinéenne
BP 391
Conakry
tel +224 441 410
fax +224 443 998
tlx 22 341
□ national television service,
broadcasting in French and local
languages.

RTG · TECHNICAL TERM
- radio-isotope thermo-electric
generator

RTHK · HONG KONG
- Radio Television Hong Kong
30 Broadcast Drive
Kowloon
tel +852 339 6300
fax +852 338 0279
tlx 45568 RTHK HX
1928 □ television and radio
broadcasting service, providing drama,
current affairs programmes (both
English and Chinese), information and
community services, variety and game
shows, children's and youth
programmes, educational programmes,
and programmes for minority groups.

RTI · ITALY
- Reti Televisive Italiane
Viale Europa 48
Cologno Monzese 2093
tel +39 2 21 02 47 28
fax +39 2 21 02 84 76
□ television programme producers.

RTI · IVORY COAST
- Radio-Télévision Ivoirienne

Boulevard Latrille
BP 883
08 Abidjan
tel +225 43 90 39
fax +225 44 73 89
tlx 26110 Ditélé
1963 □ national television service.

RTI · UK
■ Research Technology International
Unit 6
Swan Wharf Business Centre
Waterloo Road
Uxbridge
Middlesex UB8 2RA
tel +44 895 252191
fax +44 895 274692
tlx 8954169 RTILPS G
□ manufacture of machines for
cleaning, erasing and evaluating
videotape and film.

RTL · LUXEMBOURG
■ Radio-Télévision Luxembourgeoise
Villa Louvigny
Parc Municipal
Luxembourg
tel +352 421 421
fax +352 4766 2737
tlx 1787
1931 □ television and radio
broadcasting station.

RTL · SLOVENIA
■ Radiotelevizija Ljubljana
Ljubljana
□ television and radio service.

RTL · TECHNICAL TERM
■ register transistor logic

RTM · GERMANY
■ Rundfunktechnische Mitteilungen
Institut für Rundfunktechnik (IRT)
Floriansmühlstraße 60
80939 Munich
tel +49 89 323 991
fax +49 89 323 99351
tlx 5215605 irtmd
1957 □ magazine (6 issues annually)
which publishes highly specialised
coverage of research work (by the **IRT**,
as well as other organisations/
institutions) concerning broadcast

technology.

RTM · MADAGASCAR
■ Radio-Télévision Malagasy
BP 1202
101 Antananarivo
tel +261 2 22381
fax +261 2 22506
1931 □ state television service,
broadcasting in French and Malagasy.

RTM · MALAYSIA
■ Radio Television Malaysia
Department of Broadcasting
Ministry of Information
Angkasapuri
Kuala Lumpur 50614
tel +60 3 274 5333
fax +60 3 230 4735
tlx RTMTV MA31383
1969 □ supervises television and radio
broadcasting services.

RTM · MOROCCO
■ Radiodiffusion Télévision Marocaine
BP 1042
Rabat
tel +212 7 764 871
tlx 31 010
1962 □ television and radio
broadcasting service, operating in
Arabic and French.

RTNB · BURUNDI
■ Radiodiffusion et Télévision Nationale
du Burundi
BP 1900
Bujumburura
tel +257 2 23742
tlx 5119
1960 □ radio and television
broadcasting authority.

RTNDA · USA
■ Radio-Television News Directors'
Association
Suite 615
1000 Connecticut Avenue, NW
Washington
DC 20036
tel +1 202 659 6510
fax +1 202 223 4007
1946 □ trade association which strives
to better general standards of electronic

journalism and also to uphold and campaign for journalists' rights. It promotes training in journalism and publishes *Communicator* (12) and *Intercom Newsletter* (6).

RTNM · TOGO
■ Radio Télévision Nouvelle Marche
BP 3286
Lomé
tel   +228 215356
fax +228 215786
□ television service.

RTO · RUSSIA
■ Radiotelevidenie Ostankino
Piatnitskaia 25
113326 Moscow
tel   +7 095 217 7260 / 217 9015 / 215 7238
fax +7 095 215 1324
tlx   411340 / 411140
1990 □ television and radio service.

RTOS · TECHNICAL TERM
■ real-time operating system

RTP · PERU
■ Empresa de Cine, Radio y Televisión Peruana, SA
Avda José Gálvez 1040
Santa Beatriz
Lima
tel   +51 14 715570
tlx   25029
□ broadcasting authority operating 27 television channels and 29 radio channels.

RTP · PORTUGAL
■ Radio Televisão Portuguesa
Avenida 5 de Outubro, 197
Apdo. 2934
1000 Lisbon
tel   +351 1 793 1774
fax +351 1 793 1758
tlx   14527
1956 □ public service television broadcaster.

RTP · SERBIA
■ Radiotelevizija Priština
see **RTVP** · SERBIA

RTR · ROMANIA
■ Radioteleviziunea Română
see **RTV** · ROMANIA

RTRC · USA
■ Radio and Television Research Council
Suite 2103
245 Fifth Avenue
New York
NY 10016
tel   +1 212 481 3038
fax +1 212 481 3071
1941 □ group of individuals working in television and radio research which offers a forum for discussion and exchange of views and information.

RTS · SEYCHELLES
■ Radio Television Seychelles
see **SBC** · SEYCHELLES

RTS · UK
■ Royal Television Society
Holborn Hall
100 Gray's Inn Road
London WC1X 8AL
tel   +44 71 430 1000
fax +44 71 430 0924
1927 □ independent, central, free-thinking forum where the politics of television are examined, debated and very often influenced. It publishes *Television* journal (8-10), a *Yearbook* and various other publications.

RTS · TECHNICAL TERM
■ rapid transmission and storage

RTSA · BOSNIA-HERCEGOVINA
■ Radiotelevizija Sarajevo
see **RTVSA** · BOSNIA-HERCEGOVINA

RTSH · ALBANIA
■ Radiotelevizioni Shqiptar
Rruga Ismail Qemali
Tirana
tel   +355 42 223239
tlx   2216
1944 □ national television and radio broadcasting service.

RTSI · SWITZERLAND
■ Radiotelevisione della Svizzera

Italiana
via Canevascini
6903 Lugano-Besso
tel +41 91 585111
fax +41 91 589150
tlx 844484
□ television service, broadcasting in Italian.
also known as Televisione della Svizzera Italiana (TSI)

RTSR · SWITZERLAND
■ Radio-Télévision (de la) Suisse Romande
20 Quai Ernest Ansermet
PO Box 234
CH-1211 Geneva 8
tel +41 22 293333
fax +41 22 204049
tlx 427701 TVR
□ television service, broadcasting in French.
also known as Télévision (de la) Suisse Romande (TSR)

RTT · TUNISIA
■ Radiotélévision Tunisienne
71 Avenue de la Liberté
Tunis
tel +216 1 287 300
fax +216 1 781 058
tlx 14 960
1966 □ television and radio broadcasting service, operating in Arabic, French and Italian.

RTV · BOSNIA-HERCEGOVINA
■ Radiotelevizija Bosnia-Herzegovina
VI Proleterske brigade 4
71000 Sarajevo
tel +71 652333
fax +71 461569
tlx 41122
1945 □ television and radio service, broadcasting in Serbo-Croatian.

RTV · ROMANIA
■ Televiziunea Română Libera
Calea Dorobanţilor 191
PO Box 63
1200 Bucharest
tel +40 0 503055 / 334710
fax +40 0 337544
tlx 11251 / 10182

1989 □ television service, operating 2 channels.
also known as RTR
previously (from 1956) Radio Televiziunea Română Libera

RTV · RUSSIA
■ Rossijskoje Televidenije Vserossijskaja Gosudarstvennaja Televizionnaja i Radioveschateljnaja Kompanija (VGTRK)
Jamskogo polja 5-ja ul. 19/12
125124 Moscow
tel +7 095 2179981
fax +7 095 2500506
1991 □ television and radio channel broadcasting throughout Russia.

RTV · TECHNICAL TERM
■ real-time video

RTVA · SPAIN
■ Radio Televisión de Andalucía
Carretera San Juan de Aznalfarache a Tomares
Km 1350
41920 San Juan de Aznalfarache
Sevilla
tel +34 5 4763111
fax +34 5 4769755
□ television broadcaster.

RTVB · SERBIA
■ Radiotelevizija Beograd
Takovska 10
11000 Belgrade
tel +38 11 342001
fax +38 11 543178
tlx 11884
1929 □ television and radio broadcasting service, operating in Serbo-Croatian.
also known as RTB and as Televizija Beograd (TVB)

RTVCG · MONTENEGRO
■ Radiotelevizija Crne Gore
Cetinjski Put BB
81000 Podgorića
tel +38 81 41800
fax +38 81 43640
tlx 61133
1944 □ television and radio service, broadcasting on 2 channels each, in

Serbo-Croat.

RTVE · SPAIN
■ Radiotelevisión Española
Apdo. 26002
Prado del Rey
28023 Madrid 1
tel   +34 91 711 0400
tlx   27694
1956 □ television and radio
broadcasting service, operating 2
national television networks - TVE-1
and LA-2 - and 5 national radio
stations.
also known as TVE

RTVM · SPAIN
■ Radio Televisión Madrid
Madrid
□ radio and television broadcasting
station.

RTVNS · SERBIA
■ Radiotelevizija Novi Sad
Žarka Zrenjanina 3
21000 Novi Sad
tel   +38 21 611588
fax   +38 21 26624
tlx   14127
1949 □ television and radio service,
broadcasting in Hungarian, Romanian,
Ruthenian, Serbo-Croatian and Slovak.

RTVP · SERBIA
■ Radiotelevizija Priština
Maršala Titt
38000 Priština
tel   +38 26255
fax   +38 25355
tlx   18134
1944 □ television and radio
broadcasting service, operating in
Albanian, Romany, Serbo-Croatian and
Turkish.
also known as RTP

RTVR · ROMANIA
■ Radio Televiziunea Română Libera
see **RTV** · ROMANIA

RTVSA · BOSNIA-HERCEGOVINA
■ Radiotelevizija Sarajevo
VI Proleterskih Brigada, 4
71000 Sarajevo

tel   +38 71 652333
fax   +38 71 461569
□ television and radio service.
also known as RTSA

RTZIZ · ST KITTS
■ Ziz Radio and Television (St Kitts and
Nevis)
PO Box 331
Springfield
tel   +1 809 465 2621
fax   +1 809 465 5202
tlx   6820 EXTNL SKB KC
1961 □ television and radio
broadcasting service.
also known as ZIZRT

RU · TECHNICAL TERM
■ remote unit

RU/UTV · UGANDA
■ Radio Uganda and Uganda Television
PO Box 7142 and 2038
Kampala
tel   +256 41 254461 / 242316 /
245376
fax   +256 41 256888
tlx   61084
1963 □ television and radio service,
aimed at providing for the education,
entertainment, information and
mobilisation of the people of Uganda.

RUT · TECHNICAL TERM
■ rooms using television

RÚV · ICELAND
■ Ríkisútvarpið-Sjónvarp
Laugavegur 176
105 Reykjavík
tel   +354 1 693900
fax   +354 1 693008
tlx   2035 vision is
1966 □ state television broadcasting
service.

RVB · TECHNICAL TERM
■ rouge vert bleu

RZ · TECHNICAL TERM
■ return to zero

S

S/I · TECHNICAL TERM
- superimpose

S/N · TECHNICAL TERM
- signal to noise ratio (*aka* S/NR)

S/NR · TECHNICAL TERM
- signal to noise ratio (*aka* S/N)

S-VHS · TECHNICAL TERM
- Super-Video Home System (*aka* SVHS)

S2PA · FRANCE
- Syndicat des Producteurs de Programmes Audiovisuels
38 rue de Moscou
75008 Paris
tel   +33 1 42 93 79 01
fax +33 1 42 93 29 04
1977 □ representation of independent production companies. It publishes *La Lettre du S2PA* (4).
also known as SPPA

S4C · UK
- Sianel Pedwar Cymru
Parc Ty Glas
Llanishen CF4 5DU
tel   +44 222 747444
fax +44 222 754444
1982 □ television service for Wales.

SA · TECHNICAL TERM
- studio address

SABC · SOUTH AFRICA
- South African Broadcasting Corporation
see **SAUK** · SOUTH AFRICA

SAC · ARGENTINA
- Sociedad Anónima Cinematográfica

SACIS · ITALY
- Società per Azioni Commerciale Iniziative Spettacolo
Via Teulada, 28
00195 Rome
tel   +39 6 374981
fax +39 6 3723492

tlx   624487
1955 □ commercial audiovisual distributor who assigns television, cinematographic and general performing rights on behalf of Radiotelevisione Italiana (**RAI**), in Italy and abroad, regarding programmes of which RAI is the producer or copyright holder. It is also active in the Italian audiovisual production industry, both with RAI and other producers, and monitors advertising trends in Italy and abroad.

SAD · TECHNICAL TERM
- solar array drive

SADA · TECHNICAL TERM
- solar array drive assembly

SADE · TECHNICAL TERM
- solar array drive electronics

SADM · TECHNICAL TERM
- solar array drive mechanism

SAE · FRANCE
- Société d'Appareillages Electroniques
Z.I. Boitardiere
37400 Amboise
tel   +33 1 47 57 32 31
fax +33 1 47 57 36 35
1960 □ manufacturers of a complete line of connectors for use in **CATV** networks.

SAFC · AUSTRALIA
- South Australian Film Corporation
3 Butler Drive
Westside Commerce Centre
Tapley's Hill Road
Hendon
SA 5014
tel   +61 8 348 9300
fax +61 8 347 1525
tlx   AA88206
□ regional film organisation.

SAFTI · SOUTH AFRICA
- South African Film and Television Institute
PO Box 3512
Halfway House
Johannesburg 1685

tel   +27 11 315 0140
fax   +27 11 315 0146
1982 □ represents producers, production houses and facilities and has various sub-committees which deal with various issues.
previously South African Film and Video Institute (SAFVI)

SAFTTA · SOUTH AFRICA
■ South African Film and TV Technicians Association
PO Box 91625
Auckland
Johannesburg 2006
1976 □ registered union seeking to raise standards, protect members from unfair treatment and negotiate better working conditions with employer bodies.

SAFVI · SOUTH AFRICA
■ South African Film and Video Institute
see **SAFTI** · SOUTH AFRICA

SAG · USA
■ Screen Actors Guild
7065 Hollywood Boulevard
Hollywood
CA 90028
tel   +1 213 465 4600
fax   +1 213 856 6603
1933 □ union representing actors working in the film and television industries. It publishes *Screen Actor* (4) and *Screen Actor Hollywood* (4).

SAI · ITALY
■ Sindacato Attori Italiani

SAM · THE NETHERLANDS
■ Stichting Audiovisuele Manifestaties
Coehoornstraat 5
1222 RR Hilversum
tel   +31 35 837709
fax   +31 35 835700
□ foundation for audiovisual events.

SAMP · USA
■ Stuntmen's Association of Motion Pictures

SAP · TECHNICAL TERM
■ separate/second(ary) audio

programme

SASC · SOUTH AFRICA
■ South African Society of Cinematographers
PO Box 17465
Sunward Park 1470
tel   +27 11 421 0942
1954 □ to advance the art and science of cinematography; to encourage, foster and strive for excellence, artistic perfection and scientific knowledge in all matters relating to cinematography; to bring together those leaders in cinematography whose achievements in that field entitle them to membership; to strive to maintain the highest possible standards.

SASWA · SOUTH AFRICA
■ South African Scriptwriters Association
PO Box 91937
Auckland Park
Johannesburg 2006
tel   +27 11 314 2080
fax   +27 11 314 2265
1983 □ to bring more equitable working conditions for scriptwriters; to act in council as arbitrators between producers and writers; to run workshops and courses.

SATIS · FRANCE
■ Salon Européen des Techniques de l'Image et du Son
16 rue de Bassano
75016 Paris
tel   +33 1 47 20 84 44
fax   +33 1 49 52 00 54
1982 □ European image and sound technical trade show.

SATPEC · TUNISIA
■ Société Anonyme Tunisienne de Production et d'Expansion Cinématographique
10 rue Ibn Khaldoum
Tunis
tel   +216 1 740944
fax   +216 1 740024
1957 □ national society for the production, distribution, import and promotion of films.

SAUK · SOUTH AFRICA
- Suid-Afrikaanse Uitsaaikorporasie
Private Bag X41
Auckland Park
Johannesburg 2006
tel +27 11 714 9111
fax +27 11 714 5055
1936 □ statutory national broadcasting organisation, with 22 radio stations and 3 television channels, broadcasting in Afrikaans, English, North and South Sotho, Tswana, Xhosa and Zulu. Its aims are to entertain, inform and educate viewers and listeners, and to provide for their cultural needs. It publishes 2 magazines - *Interkom* (12) and *Radio & TV* (12) - as well as *This Is the SABC* (1) and *Who's Where at the SABC* (1).
also known as South African Broadcasting Corporation (SABC)

SAV · SPAIN
- Sociedad Anonima del Video
Rafael Batlle 26-28
08017 Barcelona
tel +34 3 205 7412
fax +34 3 203 6155
□ video programme distributor.

SAV · TECHNICAL TERM
- start of active video

SAVC · FINLAND
- State Audio Visual Centre
- Statens Audiovisuella Central
see **VAVK** · FINLAND

SAVE · THE NETHERLANDS
- Stichting Audiovisuele Vorming
□ organisation for audiovisual training.

SAW · TECHNICAL TERM
- surface-acoustic-wave

SAWA · UK
- Screen Advertising World Association
103A Oxford Street
London W1R 1TF
tel +44 71 734 7621
fax +44 71 437 1957
tlx 25312 ADFEST G
1953 □ act as screen contractors for, and promotes the use of, advertising in the cinema.

SB · TECHNICAL TERM
- simultaneous broadcast
- single bayonet

SBC · JAPAN
- Shin-Etsu Broadcasting Co Ltd
21-24 Yoshida 1-Chome
Nagano 381
tel +81 262 59 2111
□ television station.

SBC · SEYCHELLES
- Seychelles Broadcasting Corporation
PO Box 321
Victoria
tel +248 24161
fax +248 25641
tlx 2315 INFO TVSZ
formerly Radio Television Seychelles (RTS)
also known as SEYBC
1992 □ independent television and radio corporation fulfilling the role of national broadcaster in a monopoly context. It is funded by an annual government grant in addition to the revenue it generates.

SBC · SINGAPORE
- Singapore Broadcasting Corporation
Caldecott Hill
Andrew Road
Singapore 1129
tel +65 256 0401
fax +65 253 8808
tlx RS 39265
1980 □ to inform, educate and entertain, providing programmes to satisfy the expectations of the widest audiences; to maintain balance and objectivity in its programming; to contribute to nation-building and reflect the values, aspirations and diverse cultures of the nation; to be committed to excellence in broadcasting; to nurture professional, creative and skilled staff dedicated to a quality service using advanced technology. It broadcasts weekly television programmes in Chinese (Mandarin), English, Malay and Tamil and publishes *Broadcaster* (12).

SBC · SWEDEN
- Swedish Broadcasting Corporation
Sveriges Radio
Radiohuset
Oxenstiernsgatan 20
105 10 Stockholm
tel +46 8 784 0000
fax +46 8 784 1500
tlx 10000
1925 □ television and radio
broadcasting.

SBC · SWITZERLAND
- Swiss Broadcasting Corporation
Giacomettistraße 3
CH-3000 Bern 15
tel +41 31 439111
fax +41 31 439256
tlx 911590 ssr ch
1931 □ national broadcasting
organisation producing radio and
television programmes in the 4 national
languages - French, German, Italian
and Romansch. It is a private company,
organised as an association, in the
service of the public and non-profit
making.
*also known as Schweizerische Radio-
und Fernsehgesellschaft (SRG)*
*also known as Società Svizzera di
Radiotelevisione (SSR)*
*also known as Société Suisse de
Radiodiffusion et Télévision (SSR)*

SBC · UK
- Sony Broadcast & Communications
Jays Close
Viables
Basingstoke
Hampshire RG22 4SB
tel +44 256 55011
fax +44 256 474585
tlx 858424
□ responsible for the marketing and
distribution of the Sony range of
broadcast video and professional audio
equipment, High Definition Video
Systems and products for business and
industry.

SBCA · USA
- Satellite Broadcasting and
Communications Association of
America

Suite 600
225 Reinekers Lane
Alexandria
VA 22314
tel +1 703 549 6990
fax +1 703 549 7640
1986 □ organisation which aims to
promote public interest in satellite
communications. It runs the SBCA
Satellite Trade Show and publishes
Satvision (12).
*created by merger of Direct Broadcast
Satellite Association (DBSA) and
Satellite Television Industry Association
(STIA)*

SBE · USA
- Society of Broadcast Engineers
PO Box 20450
Indianapolis
IN 46220
tel +1 317 842 0836
fax +1 317 842 1103
1963 □ organisation of some 6000
broadcast engineers and other
professionals in related areas. It
publishes a *Newsletter* (4).

SBS · AUSTRALIA
- Special Broadcasting Service
4 Cliff Street
Milson's Point
NSW 2061
tel +61 2 964 2828
fax +61 2 964 2863
tlx AA 120944
□ to provide multilingual radio and,
where authorised by regulations from
August 1978, television services.

SBS · JAPAN
- Shizuoka Broadcasting System
1-1 Toro 3-chome
Shizuoka 422
tel +81 54 284 8900
□ television station.

SBS · KOREA
- Seoul Broadcasting System Production
13-2 Yoido-Dong
Youngdungpo-Ku
Seoul 150-010
tel +2 784 1055-7 / 1067/8
fax +2 784 6660

□ television broadcaster and producer and distributor of programme material.

SBS · USA
■ Satellite Business Systems

SBT · BRAZIL
■ Sistema Brasileiro de TV
Rua Dona Santa Veloso 535
Vila Guilherme
São Paulo 02050
tel   +55 11 292 9044
fax   +55 11 264 6004
tlx   22126
□ national television broadcasting station.

SC · TECHNICAL TERM
■ sharp cut
■ single contact
■ sub-carrier

SCA · USA
■ Screen Composers of America
2451 Nichols Canyon Road
Los Angeles
CA 90046-1798
tel   +1 213 876 6040
1945 □ organisation of musical composers for film, television and radio. It seeks to monitor performances of background music used in these media on a national basis.

SCA · TECHNICAL TERM
■ subsidiary communications authorisation

SCALE · PORTUGAL
■ Small Countries Improve their Audiovisual Level in Europe
Rua D João V, 8-R/C Dto.
1200 Lisbon
tel   +351 1 386 0630 / 0982
fax   +351 1 386 0647
1991 □ by cross-border collaboration, the 7 "small" EC member states - Belgium, Denmark, Greece, Ireland, Luxembourg, The Netherlands and Portugal - are attempting to take advantage of the economies of scale offered by the new audiovisual arena. An initiative of **MEDIA.**

SCARE · FRANCE
■ Syndicat Cinémas d'Art, de Répertoire et d'Essai
22 rue d'Artois
75008 Paris
tel   +33 1 45 63 45 64
□ art, repertory and art-house cinema federation.

SCART · TECHNICAL TERM
■ Syndicat des Constructeurs d'Appareils Radio Récepteurs et Téléviseurs

SCC · TECHNICAL TERM
■ specialised common carrier

SCDA · TECHNICAL TERM
■ sub-carrier distribution amplifier

SCET · UK
■ Scottish Council for Educational Technology
74 Victoria Crescent Road
Glasgow G12 9JN
tel   +44 41 334 9314
fax   +44 41 334 6519
□ research and development agency which focusses on education and training in Scotland, including through distribution of training films and videos.

SCG · USA
■ Screen Cartoonists Guild

SCINFOMA · MALI
■ Service Cinématographique du Ministère de l'Information du Mali
see **CNPC** · MALI

SCN · CANADA
■ Saskatchewan Communications Network
800 1920 Broad Street
Château Towers
Regina
Saskatchewan S4P 3V7
tel   +1 306 787 0490
fax   +1 306 787 0496
1989 □ educational broadcasting authority, operating 2 cable networks.

SCN · PANAMA
■ Southern Command Network

Edif. 209
Fuerte Clayton
Apdo. 919
Panama
tel +507 875567
1943 □ television station.

SCP · TECHNICAL TERM
▪ set-up control panel

SCPC · TECHNICAL TERM
▪ single channel per carrier

SCR · TECHNICAL TERM
▪ silicon-controlled rectifier

SCS · USA
▪ Society for Cinema Studies
c/o Gorham Kindem
University of North Carolina
Swain Hall
CB No. 6235
Chapel Hill
NC 27599
1959 □ society concerned with the
study of the moving image and
including among its members
academics, historians, critics, film-
makers and scholars. It publishes
Cinema Journal (4).

SCSI · TECHNICAL TERM
▪ small computer system(s) interface

SCTE · UK
▪ Society of Cable Television Engineers
Fulton House
Fulton Road
Wembley Park
Middlesex HA9 OTF
tel +44 81 902 8998
fax +44 81 903 8719
1945 □ to raise the standard of cable
television engineering to the highest
technical level which may from time to
time be commercially practicable; by
cooperation amongst the membership
and by the specialised knowledge and
experience of individual members, to
elevate and improve the status and
efficiency of those engaged in that
profession who are members; to afford
to those who may be elected members
and who at the time of their election

have not attained that level of technical
skill or experience which is the
standard of the society, the opportunity
of attaining that standard. It publishes
Cable Television Engineering (4).

SCTE · USA
▪ Society of Cable Television Engineers
669 Exton Commons
Exton
PA 19341
tel +1 215 363 6888
1969

SCTV · INDONESIA
▪ Surya Citra Televisi
Jalan Raya Perjuangan
Kebun Jeruk
Jakarta 11530
tel +62 21 530 3568
fax +62 21 549 0945
□ television broadcaster.

SCU · TECHNICAL TERM
▪ shutter control unit

SD · TECHNICAL TERM
▪ serial drag

SDDS · TECHNICAL TERM
▪ Sony Dynamic Digital Sound™

SDF · SWITZERLAND
▪ Schweizerischer Verband für Spiel-
und Dokumentarfilmproduktion
▪ Association Suisse des Producteurs de
Films de Fiction et de Documentaires
(FFD)
Zinggstr. 16
3007 Bern
tel +41 31 46 40 01
fax +41 31 46 40 53
□ association for producers of feature
and documentary films.

SDG · USA
▪ Screen Directors Guild

SDI · TECHNICAL TERM
▪ serial digital interface

SDIF · TECHNICAL TERM
▪ Sony digital interface format

SDIG · USA
- Screen Directors International Guild

SDT · JAPAN
- Shizuoka Daiichi Television
Corporation
563 Nakahara
Shizuoka 422
tel +81 54 283 8111
□ television station.

SE · TECHNICAL TERM
- sound effects (*aka* SFX)

SECAM · TECHNICAL TERM
- séquence couleur à/avec mémoire

SEE · BELGIUM
- Signal Engineering & Electronics
Avenue Reine Astrid, 1
1440 Wauthier-Braine
tel +32 2 366 9974
fax +32 2 366 2328
1972 □ its activities are design,
manufacturing and sales of CATV
products for the European, specialising
in those for CATV signal distribution on
a fixed (coax or fibre) medium.

SEG · USA
- Screen Extras Guild, Inc
3629 Cahuenga Boulevard W
Los Angeles
CA 90068
tel +1 213 851 4301
fax +1 213 851 0262
1945 □ union of those who work as
extras in the film and television
industries.

SEG · TECHNICAL TERM
- special effects generator

SEKAM · THE NETHERLANDS
- Stichting ter Exploitatie van
Kabeltelevisierechten
PO Box 75048
1070 AA Amsterdam
tel +31 20 676 5088
fax +31 20 676 5837
□ foundation for the exploitation of
cable television rights.

SEP · USA

- Sony Electronic Publishing
see **SEPC** · USA

SEPC · USA
- Sony Electronic Publishing Company
Marketing Communications
9 West 57th Street
New York
NY 10019
*also known as Sony Electronic
Publishing (SEP)*

SEPMAG · TECHNICAL TERM
- separate magnetic soundtrack

SEPOPT · TECHNICAL TERM
- separate optical soundtrack

SEPT · FRANCE
- Société d'Edition de Programmes de
Télévision
35 Quai André Citroën
75015 Paris
tel +33 1 40 59 39 77
fax +33 1 45 78 09 27
1986 □ cultural television channel
broadcasting by satellite.

SES · LUXEMBOURG
- Société Européenne des Satellites
Château de Betzdorf
6815 Luxembourg
tel +352 717251
fax +352 71725 324/227
tlx 60625 ASTRA LU
1985 □ operates the ASTRA satellite
system, Europe's first private television
system.

SESAM · TURKEY
- Sinema Eserleri Sahlpieri Meslek
Birligi

SEYBC · SEYCHELLES
- Seychelles Broadcasting Corporation
see **SBC** · SEYCHELLES

SF · SWEDEN
- AB Svensk Filmindustri
S-117 88 Stockholm
tel +46 8 658 7500
fax +46 8 658 3704
1919 □ film distributor and producer.

SF · TECHNICAL TERM
- science fiction
- soft focus

SFA · FRANCE
- Syndicat Français des Artistes
Interprètes
21 bis rue Victor Massé
75009 Paris
tel   +33 1 42 85 88 11
fax +33 1 45 26 47 21
◻ union for the defence and promotion
of the interests of professional actors,
dancers, singers, variety artists, circus
performers and others. It publishes
Plateaux (4).

SFA · UK
- Scottish Film Archive
Dowanhill
74 Victoria Crescent Road
Glasgow G12 9JN
tel   +44 41 334 4445
fax +44 41 334 8132
1976 ◻ film archive with material
dating from 1897 and concerning
aspects of Scottish social, cultural and
industrial theory.

SFA · TECHNICAL TERM
- still frame audio

SFB · GERMANY
- Sender Freies Berlin
Masuren Allee 8-14
14057 Berlin
tel   +49 30 3031-0
fax +49 30 3015062
tlx   182813
1953 ◻ public radio and television
broadcasting company.

SFC · DENMARK
- Statens Filmcentral
27 Vestergade
1456 Copenhagen V
tel   +45 33 13 26 86
fax +45 33 13 02 03
1939 ◻ as the National Film Board of
Denmark, regulated by the Ministry of
Culture, it produces, purchases and
rents out short films and documentaries
on 16mm and video to educational
institutions and libraries. It publishes

various annual catalogues.

SFC · UK
- Scottish Film Council
Dowanhill
74 Victoria Crescent Road
Glasgow G12 9ST
tel   +44 41 334 4445
fax +44 41 334 8132
1934 ◻ the provision of public access
to the widest possible range of cinema
facilities and activities; the development
of the study of film and related media
in both formal and informal education;
the stimulation and development of
film, video and television production in
Scotland; the collection and
preservation, through the operation of
the Scottish Film Archive (**SFA**), of
films, video tapes, artefacts and other
materials which are relevant to the
history and development of these media
in Scotland and to contemporary
Scottish culture and society.

SFD · UK
- Society of Film Distributors Ltd
Royalty House
72-73 Dean Street
London W1V 5HB
tel   +44 71 437 4383
fax +44 71 734 0912
1915 ◻ to promote and protect the
interests of film distributors and to
devise means to promote cooperation
amongst those engaged in film
distribution for the protection of their
mutual interests.

SFI · SWEDEN
- Svenska Filminstitutet
- Swedish Film Institute
Filmhuset
Borgvägen 1-5
PO Box 27126
S-102 52 Stockholm
tel   +46 8 665 1100
fax +46 8 661 1820
tlx   13326 FILMINS S
1963 ◻ national film institute, intended
to be a central organisation for Swedish
film and cinematic culture. An
agreement between the Swedish
government and the film and video

industries stipulates the purposes of the institute: to promote the production of Swedish films; to increase public interest in films; to promote the distribution and exhibition of quality films; to monitor technological development in the film sector; to disseminate knowledge about films; to contribute to the preservation of films and material of interest to film and cultural history; to encourage international cooperation in all these areas; to represent the interest of cinema in Sweden and abroad; to support other objectives in the field of cinema.

SFK · GERMANY
- Verband der Szenenbildner, Filmarchitekten und Kostümbildner
Bavariafilmplatz 7
82031 Geiselgasteig
tel   +49 89 6493139
□ association of set, production and costume designers for the cinema.

SFP · FRANCE
- Société Française de Production
36 rue des Alouettes
75019 Paris
tel   +33 1 40 03 50 00
fax   +33 1 42 03 18 35
tlx   240888
1975 □ producer of major programmes for television and the cinema.

SFP · SWEDEN
- Föreningen Sveriges Filmproducenter
Ankdammagatan 5 H
Box 1008
171 21 Solna
tel   +46 8 7305780
fax   +46 8 273745
□ trade association for Swedish film producers.

SFSIC · FRANCE
- Société Française des Sciences de l'Information et de la Communication
c/o MSH
54 Boulevard Raspail
75270 Paris Cedex 06
□ society whose objectives are: to promote new exchanges between professionals and universities regarding communication and culture; to represent members of the association.

SFTV · SWITZERLAND
- Schweizerischer Filmtechnikerinnen- und Filmtechniker Verband
- Association Suisse des Techniciennes et Techniciens du Film (ASTF)
Josefstrasse 106
Postfach 3274
8031 Zürich
tel   +41 1 272 2149
fax   +41 1 271 3350
□ association of film technicians.

SFV · SWITZERLAND
- Schweizerischer Filmverleiher-Verband
- Association Suisse des Distributeurs de Films (ASDF)
Effingerstr. 11
Postfach 8175
3001 Bern
tel   +41 31 25 50 77
fax   +41 31 26 03 73
□ to represent the interests of distributors in relation to cinema exhibitors and authorities.

SFW-AVA · THE NETHERLANDS
- Stichting Film en Wetenschap-Audio Visueel Archief
Zeeburgerkade 8
1019 HA Amsterdam
tel   +31 20 665 2966
fax   +31 20 665 9086
1970 □ the archiving of moving image and sound material and of documentation in this field, particularly material that is considered to be of interest to scientific research and education in The Netherlands; to contribute to research into historical audiovisual material, in particular in higher education and scientific research, and to promote its responsible use. It publishes the *SFW Yearbook*.

SFX · TECHNICAL TERM
- sound effects (*aka* SE)
- special effects (*aka* FX, SPEFX, SPFX)

SG · TECHNICAL TERM

- stereo generator
- synch generator

SHB · TECHNICAL TERM
- super high-band

SHBA · TECHNICAL TERM
- super high-band aperture

SHF · TECHNICAL TERM
- super high frequency

SHIVKV · BELGIUM
- Stedelijk Hoger Instituut voor Visuele Kommunikatie en Vormgeving
Weg Naar As, 50
3600 Genk
tel +32 11 359951
fax +32 11 357705
□ institution offering education in film, video and animation.

SHL · TECHNICAL TERM
- studio to headend link

SI · SWEDEN
- Svenska Institutet
- Swedish Institute
PO Box 7434
S-103 91 Stockholm
tel +46 8 789 2000
fax +46 8 207248
tlx 10025 swedins s
□ government-financed foundation established primarily to disseminate knowledge about Sweden's social and cultural life abroad. It offers international non-commercial distribution of short films, organises film weeks and serves as the contact organisation in Sweden for international film festivals.

SI · TECHNICAL TERM
- sponsor identification
- station identification

SIA · TECHNICAL TERM
- storage instantaneous audimeter

SIAE · ITALY
- Società Italiana degli Autori ed Editori
Viale della Letteratura 30
00144 Rome
tel +39 6 59901
fax +39 6 5923351
tlx 611423
1882 □ mediator in the management of its members copyright matters; studying problems of copyright and diffusion of the Italian artistic inheritance; collection services on behalf of several organisations; collection of the "blank tape" levy and distribution of this income to the copyright's owners; keeping the Public Cinematographic Register, in which all Italian films (complete with data) are recorded, and where transfers of the utilisation rights in the work are successively recorded; keeping a record of the receipts of every Italian film as it circulates, both for the State and for the producer. It publishes *SIAE Bulletin* (6), *Il Diritto d'Autore* (4), *Lo Spettacolo* (4), *Lo Spettacolo in Italia* (1) and *Il Teatro in Italia* (1).

SIARTE · PORTUGAL
- Sindicato das Artes e Espectaculos

SIAS · TECHNICAL TERM
- strokes interpreted animated sequences

SIBC · SOLOMON ISLANDS
- Solomon Islands Broadcasting Corporation
PO Box 654
Honiara
tel +677 20051
fax +677 23159
tlx 66406
1977 □ to transport by television or radio, mainly in Pidgin and some English, any matter or message to inform, educate or entertain the population of the Solomon Islands.

SIC · PORTUGAL
- Sociedade Independente de Comunicação
Rua Castilho 65-1º
1200 Lisbon
tel +351 1 315 2960
fax +351 1 315 2959
1992 □ private television broadcasting channel.

SICOLTRACINE · COLOMBIA
- Sindicato Colombiano de
Trabajadores de Cine
Cra 5 No 18-81
Of 404, PO Box 55480
Bogota

SIDEC · SENEGAL
- Société d'Importation de Distribution
et d'Exploitation Cinématographique
see **CIDC** · SENEGAL

SIFF · SINGAPORE
- Singapore International Film Festival
168 Kim Seng Road
Singapore 0923
tel   +65 3368706
fax +65 3368713
□ film festival.

SIFF · USA
- Seattle International Film Festival
801 East Pine Street
Seattle
Washington
DC 98122
tel   +1 206 324 9996
fax +1 206 324 9998
tlx   329 473 BURGESS SEA
1974 □ annual film festival, held in
May/June, screening over 140 feature
films and over 50 short films.

SIFT · UK
- Summary of Information on Film and
Television
c/o Library and Information Services
British Film Institute
21 Stephen Street
London W1P 1PL
tel   +44 71 255 1444
fax +44 71 436 7950
tlx   27624 BFILDNG
1989 □ information and references on
400 000 films, television programmes
and videos, 28 000 personalities, 115
000 organisations and 5000 events.
Every year another 11 000 titles are
added.

SII · TECHNICAL TERM
- sponsor identification index

SIIS · FRANCE

- Société Internationale de l'Image et
de Son
44 rue Cauchy
94110 Arcueil
tel   +33 1 47 40 82 82
fax +33 1 47 40 82 83
□ international society for image and
sound.

SÍK · ICELAND
- Samband Ísland
Kvikmyndaframleidanda
Pósthússtræti 13
PO Box 476
121 Reykjavík
tel   +354 1 28188 / 628188
fax +354 1 623424
□ association of Icelandic film
producers.

SILEX · TECHNICAL TERM
- semiconductor laser intersatellite link
experiment

SILVTR · TECHNICAL TERM
- silent videotape recording

SIMAVELEC · FRANCE
- Syndicat des Industries de Matériels
Audiovisuels Electroniques
11 rue Hamelin
75783 Paris Cedex 16
tel   +33 1 45 05 71 81
fax +33 1 45 05 71 72
tlx   611045
□ union for industries involved in
electronic audiovisual materials.

SIMPP · USA
- Society of Independent Motion
Picture Producers

SIN · USA
- Spanish International Network

SINART · COSTA RICA
- Sistema Nacional de Radio y
Televisión Cultural
Apdo. 7-1980
1000 San José
tel   +506 31 0839
fax +506 31 6604
tlx   0376 2374 sincom cr
□ government-owned cultural television

broadcaster.

SIP · TECHNICAL TERM
- station independence programme

SIS · FRANCE
- Société Industrielle de Sonorisation

SIS · UK
- Satellite Information Services Ltd
Satellite House
17 Corsham Street
London N1 6DR
tel +44 71 253 2232
fax +44 71 251 3737
□ supplier of satellite services to the
European and international broadcast
industry. It specialises in the hire and
operation of satellite links for the live
transmission of television pictures for
SNG and planned **OB** events.

SIS · TECHNICAL TERM
- sound in synch

SISCOMS · FRANCE
- Secrétariat International Spiritain de
Communications Sociales par l'Audio
Visuel

SIT · TECHNICAL TERM
- silicon-intensified/intensifier target

SITE · TECHNICAL TERM
- satellite instructional television
experiment

SITI · FRANCE
- Salon International des Techniques de
l'Image
5 bis rue Jacquemont
75017 Paris

SIU · TECHNICAL TERM
- sets in use

SIV · SWITZERLAND
- Semaine Internationale de Vidéo
Saint-Gervais Genève
5 rue du Temple
1201 Geneva
tel +41 22 732 2060
fax +41 22 738 4215
1985 □ international video week, held

every other year, attracting more than
500 video works from many countries.
Some 40 video works are selected to
compete.

SKT · JAPAN
- Shizuoka Kenmin Television Co Ltd
13 Shichiken-cho
Shizuoka 420
tel +81 54 251 3300
□ television station.

SKV · SWITZERLAND
- Schweizerischer Kino-Verband
- Association Cinématographique
Suisse (ACS)
- Associazione Svizzera dei Cinema
Effingerstr. 11
Postfach 8175
CH-3001 Bern
tel +41 31 381 5077
fax +41 31 382 0373
1925 □ association of exhibitors.

SLBC · SRI LANKA
- Sri Lanka Broadcasting Corporation
PO Box 574
Colombo 7
tel +94 1 697491 / 697500
fax +94 1 695488
tlx 21408 SLABCOR CE
1967 □ controls television and radio
broadcasting.

SLBS · SIERRA LEONE
- Sierre Leone Broadcasting Service
New England
Freetown
tel +232 222 40123
tlx 3334 RADTEX SL
1934 □ government-controlled
television and radio broadcasting
service, operating mainly in English and
4 vernacular languages - Krio, Limba,
Mende and Temne. It also has a weekly
broadcast in French.

SLCB · TECHNICAL TERM
- single line colour bar

SLF · TECHNICAL TERM
- safelight filter - film

SLG · TECHNICAL TERM

■ safelight filter - glass

SLP · TECHNICAL TERM
■ standard long play

SLR · TECHNICAL TERM
■ single lens reflex

SLRC · SRI LANKA
■ Sri Lanka Rupavahini Corporation
(Television)
Independence Square
Colombo 7
tel   +94 1 501050/4 / 580131 /
587722
fax +94 1 580929
tlx   22148 SLTV CE
1982 □ television service, broadcasting
in English, Sinhalese and Tamil.

SLSC · TECHNICAL TERM
■ split-luminance/split chrominance

SLV · TECHNICAL TERM
■ satellite launch vehicle

SM · TECHNICAL TERM
■ service module
■ spectrum management
■ stage manager
■ station manager

SMAC · TECHNICAL TERM
■ slung microphone aiming control

SMARTS · USA
■ Selective Multiple Address Radio and
Television Service

SMATV · TECHNICAL TERM
■ satellite (to) master antenna television

SMID · DENMARK
■ Sammenslutningen af Medieforskere i
Danmark
Per Jauert, President
Aarhus Universitet
Niels Juelsgade 84
8200 Aarhus
tel   +45 8613 6711
fax +45 8610 4680
1976 □ association for the study of
mass communication, with some 140
members. It publishes *Mediekultur* (2).

SMMO · THE NETHERLANDS
■ Stichting Migranten Media Onderwijs
Arie Bimondstraat 109
1054 PD Amsterdam
tel   +31 20 852259
□ institution offering courses in media.

SMO · UK
■ Sony Music Operations
Rabans Lane
Aylesbury
Bucks HP19 3BX
tel   +44 296 26151
fax +44 296 81009
□ distributors of Sony video, CD and
record products.

SMPIA · CANADA
■ Saskatchewan Motion Picture
Association
2431 8th Avenue
Regina
Saskatchewan S4R 5J7
tel   +1 306 525 9899
fax +1 306 569 1818
1985 □ non-profit organisation
representing the interests of the film
and video community in Saskatchewan.
Collectively, the members of the
organisation have worked to improve
opportunities for education, production,
promotion and appreciation of film and
video activity in Saskatchewan.

SMPS · TECHNICAL TERM
■ switched mode power supply

SMPTAD · USA
■ Society of Motion Picture and
Television Art Directors
Suite 315
11365 Ventura Boulevard
Studio City
CA 91604
tel   +1 818 762 9995
1968 □ organisation of those working
professionally in the construction, décor
and design of film and television
products.

SMPTE · USA
■ Society of Motion Picture and
Television Engineers
595 West Hartsdale Avenue

White Plains
NY 10607-1824
tel +1 914 761 1100
fax +1 914 761 3115
1916 □ to foster the advancement of engineering and technical aspects of motion pictures, television, multimedia and allied arts and sciences; to disseminate scientific information in these areas; to sponsor lectures, exhibitions, classes and conferences. Membership is open to those with a clearly defined interest in the field. It publishes *SMPTE Journal* (12).

SMS · USA
■ Subscriber Management Systems

SMT · TECHNICAL TERM
■ surface mount technology

SNA · PORTUGAL
■ Secretariado Nacional para o Audiovisual
Rua S. Pedro de Alcântara 45 (1H)
1200 Lisbon
tel +351 1 848 4491 / 848 6095 / 847 3077
fax +351 1 808 170

SNC · FRANCE
■ Société Nouvelle de Cinématographie

SNC · USA
■ Satellite News Channels

SNCCI · ITALY
■ Sindacato Nazionale Critici Cinematografici Italiani
Via Yser 8
00198 Rome
□ national union of Italian film critics.

SNG · TECHNICAL TERM
■ satellite news gathering

SNGCI · ITALY
■ Sindacato Nazionale Giornalisti Cinematografici Italiani
Via Basento 52/d
00198 Rome
□ national union of Italian cinema journalists.

SNPC · SENEGAL
■ Société Nouvelle de Production Cinématographique
Bureau du Cinéma
Ministère de la Culture et de la Communication
BP 4027
Dakar
tel +221 210527
□ official organisation for cinema.

SNR · TECHNICAL TERM
■ subject to non-renewal

SNTC · CANADA
■ Syndicat National des Travailleurs et Travailleuses en Communication
6845 rue Saint-Denis
Montreal
Quebec H2S 2S3
tel +1 514 276 8591
fax +1 514 276 6413
□ national union of workers in the communication sectors.

SNTPCAT · FRANCE
■ Syndicat National des Techniciens et Travailleurs de la Production Cinématographique et de Télévision (Audio-Visuel)
10 rue de Trétaigne
75018 Paris
tel +33 1 42 55 82 66
fax +33 1 42 52 56 26
1937 □ to help and inform film and television technicians and workers about conditions of work and collective guarantees. It publishes a *Newsletter* (4/5).
also known as SNTPCT

SNTPCT · FRANCE
see **SNTPCAT** · FRANCE

SNTR · FRANCE
■ Syndicat National des Techniciens et Réalisateurs de la Production Cinématographique et Télévisuelle
14-16 rue des Lilas
75019 Paris
tel +33 1 42 00 48 49
□ national union of film and television directors and technicians.

SNTV · NICARAGUA
- Sistema Nacional de Televisión
Km 3½
Carretera Sur.
Las Palmas
Apdo. 1505
Managua, JR
tel +505 2 660879
fax +505 2 666522
tlx 1226
□ national television broadcasting organisation.

SNV · TECHNICAL TERM
- satellite news vehicle

SOBA · UK
- Schools Olympus Broadcasting Association
c/o Terry Brockley
Technology Centre
Bridge Street
Llangefni
Gwynedd LL77 7TW
1991

SODRE · URUGUAY
- Servicio Oficial de Difusión de Radiotelevisión y Espectáculos
Sarandl 430
Montevideo 11600
tel +598 2 955758
tlx UY 6553
□ television broadcasting station.

SOF · TECHNICAL TERM
- sound on film

SOFRATEV · FRANCE
- Société Française d'Etudes et de Réalisations d'Équipements de Radiodiffusion et de Télévision

SOGIC · CANADA
- Société Générale des Industries Culturelles Québec
Bureau 200
1755 Boulevard René-Lévesque Est
Montreal
Quebec H2K 4P6
tel +1 514 873 7768
fax +1 514 873 4388
tlx 055 61675
1988 □ by means of financial

assistance and investment, it helps support the Quebec film industry and distributes and promotes its films to the international market.

SONACIB · BURKINA FASO
- Société Nationale de Distribution et d'Exploitation Cinématographique du Burkina
BP 206
Ouagadougou
tel +226 306182 / 302284
□ national body responsible for the promotion and distribution of films.

SOPACIA · FRANCE
- Société de Participations Cinématographiques Africaines
1973 □ film distribution project.

SOS · TECHNICAL TERM
- sound on sound

SOT · TECHNICAL TERM
- sound on tape

SOURCES · THE NETHERLANDS
- Stimulating Outstanding Resources for Creative European Screenwriting
Jan Luykenstraat 92
1071 CT Amsterdam
tel +31 20 672 0801
fax +31 20 672 0399
1992 □ a **MEDIA** initiative established to contribute to a higher standard of European film and television production by means of script-doctoring workshops for professional scriptwriters and other activities that stimulate and improve the craft of screenwriting in Europe.

SOV · TECHNICAL TERM
- sound on vision

SOVT · TECHNICAL TERM
- sound on videotape

SP · TECHNICAL TERM
- service provider
- single perforated
- standard play
- superior performance
- supervising producer

SPAA · AUSTRALIA
▪ Screen Production Association of Australia
Suite 2, 1st floor
144 Riley Street
East Sydney
NSW 2010
tel   +61 2 360 4900
fax +61 2 360 7106
1956 □ national body representing the interests of independent film and television producers: representing members' views to government, statutory authorities, industry groups and the general public; developing industrial policies which are workable between all parties and supportive of the industry; providing industrial representation and advice; sustaining a high level of awareness to the industry and its public which reflects both cultural and commercial viability. It publishes *Above the Line* magazine (12) and *Location Australia* (1).

SPC · TECHNICAL TERM
▪ station programme cooperative

SPCV · PORTUGAL
▪ Sociedade Portuguesa de Cinematografia e Video

SPD · TECHNICAL TERM
▪ spectral power distribution

SPECTRE · TECHNICAL TERM
▪ special purpose extra channels for terrestrial radio-communications enhancements

SPEFX · TECHNICAL TERM
▪ special effects (*aka* FX, SFX, SPFX)

SPF · CZECH REPUBLIC
▪ Slovenská Požičovna Filmov

SPFM · USA
▪ Society for the Preservation of Film Music

SPFP · FRANCE
▪ Syndicat des Producteurs de Films Publicitaires
64 rue du Château

92100 Boulogne
tel   +33 46 04 95 33
fax +33 46 05 14 24
1985 □ association of French advertising film producers.

SPFX · TECHNICAL TERM
▪ special effects (*aka* FX, SFX, SPEFX)

SPG · TECHNICAL TERM
▪ synchronising pulse generator

SPIA · USA
▪ Society for Photo-Optical Instrumentation Engineers
1000 200th Street
Bellingham
WA 98225
tel   +1 206 676 3290

SPL · TECHNICAL TERM
▪ sound pressure level

SPN · USA
▪ Satellite Programming Network

SPP · TECHNICAL TERM
▪ synchronised power pack

SPPA · FRANCE
▪ Syndicat des Producteurs de Programmes Audiovisuels
see **S2PA** · FRANCE

SPSS · PORTUGAL
▪ Scale Producers Support System
Rua D João V, 8-R/C Dto.
1200 Lisbon
tel   +351 1 386 0630 / 0982
fax +351 1 386 0647
1992 □ to strengthen the independent production of small European countries, by supporting industrial management and consolidation as well as by their ability to cooperate with their European partners. It offers 3 types of loan, including the Company Overhead Loan (**COL**).

SPTV · RUSSIA
▪ Sankt-Peterburgskoje Televidenije
□ television broadcasting service.

SQPB · TECHNICAL TERM

- super quality playback
- Super VHS quasi playback

SR · GERMANY
- Saarländischer Rundfunk-Fernsehen
Funkhaus Halberg
Postfach 1050
6600 Saarbrücken
tel   +49 681 6020
fax   +49 681 6023874
tlx   4428977
□ regional broadcasting organisation.

SR · TECHNICAL TERM
- shared resource
- silent reflex
- spectral recording
- system remote

SRC · CANADA
- Société Radio-Canada
1500 avenue Bronson
CP 8478
Ottawa
Ontario K1G 3J5
tel   +1 613 724 1200
fax   +1 613 738 6742
tlx   053 4260
1936 □ provides a national
broadcasting service in the French
language.

SRCTA · FRANCE
- Syndicat des Réalisateurs et Créateurs
du Cinéma, de la Télévision et de
l'Audiovisuel
c/o SFP P.2388
36 rue des Alouettes
75019 Paris
tel   +33 1 41 41 23 67 / 44 21 56 08 /
44 21 56 48
fax   +33 1 44 21 56 35
1978 □ union of directors.

SRF · FRANCE
- Société des Réalisateurs de Film
215 rue du Faubourg St-Honoré
75008 Paris
tel   +33 1 45 63 96 30
fax   +33 1 40 74 07 96
□ association of French film directors.

SRG · SWITZERLAND
- Schweizerische Radio- und
Fernsehgesellschaft
see **SBC** · SWITZERLAND

SRG · USA
- Station Research Group

SS · TECHNICAL TERM
- solid state
- stock shot

SSA · SWITZERLAND
- Société Suisse des Auteurs
- Schweizerische Autoren-Gesellschaft
12/14 rue Centrale
Case postale 3893
1002 Lausanne
tel   +41 21 312 6571
fax   +41 21 312 6582
tlx   454812
1963 □ protects the rights of authors -
scriptwriters, adaptors, directors -
working in the audiovisual media.

SSA · TECHNICAL TERM
- subscriber service amplifier

SSB · TECHNICAL TERM
- single sideband

SSBSC · TECHNICAL TERM
- single sideband suppressed carrier
case

SSFF · NORWAY
- Statens Studiesenter for Film
Storengveien 8 B
1342 Jar
tel   +47 67 53 00 33
fax   +47 67 12 48 65
1985 □ to organise advanced training
workshops, courses and seminars for
professionals throughout the industry
and also provide basic education in
media for students who have received
some form of basic training in the
audiovisual media.

SSG · TECHNICAL TERM
- synch signal generator

SSI · TECHNICAL TERM
- small-scale integration

SSL · UK

■ Solid State Logic Ltd
Begbroke
Oxford OX5 1RU
tel   +44 865 842300
fax +44 865 842 842118
tlx   837400 SSL OXG
1969 □ leading designer and
manufacturer of audio systems for the
music recording, video, film and
broadcasting industries.

SSM · TECHNICAL TERM
■ second surface mirror

SSO · TECHNICAL TERM
■ single system operator

SSPA · TECHNICAL TERM
■ solid state power amplifier

SSPS · TECHNICAL TERM
■ satellite power station

SSQAM · TECHNICAL TERM
■ spectrally shaped quadrature
amplitude modulator

SSR · SWITZERLAND
■ Società Svizzera di Radiotelevisione
see **SBC** · SWITZERLAND

SSR · SWITZERLAND
■ Société Suisse de Radiodiffusion et
Télévision
see **SBC** · SWITZERLAND

SSS · TECHNICAL TERM
■ swift servo system

SSTDMA · TECHNICAL TERM
■ satellite-switched time division
multiple access

SSTV · TECHNICAL TERM
■ slow-scan television

SSVC · UK
■ Services Sound and Vision
Corporation
Chalfont Grove
Chalfont St Peter
Gerrards Cross
Bucks SL9 8TN
tel   +44 494 874461

fax +44 494 872982
tlx   837254 SSVC G
1982 □ to provide training films for the
British Armed Forces and corporate
video customers; to provide UK
servicemen and women abroad with
UK television and own television
services; to provide HM ships at sea
and isolated military detachments with
UK television programmes on cassettes;
to provide entertainment, videos and
films for service audiences worldwide;
to provide a single source solution for
customers' training needs - video,
audiovisual and interactive video; to
offer our production facilities to
external customers.

SSVR · TECHNICAL TERM
■ solid state video recorder

ST · SLOVAKIA
■ Slovenská Televizia
see **STV** · SLOVAKIA

ST · TECHNICAL TERM
■ screw terminal
■ slide-tape
■ superior tape

STA · USA
■ Subscription Television Association

STA · TECHNICAL TERM
■ special temporary authorisation

STAM · TECHNICAL TERM
■ sequential thermal anhysteric
magnetisation

STAR TV · HONG KONG
■ Satellite Television Asian Region Ltd
12th floor
Hutchinson House
10 Harcourt Road
Hong Kong
tel   +852 532 1888
fax +852 523 5999 / 537 1704
1991 □ international satellite television
service, broadcasting in English and
Mandarin, established in order to meet
the increasing need for television
information and entertainment in the
Asian market.

STC · TECHNICAL TERM
- single time code

STCVQ · CANADA
- Syndicat des Techniciennes et Techniciens du Cinéma et Vidéo du Québec
Bureau 911
4200 Boulevard Saint-Laurent
Montreal
Quebec H2W 2R2
tel   +1 514 985 5751
fax +1 514 985 2227
□ group of film and video technicians.

STDN · TECHNICAL TERM
- space tracking and data network

STER · THE NETHERLANDS
- Stichting Ether Reclame
PB 344
Laapersveld 70
1200 AH Hilversum
tel   +31 35 725500
fax +31 35 246691
1966 □ selling television and radio airtime for commercial purposes (commercials), in favour of the Dutch public broadcasting system. It publishes *STER Nieuws* (c10) and an *Annual Report.*

STFG · SWITZERLAND
- Schweizer Trickfilmgruppe
- Groupement Suisse du Film d'Animation (GSFA)
Claude Ogiz
7 rue de la Place
2720 Tramelan
tel   +41 32 97 66 22
fax +41 32 97 41 69
□ to promote and support animated cinema in Switzerland.

STIA · USA
- Satellite Television Industry Association
see **SBCA** □ USA

STIC · MEXICO
- Sindicato de Trabajadores de la Industria Cinematográfica, Similares y Conexos de la R.M.
Pirineos 234

Santa Cruz Atoyac
C.P. 03310
Mexico 13, D.F.
tel   +52 5 604 1091 / 688 1472
fax +52 5 688 8129
□ labour union.

STL · TECHNICAL TERM
- studio-transmitter link

STOC-TV · USA
- Satellite Technical and Operational Committee Television

STPC · MEXICO
- Sindicato de Trabajadores Técnicos y Manuales de Estudios y Laboratorios de la Producción Cinematográfica S.I.C. de la R.M.
Fresas No. 12
Col Del Valle
tel   +52 5 575 0655
fax +52 5 559 9086
□ labour union.

STS · JAPAN
- Saga Television System
6-10 Joonai 1-chome
Saga 840
tel   +81 952 23 9111
□ television station.

STS · USA
- Specialised Telecommunication Service

STS · TECHNICAL TERM
- space transportation system

STV · JAPAN
- Sapporo Television Broadcasting Co Ltd
Kita Ichijo
Nishi 8-1-1
Chuo-ku
Sapporo 060-91
tel   +81 11 241 1181
□ television station.

STV · SLOVAKIA
- Slovenská Televizia
Asmolovova 28
845 45 Bratislava
tel   +42 7 721940

fax +42 7 322252
tlx 92277
□ Slovak television service.
also known as ST

STV · UK
■ Scottish Television plc
Cowcaddens
Glasgow G2 3PR
tel +44 41 332 9999
fax +44 41 332 6982
tlx 77388
1957 □ provides an independent
television service for central Scotland.

STV · TECHNICAL TERM
■ satellite television
■ subscription television

STVA · SWAZILAND
■ Swaziland Television Authority
PO Box A146
Mbabane
tel +268 43036-7
fax +268 42093
tlx 2138 WD
1983 □ government-owned television
corporation.

STVRC · USA
■ Satellite Television Viewing Rights
Coalition

STVS · SURINAME
■ Surinaamse Televisie Stichting
Cultuurtuinlaan
PO Box 535
Paramaribo
tel +597 73100
fax +597 77216
tlx 271
1965 □ government-owned
broadcasting station, operating services
in Dutch and English, as well as local
languages.

SUN · JAPAN
■ Sun Television Co Ltd
9-1 Minatojima Nakamachi 6-chome
Chuo-ku
Kobe 650
tel +81 78 303 3130
□ television station.

SVF · BELGIUM
■ Stichting Vlaamse Filmproductie
□ organisation which helps to provide
script and production funds to film-
makers.

SVFJ · SWITZERLAND
■ Schweizerischer Verband der
Filmjournalisten
■ Association Suisse des Journalistes
Cinématographiques (ASJC)
c/o Robert Richter
Werdtweg 8
3007 Bern
tel +41 31 371 3272
fax +41 31 371 1261
□ association of film critics.

SVG TV · ST VINCENT AND THE
GRENADINES
■ Saint Vincent and the Grenadines
Television
Dorsetshire Hill
PO Box 617
Kingstown
tel +1 809 61078
fax +1 809 61015
□ television station broadcasting both
American and local programmes.

SVGA · TECHNICAL TERM
■ super video graphics array

SVIP · SWEDEN
■ Sveriges Film och Videoproducenters
Förening
Malmvägen 15
S-115 41 Stockholm
1973 □ Swedish film and video
producers association.

SVKF · SWITZERLAND
■ Schweizerischer Verband für Kino
und Filmverleih
■ Association Suisse des Exploitants et
Distributeurs de Films (ASED)
Effingerstr. 11
Postfach 8175
CH-3001 Bern
tel +41 31 381 5077
fax +41 31 382 0373
□ association of Swiss film exhibitors
and distributors.

SVM · TECHNICAL TERM
- scanning velocity modulation

SVT · SWEDEN
- Sveriges Television AB
Oxenstiernsgatan 26-34
S-105 10 Stockholm
tel   +46 8 784 0000 / 7400
fax +46 8 784 1500
tlx   10000
□ public service broadcaster, operating 2 terrestrial, non-commercial national television channels.

SW · TECHNICAL TERM
- short wave
- super wide

SWABC · NAMIBIA
- South West African Broadcasting Corporation
see **NBC** · NAMIBIA

SWB · UK
- Summary of World Broadcasts
BBC Monitoring
Caversham Park
Reading
Berks RG4 8TZ
tel   +44 734 472742
fax +44 734 463823
tlx   848318
□ publication providing accurate coverage of international, political and economic affairs. It is available in 4 parts covering different regions. Summaries of broadcasts and news bulletins, or the complete text, are published without additional comment or interpretation to ensure impartial reporting.

SWF · GERMANY
- Südwestfunk
Hans-Bredow-Straße
76530 Baden-Baden
tel   +49 7221 920
fax +49 7221 922 010
tlx   787810
□ regional television station.

SWG · USA
- Screen Writers Guild
□ union of writers working in the film

and television industries.

SWIFT · AUSTRALIA
- Sources of Women Working In Film, Television and Video
see **WIFT** · AUSTRALIA

SWOM · THE NETHERLANDS
- Stichting ter Bevordering van het Wetenschappelijk Onderwijs in de Mediakunde
Drs M C Westermann, Secretary
Katholieke Universiteit Brabant
Postbus 90153
5000 LE Tilburg
tel   +33 13 662650 / 662508
1985 □ foundation for the promotion of university education in media science.

SWR · TECHNICAL TERM
- standing wave ratio

SWS · TECHNICAL TERM
- slow wave structure

SWT · TECHNICAL TERM
- short wave transmitter

SZDSZ · HUNGARY
- Színházi Dolgozók Szakszervezete
Gorkij Fasor 38
1068 Budapest 4
tel   +36 1 121 1120
fax +36 1 122 5412
□ federation of professional actors.

T

T&SG · USA
- Television and Screen Writers' Guild

TA · TECHNICAL TERM
- total audience

TAC · UK
- Teledwyr Annibynnol Cymru
Gronant
Caernarfon
Gwynedd LL55 1NS
tel   +44 286 671123
fax +44 286 678890
1983 □ trade association representing

the interests of Welsh independent producers.

TACET · USA
■ Television Advisory Committee for Educational Television

TACOMA · USA
■ Television Advisory Committee of Mexican Americans

TAF · TECHNICAL TERM
■ telecine analysis film

TAM · VENEZUELA
■ Televisora Andina de Mérida
Palacio Arzobispal
Plaza Bolívar
Apdo 222
Mérida
tel   +58 74 525758
tlx   74287
1982 ◻ private television station.

TAM · TECHNICAL TERM
■ television audience measurement

TAMI · USA
■ Television Accessory Manufacturers Institute

TAP · TECHNICAL TERM
■ Theatre Alignment Program

TAPE · TECHNICAL TERM
■ television audience programme evaluation

TARIF · TECHNICAL TERM
■ technical apparatus for the rectification of indifferent film

TARPAC · USA
■ Television and Radio Political Action Committee
National Association of Broadcasters (NAB)
1771 N Street NW
Washington
DC 20036-2891
tel   +1 800 424 8806
fax   +1 202 775 2157
◻ enables broadcasters in every state to make a financial contribution, on a national basis, to those candidates who are most likely to affect the business of broadcasting. TARPAC's funds pay for activities which educate and inform both broadcasters and members of Congress on relevant issues. These funds are used to promote understanding and allow for a dialogue between legislators and broadcasters.

TAS · UK
■ Tele-Aerials Satellite Ltd
Monkswell House
1 Monkswell Park
Manse Lane
Knaresborough
N Yorks HG5 8NQ
tel   +44 423 860133
fax   +44 423 860110
◻ **DTH** activities are geared to provide a national installation and maintenance service company; commercial operations concentrate on multi-point viewing systems via **VHF**, **UHF** and **IF** systems directly to the housing and hotel markets.

TASCON · TECHNICAL TERM
■ television automatic sequence control

TASO · USA
■ Television Allocations Study Organisation

TBA · USA
■ Television Bureau of Advertising
10th floor
477 Madison Avenue
New York
NY 10022-5892
tel   +1 212 486 1111
tel   +1 212 935 5631
1954 ◻ organisation of some 700 members who are dedicated to furthering television as an effective medium for advertising.
also known as TVB

TBA · TECHNICAL TERM
■ to be announced

TBC · JAPAN
■ Tohoku Broadcasting Co Ltd
26-1 Kazumi-cho

Yagiyama
Taihaku-ku
Sendai 982
tel   +81 22 229 1111
□ television station.

TBC · TECHNICAL TERM
▪ time base corrector/correction

TBD · TECHNICAL TERM
▪ to be determined

TBE · TECHNICAL TERM
▪ time-base error

TBI · UK
▪ Television Business International
21st Century Publishing
531/533 King's Road
London SW10 OTZ
tel   +44 71 352 3211
fax   +44 71 352 4883
tlx   925030
1988 □ international magazine (10
issues annually) for television
executives dealing with all issues
relating to the international television
market, including features on
programming genres, territory guides,
detailed statistical analysis of current
trends, news analysis and in-depth
features.

TBN · ST KITTS
▪ Trinity Broadcasting Network
Bath Plain
Nevis
tel   +1 809 469 5425
fax   +1 809 469 1723
□ television broadcasting service.

TBN · USA
▪ Trinity Broadcasting Network
2442 Michelle Drive
Tustin
CA
tel   +1 714 832 2950
□ cable television network.

TBS · JAPAN
▪ Tokyo Broadcasting System, Inc
5-3-6 Akasaka
Minato-ku
Tokyo 107-06

tel   +81 3 3584 3111
tel   +81 3 3584 1584
tlx   J24883 TBSBCAST
1951 □ television station.

TBS · USA
▪ Turner Broadcasting System, Inc
1050 Techwood Avenue
PO Box 105264
Atlanta
GA 30318-5264
tel   +1 404 827 1700
fax   +1 404 827 2437
1976 □ leading supplier of
entertainment and information
programming to the cable television
industry through its ownership and
operation of a number of full-time
programming services.

TC · TECHNICAL TERM
▪ technical coordinator
▪ telecine
▪ telecommand
▪ time code
▪ title card
▪ transfer of control

TCA · USA
▪ Television Critics Association

TCF · USA
▪ Twentieth Century Fox Film
Corporation
10201 West Pico Boulevard
Los Angeles
CA 90035
tel   +1 310 277 2211
fax   +1 310 203 2349
tlx   674875 CENTFOX
1935 □ film production and
distribution.

TCI · USA
▪ Telecommunications, Inc
5619 DTC Parkway
Englewood
CO 80111
tel   +1 303 721 5500
□ cable television network.

TCI-LI · TECHNICAL TERM
▪ time compressed integration of line
colour signals

TCI-LSI · TECHNICAL TERM
- time compressed integration of luminance and line-sequential colour signals

TCIP · TECHNICAL TERM
- time code in picture

TCN · AUSTRALIA
- Television Channel Nine Pty Ltd

TCR · TECHNICAL TERM
- telemetry, command and ranging

TCU · TECHNICAL TERM
- tape/timing/transmission control unit
- tight close-up

TCV · ITALY
- Totale Cine Video

TCXO · TECHNICAL TERM
- temperature-compensated crystal oscillator

TD · TECHNICAL TERM
- technical difficulties
- technical director

TDF · FRANCE
- Télédiffusion de France
21-27 rue Barbès
92542 Montrouge Cedex
tel   +33 1 46 57 11 15
fax +33 1 45 55 35 35
tlx   25738
1975 □ body which is responsible for organising and maintaining the networks; for research and study into television and radio equipment; and for broadcasting programmes which have been produced by the production companies **A2**, **FR3** and Radio France.

TDI · FRANCE
- Thorson Digital Image
29 rue Ganneron
75018 Paris
tel   +33 1 43 87 58 58
fax +33 1 40 08 03 02

TDM · MACAO
- Teledifusão de Macau
Rua Francisco Xavier Pereira 157-A

CP 446
Macao
tel   +853 519188
fax +853 520208
tlx   88309
□ private station, offering television broadcasting in Chinese and Portuguese, as well as 2 radio channels.

TDM · TECHNICAL TERM
- time division multiplex
- tuner/demodulator

TDMA · TECHNICAL TERM
- time division multiple access

TDRS(S) · TECHNICAL TERM
- tracking and data relay satellite (system)

TDS · TECHNICAL TERM
- time delay spectrometry

TE · TECHNICAL TERM
- test equipment

TEAME · UK
- National Association of Teacher Educators and Advisors in Media Education
c/o Mary Wood
Centre for Extra-Mural Studies in Higher and Further Education
Birkbeck College
University of London
26 Russell Square
London WC1B 5DQ
tel   +44 71 631 6639
fax +44 71 631 6688
□ media education association.

TEC · USA
- The Entertainment Channel

TEC · USA
- Turner Entertainment Company
One CNN Center
PO Box 105366
Atlanta
GA 30348-5366
tel   +1 404 827 1700
fax +1 404 827 2437
1986

TED · TECHNICAL TERM
- television disc

TEG · USA
- Television Entertainment Group

TELEFE · ARGENTINA
- Televisión Federal SA
Pavón 2444
1248 Buenos Aires
tel +54 1 941 0211
fax +54 1 942 6773
1989 □ private television station.

TEM · ITALY
- Technologie Elettroniche Milanesi
Via Bruno Buozzi 18/20
20089 Rozzano
tel +39 2 892 00131
fax +39 2 892 00129
□ manufacturer of professional **FM** television and microwave equipment for the broadcasting market in the highest quality and technology range.

TEM · TECHNICAL TERM
- transverse electromagnetic wave

TEN · TECHNICAL TERM
- the electronic newsroom

TES · USA
- Turner Educational Services
One CNN Center
PO Box 105366
Atlanta
GA 30348-5366
tel +1 404 827 1700
fax +1 404 827 2437
1983 □ develops, markets and distributes Turner Broadcasting System (**TBS**) programming to schools.

TF · TECHNICAL TERM
- till forbid
- trufocus

TF1 · FRANCE
- Television Française 1
Société Nationale TF1
1 quai du Point du Jour
92656 Boulogne Cedex
tel +33 41 41 12 34
fax +33 41 41 34 00

tlx 250878
1975 □ television broadcaster.

TFE · TECHNICAL TERM
- television film exhibit

TFM · TECHNICAL TERM
- timed frequency modulation

TFN · TECHNICAL TERM
- till further notice

TFT · TECHNICAL TERM
- thin film technology

TFVA · UK
- Training Film & Video Association
2nd floor
Bolsover House
5-6 Clipstone Street
London W1P 7EB
tel +44 71 323 1004
fax +44 71 436 2606
1987 □ to meet to discuss matters of mutual interest, in particular the copyright and terms and conditions of sale/hire of training films and video programmes; to take actions jointly to protect the interests of all members; to mount any agreed promotional or public relations exercise deemed desirable by the association; to raise subscriptions to support the activities of the association; to join with other associations to further the interests of members if considered desirable; to promote the effectiveness of training programmes in the UK and overseas and to help create a suitable environment to enhance the commercial activities of its members.

THD · TECHNICAL TERM
- total harmonic distortion

THE · USA
- Turner Home Entertainment
One CNN Center
PO Box 105366
Atlanta
GA 30348-5366
tel +1 404 827 1700
fax +1 404 827 2437
1987 □ administers, sells and licenses

Turner Broadcasting System (**TBS**) products to domestic and international home video markets.

THK · JAPAN
- Taiheiyo Hoso Kyokai
Box 1000
Tokyo 100-91
tel   +81 3 329 54921
fax +81 3 323 32650
1951 ▢ association producing Christian television and radio programmes, as well as offering other services such as a correspondence course in the Bible, and the provision of studio facilities. It publishes the following magazines: *Pacific Report* (6), *PBA Dayori* (12) and *Update* (6).
also known as Pacific Broadcasting Association (PBA)

THR · USA
- The Hollywood Reporter
6715 Sunset Boulevard
Hollywood
CA 90028
tel   +1 213 464 7411
fax +1 213 469 8770
tlx   798260
1930 ▢ newspaper for the film, broadcast and entertainment industry, with 254 daily issues and some 13 000 pages published each year.

TI · TECHNICAL TERM
- terrestrial interference

TIC · TECHNICAL TERM
- timing chain

TICCIT · TECHNICAL TERM
- time-shared, interactive computer-controlled information television

TIM · TECHNICAL TERM
- transient intermodulation distortion

TIO · USA
- Television Information Office

TIROS · TECHNICAL TERM
- television infrared observing satellite

TJ · TECHNICAL TERM

- telejector

TJS · TECHNICAL TERM
- transverse-junction stripe

TKU · JAPAN
- Kumamoto Telecasting Co Ltd
440 Tokuo-machi
Kumamoto 861-55
tel   +81 96 354 3411
▢ television station.

TL · LEBANON
- Télé-Liban
PO Box 115054
Hazmieh
Beirut
tel   +961 1 450100
tlx   20923
1959 ▢ television broadcasting service, operating programmes in Arabic, English and French.

TLC · USA
- The Learning Channel
7700 Wisconsin Avenue
Bethesda
MA 20814
tel   +1 301 986 0444
fax +1 301 986 4823
▢ educational television programme channel.

TLM · FRANCE
- Télé Lyon Métropole
21 Boulevard Yves Farge
69007 Lyon
tel   +33 78 72 73 73
fax +33 72 73 15 50
▢ private television broadcasting service.

TLT · FRANCE
- Télé Toulouse
3 Place Alfonse-Jourdain
31069 Toulouse Cedex
tel   +33 61 23 65 65
fax +33 61 21 24 71
1988 ▢ local private television service which focusses on local and regional information.

TM · TECHNICAL TERM
- technical manager

- telemetry

TMBS · TECHNICAL TERM
- torque-motor-driven beam steerer

TMC · MONACO
- Télé(vision) Monte Carlo
16 Boulevard Princess Charlotte
MC 98090
tel   +3393 505940
fax +3393 250109
tlx   469823 Tele Carlo
□ television broadcasting station.

TMC · USA
- The Movie Channel

TMD · TECHNICAL TERM
- thermal magnetic duplication/thermo
magnetic video highspeed duplication

TMS · TECHNICAL TERM
- tape management and scheduling
system

TNC · CHILE
- Televisión Nacional de Chile
Casilla 16104
Bellavista 0990
Santiago
tel   +56 2 777 3692
fax +56 2 777 0339
tlx   24-1375
□ government network of television
broadcasting stations.

TNC · JAPAN
- Television Nishi Nippon Corporation
20-23 Takamiya 4-chome
Minami-ku
Fukuoka 815
tel   +81 92 525 2222
□ television station.

TNCV · CAPE VERDE
- Televisão Nacional de Cabo Verde
Acahada de Santo António
CP 2
Praia
São Tiago
tel   +238 615 829
fax +238 615 831
tlx   6030
□ national television station,

broadcasting in Créole and Portuguese.

TNN · JAPAN
- Television Niigata Networks Co Ltd
1-11 Shinko-cho
Niigata 950
tel   +81 25 283 1111
□ television station.

TNT · USA
- Turner Network Television
1050 Techwood Drive, N.W.
PO Box 105264
Atlanta
GA 30318-5264
tel   +1 404 827 1519
fax +1 404 827 3134
1988 □ showcases high-quality,
original programming to cable homes,
including many of Hollywood's greatest
titles as well as high-profile sporting
events.

TOC · TECHNICAL TERM
- television operating centre

TOP · TECHNICAL TERM
- table of pages

TOS · JAPAN
- Television Oita System Co Ltd
843-25 Kasugaura
Oita 870
tel   +81 975 32 9111
□ television station.

TOS · TECHNICAL TERM
- transfer orbit stage

TP · TECHNICAL TERM
- teleplay
- television pick-up
- triple play
- two pin

TPA · ANGOLA
- Televisão Popular de Angola
CP 2604
Rua Ho Chi Minh
Luanda
tel   +244 2 320025-7
fax +244 2 391091
tlx   3238 / 4153
1975 □ national television broadcasting

service.

TPA · UK
- The Producers Association
now incorporated within Producers Alliance for Cinema and Television (PACT)

TPA · TECHNICAL TERM
- transistor power amplifier

TPEA · USA
- Television Program Export Association

TPI · INDONESIA
- Pt Cipta Televisi Pendidikan
Indonesia
Wisma Tungu II
6 Jalan HR Rasuna Said Kav Kuningan
Jakarta 12940
tel   +62 21 749 2747
1991 ☐ private television channel, supported by commercial advertising.

TPIB · USA
- Technical Panel for International Broadcast
☐ government committee.

TPIB · TECHNICAL TERM
- tuned port infinite baffle

TPO · TECHNICAL TERM
- transmitter power output

TPS · USA
- Turner Program Services
One CNN Center
PO Box 105366
Atlanta
GA 30348-5366
tel   +1 404 827 1700
fax   +1 404 827 2437
1981 ☐ syndication division of Turner Broadcasting System (**TBS**).

TPT · TECHNICAL TERM
- total prime time

TPV · USA
- The Perfect Vision
2 Glen Avenue
PO Box 357
Sea Cliff

New York
NY 11579
tel   +1 516 676 2830
fax   +1 516 676 5469
1986 ☐ quarterly magazine devoted to superior film viewing at home, including reports on laserdisc and video releases, and state-of-the-art technology.

TQS · CANADA
- Réseau de Télévision Quatre-Saisons
405 Avenue Ogilvy
Montreal
Quebec H3N 2Y4
tel   +1 514 271 3535
fax   +1 514 271 6231
tlx   058 25698
1986 ☐ French-language television broadcaster, operating on 2 channels throughout Quebec.

TRC · TECHNICAL TERM
- transient recovery circuit

TRIC · UK
- Television and Radio Industries Club
c/o Barrie Hall
Corbetts House
Norwood End
Fyfield
Chipping Ongar
Essex CM5 0RW
tel   +44 277 899337
fax   +44 277 899691
1931 ☐ to promote mutual understanding and goodwill amongst those engaged in the audio, visual and allied industries. It publishes a *Yearbook*.

TRMA · TECHNICAL TERM
- time random multiple access

TROM · TECHNICAL TERM
- teletext read-only memory

TROS · THE NETHERLANDS
- Televisie- en Radio- Omroepstichting
PO Box 450
1200 AL Hilversum
tel   +31 35 715715
fax   +31 35 715317
tlx   73070

1964 □ independent broadcasting company.

TRS-ID · TECHNICAL TERM
▪ timing reference signal and line identification

TRT · TURKEY
▪ Türkiye Radyo Televizyon Kurumu
▪ Turkish Radio and Television Corporation
TRT-TV Department
Nevzat Tandogan Caddesi 2
Kavaklidere
Ankara
tel   +90 4 428 2230
fax +90 4 468 0420
tlx 42-374
1964 □ national television and radio broadcasting company.

TRT · TECHNICAL TERM
▪ total running tape/time

TRUST · TECHNICAL TERM
▪ television relay using small terminals

TS · TECHNICAL TERM
▪ tape stabilising

TSA · TECHNICAL TERM
▪ total survey area

TSB · JAPAN
▪ TV Shinshu Broadcasting Co Ltd
4-18 Marunouchi
Matsumoto 390
tel   +81 263 36 2002
□ television station.

TSC · JAPAN
▪ TV Setouchi Broadcasting Co Ltd
8-8 Noda 5-chome
Okayama 700
tel   +81 862 44 2300
□ television station.

TSI · SWITZERLAND
▪ Televisione della Svizzera Italiana
see **RTSI** · SWITZERLAND

TSK · JAPAN
▪ San-In Chuo Television Broadcasting Co Ltd

721 Nishikawazu-cho
Matsue 690
tel   +81 852 23 3434
□ television station.

TSL · UK
▪ Television Systems Ltd
Unit 3
Kings Grove
Maidenhead
Berks SL6 4DP
tel   +44 628 773904
fax +44 628 773635
□ specialist systems design and installation company providing technical consultancy, systems design, installation and manufacturing services to the broadcast and allied industries.

TSN · CANADA
▪ The Sports Network
1155 Leslie Street
Don Mills
Ontario M3C 2J6
tel   +1 416 449 2244
fax +1 416 391 8210
□ sports broadcasting.

TSR · SWITZERLAND
▪ Télévision (de la) Suisse Romande
see **RTSR** · SWITZERLAND

TSS · JAPAN
▪ Shin Hiroshima Telecasting Co Ltd
3-19 Deshio 2-chome
Minami-ku
Hiroshima 734
tel   +81 82 255 1111
□ television station.

TST · THAILAND
▪ Thai Sky TV
21 Pacific Tower
9/10th floors
Viphavadadi-rangsit Road
Jatujak
Bangkok 10900
tel   +66 2 273 8977
□ television broadcasting.

TST · TECHNICAL TERM
▪ total story tape

TSV · TECHNICAL TERM

■ time spent viewing

TT · TECHNICAL TERM
■ teletype

TTC · USA
■ Television Technology Corporation
650 South Taylor Avenue
Louisville
CO 80027
tel +1 303 665 8000
fax +1 303 673 9900
1967 □ manufacturer of radio and
television transmitters and transposers.

TTC · TECHNICAL TERM
■ telemetry, tracking and command

TTL · TECHNICAL TERM
■ through the lens
■ transistor-transistor logic

TTR · TECHNICAL TERM
■ television translator relay

TTT · TRINIDAD AND TOBAGO
■ Trinidad & Tobago Television
Company
PO Box 665
Port of Spain
tel +1 809 62 24141
fax +1 809 62 20344
tlx 22664 TTTV WG
1962 □ television broadcasting service.

TTTV · UK
■ Tyne Tees Television
The Television Centre
City Road
Newcastle-upon-Tyne NE1 2AL
tel +44 91 261 0181
fax +44 91 261 2302
tlx 53279
1959 □ provides an independent
television service for North-East
England, an area covering Cleveland,
Durham, Tyne and Wear and North
Yorkshire.

TTV · FINLAND
■ Tampereen Tietoverkko

TTV · TAIWAN
■ Taiwan Television Enterprise

10 Pa Teh Road
Sec. 3
Taipei
tel +886 2 7711515
fax +886 2 7759626
tlx 25714
1962 □ television broadcaster.

TU · TECHNICAL TERM
■ tape unit
■ timing unit

TUF · JAPAN
■ TV-U Fukushima Inc
1-1 Nishi-Chuo
Fukushima 960
tel +81 245 31 5111
□ television station.

TUG · UK
■ Television Users' Group
see **CPBF** · UK

TUT · JAPAN
■ Tulip-TV Inc
6-1 Hirokoji
Takaoka 933
tel +81 766 26 6000
□ television station.

TUY · JAPAN
■ TV-U Yamagata Inc
4-22 Kamihon-cho
Sakata
Yamagata 998
tel +81 234 23 8111
□ television station.

TV · TECHNICAL TERM
■ television

TVA · JAPAN
■ Television Aichi Corporation
4-8 Osu 2-chome
Naka-ku
Nagoya 460
tel +81 52 203 0250
□ television station.

TVAH · ARGENTINA
■ Tres Américas Video Home

TVB · HONG KONG
■ Television Broadcasts Ltd

Complex Building
Lot no. 214
Clearwater Bay Road
Kowloon
tel   +852 3 7194828
fax +852 3 581300
tlx   43596 HX
□ television broadcasting service.

TVB · SERBIA
▪ Televizija Beograd
see **RTVB** · SERBIA

TVB · USA
▪ Television Bureau of Advertising
see **TBA** · USA

TVBS · TECHNICAL TERM
▪ television broadcast satellite

TVC · SPAIN
▪ Televisió de Catalunya
Jacint Verdaguer s/n
08970 Sant Joan Despí
Barcelona
tel   +34 3 499 9333
fax +34 3 473 0671
tlx   97990 TVCT E
1983 □ regional television broadcasting
in Catalan on 2 channels to north-east
Spain.

TVC · UK
▪ TV Cartoons
39 Grafton Way
London W1P 5LA
tel   +44 71 388 2222
fax +44 71 383 4192
1957 □ animation film company,
specialising in half-hour films.

TVCF · BELGIUM
▪ Radio-Télévision de la Communauté
Française
Boulevard A Reyerslaan 52
1043 Brussels
tel   +32 2 737 2545
fax +32 2 734 4381
tlx   21-437
□ French-language radio and television
broadcasting station.

TVE · MOZAMBIQUE
▪ Televisão Experimental

Avda Julius Nyerere 930
CP 2675
Maputo
tel   +258 491365
tlx   6346
1981 □ television broadcasting.

TVE · SPAIN
▪ Radiotelevisión Española
see **RTVE** · SPAIN

TVE · UK
▪ Television Trust for the Environment
46 Charlotte Street
London W1P 1LX
tel   +44 71 323 1376
fax +44 71 580 2308
tlx   291721
1984 □ non-profit organisation,
sponsored by the United Nations
Environment Programme (UNEP),
Central Television and the World Wide
Fund for Nature (WWF) to promote
global awareness of environment and
development issues via television. It co-
finances environmental documentaries,
with an emphasis on coverage of issues
in the Global South. It publishes
Moving Pictures Bulletin (4) and *Green
Film Catalogue* (database).

TVG · BRAZIL
▪ TV Globo Ltda
Rua Lopes Quintas 303
Jardin Botanico
22463 Rio de Janeiro
tel   +55 21 529 2000
fax +55 21 294 2042
tlx   22795
1965 □ national network of television
and radio stations.

TVG · SPAIN
▪ Televisión de Galicia
Apdo. 707
San Marcos
15780 Santiago de Compostela
tel   +34 81 564400
fax +34 81 586577
tlx   97012
1985 □ independent Galician-language
television broadcasting station.
*also known as Compañía de Radio
Televisión de Galicia (CRTVG or*

CRTG)

TVGA · TECHNICAL TERM
■ television graphics adaptor

TVH · JAPAN
■ Television Hokkaido Co Ltd
12-4 Odori-higashi 6-chome
Chuo-ku
Sapporo 060
tel +81 11 232 1117
□ television station.

TVHD · TECHNICAL TERM
■ télévision à haute définition

TVHH · TECHNICAL TERM
■ television households

TVI · BELGIUM
■ Télévision Indépendante
67 Avenue Franklin Roosevelt
1050 Brussels
tel +32 2 640 5150
fax +32 2 627 1712
tlx 64430
□ commercial television station
broadcasting in French.

TVI · JAPAN
■ Television Iwate Corporation
2-10 Uchimaru
Morioka 020
tel +81 196 24 1166
□ television station.

TVI · PORTUGAL
■ Televisão Independente
Edificio Altejo
Rua 3, Piso 6
Sala 609
Matinha
1900 Lisbon
tel +351 1 858 8000
fax +351 1 858 7969
1992 □ private television broadcasting
channel.

TVI · TECHNICAL TERM
■ television interference
■ tutored video instruction

TVIC · THAILAND
■ Television Information Centre

998/1 Soi Ruamsirimitr Phaholyothin
Road
Ladyao Jattujak
Bangkok 10900
tel +66 2 278 1255-60 / 2799280-4
fax +66 2 270 1975
tlx 82730 BBTV TH
1990 □ leading in television
information systems; also a television
archive.

TVK · CAMBODIA
■ TV Kampuchean
Road 106
Boulevard Tou Samuth
Phnom-Penh
tel +855 22 969
□ television station.

TVK · JAPAN
■ Television Kanagawa Co Ltd
69-1 Yamashita-cho
Naka-ku
Yokohama 231
tel +81 45 651 1711
□ television station.

TVL · TECHNICAL TERM
■ television lines

TVM · TECHNICAL TERM
■ TV movie

TVN · JAPAN
■ Nara Television Co Ltd
1699-1 Horen-cho
Nara 630
tel +81 742 23 4601
□ television station.

TVNC · CANADA
■ Television Northern Canada
Box 1630
Iqaluit
N.W.T. X0A 0H0
tel +1 819 979 1707
fax +1 819 979 1708
1991 □ television broadcaster.

TVNZ · NEW ZEALAND
■ Television New Zealand Ltd
Television Centre
100 Victoria Street West
Box 3819

Auckland
tel   +64 9 377 0630
fax +64 9 375 0916
tlx NZ 60056
1960 □ aims to operate a commercially
successful electronic communications
business, acting with social responsibility in the provision of quality
services, including the provision of
television programmes which reflect
and foster New Zealand's identity and
culture. It publishes *Networks* (26) and
Televiews (12).

TVO · CANADA
▪ TVOntario
Box 200
Station Q
Toronto
Ontario M4T 2T1
tel   +1 416 484 2600
fax +1 416 484 6285
1970 □ to provide equal access for all
Ontarians to television-based learning
opportunities. It is the leader in the
production and distribution of
television-based learning systems and is
an integral part of the educational and
cultural fabric of Ontario, Canada and
the world. It provides viewers with a
wide and enriching selection of
programming from around the world in
productions and co-productions with
national and international producers
and broadcasters, as well as high-
quality acquisitions. It publishes *Signal*
(12).

TVO · JAPAN
▪ Television Osaka Inc
2-18 Otemae 1-chome
Chuo-ku
Osaka 540-19
tel   +81 6 947 0019
□ television station.

TVP · RUSSIA
▪ Televidenie Peterburg
ul. Ital'anskaja 27
1910011 St Petersburg
1992 □ television station.

TVQ · JAPAN
▪ TXN Kyusyu Co Ltd

2-3-1 Sumiyoshi
Hakata-ku
Fukuoka 812
tel   +81 92 262 0019
□ television station.

TVR · TECHNICAL TERM
▪ tele(vision) recording

TVRI · INDONESIA
▪ Yayasan Televisi Republik Indonesia
Jalan Gerbang Pemuda Senayan
Jakarta 10270
tel   +62 21 581 125 / 582 328
fax +62 21 583 132
tlx 46154
1962 □ state-owned television station.

TVRO · TECHNICAL TERM
▪ television receive-only (terminal)

TVS · JAPAN
▪ Television Saitama Co Ltd
36-4 Tokiwa 6-chome
Urawa 336
tel   +81 48 824 3131
□ television station.

TVS · SLOVENIA
▪ Televizija Slovenija
Moše Pijade 5
61000 Ljubljana
tel   +38 61 311922
fax +38 61 319971
tlx 32283
1928 □ television and radio
broadcasting service, operating in
Italian and Slovenian.

TVSK · MACEDONIA
▪ Radiotelevizija Skopje
Goce Delčev BB
91000 Skopje
tel   +38 91 227711
fax +38 91 236856
tlx 51157
1944 □ television (2 channels) and
radio (3 channels) broadcasting service,
operating in Albanian, Macedonian and
Turkish.

TVT · THAILAND
▪ Television of Thailand
Thanon Petchburi

Bangkok 10200
tel   +66 2 314 4001
tlx   72243
□ television broadcaster.

TVT · TOGO
■ Télévision Togolaise
BP 3286
Lomé
tel   +228 215356
fax +228 215786
tlx   5320
□ television broadcaster.

TVT · TECHNICAL TERM
■ television terminal
■ television typewriter

TVV · SPAIN
■ Televisió Valenciana
Polígono de Acceso a Ademuz s/n
46100 Burjassot
Valencia
tel   +34 6 364 1100
fax +34 6 363 9516
tlx   61023
1989 □ regional television broadcasting
station.

TWA · TECHNICAL TERM
■ travelling wave amplifier

TWE · USA
■ Transworld Entertainment

TWI · UK
■ Trans World International
TWI House
23 Eyot Gardens
London W6 9TR
tel   +44 81 846 8070
fax +44 81 746 5334
tlx   267486
1966 □ film, television and video
division of International Management
Group (IMG), it serves as an
independent producer of sports
programming, with an output of over
600 hours per year.

TWIFT · CANADA
■ Toronto Women in Film and
Television
Suite 219

150 John Street
Toronto
Ontario M5V 3C3
tel   +1 416 348 9578
fax +1 416 973 6318
□ non-profit association of professional
women established to improve the
status and depiction of women in film
and television and to celebrate their
achievements.

TWT · TECHNICAL TERM
■ travelling wave tube

TWTA · TECHNICAL TERM
■ travelling wave tube amplifier

TYS · JAPAN
■ Television Yamaguchi Co Ltd
1277 Mihori
Ouchi
Yamaguchi 753-02
tel   +81 839 23 6111
□ television station.

U

UAR · TECHNICAL TERM
■ universal asynchronous receiver

UART · FRANCE
■ Union des Auteurs, Réalisateurs et
Techniciens du Cinéma et de la
Télévision
7 rue Henri Rochefort
75017 Paris
tel   +33 1 44 15 24 24
fax +33 1 44 15 24 20
□ association of cinema and television
authors, directors and technicians.

UART · TECHNICAL TERM
■ universal asynchronous receiver-
transmitter

UCAHM · FRANCE
■ Union des Cinéastes Amateurs
Huitistes Mondiaux
□ organisation of 8mm amateur film-
makers.

UCCA · ITALY

■ Union Circoli Cinematografici Arci Nova
Via Francesco Carrara 24
00196 Rome
tel   +39 6 321 6878
fax   +39 6 321 6877
1967 □ non-profit organisation of 160 cineclubs throughout Italy which organises and promotes exhibitions of first quality pictures in Italy and abroad, publishes books and catalogues concerning films, authors and cinema, both present and past. It publishes *UCCA News* (6).

UCI · UK
■ United Cinemas International
1st floor
Bridgewater House
Whitworth Street
Manchester M60 1LS
tel   +44 61 236 5660
fax   +44 61 236 5708
1985 □ cinema exhibitor whose philosophy is to offer a complete cinematic entertainment package to every member of the family, and, in so doing, become an important part of the community.

UCINA · SENEGAL
■ Union Cinématographique Africaine
□ private organisation for cinematographic production.

UCLA · USA
■ University of California Los Angeles
Dept of Theater, Film and Television
MacGowan Hall
405 Hilgard Avenue
Los Angeles
CA 90024
tel   +1 310 825 7741 / 206 6465
fax   +1 310 825 3383
1919 □ higher educational institution offering courses in film.

UCM · TECHNICAL TERM
■ user communications manager

UCP · USA
■ United Cable Programmes

UDC · TECHNICAL TERM

■ universal decimal classification

UDD · TECHNICAL TERM
■ ultra dispersion and durability

UDTV · TECHNICAL TERM
■ ultra high definition television

UER · SWITZERLAND
■ Union Européenne de Radio-Télévision
Ancienne Route 17A
Case postale 67
CH-1218 Grand Saconnex/Geneva
tel   +41 22 717 2111
fax   +41 22 798 5897
tlx   415700 ebu ch
1950 □ professional association of national broadcasters with 114 members in 79 countries. The purpose is to promote cooperation between its members and broadcasting organisations of the entire world and to represent the interests of its members with broadcasting organisations worldwide and to represent the interests of its members in the programme, legal, technical and other fields. The activities of the UER are channelled through the Television Programme Committee, the Radio Programme Committee, the Legal Committee and the Technical Committee, with their working parties, sub-groups and ad hoc groups. It publishes the magazines *Diffusion* (4) and *EBU Technical Review* (4), as well as other publications.
also known as European Broadcasting Union (EBU)

UESC · BELGIUM
■ Union Européenne du Spectacle Cinématographique
■ Unione Europea dello Spettacolo Cinematografico
Chaussée de Haacht 35
1030 Brussels
1962 □ European film union.

UFAT · FRANCE
■ Union Fédérale des Associations de Téléspectateurs
22 rue Docteur Germain Sée
75016 Paris

□ federal union of televiewers' associations.

UFB · TECHNICAL TERM
■ unfit for broadcast

UFBG · USA
■ Up-Front Buying Guide
Nielsen Media Research
1290 Avenue of the Americas
New York
NY 10104
tel   +1 212 708 7500
fax +1 212 708 7795
□ quarterly report which provides estimates of household and persons television usage and network audiences by daypart and by half-hour time periods for: each evening in primetime; Mon-Fri averages - daytime and late fringe; weekend daytime. It also contains Network Programme Schedules by ½ hours as well as the most recent 5 quarters of audience data.

UFCA · FRANCE
■ Union pour le Financement du Cinéma et de l'Audiovisuel
Paris

UFCCI · FRANCE
■ Unité Fonctionnelle Cinéma Communication Information
Tour 34-24
2 Place Jussieu
75251 Paris Cedex
tel   +33 44 27 68 75
□ educational institution.

UFFEJ · FRANCE
■ Union Française du Film pour l'Enfance et la Jeunesse
25 rue Raymond Losserand
75014 Paris
tel   +33 1 43 35 54 02
fax +33 1 43 21 79 61
1990 □ to promote the cinema and audiovisual media amongst children and young people. It publishes *Zéro de Conduite* magazine (4).

UFITA · GERMANY
■ Archiv für Urheber-, Film, Funk- und Theaterrecht
□ archive for rights relating to authors, films, radio and theatre.

UFOLEIS · FRANCE
■ Union Française des Œuvres Laïques d'Education par l'Image et par le Son
21 rue St-Fargeau
75020 Paris
□ society for secular educational work through image and sound.

UFVA · USA
■ University Film and Video Association
c/o Communication Arts Department
Loyola Marimount University
Loyola Boulevard at West 80th Street
Los Angeles
CA 90045
tel   +1 213 338 7532
fax +1 213 338 3030
1947 □ association concerned with the study and production of film in universities and colleges.

UFVF · USA
■ University Film and Video Foundation
Dept of Radio-TV-Film
North Texas State University
PO Box 13138
Denton
TX 76203
tel   +1 817 565 2537
fax +1 817 565 2518
1958 □ organisation which promotes and supports film and video production within universities.

UGC · FRANCE
■ Union Générale Cinématographique
24 avenue Charles de Gaulle
Neuilly-sur-Seine 92522
tel   +33 1 46 40 44 30/32
fax +33 1 46 24 37 28
tlx   UGC SHOW 614487
□ major film and television programme distributors and exhibitors.

UHF · TECHNICAL TERM
■ ultra high frequency

UICC · ITALY
■ Unione Italiana Circolo del Cinema

Casella Postale 10395
00144 Rome
□ Italian union of cinema clubs.

UIH · USA
■ United International Holdings
4643 South Ulster Street
Suite 1300
Denver
CO 80237
tel +1 303 770 4001
fax +1 303 770 4207
□ international cable company.

UIP · UK
■ United International Pictures
Mortimer House
37-41 Mortimer Street
London W1A 2JL
tel +44 71 636 1655
fax +44 71 323 0121
□ film distributor.

UIT · SWITZERLAND
■ Union Internationale des
Télécommunications
see **ITU** · SWITZERLAND

UJ · TECHNICAL TERM
■ uni-junction transistor

ULA · TECHNICAL TERM
■ uncommitted logic array

ULPA · LUXEMBOURG
■ Union Luxembourgeoise des
Producteurs Audiovisuels
BP 2006
L-1024 Luxembourg
tel +352 251717
fax +352 251895
1991 □ to represent independent
producers in Luxembourg and
internationally, as well as to provide a
meeting place for the exchange of
information.

ULSI · TECHNICAL TERM
■ ultra large-scale integration

UMK · JAPAN
■ Television Miyazaki Co Ltd
2-78 Gion
Miyazaki 880

tel +81 985 31 5111
□ television station.

UNAC · ITALY
■ Unione Nazionale Autori e
Cinetecnici
Via di Villa Emiliani 24
00197 Rome
□ national union of screenwriters and
film technicians.

UNCB · BURKINA FASO
■ Union Nationale des Cinéastes
Burkinabés
c/o Pierre Rouamba
Direction de l'Education en Matière de
Population
BP 4901
01 Ouagadougou
□ professional film-makers' organisation, defending the moral and
economic interests of its members.

UNDF · ITALY
■ Unione Nazionale Distributori Film
Viale Regina Margherita 286
00198 Rome
tel +39 6 884 1271
fax +39 6 440 4128
1944 □ national association of film
distributors.

UNEFA · ITALY
■ Unione Nazionale Esportatori Film e
Audiovisivi
Viale Regina Margherita 286
00198 Rome
tel +39 6 884 1271
fax +39 6 884 8789
tlx 624659
□ film export association.

UNIATEC · FRANCE
■ Union Internationale des Associations
Techniques Cinématographiques
11 rue Galilée
75016 Paris
tel +33 1 47 20 55 69
1956 □ international union of
cinematographic technical associations.

UNIC · FRANCE
■ Union Internationale des Cinémas
■ Unione Internazionale dei Cinema

- International Union of Cinemas
- Internationale Filmtheaterunion
10 rue de Marignan
75008 Paris
tel +33 1 43 59 16 76
fax +33 1 40 74 08 64
1953 □ defends the interests of cinema exhibitors worldwide, particulary in matters of law and economics. It publishes *UNIC News* and a *Bulletin* (6).

UNICC · FRANCE
- Union Nationale Inter Ciné-Clubs
c/o Janine Bertrand
12 rue des Lyonnais
75005 Paris
tel +33 1 45 35 35 39
fax +33 1 47 07 81 20
□ national federation of film clubs.

UNICS · ITALY
- Unione Nazionale Industrie Cinetelevisive Specializzate
Viale Regina Margherita 286
00198 Rome
tel +39 6 884 1271
fax +39 6 440 4128
1944 □ association of specialised cinema and television organisations.

UNITC · ITALY
- Unione Nazionale Industrie Tecniche Cinetelevisive
Viale Regina Margherita 286
00198 Rome
tel +39 6 884 1271
fax +39 6 440 4128
1944 □ association of cinema and television technical organisations.

UNPF · ITALY
- Unione Nazionale Produttori Film
Viale Regina Margherita 286
00198 Rome
tel +39 6 884 1271
fax +39 6 440 4128
1944 □ association of film producers.

UNSCF · FRANCE
- Union National Syndicale des Cinémas Familiaux
86 bis, rue Rachais
69007 Lyon

tel +33 78 69 03 70

UNTV · USA
- United Nations Television
Department of Public Information
United Nations
New York
NY 10017
tel +1 212 963 6945 / 6947 / 6970
fax +1 212 963 9765 / 1307 / 3860
tlx 420544 UNH UI
1949 □ covers meetings of the General Assembly, the Security Council and other official meetings, as well as events at Headquarters. Television coverage materials are also made available for use in feature productions and for archival purposes. It also assists television journalists who wish to cover the UN.

UNUPADEC · ITALY
- Unione Nazionale Unitaria Professionale Autori Drammatici e Cinematografici
Via Cardinale Mistrangelo 10
00155 Rome
tel +39 6 62 21 409
□ national professional union of screenwriters and playwrights.

UOO · TECHNICAL TERM
- unavailable, on order

UPCT · SPAIN
- Unión de Productores de Cine y Televisión
C/Pintor Juan Gris, 5-1° B
28020 Madrid
tel +34 1 555 4477 / 555 4580
fax +34 1 597 3807
1983 □ representation and defence of the professional interests of companies involved in cinematographic and audiovisual production.

UPF · FRANCE
- Union des Producteurs de Films
1 Place des Deux Ecus
75001 Paris
tel +33 1 40 28 01 38
fax +33 1 42 21 17 00
1987 □ professional organisation of film producers.

UPPT · BELGIUM
- Union des Producteurs de Programmes de Télévision
12 avenue Ariane
1200 Brussels
tel   +32 2 773 4811
fax +32 2 773 4888
1987 □ association of television programme producers whose objectives are: to promote production, foster good relations between producers and undertake joint activities, and to develop contacts on an international basis.

URTI · FRANCE
- Université Radiophonique et Télévisuelle Internationale
- Universidad Radiofonica y Televisual Internacional
- Universidade Radiofonica e Televisiva Internacional
Maison de Radio France
116 Avenue du Président-Kennedy
75786 Paris Cedex 16
tel   +33 1 42 30 23 61 / 42 30 39 98 / 42 30 23 64
fax +33 1 40 50 89 99
tlx   200 002 F
also known as International Radio and Television University (IRTU)
1949 □ association of television and radio organisations whose aim is to exchange and broadcast several hundred cultural programmes each year, in the sciences, history, literature and the arts. It publishes *La Lettre de l'URTI*.

URTNA · KENYA
- Union des Radiodiffusion Télévisions Nationales d'Afrique
PO Box 50518
Nairobi
tel   +254 2 219661
fax +254 2 219662
□ organisation for the exchange and distribution of television programmes to some 40 African television channels.

USA · USA
- United Scenic Artists
575 Eighth Avenue
New York

NY 10018
tel   +1 212 736 4498
fax +1 212 736 4681
□ union consisting of some 2000 scenic designers and artists, as well as lighting and costume designers who work in the industries of television, film and the theatre.

USART · TECHNICAL TERM
- universal synchronous/asynchronous receiver-transmitter

USC · USA
- University of Southern California School of Cinema and Television
University Park
Los Angeles
CA 90089-2211
tel   +1 213 740 2804 / 3317
fax +1 213 740 7682
1879 □ higher educational institution offering courses in film.

USEFF · USA
- US Environment Film Festival
1026 West Colorado Avenue
Colorado Springs
CO 80904
tel   +1 719 520 1952
fax +1 719 520 9157
□ annual film festival devoted solely to environmental films.

USPA · FRANCE
- Union Syndicale de la Production Audiovisuelle
59 rue de Châteaudun
75009 Paris
tel   +33 1 44 53 03 03
fax +33 1 49 95 99 80
1961 □ answers technical, administrative and professional questions faced by producer members; represents the common interests of production companies internationally through their relations with government administrations, professional unions of artistes, authors, directors and technicians, and with the CNC, the EC and the Council of Europe; supports and reinforces the identity and professional standing of television producers in France through various

agents. It publishes an annual list of French producers and distributors.

UT · UKRAINE
- Ukrajinska Telebačennja
ul. Chreščatik 26
252001 Kiev
tel   +42 2 410 7111
fax +42 2 425 484
tlx 122747
☐ television service.

UTV · UK
- Ulster Television plc
Havelock House
Ormeau Road
Belfast
N Ireland BT7 1EB
tel   +44 232 328122
fax +44 232 246695
tlx 74654
1959 ☐ provides an independent television service for Northern Ireland, broadcasting on Channel 3.

UV · TECHNICAL TERM
- ultra-violet

V

V/VH · TECHNICAL TERM
- viewers per viewing household (*aka* VPVH)

VA · TECHNICAL TERM
- voltampere(s)

VAI · TECHNICAL TERM
- video-assisted instruction

VAM · AUSTRIA
- Verwertungsgesellschaft für Audiovisuelle Medien

VAMG · THE NETHERLANDS
- Vereniging van Audiovisuele Medewerkers in de Gezondheidszorg
Postbus 64711
2506 CC 's-Gravenhage
☐ association of audiovisual employees in the health service.

VAP · THE NETHERLANDS
- Verenigde Audiovisuele Produktiebedrijven
p/a H A F Wennink
Mozartlaan 27
1217 CM Hilversum
tel   +31 35 238677
fax +31 35 238674
☐ association of audiovisual production companies.

VAR · BELGIUM
- Vlaamse Audiovisuele Regie
Tollaan 107b bus 3
1932 St-Stevens-Woluwe
tel   +32 2 725 0524
fax +32 2 725 3977
1990 ☐ responsible for selling sponsorship on the public television channels Belgische Radio en Televisie (**BRT**) and TV2.

VARA · THE NETHERLANDS
- Vereniging van Arbeiders-Radio-Amateurs
PO Box 175
1200 AD Hilversum
tel   +31 35 711370
fax +31 35 711378
tlx 73062
1925 ☐ broadcasting company.

VAVK · FINLAND
- Valtion audiovisuaalinen keskus
Hakaniemenkatu 2
SF-00530 Helsinki
tel   +358 0 7747 7022
fax +358 0 7747 7475
also known as State Audio Visual Centre and Statens Audiovisuella Central (both SAVC)
1976 ☐ to promote the use of audiovisual media in education. It produces and acquires audiovisual material from Finland and abroad and acts as a nationwide distribution centre. It follows the development in audiovisual media, reporting on new developments in its journal. It publishes *Oppima* (6).

VBI · TECHNICAL TERM
- vertical blanking interval

VBS · UK
■ Visual Broadcast Services
5th floor
Haddon House
2-4 Fitzroy Street
London W1P 5AD
tel   +44 71 728 5137
fax +44 71 728 5150
❑ provides broadcasters globally with
full-time satellite access to distribute
programming to customers.

VBS · TECHNICAL TERM
■ video, blanking and synchs

VBV · TECHNICAL TERM
■ video-black-video

VCA · TECHNICAL TERM
■ voltage-controlled amplifier/attenuator

VCC · TECHNICAL TERM
■ viewers' consultative council

VCCFT · AUSTRALIA
■ Victorian Council for Children's Films
and Television Ltd
17 St Andrew's Place
East Melbourne
VIC 3002
tel   +61 3 651 1919
fax +61 3 651 1238
1940 ❑ to stimulate and maintain
public interest in the provision of
suitable film, television and video
entertainment for children.

VCHP · TECHNICAL TERM
■ variable conductance heat pipe

VCI · UK
■ Video Collection International
Strand VCI House
36 Caxton Way
Watford
Herts WD1 8UF
tel   +44 923 255558
fax +44 923 816744
1985 ❑ publishing company marketing
pre-recorded video cassettes, which are
sold retail and by mail order. It is a
market-leader and has some 2000 titles
available.

VCIU · UK
■ Video Courses in Industry Unit
Aston University
Continuing Education Service
Aston Triangle
Birmingham B4 7ET
tel   +44 21 359 3611 x4958
fax +44 21 359 6427
1988 ❑ to encourage the production
and use of 55 video-based distance
learning programmes in electronic
systems and equipment, electronic
design, information technology,
software engineering and
manufacturing. Courses have been
provided by universities, polytechnics,
training bodies and private companies
throughout the UK and are all available
from the VCIU, which is part of the
Continuing Education Service (**CES**).
VCIU publishes *Current Titles* (portfolio
of 59 video courses).

VCO · TECHNICAL TERM
■ voltage-controlled oscillator

VCP · THE NETHERLANDS
■ Verenigde Commercial Producenten
Torenhof 14
3742 CT Baarn
tel   +31 2154 23876
fax +31 2154 23568
❑ group of commercial producers.

VCPS · UK
■ Video Copyright Protection Society

VCR · TECHNICAL TERM
■ video cassette/cartridge recorder

VCS · TECHNICAL TERM
■ videocassette

VCU · TECHNICAL TERM
■ very close-up

VDA · TECHNICAL TERM
■ video distribution amplifier

VDF · GERMANY
■ Verband der Filmverleiher
Kreuzberger Ring 56
65205 Wiesbaden
tel   +49 611 7 78 92 21

fax +49 611 7 78 92 12
1947 □ to support film distributors and to negotiate with authorities and other sectors of the industry.

VDP · TECHNICAL TERM
▪ video display processor

VDR · TECHNICAL TERM
▪ vertical drive
▪ video disc recorder
▪ voltage-dependent resistor

VDS · GERMANY
▪ Verband Deutscher Spielfilmproduzenten
Beichstraße 8-9
80802 Munich
tel +49 89 34 86 02
tlx 5216421
□ organisation of feature film producers.

VDSQ · TECHNICAL TERM
▪ video data sequence

VDT · TECHNICAL TERM
▪ video display terminal

VDU · TECHNICAL TERM
▪ video/visual display unit

VEC · THE NETHERLANDS
▪ Video Education Centre
Bergstraat 51-53
7411 ES Deventer
tel +31 5700 16536
□ educational video centre.

VER · ARGENTINA
▪ Video Editora República

VERA · TECHNICAL TERM
▪ videotape/vision electronic recording apparatus

VET · TECHNICAL TERM
▪ video editing terminal

VEVAM · THE NETHERLANDS
▪ Vereniging ter Exploitatie van Vertoningsrechten op Audiovisueel Materiaal
PO Box 581

1000 AN Amsterdam
tel +31 20 676 5088
fax +31 20 676 5837
1983 □ collecting and distributing royalties for the film and television industry.

VF · TECHNICAL TERM
▪ video frequency
▪ viewfinder (*aka* V/F)
▪ voice frequency

VFA · USA
▪ Video Free America
442 Shotwell Street
San Francisco
CA 94110
tel +1 415 648 9040
fax +1 415 648 0961
1970 □ serves as a place for experimentation and innovation for new artists and audiences.

VFF · GERMANY
▪ Verwertungsgesellschaft der Film- und Fernsehproduzenten
Widenmayerstraße 32
80538 Munich
tel +49 89 223535
fax +49 89 2285562
1979 □ collection agency which handles royalties for producers which they receive under German copyright law in the form of a levy payable on videocassettes and video recordings.

VFL · TECHNICAL TERM
▪ variable focal length/lens

VFS · AUSTRIA
▪ Verwertungsgesellschaft Filmschaffende
Johannesgasse 12
1010 Vienna
tel +43 1 512 3284
fax +43 1 513 3907
□ collecting society for film directors, editors and cinematographers.

VFX · TECHNICAL TERM
▪ visual effects

VGA · TECHNICAL TERM
▪ video graphics array

- visual graphics adaptor

VGF · GERMANY
- Verwertungsgesellschaft für Nutzungsrechte an Filmwerken MbH
Kreuzberger Ring 56
65205 Wiesbaden
tel +49 611 7789 222
fax +49 611 7789 214
1981 □ copyright collecting agency which represents film producers and directors with regard to certain claims for remuneration granted by German copyright law.

VGIK · RUSSIA
- Vsesoiuznyi Gosudarstvennyi Institut Kinematografii
Wilhem Piecka 3
129128 Moscow
tel +7 095 181 3868 / 181 1806
fax +7 095 187 7174
tlx 411417 KINO SU
1919 □ film school.

VGTRK · RUSSIA
- Vserossijskaja Gosudarstvennaja Televizionnaja i Radioveschateljnaja Kompanija
Jamskogo polja 5-ja ul. 19/12
125124 Moscow
tel +7 095 2179981
fax +7 095 2500506
1991 □ produces the television channel Rossijskoje Televidenije (**RTV**) which broadcasts throughout Russia.

VHD · TECHNICAL TERM
- video/very high density

VHF · TECHNICAL TERM
- very high frequency

VHM · TECHNICAL TERM
- virtual hardware monitor

VHS · TECHNICAL TERM
- Video Home System

VI · TECHNICAL TERM
- volume indicator

VIBGYOR · TECHNICAL TERM
- violet, indigo, blue, green, yellow, orange, red

VIDA · USA
- Video Industries Distributors Association

VIDEX · TECHNICAL TERM
- viewfinder information display extension

VIEW · TECHNICAL TERM
- visually integrated edit workstation

VIMCAS · TECHNICAL TERM
- vertical interval multi-channel audio system

VIPS · TECHNICAL TERM
- visual information processing system

VIR · TECHNICAL TERM
- vertical interval reference

VIRS · TECHNICAL TERM
- vertical interface reference signal

VISC · TECHNICAL TERM
- vertical interval cub-carrier

VISS · TECHNICAL TERM
- video/visual index search system

VISTA · TECHNICAL TERM
- visual system transmission algorithm

VITC · TECHNICAL TERM
- vertical interval/information time code

VITEAC · USA
- Video Transmission Engineering Advisory Committee

VITS · TECHNICAL TERM
- vertical interval test signal

VLAD · TECHNICAL TERM
- very low-angle dolly

VLAM · THE NETHERLANDS
- Vereniging van Leveranciers van Audio-Visuele Media
Hyacintenlaan 7
6866 DL Heelsum

tel +31 8373 14449
1970 □ association of suppliers of audiovisual materials.

VLF · TECHNICAL TERM
- very low frequency

VLP · TECHNICAL TERM
- very long play
- videodisc long player

VLS · TECHNICAL TERM
- very long shot

VLSI · TECHNICAL TERM
- very large-scale integration

VLT · TECHNICAL TERM
- video layout terminal

VLV · UK
- Voice of the Listener and Viewer
101 King's Drive
Gravesend
Kent DA12 5BQ
tel +44 474 352835
fax on request
incorporating Broadcasting Research Unit (BRU)
1983 □ independent non-profit-making consumer association, speaking out for quality in broadcasting. Its aims are: to raise awareness of the importance of our broadcasting services in our national and community life and culture and the influence they have on our heritage of speech, art, drama, literature, music and democracy; to maintain the principles of public service within British broadcasting; to provide viewers with a collective voice and the means to engage in dialogue and decision-making with relevant bodies. It holds regular public lectures, seminars and conferences about broadcasting issues and provides an independent forum where all with an interest in broadcasting can meet on equal terms. It publishes a *Newsletter* (4).

VMOS · TECHNICAL TERM
- vertical metal-oxide-silicon

VNA · TECHNICAL TERM
- video noise analyzer

VNII · RUSSIA
- Vsesojuzny Nauchno-Issledovateljsky Institut Isskusstvoznanija
Dedtiarni per 8
103050 Moscow
tel +7 095 299 4309
1944

VNIIK · RUSSIA
- Vsesojuzny Nauchnoissledovateljsky Institut Kinoiskusstva
1973 □ cinematographic and scientific research institution.

VNIITR · RUSSIA
- Vsesojuzny Nauchnoissledovateljsky Institut Televidenija i Radioveschanija
3d Khoroschevskaya 12
123298 Moscow
tel +7 095 943 0006
1944 □ television and radio research institution.

VNR · TECHNICAL TERM
- video noise reduction

VNRT · VIETNAM
- Vietnam Radio and Television
□ television broadcasting service.

VO · TECHNICAL TERM
- video operator
- vision operator
- voice-over (*aka* V/O, V.O.)

VOC · TECHNICAL TERM
- voice-over credits

VOO · THE NETHERLANDS
- Veronica Omroep Organisatie
Laapersveld
1213 VB Hilversum
tel +31 35 716716
fax +31 35 249771
tlx 43027
1976 □ broadcasting company.

VP · SPAIN
- Video Professional
Consejo de Ciento
83 6a Planta

08015 Barcelona
tel +34 3 426 2394
fax +34 3 426 1450
1989 □ magazine (11 issues annually) covering video.

VPH · TECHNICAL TERM
- viewers per household

VPI · USA
- Videfilm Producers International Ltd
250 West 57th Street
Suite 1701
New York
NY 10107
tel +1 212 581 0400
fax +1 212 581 2752
1988 □ worldwide distribution and production company of video, television and filmed entertainment in the areas of music, performing arts, cultural documentaries, family entertainment, drama and feature film. It publishes a *Catalogue of Programmes in Distribution* (1).

VPL · UK
- Video Performance Ltd
Ganton House
14-22 Ganton Street
London W1V 1LB
tel +44 71 437 0311
fax +44 71 734 9797
1984 □ established by the majority of music video-producing companies record companies in order to administer the public performance and broadcast rights in music videos on behalf of these record companies.

VPRO · THE NETHERLANDS
- Vrijzinnig Protestantsche Radio-Omroep
Postbus 11
1200 JC Hilversum
tel +31 35 712911
fax +31 35 712252
tlx 43014
1926 □ Protestant broadcasting company.

VPS · TECHNICAL TERM
- viewers per set

VPT · TECHNICAL TERM
- video programming by teletext

VPVH · USA
- Viewers-Per-1000 Viewing Households
see **PTR** · USA

VPVH · TECHNICAL TERM
- viewers per viewing household (*aka* V/VH)

VQT · USA
- Viewers for Quality Television

VR · TECHNICAL TERM
- virtual reality

VRAM · TECHNICAL TERM
- volatile random-access memory

VRC · TECHNICAL TERM
- video recording camera

VRFF · GERMANY
- Vereinigung der Rundfunk-, Film- und Fernsehschaffenden
Lerchenberg
Postfach 31 01 25
55062 Mainz
tel +49 6131 7533
□ association of radio, film and television producers.

VRP · TECHNICAL TERM
- vertical radiation pattern

VS · TECHNICAL TERM
- video signal
- vision supervisor

VSAT · TECHNICAL TERM
- very small aperture terminal

VSB · TECHNICAL TERM
- vestigial sideband

VSDA · USA
- Video Software Dealers Association
303 Harper Drive
Moorstown
NJ 08057-3229
tel +1 609 231 7800
fax +1 609 231 9791

1981 □ organisation whose main members are distributors and retailers of both videocassettes and videodiscs and whose primary aim is to serve as a voice for the video software merchandising industries. It publishes *VSDA Report* (12), as well as other reports and publications.

VSFG · SWITZERLAND
- Verband Schweizerischer Filmgestalter/innen
- Association Suisse des Réalisateurs/trices de Films (ASRF)
Brigitte Wicki
Postfach
8340 Hinwil
tel   +41 1 937 23 16
fax   +41 1 938 1357
□ association of Swiss film-makers.

VSI · TECHNICAL TERM
- visual station identification

VSIS · TECHNICAL TERM
- V-groove substrate inner stripe

VSM · TECHNICAL TERM
- video status memory

VST · TECHNICAL TERM
- voltage synthesis tuning

VSU · TECHNICAL TERM
- variable speed unit

VSWR · TECHNICAL TERM
- voltage standing wave ratio

VT · TECHNICAL TERM
- video terminal
- videotape

VTA · UK
- Video Trade Association
54D High Street
Northwood
Middlesex HA6 1BL
tel   +44 923 829122
fax   +44 923 835980
1981 □ represents video retailers and acts on their behalf. It publishes *Video Dealer* (12).

VTI · FRANCE
- Vidéotransmission Internationale

VTM · BELGIUM
- Vlaamse Televisie Maatschappij
Medialaan 1
B-1800 Vilvoorde
tel   +32 2 255 3211
fax   +32 2 252 3787
tlx   62020
1989 □ private commercial cable television station, broadcasting in Dutch.

VTO · TECHNICAL TERM
- voltage-tuned oscillator

VTOL · TECHNICAL TERM
- video tape on line

VTP · TECHNICAL TERM
- videotape player

VTR · TECHNICAL TERM
- videotape player
- videotape recorder/recording

VTRS · TECHNICAL TERM
- videotape recording system

VTS · TECHNICAL TERM
- video tuning system

VU · TECHNICAL TERM
- volume unit

VVV · TECHNICAL TERM
- video-video-video

W

W/G · TECHNICAL TERM
- waveguide

WA · TECHNICAL TERM
- wide angle

WACB · USA
- World Association for Christian Broadcasting

WACC · UK

■ World Association for Christian Communication
357 Kennington Lane
London SE11 5QY
tel   +44 71 582 9139
fax   +44 71 735 0340
tlx   8812669 WACC
□ group of international organisations dedicated to Christian media and communication. It publishes *ACTION Newsletter* (10) and *Media Development* (4).

WACK · TECHNICAL TERM
■ write address clock

WAMM · UK
■ Women Against Media Myths
□ pressure group.

WASEC · USA
■ Warner Amex Satellite Entertainment Company

WAVES · UK
■ Women's Audio Visual Education Scheme
London Women's Centre
4 Wild Court
London WC2B 5AU
tel   +44 71 430 1076
1991 □ to promote and train women to work in the audio and visual media industries and to make their own independent work. It publishes a *Newsletter* (6).

WB · USA
■ Warner Brothers Inc
4000 Warner Boulevard
Burbank
CA 91522
tel   +1 818 954 6000
fax   +1 818 954 2464
tlx   4720389
1923 □ motion picture production and distribution.

WB · TECHNICAL TERM
■ wave band
■ white balance

WBF · GERMANY
■ Institut für Weltkunde in Bildung und

Forschung, gemeinnützige Gesellschaft mbH
Jüthornstraße 33
22043 Hamburg
tel   +49 40 687161
fax   +49 40 687204
1962 □ non-profit making organisation producing 16mm educational films and videos for use in schools, in the subjects of biology, geography, history and religion.

WBFM · TECHNICAL TERM
■ wideband FM

WBI · BELGIUM
■ Wallonie-Bruxelles Images
61 rue Marché aux Herbes
1000 Brussels
tel   +32 2 504 0266
fax   +32 2 514 4136
□ group of film production companies and centres operating in French-speaking Belgium.

WBI · UK
■ World Broadcasting Information
BBC Monitoring
Caversham Park
Reading
Berks RG4 8TZ
tel   +44 734 472742 / 469261
fax   +44 734 461993
tlx   848318
1973 □ weekly publication giving a complete picture on world developments in radio, television, satellite communications, cable and news agencies throughout the world. It provides details of broadcasting behaviour, technical developments, programming policy and future plans in the form of editorial material and verbatim transcripts or translations of relevant items. The vast amount of research undertaken also produces detailed operational programme and frequency schedules of most of the world's broadcasters; these schedules are issued as separate appendixes. It publishes the *WBI Directory*.

WBVTR · TECHNICAL TERM
■ wideband videotape recorder

WDR · GERMANY
- Westdeutscher Rundfunk Köln
Appellhofplatz 1
PO Box 101950
50600 Cologne
tel +49 221 2201
fax +49 221 220 4800
tlx 8882575
1954 □ radio and television
broadcasting station with the objective
of providing information, education and
entertainment in picture and sound
broadcasting. It publishes *Information
zum Radioprogramm* (12), *Print* (12),
Hörspielkatalog (2), *Jahresbericht* (1)
and other publications.

WFA · UK
- Workers Film Association
9 Lucy Street
Manchester M15 4BX
tel +44 61 848 9782
fax +44 61 848 9783
1974 □ media and culture centre
which is a registered educational cooperative for the benefit of the
community. It offers training courses,
provides video production and
distribution, and organises exhibitions,
a film society and a social club. It
publishes a *Newsletter* (2).

WFD · TECHNICAL TERM
- wide field acquisition detector

WFM · TECHNICAL TERM
- wave form monitor

WFS · GERMANY
- Werbefunk Saar GmbH
Funkhaus Halberg
6600 Saarbrücken
tel +49 681 687920
fax +49 681 6879221
□ regional sales of television and radio
advertising.

WTFDA · USA
- Worldwide Television-FM DX
Association

WFTVN
- Women's Film, Television and Video
Network

WGAE · USA
- Writers' Guild of America East, Inc
555 West 57th Street
New York
NY 10019
tel +1 212 767 7800
fax +1 212 582 1909
1954 □ union.

WGAW · USA
- Writers' Guild of America West, Inc
8955 Beverly Boulevard
West Hollywood
CA 90048
tel +1 310 550 1000
fax +1 310 550 8185
1954 □ union.

WGC · CANADA
- Writers' Guild of Canada
3rd floor
35 McCaul Street
Toronto
Ontario M5T 1V7
tel +1 416 979 7907
fax +1 416 979 9273
□ represents writers who are working
in the fields of film, television, radio
and the recorded media.

WIC · CANADA
- Western International
Communications Ltd
1960 - 505 Burrard Street
Vancouver
British Columbia V7X 1M6
tel +1 604 687 2844
fax +1 604 687 8271
1985 □ broadcaster (television, PAY TV,
radio, satellite network services).

WIC · USA
- Women in Cable

WIFT · AUSTRALIA
- Women in Film and Television Inc
66 Albion Street
Surry Hills
NSW 2010
tel +61 2 281 2058
fax +61 2 281 1968 *(by arrangement)*
1982 □ to promote and encourage the
participation of women working in film,
television and video; to establish an

industry-based information and communication network and support group for women; to hold film and video screenings and seminars relevant to women working in these media; to support or run training programmes which will enhance women's skills and knowledge; to act as a lobby group; to encourage and produce publicity to promote a better climate for the advancement of women working in film, television and video; to eliminate sexism in the portrayal of women in film, television and video and encourage a more diverse representation of women in those media. It publishes a *Newsletter* (6) and the *SWIFT Directory* (1).

WIN · USA
■ World International Network
Suite 300
301 North Canon Drive
Beverly Hills
CA 90035
tel   +1 310 859 2700
fax   +1 310 859 3928
□ television and video programme producers and distributors.

WIP · BELGIUM
■ Wallonie Image Production
6 rue des Fories
4020 Liège
tel   +32 41 43 11 27
fax   +32 41 43 07 29
□ film production.

WIS · GERMANY
■ Werbung in Südwestfunk GmbH
Hans-Bredow-Straße 20
76530 Baden-Baden
tel   +49 7221 92-0
fax   +49 7221 924141
□ regional sales of television and radio advertising.

WIT · USA
■ Western Instructional Television, Inc
18/1438 North Gower Street
Los Angeles
CA 90028
tel   +1 213 466 8601
fax   +1 213 466 8895

1970 □ production and distribution of instructional television programmes in art, science, music, history, arts and social sciences - available for broadcast or cablecast, as well as on videocassette.

WL · TECHNICAL TERM
■ wavelength

WMM · USA
■ Women Make Movies

WMP · USA
■ Women's Media Project

WMPI · USA
■ Women in the Motion Picture Industry

WMRP · UK
■ Women's Media Resource Project
89a Kingsland High Street
London E8 2PB
tel   +44 71 254 6536
1985

WOK · TECHNICAL TERM
■ write OK

WOMPI · USA
■ Women of the Motion Picture Industry International

WORM · TECHNICAL TERM
■ write once, read many

WP · TECHNICAL TERM
■ workprint

WRTH · THE NETHERLANDS
■ World Radio and Television Handbook
PO Box 9027
1006 AA Amsterdam
tel   +31 20 669 1911
fax   +31 20 669 1941
□ practical reference guide to the world's radio and television services.

WS · TECHNICAL TERM
■ wide shot

WSBD · ITALY

■ World Broadcasting Syndication
Distribution
Via Cesare Ferrero Di Cambiano 82
00191 Rome
tel +39 6 329 6917
fax +39 6 329 6903
□ television broadcasting company.

WST · TECHNICAL TERM
■ world system teletext

WTN · UK
■ Worldwide Television News
The Interchange
Oval Road
Camden Lock
London NW1 7EP
tel +44 71 410 5200
fax +44 71 413 8302 / 413 8303
tlx 23915
1952 □ international television news
agency which aims to provide
comprehensive television services to
broadcasters, production companies,
commercial organisations, governments
and international corporations. It offers:
daily satellite news feeds; camera crews
and reporters on call 24 hours a day in
every major world capital; programme
production (current affairs, environment, health, sports, entertainment and
youth programmes); international video
coverage and distribution; video news
releases; satellite conferences; satellite
media tours; comprehensive archives;
studios and facilities; special shooting
and commercial productions division. It
publishes the *WTN Newsletter* (4).

WTV · JAPAN
■ Wakayama Telecasting Corporation
151 Sakaedani
Wakayama 640
tel +81 734 55 5711
□ television station.

WVC · THE NETHERLANDS
■ Welzijn, Volksgezondheid en Cultuur
Ministry of Welfare, Public Health and
Cultural Affairs
Film Division
Sir Winston Churchilllaan 366-368
PO Box 3009
2280 ML Rijswijk

tel +31 70 340 6148
fax +31 70 340 5742
1982 □ the Dutch government supports
film because of the importance of this
medium as an autonomous professional
art form and because of its contribution
to Dutch cultural identity. The policy of
the Ministry of Welfare, Public Health
and Cultural Affairs is directed at the
improvement of the quality and
diversity of Dutch film.

WWEN · UK
■ Worldwide Entertainment News
Mentorn House
140 Wardour Street
London W1V 3AV
tel +44 71 287 4545
fax +44 71 287 3728
1992 □ global entertainment news
service.

WWF · GERMANY
■ Westdeutsches Werbfernsehen GmbH

WWVF · THE NETHERLANDS
■ World Wide Video Festival
Noordeinde 140
2514 GP The Hague
tel +31 70 364 4805
fax +31 70 361 4448
1975 □ to present and promote
independent video, produced in all
parts of the world. Video productions
are selected because of their quality,
originality and the way in which they
further the creative use of the electronic
media.

X

XCU · TECHNICAL TERM
■ extreme close-up (*aka* ECU)

XHS · TECHNICAL TERM
■ extreme high shot (*aka* EHS)

XLS · TECHNICAL TERM
■ extreme long-shot (*aka* ELS)

XT · TECHNICAL TERM
■ X-carved tablet

Y

YBC · JAPAN
- Yamagata Broadcasting Co Ltd
2-5 Hatago-machi
Yamagata 990
tel   +81 236 22 6161
□ television station.

YBS · JAPAN
- Yamanashi Broadcasting System
6-10 Kitaguchi 2-chome
Kofu 400
tel   +81 552 31 3000
□ television station.

YCM · TECHNICAL TERM
- yellow cyan magenta

YEM · JAPAN
- Yamashita Engineering Manufacture
Inc
1926 Okata
Atsugi-shi
Kanagawa 243
tel   +81 462 28 8692 / 28 8883
fax +81 462 29 1944 / 28 3044
1979 □ manufacturing and marketing
of TV test signal generators, TV synch
signal generators, electronic image
processors, as well as designing,
developing and manufacturing audio
and visual components, digital
equipment, system control equipment,
and software programming.

YTS · JAPAN
- Yamagata Television Station
4-1 Shironishi-machi 5-chome
Yamagata 990
tel   +81 236 45 1211
□ television station.

YTV · JAPAN
- Tomiuri Telecasting Corporation
2-33 Shiromi 2-chome
Chuo-ku
Osaka 540-10
tel   +81 6 947 2111
□ television station.

YTV · UK

- Yorkshire Television
The Television Centre
Leeds
W Yorks LS3 1JS
tel   +44 532 438283
fax +44 532 445107
tlx   557232
1968 □ provides an independent
television service on Channel 3 for the
areas of Humberside, North Derbyshire,
North Lincolnshire and Yorkshire.

Z

ZB · TECHNICAL TERM
- zoom back

ZBC · ZIMBABWE
- Zimbabwe Broadcasting Corporation
PO Box HG 444
Highlands
Harare
tel   +263 4 707222 / 729661/2
fax +263 4 795698 / 702940 / 729684
tlx   24175 ZBC HOV ZW
1957 □ television and radio
broadcasting service.

ZDF · GERMANY
- Zweites Deutsches Fernsehen
PO Box 4040
55030 Mainz
tel   +49 6131 701
fax +49 6131 702157
tlx   4187930 zdf d
1963 □ public service broadcaster,
supplying the nation's second channel.
It is a non-profit making organisation
regulated by a board but independent
of the State and funded by both a
licence fee and advertising.

ZEAM · GERMANY
- Zentraleinrichtung für AV-Medien
Malteserstr. 74-100
12249 Berlin
tel   +49 30 779 2420
□ institution offering practical courses
in film-making.

ZFVA · ZIMBABWE
- Zimbabwe Film and Video

Association

ZI · TECHNICAL TERM
▪ zoom in

ZIF · TECHNICAL TERM
▪ zero insertion force

ZIFTAWU · ZIMBABWE
▪ Zimbabwe Film, Television and Allied
Workers Union
PO Box 6160
Harare
tel   +263 4 28262
fax +263 4 724226
1985 □ to protect and promote the
interests of all Zimbabweans working
on film productions, both foreign and
local. It also offers services such as
crew, technicians, location scouting
and any other information required by
producers wanting to film in
Zimbabwe.

ZIZRT · ST KITTS
▪ Ziz Radio and Television (St Kitts and
Nevis)
see **RTZIZ** · ST KITTS

ZNBC · ZAMBIA
▪ Zambia National Broadcasting
Corporation
Mass Media Complex
PO Box 50015
Lusaka
tel   +260 1 220860 / 220874
fax +260 1 254013 / 252391
tlx   41221
1966 □ television and radio service.

ZNM · SWITZERLAND
▪ Zentrum für Neue Medien
Wagistrasse 4
8952 Schlieren-Zürich
tel   +41 1 730 2004
fax +41 1 730 4347
□ media centre and educational
institution.

ZO · TECHNICAL TERM
▪ zoom out

Indexes

Full Name Index

This index includes the full descriptive name(s) of each acronym listed in the main part of the book; all technical terms are shown in italic type. It has been compiled in a word-for-word alphabetical order, for which purpose all accents, diacritical marks, brackets and commas have been ignored. Any definite or indefinite articles prefacing the full name have similarly been disregarded. Therefore, for example, "The Children's Channel" is listed under "Children's Channel, The". Hyphenated entries and those broken by "/" are treated as two words. Entries containing an apostrophe are arranged such that, for example, those beginning with "director's" appear after all those beginning with "director". Ampersands (&) are treated as the word "and". Where in the main part of the book identical acronyms are listed (for example **AAV**), in this index the country has been added for clarification. If identical acronyms originate from the same country, no distinction is made.

3-dimensional	*3-D*

A

A C Nielsen Company	ACN
Abonnee Televisie Nederland	ATN · SURINAME
Academy Award®	*AA*
Academy of Motion Picture Arts And Sciences	AMPAS
Academy of Science Fiction, Fantasy and Horror Films	ASFFHF
Academy of Television Arts and Sciences	ATAS
acceptable quality level	*AQL*
Access for Disabled People to Arts Premises Today	ADAPT
Accuracy in Media, Inc	AIM · USA
acoustic surround processors	*ASP*
acquisition of signal	*AOS*
acquisition, tracking and pointing	*ATP*
Acrodyne's digital amplitude modulation	*ADAM™*
Actiengesellschaft für Anilin-Fabrikation-Gevaert	AGFA-Gevaert
Action for Children's Television	ACT · USA
action print only	*APO*
active communications satellite	*ACS*
active nutation damping	*AND*
active sideband optimum	*ASO*
activity release monitor	*ARM*
Actors Training to Improve New Generation	ACTING
Actors' Equity Association	AEA
Actors' Fund of America	AFA
adaptive delta modulation	*ADM*
adaptive delta pulse code modulation	*ADPCM*
adaptive differential pulse code modulation	*ADPCM*
additional dialogue replacement	*ADR*
additive white Gaussian noise	*AWGN*
adjacent channel interference	*ACI*

Administración Nacional de Telecomunicaciones	ANTEL
Adult Video Association	AVA · USA
Advanced Audio Visual Systems	AAVS
Advanced Broadcasting Electronics	ABE
advanced charging system	*ACS*
advanced circuit technology	*ACT*
advanced communications technology satellite	*ACTS*
advanced compatible television	*ACTV*
advanced conversion equipment	*ACE*
advanced data communications control	*ADCCP*
advanced digital adaption converter	*ADAC*
advanced digital television	*ADTV*
advanced interactive video	*AIV*
advanced robotic control (system)	*ARC*
advanced systems and technology mission satellite	*ARTEMIS*
advanced telecommunications service	*ATS*
advanced television	*ATV*
Advanced Television Markets	ATM · UK
Advanced Television Services	ATS
Advanced Television Systems Committee	ATSC
Advanced Television Test Center	ATTC
Advertiser Syndicated Television Association	ASTA
advertising control for television	*AC-T*
Advertising Film and Videotape Producers' Association	AFVPA
Advisory Committee on Advanced Television Service	ACATS
Aerial Video Systems	AVS
aeronautical mobile satellite service	*AMSS*
African Film and Television Collective	AFTC
African Women in Film & Video Association	AWIFAV
Agence Française pour le Développement de la Télévision en Arabie Séoudite	ADETE
Agence Francophone d'Images et de Télévision	AFIT
Agence Internationale d'Images TV de RFO	AITV
Agence pour le Développement Régional du Cinéma	ADRC · FRANCE
Agence Spatiale Européenne	ASE
Agency for Instructional Television	AIT
Agrupació Catalana de Productors Cinematogràfics	ACPC
airborne flight test system	*AFTS*
Akita Asahi Broadcasting Co	AAB
Akita Broadcasting System	ABS · JAPAN
Akita Television Co Ltd	AKT
Aktion Funk und Fernsehen	AFF
Alberta Motion Picture Development Corporation	AMPDC
Alberta Motion Picture Industries Association	AMPIA
Algemene Vereniging Radio-Omroep	AVRO
All-Channel Television Society	ACTS
All-Industry Marketing for Cinema	AIM · UK
Alliance Europe pour la TV et la Culture	AETC
Alliance Internationale de la Distribution par Câble	AID
Alliance of Canadian Cinema, Television and Radio Artists	ACTRA
Alliance of Motion Picture & Television Producers	AMPTP
Alliance of Television Film Producers	ATFP
Alo Radio and Television Company	ART · TURKEY
Alpha Repertory Television Service	ARTS
alternate-mark-inversion	*AMI*

Alternatieve Televisie Verzorging	ATV · SURINAME
alternating current	*AC*
Aluminium-Gallium Arsenide	*AL-GA-AS*
Amalgamated Engineering and Electrical Union - Electrical and Electronic Telecommunication and Plumbing Union Division	AEEU-EETPU
Amateur Film & Video Maker	AFVM
American Association of Cable Television Owners	AACTO
American Broadcasting Company	ABC · USA
American Cable Network, Inc	ACN
American Christian Television System	ACTS
American Cinema Editors Inc.	ACE
American Citizens' Television Committee, Inc	ACT · USA
American Community Service Network	ACSN
American Council for Better Broadcasts	ACBB
American Federation of Television and Radio Artists	AFTRA
American Film and Video Association	AFVA
American Film Institute	AFI · USA
American Film Market	AFM
American Film Marketing Association	AFMA
American Guild of Musical Artists	AGMA
American Guild of Variety Artists	AGVA
American Motion Picture Export Company	AMPEC
American Movie Classics	AMC · USA
American Multi Cinema	AMC · USA
American National Standards Institute	ANSI
American Public Television Producers Association	APTPA
American Science Film Association	ASFA
American Society of Cinematographers	ASC
American Society of Television Cameramen, Inc	ASTVC
American Standards Association	ASA
American Telephone and Telegraph Company	AT&T
American Television & Communications Corporation	ATC · USA
American Television Society	ATS
American Video Association	AVA · USA
American Women in Radio and Television, Inc	AWRT
Amicale des Cadres de l'Industrie Cinématographique	ACIC
amplex digital optics	*ADO*™
amplitude modulated link	*AML*
amplitude modulated transmitter	*AMT*
amplitude modulation	*AM*
amplitude shift keying	*ASK*
Anadolu Radio Television Corporation	ART · UK
analogue component link equipment	*ACLE*
analogue to digital	*A/D*
analogue-to-digital convertor/coding	*ADC*
analogue write once	*AWO*
Anambra State Television	ABS-TV
angled shot	*AS*
angstrom unit	*AU*
animated graphics system	*AGS*
announce booth	*AB*
annual licence fee	*ALF*
annular control electrode	*ACE*
antenna noise temperature	*ANT*

Antenne des Téléspectateurs Actifs	ANTEA
Anthropology Film Center Foundation	AFCF
anti comet-tail	*ACT*
anti-flicker processor	*AFP*
Antigua and Barbuda Broadcasting Service	ABBS / ABS · ANTIGUA AND BARBUDA
Aomori Television Co Ltd	ATV · JAPAN
apogee boost motor	*ABM*
apogee engine firing	*AEF*
apogee kick motor	*AKM*
apogee motor firing	*AMF*
Appalachian Community Service Network	ACSN
application specified integrated circuit	*ASIC*
application(s) technology satellite	*ATS*
Applied Research and Technology, Inc	ART · USA
appreciation index	*AI*
Aquila Broadcasting Sets SpA	ABS · ITALY
Arab States Broadcasting Union	ASBU
Arbeitsgemeinschaft der öffentlich-rechtlichen Rundfunkanstalten der Bundesrepublik Deutschland	ARD
Arbeitsgruppe Kommunikationsforschung München	AKM
Arbeitskreis Wissenschaftlicher Film	AWF
Archiv für Urheber-, Film, Funk- und Theaterrecht	UFITA
area of dominant influence	*ADI*
Argentina Televisora Color	ATC · ARGENTINA
Argentina Video Home	AVH
Armed Forces Broadcasters Association	AFBA
Armed Forces Network	AFN · USA
Armed Forces Radio and Television Service	AFRTS
Armed Forces Television Service	AFTS · USA
Arnold & Richter Cine Technik	ARRI
array shunt regulator	*ASR*
Arri precision exposure control	*APEC*
art director	*AD*
artificial intelligence	*AI*
Artists and Music Consultants	AMC · BELGIUM
Arts and Entertainment Network	A&E
Asahi Broadcasting Aomori Co	ABA · JAPAN
Asahi Broadcasting Corporation	ABC · JAPAN
Asahi National Broadcasting Co	ANB
Asesoramiento y Servicios Técnicos Industriales, SA	ASTISA
Asia-Pacific Broadcasting Union	ABU · MALAYSIA
Asia-Pacific Institute for Broadcasting Development	AIBD
Asia Television Ltd	ATV · HONG KONG
Asia Television Network	ATN · INDIA
Asian Motion Picture Producers Association	AMPPA
Asociación Colombiana de Distribudores y Exhibidores de Cine	ACOCINE
Asociación de Cinematográficas Colombianas	ACCO
Asociación de Distribuidores y Importadores Cinematográficos de Ambito Nacional	ADICAN
Asociación de Distribuidores y Importadores Videográficos de Ambito Nacional	ADIVAN
Asociación de Teleradiodifusoras Argentinas	ATA
Asociación de Videoeditores Independientes de la Argentina	AVIA
Asociación Fonográfica y Videográfica Española	AFYVE

Asociación Independiente de Productores Vascos	AIPV
Asociación Internacional de Radiodifusión	AIR
Asociación Mexicana de Filmadoras	AMFI
Asociación Nacional de Broadcasters Uruguayos	ANDEBU
Asociación Nacional de Trabajadores de Radio y Televisión	ANALTRARADIO
Asociación Nacional Empresas Produccion Audiovisual	ANEPA
Asociación Videográfica Española	AVE
aspect ratio	*AR*
aspect ratio controller	*ARC*
ass on curb	*AOC*
assembly, integration and test	*AIT*
Assistance Audio-Visuelle	AAV · BELGIUM
assistant cameramen	*AC*
assistant director	*AD*
assistant film cameraman	*AFC*
assistant film recordist	*AFR*
assistant floor manager	*AFM*
assistant stage manager	*ASM*
Associação Brasileira das Empresas de Video Comunicação	ABEVC
Associação de Produtores/Realizadores de Filmes Publicitarios	APRFP
Associació Nacional de Distribuidors Cinematogràfics de Catalunya	ANDICCA
associate director	*AD*
associate producer	*AP*
Associated Actors and Artistes of America	AAAA
Associated Press Broadcasters	APB
Association Canadienne d'Etudes Cinématographiques	FSAC
Association Canadienne de la Radio et de la Télévision de Langue Française Inc	
	ACTRF
Association Canadienne de Production de Film et Télévision	ACPFT
Association Canadienne de Télévision par Câble	ACTC
Association Cinématographique Professionnelle de Conciliation et d'Arbitrage	ACPCA
Association Cinématographique Suisse	ACS · SWITZERLAND
Association Cinématographique Suisse Romande	ACSR
Association de Créateurs pour l'Audio-Visuel	ACA
Association de Gestion Internationale Collective des Œuvres Audiovisuelles	AGICOA
Association de Lutte Contre la Piraterie Audiovisuelle	ALPA
Association de Préfiguration du Centre Européen de l'Image et du Son	APCEIS
Association de Télévision Educative au Canada	ATEC
Association des Auteurs-Réalisateurs-Producteurs	ARP
Association des Cinéastes Gabonais	ACG
Association des Cinéastes Sénégalais	ACS · SENEGAL
Association des Cinémas de Recherche de l'Ile-de-France	ACRIF
Association des Correspondants des Radios et Télévisions Etrangères à Paris	CRETE
Association des Producteurs de Films et de Télévision du Québec	APFTQ
Association des Producteurs de Films et de Vidéo du Québec	APFVQ
Association des Professeurs pour la Promotion de l'Education Cinématographique	
	APEC
Association des Professionnel-le-s de la Vidéo du Québec	APVQ
Association des Propriétaires de Cinémas du Québec, Inc	APCQ
Association des Réalisateurs de Télévision Exerçant en Régions	ARTER
Association des Responsables et Spécialistes Audiovisuels des Etablissements	
d'Enseignement Supérieur	ARAS
Association des Télévisions Commerciales Européennes	ACT · ITALY
Association des Trois Mondes	ATM · FRANCE

Association des Vidéo Clubs Professionnels	AVCP
Association du Droit de Retransmission Canadien	ADRC · CANADA
Association du Festival International de Films de Femmes	AFIFF
Association Européenne du Film d'Animation	AEFA
Association Européenne pour l'Education aux Médias Audiovisuels	AEEMA
Association for Competitive Television	ACT · USA
Association for Education by Radio-Television	AERT
Association for Education in Journalism and Mass Communications	AEJMC
Association for Independent Video and Film-Makers	AIVF
Association for Maximum Service Television	AMST
Association for Media Education in England	AME
Association for Media Education in Scotland	AMES
Association for Media, Film and Television Studies in Further and Higher Education	AMFIT
Association for Tele-Education in Canada	ATEC
Association Française de Normalisation	AFNOR
Association Française de Recherche sur l'Histoire du Cinéma	AFRHC
Association Française des Cinémas d'Art-et-Essai	AFCAE
Association - Française - des Cinémas de Recherche Indépendants de la Région Alpine	ACRIRA
Association Française des Directeurs de la Photographie Cinématographique	AFC · FRANCE
Association Française des Producteurs de Films et de Programmes Audiovisuels	AFPF
Association Française du Cinéma d'Animation	AFCA
Association Internationale de Radiodifussion	AIR
Association Internationale des Auteurs de l'Audiovisuel	AIDAA
Association Internationale des Etudes et Recherches sur l'Information	AIERI
Association Internationale du Film d'Animation	ASIFA
Association Internationale pour la Vidéo dans les Arts et la Culture	AIVAC
Association Littéraire et Artistique Internationale	ALAI
Association Nationale de Gestion des Œuvres Audiovisuelles	ANGOA
Association Nationale des Téléspectateurs et Auditeurs	ANTEA
Association Nationale pour la Défense de la Télévision	ANADET
Association of America's Public Television Stations	APTS / AAPTS
Association of Black Film and Video Workshops	ABW
Association of Black Motion Picture and Television Producers	ABMPTP
Association of Cable Television Suppliers	ACTS
Association of Canadian Film Craftspeople	ACFC
Association of Catholic Television and Radio Syndicators	ACTRS
Association of Christians in Local Broadcasting	ACLB
Association of Cinema and Video Laboratories, Inc	ACVL
Association of Cinematograph, Television and Allied Technicians	ACTT
Association of College and University Broadcasting Stations	ACUBS
Association of Commercial Television in Europe	ACT
Association of Film Commissioners International	AFCI
Association of Independent Cinemas	AIC · UK
Association of Independent Commercial Editors	AICE
Association of Independent Commercial Producers, Inc	AICP · USA
Association of Independent Metropolitan Stations	AIMS
Association of Independent Television Stations, Inc.	AITS · USA
Association of Local TV Operators	ALTO
Association of Maximum Service Telecasters	AMST / MST
Association of Moving Image Archives	AMIA
Association of Professional Recording Services Ltd	APRS

Association of Radio and Television News Analysts	ARTNA
Association pour la Création Française et Européenne dans l'Audiovisuel	ACFEA
Association pour la Diffusion du Cinéma d'Expression Latine	ADICIEL
Association pour la Fondation Internationale du Cinéma et de la Communication Audiovisuelle	AFICCA
Association pour la Formation aux Métiers de l'Audio-Visuel	AFOMAV
Association pour la Promotion de l'Image	API
Association pour la Promotion des Professionnels de l'Image et de la Communication de la Côte d'Azur	APRICA
Association pour le Développement de l'Audio-Visuel et du Court Métrage	ADACOM
Association pour le Festival de Cinéma d'Animation de Baillargues	AFCAB
Association Professionnelle des Réalisateurs d'Œuvres Audiovisuelles de Commande	APRAC
Association Professionnelle du Spectacle et de l'Audio-Visuel	APDS
Association Québécoise de l'Industrie du Disque, du Spectacle et de la Vidéo	ADISQ
Association Québécoise des Critiques de Cinéma	AQCC
Association Québécoise des Etudes Cinématographiques	AQEC
Association Québécoise des Réalisateurs et Réalisatrices de Cinéma et de Télévision	AQRRCT
Association Rélative à la Télévision Européenne	ARTE
Association Romande du Cinéma	ARC
Association Sénégalais des Critiques de Cinéma	ASSECCI
Association Suisse des Distributeurs de Films	ASDF
Association Suisse des Exploitants et Distributeurs de Films	ASED
Association Suisse des Industries Techniques Cinématographiques	ITC · SWITZERLAND
Association Suisse des Journalistes Cinématographiques	ASJC
Association Suisse des Producteurs de Films de Fiction et de Documentaires	FFD · SWITZERLAND
Association Suisse des Réalisateurs/trices de Films	ASRF
Association Suisse des Techniciennes et Techniciens du Film	ASTF
Association Suisse du Film de Commande et de l'Audiovision	FCA
Association Universitaire pour le Développement, l'Education et la Communication en Afrique et dans le Monde	AUDECAM
Associazione Cattolica Esercenti Cinema	ACEC
Associazione Generale Italiana dello Spettacolo	AGIS
Associazione Internazionale del Cinema Comico d'Arte	AICCA
Associazione Italiana Amici del Cinema d'Essai	AIACE
Associazione Italiana Autori della Fotografia	AIC · ITALY
Associazione Italiana Cineoperatori Professionisti	AICP · ITALY
Associazione Italiana Cultura Cinematografica	AICC
Associazione Italiana Dialoghisti Adattatori Cinetelevisivi	AIDAC
Associazione Italiana Lavoratori Spettacolo	AILS
Associazione Italiana Maestranze Cinematografiche	AIMC
Associazione Italiana Studi Cineaudiovisivi	AISCA
Associazione Italiana Tecnici del Suono	AITS · ITALY
Associazione Italiana Telecineoperatori	AITC
Associazione Nazionale Circoli Cinematografici Italiani	ANCCI
Associazione Nazionale Distributori Televisivi e Affini	ANDTA
Associazione Nazionale Esercenti Cinema	ANEC
Associazione Nazionale Imprese Pubblicità Audiovisiva	ANIPA
Associazione Nazionale Industrie Cinematografiche e Audiovisive	ANICA
Associazione Nazionale Studi Effetti Ottici Cinetelevisivi	ANSEOC
Associazione Nazionale Teleradio Indipendenti	ANTI
Associazione Operatori Cinematografici Italiani	AOCI

Associazione Produttori Indipendenti Cinematografico Elettronici	APICE
Associazione Svizzera dei Cinema	SKV
Associazione Tecnica Italiana per la Cinematografia e la Televisione	ATIC
Associção Brasileira de Emissoras de Rádio e Televisão	ABERT
asymmetric sideband	*ASB*
asynchronous pulse code modulation	*APCM*
Atelier de Recherches Audiovisuelles	ARAV
Atlantic Entertainment Group	AEG
Atlantic Independent Film and Video Association	AIFVA
attitude and orbital control system	*AOCS*
attitude control electronics	*ACE*
attitude control system	*ACS*
Attività Cinetelevisive, Audio, Distribuzione Film	ACTA
audience appreciation	*AA*
audience research	*AR*
Audience Research & Development	AR&D
Audience Studies, Inc	ASI
audio cassette recorder	*ACR*
audio description of television	*AUDETEL*
Audio Engineering Society	AES
audio follow	*AF*
audio follow(s) video	*AFV*
audio tape recorder	*ATR*
audio test signal generator	*ASG*
audio/video	*AV*
audio, video, control	*AVC*
audio video interactive	*AVI*
audio video interactive development	*AVID*
Audio Visual Arts Ltd	AVA · UK
Audio Visual Association	AVA · UK
Audio Visual Distributors Association of Australia	AVDAA
Audio Visual Library Services	AVLS
audiovisual	*AV*
audiovisual communications	*AVC*
Audiovisuel Multimedia International	AMI
Audiovisuele Federatie Nederlands	AFN · THE NETHERLANDS
AudioVisuelle Media	AVM
Audiovisuelle Medienzentrum	AVMZ
augmentation signal package	*ASP*
Australian Broadcasting Authority	ABA · AUSTRALIA
Australian Broadcasting Control Board	ABCB
Australian Broadcasting Corporation	ABC · AUSTRALIA
Australian Broadcasting Tribunal	ABT · AUSTRALIA
Australian Children's Television Action Committee	ACTAC
Australian Children's Television Foundation	ACTF
Australian Council for Children's Films and Television	ACCFT
Australian Federation of Commercial Broadcasting Stations	AFCBS
Australian Film and Television School	AFTS · AUSTRALIA
Australian Film Commission	AFC · AUSTRALIA
Australian Film Finance Commission	AFFC
Australian Film Finance Corporation	AFFC / FFC
Australian Film Fund Management	AFFM
Australian Film Institute	AFI · AUSTRALIA
Australian Film, Television and Radio School	AFTRS

Australian National Television Council	ANTC
Australian Screen Directors Association	ASDA
Australian Teachers of Media	ATOM
auto channel programming	*ACP*
auto chase focus	*ACF*
auto-convergence alignment system	*ACON*
auto music scan	*AMS*
auto programme find	*APF*
auto ranging	*AR*
auto tape time select	*ATTS*
auto tracing white	*ATW*
auto tuning system	*ATS*
automated camera effects system	*ACES*
Automated Measurement of Line-Up	AMOL
automated news graphics interface system	*ANGIS*™
automated test equipment	*ATE*
automatic assemble editing	*AAE*
automatic beam control	*ABC*
automatic beam optimiser	*ABO*
automatic black level	*ABL*
automatic brightness control	*ABC*
automatic chroma control	*ACC*
automatic chrominance control	*ACC*
automatic colour control	*ACC*
automatic contrast control	*ACC*
automatic dependent surveillance	*ADS*
automatic dialogue replacement	*ADR*
automatic editing function	*AEF*
auto(matic) exposure	*AE*
automatic (fine) frequency control	*AFC*
automatic fine tuning	*AFT*
automatic gain control	*AGC*
automatic lamp changer	*ALC*
automatic level control	*ALC*
automatic music programme search	*AMPS*
automatic phase control	*APC*
automatic picture control	*APC*
automatic power control	*APC*
automatic reconfiguration mode	*ARM*
automatic remote cassette handler	*ARCH*
automatic scan tracking	*AST*
automatic sequence register	*ASR*
automatic slope control	*ASC*
automatic test equipment	*ATC*
automatic track finding/following	*ATF*
automatic transmission system	*ATS*
automatic volume control	*AVC*
auto(matic) white balance	*AWB*
avalanche photodiode	*APD*
average audience	*AA*
average picture level	*APL*
average quarter hour	*AQH*
Award for Cablecasting Excellence	ACE
axial front projection	*AFP*

B

baby N connector	*BNC*
back light compensation	*BLC*
back projection	*BP*
Back to the Bible Broadcast	BBB
background	*BG / BKG*
background music	*BGM*
background video	*BGV*
Bâlgarska Televizija	BT / BTV · BULGARIA
Bangkok Broadcasting and Television Company Ltd	BBTV
Bangladesh National Broadcasting Authority	BNBA
Bangladesh Television	BTV · BANGLADESH
Barn och ungdomsfilmfestivalen i Malmö	BUFF
Bart Omroep Organisatie Stichting	BOOS
Bath Community Television Ltd	BCTV
Bay Area Video Coalition	BAVC
Bayerische Rundfunkwerbung GmbH	BRW
Bayerischer Rundfunk	BR
bayonet base	*BB*
bayonet connector	*BNC*
Bayrak Radio and Television Corporation	BRTK
beginning of tape	*BOT*
behind the lens	*BTL*
Beijing Broadcasting Institute	BBI
Belgische Radio en Televisie	BRT / BRTN
below minimum standards	*BMS*
Bendel State Television	BTV · BENIN
Beroepvereniging van Film- en Televisiemakers	NBF
best time available	*BTA*
Betacam Standard Play	*BCSP*
big character select	*BCS*
big close-up	*BCU*
big fat wide shot	*BFWS*
binary-coded decimal	*BCD*
binary phase-shift keying	*BPSK*
binary synchronous communication	*BSC*
biochemical oxygen demand	*BOD*
bit error rate	*BER*
bit error rate testing	*BERT*
bit map	*BMP*
bit-rate reduction	*BRR*
Biwako Broadcasting Co Ltd	BBC · JAPAN
black and white	*BW*
Black Audio Film Collective	BAFC
black burst	*BB*
Black Citizens for a Fair Media	BCFM
Black Efforts for Soul in Television	BEST
Black Entertainment Television	BET
Black Film Bulletin	BFB
Black Media Training Trust	BMTT

black range	*BR*
Black Variety Television	BVTV
black-video-black	*BVB*
block down	*BD*
block termination	*BT*
Board for International Broadcasting	BIB
Bombay International Film Festival	BIFF
Border Broadcasters' Collective	BBC · CANADA
Borno State Radio and Television Corporation	BRTV
Bose-Chaudhuri-Hocquenghem	*BCH*
box office	*BO*
break tape manager	*BTM*
British Academy of Film and Television Arts	BAFTA
British Action for Children's Television	BAC TV
British Amateur Television Club	BATC
British Amateur Video Awards	BAVA
British Board of Film Censors	BBFC
British Board of Film Classification	BBFC
British Broadcasting Corporation	BBC · UK
British Broadcasting Corporation - World Service Television	BBC-WSTV
British Columbia Motion Picture Association	BCMPA
British Federation of Film Societies	BFFS
British Film & Television Producers Association	BFTPA
British Film Commission	BFC
British Film Designs Guild	BFDG
British Film Institute	BFI · UK
British Forces Broadcasting Service	BFBS
British Industrial & Scientific Film Association	BISFA
British Interactive Multimedia Association	BIMA
British Kinematograph Sound and Television Society	BKSTS
British Radio and Electronic Equipment Manufacturers Association	BREMA
British Satellite Broadcasting	BSB
British Screen Advisory Council	BSAC
British Screen Development	BSD
British Screen Finance Ltd	BSF
British Sky Broadcasting	BSKYB
British Society of Cinematographers	BSC
British Universities Film & Video Council	BUFVC
British Video History Trust	BVHT
British Videogram Association	BVA
broadband communications network	*BCN*
broadband integrated services digital network	*BISDN*
broadcast	*BC*
Broadcast Advertisers Reports	BAR
Broadcast Advertising Producers Society of America	BAPSA
Broadcast Bureau of Measurement	BBM
Broadcast Cable Credit Association	BCCA
Broadcast Cable Financial Management Association	BCFMA
Broadcast Designers Association, Inc	BDA
Broadcast Education Association	BEA
Broadcast Equipment Rental Company	BERC
Broadcast Institute of North America	BINA
Broadcast Music, Inc	BMI
Broadcast Pioneers	BP

Broadcast Pioneers Educational Fund, Inc	BPEF
Broadcast Pioneers Library	BPL
Broadcast Programming Centre of Japan	BPCJ
Broadcast Promotion and Marketing Executives	BPME
Broadcast Rating Council	BRC
broadcast satellite	*BS*
Broadcast Technology Society	BTS · USA
Broadcast Television Recording Engineers	BTRE
Broadcast Television Systems Committee	BTSC
Broadcast Television Systems GmbH	BTS · GERMANY
broadcast video	*BV*
broadcast video editing	*BVE*
Broadcast Video Engineering Ltd	BVE
broadcast video monitor	*BVM*
broadcast video switcher	*BVS*
broadcast video U-matic®	*BVU*
Broadcasters' Audience Research Board Ltd	BARB
Broadcasters' Foundation, Inc	BFI · USA
Broadcasting Across the Barriers of European Language	BABEL
Broadcasting and Entertainment Trades Alliance	BETA
Broadcasting and Film Commission/National Film Council of the Churches of Christ	
	BFC/NCC
Broadcasting Complaints Commission	BCC · UK
Broadcasting Corporation of Belize	BCB · BELIZE
Broadcasting Corporation of China	BCC · TAIWAN
Broadcasting Corporation of Oyo State	BCOS
Broadcasting Corporation of the Bahamas	BCB · BAHAMAS
Broadcasting Entertainment Cinematograph and Theatre Union	BECTU
Broadcasting Foundation of America	BFA
Broadcasting Organisations of the Non-Aligned Countries	BONAC
Broadcasting Press Guild	BPG
Broadcasting Research Unit	BRU
broadcast(ing) satellite service	*BSS*
Broadcasting Standards Council	BSC
Broadcasting Support Services	BSS · UK
Broadcasting System of Niigata Inc	BSN
Broadcasting System of San-In	BSS · JAPAN
build-up	*BU*
built-in time code	*BITC*
Bund Freischaffender Foto-Designer	BFF
Bundes Deutscher Filmamateure	BDFA
Bundesverband Deutscher Fernsehproduzenten	BDF
Bundesverband Filmschnitt Cutter	BFS
Bundesverband HDTV	BHDTV
Bundesverband Jugend und Film eV	BJF
Bundesverband Kable und Satellite	BKS
Bureau de Développement des Télécommunications	BDT
Bureau de Liaison de l'Industrie Cinématographique	BLIC
Bureau de Liaison Européen du Cinéma	BLEC
Bureau Européen du Cinéma et de la Télévision	BECT
Bureau International de Liaison des Instituts du Film d'Animation	BILIFA
buried heterostructure	*BH*
business band service	*BBS*
business television	*BTV*

C

Cable and Broadcast Productions	CBP
Cable Arts Foundation, Inc	CAF
Cable Authority	CA
cable diffusion service	*CDS*
Cable Health Network	CHN
cable households using television	*CHUT*
Cable National Audience Demographics	CNAD
Cable News Network	CNN
Cable Satellite Public Affairs Network	C-SPAN
Cable Sport and Leisure	CSL
cable television	*CTV / CATV*
Cable Television Administration and Marketing Society	CTAM
Cable Television Advertising Bureau, Inc	CAB · USA / CTAB
Cable Television Association	CTA · UK
Cable Television Information Center	CTIC
cable television relay service	*CARS*
Cable Television Technical Advisory Committee	CTAC
cadmium disulphide	*CDS*
Caisse de Prévoyance et de Retraite de l'Industrie Cinématographique, des Activités du Spectacle et de l'Audiovisuel	CAPRICAS
Caisse de Retraite des Cadres de l'Industrie Cinématographique, des Activités du Spectacle et de l'Audiovisuel	CARCICAS
California Film Commission	CFC
Cámara Nacional de Medios de Comunicación Colectiva	CANAMECC
Cambodia Television	CTV · CAMBODIA
camera control unit	*CCU*
camera head unit	*CHU*
Campaign Against Racism in the Media	CARM
Campaign for Press and Broadcasting Freedom	CPBF
can go over	*CGO*
"Canada's First Multilingual Television"	CFMT
Canadian Association of Broadcasters	CAB · CANADA
Canadian Association of Motion Picture Producers	CAMPP
Canadian Audio-Visual Certification Office	CAVCO
Canadian Broadcasters Rights Agency, Inc	CBRA
Canadian Broadcasting Corporation	CBC · CANADA
Canadian Cable Television Association	CCTA
Canadian Coalition Against Video Theft	CCAVT
Canadian Film and Television Production Association	CFTPA
Canadian Film-Makers Distribution Centre	CFDC / CFMDC
Canadian Independent Film Caucus	CIFC
Canadian International Studios, Inc	CIS
Canadian Motion Picture Distributors Association	CMPDA
Canadian Radio-Television and Telecommunications Commission	CRTC
Canadian Retransmission Collective	CRC · CANADA
Canadian Retransmission Right Association	CRRA
Canadian Society of Cinematographers	CSC · CANADA
Canadian Television	CTV · CANADA
Canadian Television Series Development Foundation	CTSDF
Canadian Women in Radio and Television	CWRT
Canal France International	CFI · FRANCE

candela-meter-second	*CMS*
candle power	*CP*
Canterbury Television	CTV · NEW ZEALAND
capacitance electronic disc	*CED*
capacitive electronic disc	*CED*
Cape Film and Video Foundation	CFVF · SOUTH AFRICA
Cape Independent Film-Makers Forum	CIFF
Capital Cost Allowance	CCA · CANADA
caption projection unit	*CPU*
Caribbean Broadcasting Corporation (Barbados)	CABC / CBC · BARBADOS
Caribbean Broadcasting Union	CBU
Caribbean Film and Video Foundation	CFVF · MARTINIQUE
Caribbean Institute of Mass Communication	CARIMAC
carrier/interference	*C/I*
carrier-to-noise ratio	*C/N / CNR*
cartridge tape	*CT*
cartridge video recorder	*CVR*
cassette preparation system	*CPS*
cassette tape recorder	*CTR*
cathode-potential stabilised-target scanning	*CPS*
cathode ray oscilloscope	*CRO*
cathode ray tube	*CRT*
Catholic Apostolate of Radio, Television and Advertising	CARTA
Catholic Media Council	CAMECO
CBS Broadcast International	CBI
centimetres visible	*CMV*
central aerial television	*CATV*
central apparatus room	*CAR*
Central Australian Aboriginal Media Association	CAAMA
Central Board of Film Censors	CBFC
central control room	*CCR*
central control unit	*CCU*
Central Film Library	CFL
Central Motion Picture Corporation	CMPC
Central Organisation of Finnish Film Producers	COFFP
central processing unit	*CPU*
Central Television Enterprises	CTE
Centralnoje Televidenije	CT · RUSSIA
Centre Bruxellois de l'Audiovisuel	CBA · BELGIUM
Centre Cinématographique Marocain	CCM
Centre Commun d'Etudes de Télédiffusion et de Télécommunications	CCETT
Centre d'Enseignement et de Recherche Audiovisuel	CERAV
Centre d'Etudes des Sciences et Techniques de l'Information	CESTI
Centre d'Etudes et de Recherches de l'Image et du Son	CERIS
Centre d'Information d'Orientation de l'Association Professionnelle du Spectacle et de l'Audiovisuel	CIOAPDS
Centre d'Initiation au Cinéma, aux Communications et aux Moyens Audiovisuels	CIC · FRANCE
Centre de Recherche et d'Etudes sur les Arts du Texte, de l'Image et du Spectacle	CREATIS
Centre de Recherche sur les Arts de la Communication	CRAC
Centre de Recherches Cinéma, Rites et Mythes Contemporains	CRMC
Centre de Recherches d'Esthétique du Cinéma et des Arts Audiovisuels	CRECA
Centre de Sociologie de l'Innovation	CSI

Centre Européen de l'Image et du Son	CEIS
Centre for Mass Communication Research	CMCR
Centre for Telecommunications Development	CTD
Centre for the Study of Communication and Culture	CSCC
Centre Interdisciplinaire de Recherche en Communication Audiovisuelle	CIRCAV
Centre International Audiovisuel d'Etudes et de Recherches	CIAVER
Centre International de Création Video	CICV
Centre International de Documentation Cinématographique	CIDC · BELGIUM
Centre International de Documentation et d'Echanges sur le Cinéma et la Communication Audiovisuelle	CIDECCA
Centre International de Liaison des Ecoles de Cinéma et de Télévision	CILECT
Centre International du Cinéma d'Animation	CICA
Centre International du Film pour l'Enfance et la Jeunesse	CIFEJ
Centre Méditérranéen de la Communication Audiovisuelle	CMCA
Centre National de la Cinématographie	CNC · FRANCE
Centre National de l'Audiovisuel	CNA · LUXEMBOURG
Centre National de Production Cinématographique	CNPC
Centre National des Archives de la Publicité	CNAP
Centre National du Cinéma *(Gabon)*	CENACI
Centre National du Cinéma *(Ivory Coast)*	CNC
Centre National du Cinéma Burkinabé	CNCB
Centre National du Cinéma du Burkina Faso	CNCB
Centre Nationale Français du Film pour l'Enfance et la Jeunesse	CFEJ
Centro Cattolico Cinematografico	CCC · ITALY
Centro Cattolico Televisivo	CCTV · ITALY
Centro de Capacitación Cinematográfica	CCC · MEXICO
Centro de Estudios de la Imagen y del Video	CEV
Centro de Experimentación y Realización Cinemtográfica	CERC
Centro de Información Cinematográfica	CIC · CUBA
Centro Internacional del Audiovisual Universitario	CIAVU
Centro Italiana Addestramento Cinematografico	CIAC
Centro Italiano Studi sull'Arte dello Spettacolo & TV	CISAS
Centro Mediterrãneo da Comuniçăo Audiovisual	CMCA
Centro Sperimentale di Cinematografia	CSC · ITALY
Centro Studi Cinematografici	CSC · ITALY
Centro Studi Cinetelevisivi	CSCTV
Centro Telecinematografica Culturale	CTC · ITALY
Centro Televisivo Vaticano	CTV · ITALY
Centro Universitario de Estudios Cinematográficos	CUEC
Centrum voor Omroep en Media	COM
Çerrato Compagnia Cinematografico	CCC · ITALY
Česká Televize	ČST · CZECH REPUBLIC
Cesko & Slovenske Televize	ČSTV
CETA Electronic Design (UK) Ltd	CED
CFL Vision	CFL
chain break	*CB*
Chambre Professionnelle Belge de la Cinématographie	CPBC
Chambre Syndicale de l'Edition Audiovisuelle	CSEA
Chambre Syndicale des Producteurs et Exportateurs de Films Français	CSPEFF
change-over	*CO*
channel compatible digicypher	*CCDC*
Channel Forty Seven Television	CFMT
Channel Four Television Company Ltd	C4
channel stops	*CS*

Channel Television	CTV · UK
channelled substrate plomar	*CSP*
character background generator	*CBG*
character generator	*CG*
charge coupled device	*CCD*
Chiba Television Broadcasting Corporation	CTC · JAPAN
Chicago Children's Film Centre	CCFC
Chicago International Children's Film Festival	CICFF
chief engineer	*CE*
Children's Channel, The	CC
children's feature/film	*CF*
Children's Film and Television Center	CFTCA
Children's Film and Television Foundation Ltd, The	CFTF
Children's Film Unit, The	CFU
Children's Television Workshop	CTW
China Central Television	CCTV · CHINA
China Television Company	CTV · TAIWAN
Chinese Television System	CTS
Christian Broadcasting Network	CBN
Christian Broadcasting System Korea	CBSK
Christian European Visual Media Association	CEVMA
Christian Film Distributors' Association	CFDA
Christian Leaders for Responsible Television	CLEARTV
Christian Television Mission	CTM
chroma crawl free	*CCF*
chroma light and dark	*CDK*
chroma timer/time compressed multiplex	*CTCM*
chrominance noise reducer	*CNR*
Chubu-Nippon Broadcasting Co Ltd	CBC · JAPAN
Chugoku Broadcasting Co Ltd	RCC
Chukyo Television Co Ltd	CTV · JAPAN
Churches Advisory Council for Local Broadcasting	CACLB
Churches TV Centre	CTVC
Cine Guild of Great Britain	CGGB
Cinéastes Sénégalaises Associés, Les	CINESEAS
Cinecircoli Giovanili Socio-Culturali	CGS
Cineforum Italiano	CINIT
Cinema Advertising Association	CAA · UK
Cinema and Television Benevolent Fund	CTBF
Cinema and Video Industry Audience Research	CAVIAR
Cinema Digital Sound®	*CDS*
Cinema Exhibitors Association	CEA
Cinema International Corporation	CIC · USA
Cinema Romana Cineproduzione	CRC · ITALY
Cinema Theatre Association	CTA · UK
CinemaScope	*CS*
Cinématographie, Representation, Communication Audiovisuelle	CIRCA
Cineteleaudio Cooperativa	CTA · ITALY
circular polarisation	*CP*
circularly polarised	*CP*
Citizens for Cable Awareness	CCA · USA
Classics Video Cinema Collector's Club	CVCCC
Classification and Rating Administration	CARA
clean, clear coat	*C³*

clear colour screen	*CCS*
close medium shot	*CMS*
close shot	*CS*
close-up	*CU*
close-up shot	*CS*
closed captioning	*CC*
closed-circuit (cable) television	*CCTV*
Closed-Circuit Television Manufacturers Association	CCTMA
Club Deutscher Film- und Fernseh-Maskenbildner Sektion München	CDFM
co-channel interference	*CCI*
co-producer	*CP*
Coalition Opposing Signal Theft	COST · USA
coaxial cable information system	*CCIS*
code division multiple access	*CDMA*
coherent phase shift keying	*CPSK*
colour actuance improvement	*CAI*
colour aperture improvement	*CAI*
colour compensating	*CC*
colour control panel	*CCP*
colour graphics adaptor	*CGA*
colour index	*CI*
colour look-up table	*CLUT*
colour mobile central control room	*CMCCR*
colour mobile control room	*CMCR*
colour phase alternation	*CPA*
colour print(ing)	*CP*
colour rendering index	*CRI*
colour reversal intermediate	*CRI*
colour roving eye	*CRE*
colour separation overlay	*CSO*
colour temperature	*CT*
colour temperature control	*CTC*
colour transient improvement/improver	*CTI*
colour, video, blanking and synchs	*CVBS*
Columbia Broadcasting System, Inc	CBS
Comataidh Telebhisein Gàidhlig	CTG
combined propulsion system	*CPS*
Comisión Organizadora Festival Americano de Cine de Los Pueblos Indígenas	CLACPI
Comitato Cinematografia Ragazzi	CCR
Comitato Ecumenico per le Comunicazioni Sociali	CECS
Comitato Nazionale Diffusione Film d'Arte e Cultura	FAC
Comité Africain de Cinéastes	CAC
Comité Consultatif International de Radiocommunications	CCIR
Comité Consultatif International de Téléphone et de Télégraph	CCITT
Comité des Industries Cinématographiques et Audiovisuelles des Communautés Européennes et de l'Europe Extracommunautaire	CICCE
Comité Directeur sur les Moyens de Communication de Masse	CDMM
Comité International pour la Diffusion des Arts et des Lettres par le Cinéma	CIDALC
commercial announcement	*CA*
Commercial Art Directors Association	CADA
commercial continuity	*CC*
commercial matter	*CM*
Commercial Producers Association	CPA
Commission Internationale d'Eclairage	CIE

Commission Nationale de la Communication et des Libertés	CNCL
Commission Supérieure Technique de l'Image et du Son	CST · FRANCE
Committee for Competitive Television	CCT
Committee on Children's Television, Inc	CCTI
Committee on Local Television Audience Measurement	COLTAM
Committee on Nationwide Television Audience Measurement	CONTAM
Committee to Preserve American Color Television	COMPACT
Commodore dynamic total vision	*CDTV*
common channel signalling	*CCS*
common mode rejection ratio	*CMRR*
Commonwealth Broadcasting Association	CBA · UK
Commonwealth Fund for Technical Cooperation	CFTC
communication technology satellite	*CTS*
Communication Workers of America	CWA
Communications Coordination Committee for the United Nations	CCC/UN
communications module	*CM*
communications satellite	*CS*
community antenna relay service	*CARS*
community antenna television	*CATV*
Community Antenna Television Association	CATA
Community Broadcasters Association	CBA · USA
community programmes unit	*CPU*
community television	*CTV*
Community Video School	CVS
compact disc	*CD*
compact disc-interactive	*CD-I*
compact disc read-only memory	*CD-ROM*
compact disc read-only memory extended architecture	*CD-ROM XA*
compact disc real-time operating system	*CD-RTOS*
compact disc-video	*CD-V*
compact disc write once	*CDW*
compact indium discharge	*CID*
compact iodide, daylight	*CID*
compact iodine discharge	*CID*
compact laser disc player	*CLD*
compact recording videodisc	*CRV*
compact source iodide	*CSI*
compact video cartridge	*CVC*
compact video disc	*CVD*
Compagnia Distribuzione Audiovisivi	CDA
Compagnia Distribuzione Internazionale	CDI
Compagnie Artistique de Productions et d'Adaptations Cinématographiques	CAPAC
Compagnie Française Cinématographique	CFG
Compagnie Générale de Télécommunication Téléservice	CGVT
Compagnie Luxembourgeoise de Télédiffusion	CLT
Compagnie São-Toméenne de Télécommunications	CST · SÃO TOMÉ AND PRINCIPE
Compañía de Fomento Cinematográfico	FOCINE
Compañía de Radio Televisión de Galicia	CRTG / CRTVG
Compañía Operadora de Teatros	COTSA
Company Overhead Loan	COL
compatible-quadrature amplitude modulator	*C-QUAM*
complementary metal-oxide semiconductor/silicon	*CMOS*
Completion Bond Company, Inc	CBC · USA
completion guarantor	*CG*

component analogue video	CAV
component recorded/recording video(disc)	CRV
component tape drive	CTD
composite magnetic	COMMAG
composite optical	COMOPT
composite video, burst and synchs	CVBS
compressed digital video	CD-V
compressed time division multiple(x)	CTDM
Compte de Soutien à l'Industrie des Programmes	COSIP
computer-aided/assisted design	CAD
computer-aided/assisted design and manufacture	CADAM
computer-assisted interactive video	CAIV
computer-assisted makeup and imaging system	CAMIS
computer assisted traditional animation	CATA
computer controlled (tele)text	CCT
computer-generated holograms	CGH
computer-generated image(ry)	CGI
computer graphics	CG
computer interface for tuning and analogue control	CITAC
computer video synchronizer	CVS
Confédération Internationale des Cinémas d'Art-et-Essai Européens	CICAE
Confédération Internationale des Industries Techniques du Cinéma	CIITC
Confédération Laïque de l'Audiovisuel	CLAV
Confédération Nationale de la Publicité Audiovisuel	CNPA
conférence administrative mondiale des radiocommunications	CAMR
Conferencia de Autoridades Cinematográficas Iberoamericanas	CACI
confirmation of broadcast order	CBO
Connoisseur Video	CV
Conseil de la Radiodiffusion et des Télécommunications Canadiennes	CRTC
Conseil International des Radios-Télévisions d'Expression Française	CIRTEF
Conseil International du Cinéma, de la Télévision et de la Communication Audiovisuelle	CICT · FRANCE
Conseil National de l'Audiovisuel	CNA · SENEGAL
Conseil National des Télécommunications	CONATEL
Conseil Supérieur de l'Audiovisuel (Algeria)	CSA
Conseil Supérieur de l'Audiovisuel (France)	CSA
Conservatoire Libre du Cinéma Français	CLCF
Conservatoire National Supérieur d'Art Dramatique	CNSAD
Conservatorio Internazionale di Scienze Audiovisive	CISA
Consiglio Internazionale Cinema e TV	CICT · ITALY
Consolidated Film Industries	CFI · USA
Consortium de Communication Audiovisuelle en Afrique	CCA · SENEGAL
Consortium de Télévision Québec-Canada	CTQC
Consortium Interafricain de Distribution Cinématographique	CIDC · SENEGAL
Consortium of Media Exhibitors	COMEX
Consortium of University Film Centers	CUFC
constant angular velocity	CAV
constant conductance heat pipe	CCHP
constant linear velocity	CLV
constricted double heterojunction	COH
construction permit	CP
Consumer News & Business Channel	CNBC
Contactgroep Audiovisuele Centra Wetenschappelijk Onderwijs	CAWO
Continuing Education and Training	CET

Continuing Education Service, The	CES
continuous wave	*CW*
contrast transfer function	*CTF*
control and data/delay channel	*CDC*
control diagnostic panel	*CDP*
control electronics unit	*CEU*
control lens motor	*CLM*
control track	*CT*
control unit	*CU*
controlled light diffusion	*CLD*
conventional amplitude modulation	*CAM*
Cook Islands Broadcasting Corporation	CIBC
Cooperativa Lavoratori del Cinema e del Teatro	CLCT
Cooperative Nouveau Cinéma	CNC · BELGIUM
Coopérative Régionale du Cinéma Culturel de Strasbourg	CRCC
Coordination des Fédérations de Ciné-Clubs	COFECIC
Coordination Européenne des Producteurs Indépendants	CEPI
Coproduktiefonds Binnenlandse Omroep	COBO
Copyright Collective of Canada	CCC · CANADA
Corporació Catalana de Ràdio i Televisió	CCRTV
Corporation for Public Broadcasting	CPB
Council for Children's Television and Media	CCTM
Council of Motion Picture Organisations	COMPO
Council on International Non-Theatrical Events	CINE
Country Music Television	CMT
Coventry's Own Local Television	COLT
Creative Artists Agency Inc	CAA · USA
Creative Technology	CT · UK
critical hours	*CH*
critical young televiewer	*CYT*
cross-interleave code	*CIC*
cross-interleaved Reed-Solomon code	*CIRC*
cross-modulation products	*CMP*
current transfer ratio	*CTR*
Custom Electronic Design and Installation Association	CEDIA
customer premises equipment	*CPE*
cycles per minute	*CPM*
cycles per second	*CPS*
cyclic redundancy check (code)	*CRC(C)*
cyclic redundancy code	*CRC*
Cyprus Broadcasting Corporation	CBC · CYPRUS / CYBC

D

daily electronic feed	*DEF*
daily production report	*DPR*
Dance Films Association	DFA · USA
Danish Film Institute	DFI
Danmarks Radio	DR
Dansk Management Center	DMC
dark line defect	*DLD*
data cassette recording system	*DCRS*
David Barker Associates Television Ltd	DBA Television

day for night	*D/N*
daylight savings time	*DST*
de-spin active nutation damping electronics	*DANDE*
Deaf Broadcasting Council	DBC
decibel	*DB*
decibel meter	*DBM*
defence service communications satellite	*DSCS*
delay modulation	*DM*
delayed broadcast	*DB*
delayed electronic feed	*DEF*
delta modulation	*DM*
demand assigned/assignment multiple access	*DAMA*
demographic adjustment factor	*DAF*
density ratio	*DR*
Denver International Film Festival	DIFF · USA
depth of discharge	*DOD*
depth of field	*DF / D/F*
designated market area	*DMA*
Designers and Art Directors Association	D&AD
desk top video	*DTV*
Deutsche Fernsehnachrichten Agentur	DFA · GERMANY
Deutsche Film- und Fernsehakademie Berlin	DFFB
Deutsche Gesellschaft für Medien und Geschichte	DGMG
Deutsche Industrie-Norm	DIN
Deutsche Industriefilm-Zentrale	DIZ
Deutsche Sports Fernsehen	DSF
Deutsche und Rätoromanische Schweiz	DRS
Deutsche Welle	DW
Deutsches Institut für Fernstudien	DIFF · GERMANY
Developing European Learning Through Technological Advance	DELTA
dialogue, music and effects	*DME*
dialogue music effects and foley	*DMEF*
dialogue-to-analogue converter/conversion	*DAC*
dielectric stabilised oscillator	*DSO*
differential gain	*DG*
differential pulse code modulation	*DPCM*
differential quadrature phase shift keying	*DQPSK*
differential survey treatment	*DST*
differentially coherent pulse code modulation	*DCPCM*
Diffusione Internazionale Film Informativi	DIFI
digital audio broadcasting	*DAB*
digital audio disc	*DAD*
digital audio for television	*DATE*
digital audio stationary head	*DASH*
digital audio tape	*DAT*
digital cartridge player	*DCP*
digital channel stereo	*DCS*
digital compact cassette	*DCC*
digital component tape	*DCT*
digital disc recorder	*DDR*
digital image stabiliser	*DVIS*
digital intercontinental conversion equipment	*DICE*
digital multi-effects	*DME*
digital noise reducer	*DNR*

digital optical recording	DOR
digital panel meter	DPM
digital picture exchange	DPX
digital production effects	DPE
digital programme search system	DPSS
digital scene detection	DSD
digital scene simulation	DSS
digital signal processing/processor	DSP
digital spectrum compatible	DSC
digital studio-transmitter link	DSTL™
digital sum variation	DSV
digital surround processor/processing	DSP
digital television for terrestrial broadcasting	DTTB
digital television tape recorder	DTTR
digital termination service	DTS
digital terrestrial television broadcasting	DTTB
digital-to-analogue	D-A
digital video adaptor	DVA
digital video effects	DVE
digital video interactive	DVI®
digital video processors	DVPC
digital video recording	DVR
digital videotape recorder	DVTR
digitally assisted television	DATV
diode-transistor logic	DTL
direct access management system	DAMS
Direct Broadcast Satellite Association	DBSA
direct broadcast(ing) (by/from) satellite	DBS
direct current	DC
direct domestic reception	DDR
direct drive	DD
direct exchange line	DEL
direct memory access	DMA
direct-read-after-write	DRAW
direct serial interfacing	DSI
direct to disc optical	DDO
direct to home	DTH
direct voice	DV
Directing Workshop for Women	DWW
Direction de la Production Cinématographique	DIPROCI
directional antenna	DA
director of photography	DOP / DP
director's fresh instruction	DFI
Directors' Guild of America	DGA
Directors' Guild of Canada	DGC
Directors' Guild of Great Britain	DGGB
discrete cosine transform	DCT
display control programme	DCP
distributed Bragg reflector	DBR
distributed feedback	DFB
distribution amplifier	DA
distributor control unit	DCC
Distribuzione Angelo Rizzoli Cinematografica	DARC
dolly in	DI

dolly out	*DO*
dolly shot	*DS*
domestic satellite communication system	*DSCS*
domestic satellite service	*DSS*
Doordarshan (India Television)	DDI
Doppiaggio Pubblicità Televisiva	DPT
double Azimuth	*DA*
double heterostructure	*DH*
double perforated	*DP*
double play	*DP*
double sideband	*DSB*
double-sided	*D/S*
downstream keying/keyer	*DSK*
drawing exchange file	*DXF*
drop frame	*DF*
drop-out compensator	*DOC*
dual channel sound	*DCS*
dual in-line package	*DIP*
dual resolution processing	*DRP*
dual sound-in-synch	*DSIS*
dual surface shape	*DSS*
dual time code	*DTC*
Dutch Documentary and Independent Film Association	DIFA
Dwight Cavendish Developments Ltd	DC
dynamic beam control	*DBC*
dynamic beam forming	*DBF*
dynamic black level	*DBL*
dynamic comb filter	*DCF*
dynamic contrast control	*DCC*
dynamic crossed field photo multiplier	*DCFP*
dynamic lens correction	*DLC*
dynamic motion control	*DMC*
dynamic motion stimulator	*DMS*
dynamic picture optimiser	*DPO*
dynamic random-access memory	*DRAM*
dynamic range improvement	*DRI*
dynamic track following	*DTF*
dynamic tracking	*DT*
dynamically redefinable character sets	*DRCS*

E

earphone commentary	*EC*
earth leakage circuit breaker	*ELCB*
East Anglian Film Archive	EAFA · UK
East London Telecommunications	ELT
Eastern Educational Television Network	EEN
Eastman colour negative	*ECN*
easy find system	*EFS*
Ecole Française d'Enseignement Technique	EFET
Ecole Nationale Louis-Lumière	ENLL
Ecole Nationale Supérieure des Arts Décoratifs	ENSAD
Ecole Nationale Supérieure des Arts Visuels de la Cambre	ENSAV

Ecole Supérieure Communication Audiovisuelle	ESCOMA
Ecole Supérieure d'Art Visuel	ESAV
Ecole Supérieure d'Etudes Cinématographiques	ESEC
Ecole Supérieure de Cinéastes et d'Acteurs	ESCA
Ecole Supérieure de Réalisation Audiovisuelle	ESRA
Ecole Supérieure des Techniques du Cinéma et de l'Audiovisuel	ESTCA
Ecole Technique Privée de Photographie, de l'Audiovisuel et de Graphisme Publicitaire	ETPA
edge number(s)	*EN*
edge of coverage	*EOC*
Edinburgh International Film Festival	EIFF
Edinburgh International Television Festival	EITF
edit decision list	*EDL*
edit-level video	*ELV*
edit sync guide	*ESG*
edit video architecture	*EVA*
Educational and Television Films Ltd	ETV
Educational Broadcasting Council for Northern Ireland	EBC(NI)
Educational Broadcasting Council for Scotland	EBCS
Educational Broadcasting Council for the United Kingdom	EBC(UK)
educational cable television	*ECATV*
Educational Film Library Association, Inc	EFLA
Educational Film Services International	EFS
Educational Media Film & Video Ltd	EMFV
Educational Radio and Television Center	ETRAC
Educational Recording Agency Ltd, The	ERA
educational television	*ET / ETV / EDTV*
Educational Television Association	ETA
educational television by satellite	*ETVS*
Educational Television Stations	ETS
Eerste Amsterdamse Film Associatie	EAFA · THE NETHERLANDS
effective focal length	*EFL*
effective isotropic(ally) radiated power	*EIRP*
effective radiated power	*ERP*
effects	*FX*
Egyptian Radio and Television Union	ERTU
Ehime Broadcasting Co Ltd	EBC · JAPAN
eight to fourteen modulation	*EFM*
Electrical and Electronic Telecommunication and Plumbing Union	EETPU
electrical engineer	*EE*
electrical ground support system	*EGSE*
electrically alterable read-only memory	*EAROM*
electrically erasable programmable read-only memory	*EEPROM*
ElectricImage™ Animation System	*EIAS*
electro-optical	*EO*
electromagnetic interference	*EMI*
electromechanical recorder	*EMR*
electron beam recording/recorder	*EBR*
electron gun technology	*EGT*
electronic camera coverage	*ECC*
electronic character generator	*ECG*
electronic cinematographic camera	*ECC*
electronic cinematography	*EC*
electronic data interchange	*EDI*

electronic data transfer	*EDT*
electronic editing	*EE*
electronic facial identification technique	*E-FIT*
electronic field/film production	*EFP*
electronic film conforming	*EFC*
electronic funds transfer	*EFT*
Electronic Industries Association	EIA
Electronic Industries Association of Japan	EIAJ
electronic journalism	*EJ*
electronic line replacement	*ELR*
electronic marker system	*EMS*
Electronic Media Rating Council	EMRC
electronic news gathering	*ENG*
electronic newsroom, the	*TEN*
electronic newsroom system	*ENS*
electronic pin registration	*EPR*
electronic post-production	*EPP*
electronic power conditioner	*EPC*
electronic set-up	*ESU*
electronic sports gathering	*ESG*
electronic still store	*ESS*
electronic video recording/recorder	*EVR*
electronic viewfinder	*EVF*
electronically variable delay line	*EVDL*
Electronics Research, Inc	ERI
electronics to electronics	*E-E*
electrostatic discharge	*ESD*
Elleniki Radiophonia Teleorassi	ERT
Elleniki Tileorassi	ET
Emergency Broadcasting System	EBS
emitter-coupled logic	*ECL*
Empresa de Cine, Radio y Televisión Peruana, SA	RTP · PERU
Empresa Distribuidora e Exhibidora de Cinema	EDECINE
emulsion in	*EI*
emulsion out	*EO*
end of active video	*EAV*
end of life	*EOL*
end of reel	*EOR*
end of tape	*EOT*
end of transmission	*EOT*
engineer in charge	*EIC*
engineering manager	*EM*
engineering manual exchange	*EMX*
engineering model	*EM*
engineering set-up	*ESU*
enhanced definition television	*EDTV*
enhanced graphics adaptor	*EGA*
enhanced graphics interface	*EGI*
enhanced non-return to zero	*ENRZ*
enhanced vertical definition/resolution system	*EVS*
Ente Autonomo Gestione per Il Cinema	EAGC
Enterprise Nationale de Télévision	ENTV
Entertainment & Sports Programming Network, Inc	ESPN
Entertainment Business Services International	EBS

Entertainment Channel, The	TEC
Entertainment Data Inc	EDI · USA
Entertainment Programming Services	EPS
Entrepreneurs de l'Audiovisuel Européen, Les	EAVE
equivalent isotropic(ally) radiated power	*EIRP*
equivalent neutral density	*END*
equivalent noise temperature	*ENT*
erasable programmable read-only disc	*EPROD*
erasable programmable read-only memory	*EPROM*
error detection and handling	*EDH*
error detection code	*EDC*
Escuela Internacional de Cine y TV	EICTV
Espace Vidéo Européen	EVE
Espectaculo & Cultura	ETC
Establissement Cinématographique et Photographique des Armées	ECPA
Eternal Word Television Network	EWTN
Euro Media Garanties	EMG
Europäischer Gewerkschaftsausschuss für Kunst, Medien und Unterhaltung	EGAKU
Europäisches Dokumentarfilminstitut	EDI · GERMANY
European Association for an Audiovisual Independent Market	EUROAIM
European Association of Animation Film	EAFF
European Audiovisual Entrepreneurs	EAVE
European Broadcasting Union	EBU
European Business Channel	EBC · SWITZERLAND
European Cable Communications	ECC
European Cable Communications Association	ECCA
European Cinema and Television Office	ECTO
European Cinema and Television Year	ECTVY
European Co-Production Conference and Market	ECCO
European Co-Production Fund Ltd	ECF
European Communications Satellite	*ECS*
European Communities Film Libraries Association	ECFLA
European Cooperation in the Field of Scientific and Technical Research	
	COST · BELGIUM
European Coproduction Association	ECA
European Documentary Film Institute	EDI · GERMANY
European Film Academy eV	EFA
European Film and Television Studies Conference	EFTSC
European Film Distribution Office	EFDO
European Film Finance and Insurers' Association	EFFIA
European Film Finance and Marketing	EFFAM
European Group of Television Advertising	EGTA
European Institute for the Media	EIM
European Issues in Educational Media	EIEM
European MultiMedia Awards Ltd	EMMA
European Programme on Satellite	*EPS*
European Programme Providers Group	EPPG
European Research and Coordination Agency	EUREKA
European Satellite Consultancy Organisation	ESCO
European Satellite Television Association	ESTA
European Space Agency	ESA
European Strategic Programme for Research and Development in Information Technology	ESPRIT
European Telecommunications Satellite Organisation	EUTELSAT

European Video Association	EVA
European Video Independent Producers	EUROVIP
European Video Services	EVS
Eurovision News Exchange	EVN
Euskal Irrati Telebista	EITB
Euskal Telebista	ETB
Evangelische Omroep	EO
Evangelisches Zentrum für Entwicklungsbezogene Filmarbeit	EZEF
executive producer	*EP*
executive supervising producer	*ESP*
Exhibitors in Cable	EIC
expanded sample frame	*ESF*
expendable launch vehicle	*ELV*
exposure index	*EI*
exposure value	*EV*
extended clear scan	*ECS*
extended definition	*ED*
extended definition television	*EDTV*
extended industry standard architecture	*EISA*
extended mogul end prong	*EMEP*
extended play	*EP*
external Bragg reflector	*EBRL*
external synchronising unit	*ESU*
extra-big close-up	*EBCU*
extra definition television	*EDTV*
extra high frequency	*EHF*
extra high grade	*EHG*
extra-high tension	*EHT*
extreme close-up	*ECU / XCU*
extreme high shot	*EHS / XHS*
extreme long-shot	*ELS / XLS*
extreme ultra-violet	*EUV*
extremely low frequency	*ELF*

F

fade down/up	*FDU*
fade in	*FI*
fade out	*FO*
fade sound and picture out	*FSAPO*
Fællesforeningen af Danske Antenneforeninger	FDA
Fairness in Media	FIM
false alarm rate	*FAR*
Family Communications Inc	FCI
family viewing	*FV*
fan-out amplifier	*FOA*
Farabi Cinema Foundation	FCF
fast forward	*FF*
Federação Latinoamericana de Productores de Fonogramas y Videogramas	FLAPF
Federação Portuguesa de Cinema e Audio-Visuals	FPCA
Federación Antipiratería	FAP
Federación de Organismos de Radio y Televisión Autonómicos	FORTA
Federal Communications Commission	FCC

Federation Against Copyright Theft Ltd	FACT
Fédération des Cinéastes Amateurs de Belgique	FACINEB
Fédération des Clubs Français des Cinéastes	FCFC
Fédération Européenne des Associations de Téléspectateurs	FET
Fédération Européenne des Industries Techniques de l'Image et du Son	FEITIS
Fédération Européenne des Réalisateurs de l'Audiovisuel	FERA
Fédération Internationale de la Presse Cinématographique	FIPRESCI
Fédération Internationale des Acteurs	FIA
Fédération Internationale des Archives de Télévision	FIAT
Fédération Internationale des Archives du Film	FIAF
Fédération Internationale des Associations de Distributeurs de Films	FIAD
Fédération Internationale des Associations de Producteurs de Films	FIAPF
Fédération Internationale des Ciné-Clubs	FICC · SWITZERLAND
Fédération Internationale des Festivals Indépendants	FIFI
Fédération Internationale des Producteurs de Films Indépendants	FIPFI
Fédération Internationale des Syndicats des Travailleurs de l'Audiovisuel	FISTAV
Fédération Internationale du Cinéma et de la Télévision Sportifs	FICTS
Fédération Loisirs et Culture	FLEC
Fédération Nationale des Distributeurs de Films	FNDF
Fédération Nationale des Industries Techniques du Cinéma et de l'Audiovisuel	
	FITCA / FNITCA
Federation of African Media Women	FAMW
Federation of Australian Amateur Cine Societies	FAACS
Federation of Australian Commercial Broadcasters	FACB
Federation of Australian Commercial Television Stations	FACTS
Federation of Broadcasting Unions	FBU
Federation of Commercial Audiovisual Libraries Ltd	FOCAL · UK
Federation of Entertainment Unions	FEU
Federation of Irish Film Societies Ltd	FIFS
Fédération Panafricaine des Cinéastes	FEPACI
Federazione anti-Pirateria Audiovisiva	FAPAV / FAVAV
Federazione Associazioni Produttori Distributori	APD
Federazione Internazionale degli Archivi delle Immagini e dei Suoni	FIAIS
Federazione Italiana Cineclub	FEDIC
Federazione Italiana Cineforum	FIC
Federazione Italiana Cinema d'Essai	FICE
Federazione Italiana Circoli del Cinema	FICC · ITALY
Federazione Italiana Lavoratori Informazione e Spettacolo	FILIS
Federazione Nazionale Cinevideoautori	FNC
Federazione Radio Televisioni	FRT
feedback	*FB*
feet per minute	*FPM*
feet per second	*FPS / F/S*
Fernseh- und Kinotechnische Gesellschaft	FKTG
Festival du Film et de la Jeunesse de Paris	FIFEJ
Festival International de Programmes Audiovisuels	FIPA
Festival International des Films sur l'Architecture	FIFARC
Festival International du Film d'Architecture et d'Urbanisme de Lausanne	FIFAL
Festival International du Film d'Art	FIFA
Festival International du Film et des Réalisateurs des Ecoles de Cinéma	FIFREC
Festival International du Film sur l'Art	FIFART
Festival International du Film sur l'Energie	FIFEL
Festival Panafricain du Cinéma de Ouagadougou	FESPACO
fibre optic	*FO*

fibre optic cable	FOC
Fiduciaire d'Editions de Films	FIDES
field effect(s) transmitter/transistor	FET
field of travel	FOT
field of view	FOV
field strength meter	FSM
field synchronisation	FS
Film and Allied Workers Organisation	FAWO
Film and Television Institute of India	FTII
film and television technician	FTT
Film and Television Technology Institute	FTTI
Film and TV Technician	FTT
Film and Video Arts Society - Alberta	FAVA
film and video library	FVL
Film and Video Security Office	FVSO
Film Archive Management and Entertainment	FAME
Film Artistes Association	FAA
film developer	FD
Film Festival of International Cinema Students	FICCS
Film Four International	FFI
Film Institute of Ireland	FII
film library on line	FLOL
Film-Makers Association	FMA
film operations manager	FOM
Film Parlant Français	FPF
Film Society Unit	FSU
film strip	FS
Film Studies Association of Canada	FSAC
Film/Video Arts	F/VA
Filmbewertungsstelle Wiesbaden	FBW
Filmförderungsanstalt Bundesanstalt des öffentlichen Rechts	FFA
Filmová Akademie Muzických Umění	FAMU
Filmový a Televizni Svaz	FITES
Financial News Network	FNN
Financial Times Television	FTTV
fine grain	FG
finite impulse response	FIR
Finlands Filmstiftelse	FFF
Finnish Film Foundation	FFF
firm contact	FC
first-in first-out	FIFO
fit and sealed	FS
five kilowatt	FK
fixed satellite service	FSS
fixed service satellite	FSS
flat tension mark	FTM
flat(ter) square(r) tube	FST
Flemish European Media Institute	FEMI
flight model	FM
floating point unit	FPU
floor manager	FM
Florida News Network	FNN
fluorescent display panel	FDP
flying spot scan	FSS

FM improvement	*FMI*
focal length	*FL*
focal plane	*FP*
focus, aperture, shutter, tachometer	*FAST*
follow focus	*FF*
follow shot	*FS*
Fondation de Formation Continue pour le Cinéma et l'Audiovisuel	
	FOCAL · SWITZERLAND
Fondo de Fomento Cinematográfico	FONCINE
Fonds d'Assurance Formation des Activités du Spectacle et de l'Audio-Visuel	AFDAS
Fonds de l'Industrie Cinématographique	FODIC
foot candle	*FC*
footlambert	*FL*
foreground	*FF*
Foreningen af Danske Spillefilmproducenter	FDS
Föreningen Sveriges Filmproducenter	SFP · SWEDEN
Formation de Recherche Cinématographique	FRC
forward error correction/control	*FEC*
Foundation for American Communications	FACS
Foundation for Independent Video and Film	FIVF
Foundation of Motion Picture Pioneers	FMPP
Foundation To Improve Television	FIT
Foundation to Underwrite New Drama for Pay TV	FUND
fractal image format file	*FIF*
frame count cueing	*FCC*
frame inline transfer	*FIT*
frame interline transfer	*FIT*
frame store synchroniser	*FSS*
frame transfer	*FT*
frames per foot	*FPF*
frames per minute	*FPM*
frames per second	*FPS / F/S*
France Câbles et Radio	FCR
France Media International	FMI
France Regions 3	FR3
Freiwillige Selbstkontrolle der Filmwirtschaft	FSK
frequency demodulator	*FD*
frequency-division multiple access	*FDMA*
frequency division multiplex(ing)	*FDM*
frequency modulation/modulated	*FM*
frequency of audio sampling	*FAS*
frequency shift keying	*FSK*
Friedrich Ebert Stiftung	FES
front axial projection	*FAP*
front projection	*FP*
Fuji National Video Centre	FNVC
Fukui Broadcasting Co Ltd	FBC
Fukui Television Broadcasting Corporation	FTB · JAPAN
Fukuoka Broadcasting System	FBS
Fukushima Central Television Co Ltd	FCT
Fukushima Telecasting Co Ltd	FTV
full aperture	*FA*
full auto shooting	*FAS*
full-length shot	*FLS*

full level one feature	*FLOF*
full-motion video	*FMV*
full screen full motion	*FSFM*
full screen full motion video	*FSFMV*
full shot	*FS*
full width half maximum	*FWHM*
Fundacão do Cinema Brasileiro	FCB
fusible link logic array	*FLLA*
Future Film Developments	FFD · UK

G

Gaelic Television Committee	GTC
gain/temperature	*G/T*
Gallium Arsenide	*GA-AS*
Gallium Arsenide field effect transistor	*GAASFET*
gallium photo diode	*GPD*
gauged Angenieux zoom equipment	*GAZE*
general porte instruction	*GPI*
general purpose interface	*GPI*
general purpose interface bus	*GPIB*
General Screen Enterprises	GSE
general view	*G/V / GV*
Genootschap van Nederlandse Speelfilmmakers	GNS
geostationary earth orbit	*GEO*
geostationary satellite	*GSS*
geostationary satellite orbit	*GSO*
geostationary technology satellite	*GTS*
geostationary transfer orbit	*GTP*
geosynchronous equatorial orbit	*GEO*
German Film and Video Library	GFVL
Gesellschaft zur Übernahme und Wahrnehmung von Filmaufführungsrechten mbH	
	GÜFA
Gesellschaft zur Wahrnehmung von Film- und Fernsehrechten	GWFF
Ghana Broadcasting Corporation	GBC · GHANA
ghost cancellation/cancelling reference	*GCR*
Gibraltar Broadcasting Corporation	GIBBC
Gifu Broadcasting System	GBS
gigabytes	*GB*
gigacycles per second	*GC/S*
gigahertz	*GHZ*
gigawatt	*GW*
Good Morning Television	GMTV
graded index	*GRIN*
graphic user interface	*GUI*
Grass Valley Group	GVG
Great American Communications Company	GACC
Great Plains National Instructional Television Library	GPNITL
Greek Film Centre	GFC
gross average audience	*GAA*
gross impression	*GI*
gross rating points	*GRP*
group coded recording	*GCR*

Group of European Audience Researchers	GEAR
Groupe d'Etudes Historiques sur la Radiotélévision	GEHRA
Groupe de Recherche Enterprise et Communication	GREC
Groupe de Recherches et d'Essais Cinématographiques	GREC
Groupe de Recherches Sur les Enjeux de la Communication	GRESEC
Groupe Européen d'Enseignement des Métiers de l'Audiovisuel et de la Communication	GEEMAC
Groupe Européen de Réalisations Audiovisuelles pour le Développement	GRAD
Groupe pour le Développement d'une Identité Audiovisuelle de l'Europe	DAVID
Groupement de Ciné-Clubs et d'Associations Culturelles du Sud-Ouest de la France	GACSO
Groupement des Institutions Sociales du Spectacle au Service des Enterprises, des Salariés et des Retraites du Spectacle et de l'Audiovisuel	GRISS
Groupement Européen des Ecoles de Cinéma et de Télévision	GEECT
Groupement Européen des Financiers du Cinéma et de l'Audiovisuel	GEFCA
Groupement Européen pour la Circulation des Œuvres	GRECO
Groupement Informatique de l'Audiovisuel	GIA
Groupement Professionnel des Supports Magnétiques Vierges Audio et Vidéo	GPSMVAV
Groupement Suisse du Film d'Animation	GSFA
Grupo de Estudos e Realizações Lda	GER
Guild of British Animation	GBA
Guild of British Camera Technicians	GBCT
Guild of British Film Editors	GBFE
Guild of Film Production Accountants and Financial Administrators	GFPAFA
Guild of Film Production Executives	GFPE
Guild of Local Television	GOLT
Gunma Television Co Ltd	GTV
Guyana Broadcasting Corporation	GBC · GUYANA / GUYBC

H

half amplitude modulation	*HAD*
half-line offset PAL	*HLO-PAL*
half-power beam width	*HPBW*
halogen-metal-iodide	*HMI*
Hamburg Film Fonds	HFF · GERMANY
Hans Bredow Institut für Rundfunk und Fernsehen	HBI
harmonic-related carrier	*HRC*
Hauptverband Deutscher Filmtheater eV	HDF
Haute Autorité de la Communication Audiovisuelle	HA / HACA
hearing-impaired subtitles	*HIS*
heatable eyecup	*HE*
Hebrew Actors' Union	HAU
height above average terrain	*HAAT*
height/distance	*H/D*
Helen Television System	HTS
hertz	*HZ*
Hessischer Rundfunk	HR
high band saticon trinicon	*HBST*
high definition	*HD*
high definition digital framestore	*HDDF*
high definition electronic production	*HDEP*

high-definition progressive	*HDP*
high-definition progressive scanning and quincunx sampling	*HDQ*
high definition television	*HDTV*
High Definition Training Programme	HDTP
high definition video system	*HDVS®*
high density digital recording	*HDDR*
high density modulation	*HDM*
high efficiency	*HE*
high electron mobility transistor	*HEMT*
high frequency	*HF*
high grade	*HG*
high intensity	*HI*
high-intensity discharge(r)	*HID*
high-level data link control	*HDLC*
high mid frequency	*HMF*
high-power amplifier	*HPA*
high quality	*HQ*
high quality television	*HQTV*
high resolution	*HR*
high resolution television	*HRTV*
high speed complementary metal-oxide-gate semiconductor	*HCMOS*
high tension	*HT*
high voltage	*HV*
Higher Education Film & Video Library	HEFVL
Higher Education Film Library	HEFVL
highest possible frequency	*HPF*
highlight overload protection	*HOP*
Hiroshima Telecasting Co Ltd	HTV · JAPAN
Hochschule für Fernsehen und Film	HFF · GERMANY
Hochschule für Musik und Darstellende Kunst in Wien	HFMDK
Hoger Rijksinstituut voor Toneel en Cultuurspreiding	HITCS / HRITCS / RITCS
Hokkaido Broadcasting Co Ltd	HBC
Hokkaido Television Broadcasting Ltd	HTB
Hokuriku Asahi Broadcasting Co	HAB
hold for release	*HFR*
hole accumulated diode	*HAAT*
Hollywood Radio and Television Society	HRTS
Hollywood Reporter, The	THR
Home Box Office, Inc	HBO
home satellite dish	*HSD*
Home Shopping Network	HSN
Home Theatre Network	HTN
home video	*HV*
Home Video Channel	HVC
home video recorder	*HVR*
Homestead and Community Broadcasting Satellite Service	HACBSS / HACBUS
horizontal drive	*HDR*
horizontal radiation pattern	*HRP*
Horror and Fantasy Film Society	HFFS
Hoso Bunka Foundation	HBF
Household Tracking Report	HTR
households	*HH*
Households & Persons Cost Per 1000 Report	CPT
Households Using Television	HUT

Hrvatska Radio-Televizija	HRT / HRTV / HTV · CROATIA
Hughes-JVC Technology (Corporation)	HJT
Hurter & Driffield	*H&D*
hydragyrum medium iodide	*HMI*
hypothetical reference circuit	*HRC*

I

Icelandic Film Fund	IFF
identification data accessory	*IDA*
image enhancer	*IA*
image optics assembly	*IOA*
image orthicon	*IO*
image synthesis and computer animation	*ISCA*
impact avalanche and transit time	*IMPATT*
Imperial War Museum	IWM
improved definition television	*IDT / IDTV*
improved PAL	*I-PAL*
improved PAL modified	*I-PAL-M*
in vision	*I/V*
inches per second	*IPS*
incidental carrier phase modulation	*ICPM / IPM*
Incorporated Society of British Advertisers	ISBA
incue	*IC*
Independent Basque Film Producers Association	IBFPA
Independent Broadcasting Authority	IBA · UK
independent facilitator and packager	*IFP*
Independent Feature Film Market	IFFM
Independent Feature Project	IFP
Independent Feature Project/West	IFP/West
Independent Film and Video Alliance	IFAVA
Independent Film Distributors' Association	IFDA
Independent Film Producers International Association	IFPIA
Independent Film Producers of America	IFPA · USA
Independent Film Production Associates	IFPA · UK
Independent Filmmakers Cooperative of Ottawa, Inc	IFCO
independent main output	*IMO*
Independent Producers Group	IPG
Independent Programme Producers Association	IPPA
Independent Radio and Television Commission	IRTC
Independent Television	ITV · UK
Independent Television Association	ITVA · UK
Independent Television Commission	ITC · UK
Independent Television News	ITN
Independent Television News Association	ITNA
Independent Television Organisation	ITO
Independent Television Service	ITVS
Independent Television Station Association	INTV
Indian Summer Cinema and Television Multimedia Market	MIFED
inductive output tube	*IOT*
Industrial Acoustics Company	IAC · UK
industrial television	*ITV*
infinite impulse response	*IIR*

Information Film Producers of America	IFPA · USA
information technology	*IT*
infra red	*IR*
Iniziative Cinematografiche Editoriali e Commerciali	ICEC
inline transfer	*IT*
Innovation of the European Short and Documentary	IVENS
input	*I/P*
input circuit	*IC*
input multiplexer	*IMUX*
input/output	*I/O*
insertion communication equipment	*ICE*
insertion test signals	*ITS*
instant record timer	*IRT*
instant recording image system	*IRIS*
Institut de Cinématographie Scientifique	ICS · FRANCE
Institut de Coopération Audiovisuelle Francophone	ICAF
Institut de Formation aux Métiers du Cinéma	IFCA
Institut de Formation et d'Enseignement pour les Métiers de l'Image et du Son	FEMIS
Institut de l'Audiovisuel	IDA · FRANCE
Institut de l'Audiovisuel et des Télécommunications en Europe	IDATE
Institut de Recherche en Cinéma et Audiovisuel	IRCAV
Institut des Arts de Diffusion	IAD
Institut des Hautes Etudes de la Communication	IDHECOM
Institut des Hautes Etudes des Communications Sociales	IHECS
Institut des Sciences de l'Information et de la Communication	ISIC
Institut Européen d'Ecriture Audiovisuelle et Créative	IEE · BELGIUM
Institut für den Wissenschaftlichen Film	IWF
Institut für Film und Bild in Wissenschaft und Unterricht	FWU
Institut für Mediengestaltung und Medientechnologie	IMM
Institut für Rundfunktechnik	IRT
Institut für Weltkunde in Bildung und Forschung, gemeinnützige Gesellschaft	WBF
Institut Image, Médias, Informatique de la Communication	IMAC
Institut International de l'Image et du Son	IIIS
Institut Jugend Film Fernsehen	JFF · GERMANY
Institut Kesenian Jakarta	IKJ
Institut National de l'Audiovisuel	INA · FRANCE
Institut National de Radioélectricité et de Cinématographie	INRACI
Institut National Supérieur de l'Enseignement Technique	INSET
Institut National Supérieur des Arts du Spectacle et Techniques de Diffusion	INSAS
Institut pour le Financement du Cinéma et des Industries Culturelles	IFCIC
Institut Supérieur d'Etudes Cinématographiques	ISEC
Institute for Education by Radio-Television	IERT
Institute of Amateur Cinematographers	IAC · UK
Institute of Broadcast Sound	IBS · UK
Institute of Broadcasting Financial Management	IBFM
Institution of Electrical and Electronics Engineers, Inc	IEEE
Institution of Electrical Engineers	IEE · UK
Instituto Angolana de Cinema	IAC · ANGOLA
Instituto Arte de Cinematografía	IAC · ARGENTINA
Instituto Cubano de Arte e Industria Cinematográfica	ICAIC
Instituto de la Cinematografía y de las Artes Audiovisuales	ICAA
Instituto Ecuatoriano de Telecomunicaciones	IETEL
Instituto Mexicano de Cinematográfica	IMCINE
Instituto Mexicano de Televisión	IMEVISION

Instituto Nacional de Cinema	INC
Instituto Nacional de Radio y Televisión	INRAVISION
Instituto Oficial de Radiodifusión y Televisión	IORTV
Instituto Português de Cinema	IPC
instructional television	*ITV*
instructional television, fixed	*IF*
instructional television fixed service	*ITFS*
Instructional Television Funding Cooperative	ITBC
Insulated Cable Engineers Association	ICEA
insulated gate field effect transistor	*IGFET*
insulation displacement connector	*IDC*
integrated authoring system	*IAS*
integrated broadband communications	*IBC*
integrated broadcast operation	*IBO*
integrated circuit	*IC*
integrated receiver and/decoder	*IRD*
integrated services digital network	*ISDN*
intelligent picture	*IP*
intelligent quest	*IQ*
Inter-American Association of Broadcasting	IAAB
inter-orbit link	*IOL*
inter-satellite link	*ISL*
inter-satellite service	*ISS*
Inter-University History Film Consortium	IUHFC
interactive knowledge system	*IKS*
interactive laser video	*ILV*
interactive menu control	*IMC*
interactive multimedia	*IMM*
interactive photorealistic rendering	*IPR*
interactive video	*IV*
interactive video disc	*IVD*
interactive video in further education	*IVIFE*
Intercollegiate Broadcasting System, Inc	IBS · USA
Interessengemeinschaft Neue Medien	INM
interim upper stage	*IUS*
Interkerkelijke Omroep Nederland	IKON
interline transfer	*IT*
intermediate frequency	*IF*
intermediate power amplifier	*IPA*
intermodulation	*IM*
intermodulation distortion	*IMD*
internal optical system	*IOS*
International Alliance of Theatrical Stage Employees & Moving Picture Machine Operators of the United States and Canada	IA / IATSE
International Animated Film Society	IAFS
International Association for Mass Communication Research	IAMCR
International Association for Media and History	IAMHIST
International Association for Media in Science	IAMS
International Association of Amateur Film Festivals	IAFF
International Association of Broadcast Monitors	IABM · USA
International Association of Broadcasting	IAB
International Association of Broadcasting Manufacturers	IABM · UK
International Association of Independent Producers	IAIP
International Association of Satellite Users and Suppliers	IASUS

International Association of Video	IAV
International Association of Women in Radio and Television	IAWRT
International Audio-Visual Services	IAVS
International Audiovisual Society	IAS
International Bank Films	IBF
International Broadcast Engineer	IBE
International Broadcast Film Group	IBFG
international broadcast(ing)	*IB*
International Broadcasting and Television Organisation	IBTO
International Broadcasting Convention	IBC · UK
International Broadcasting Corporation Ltd	IBC · THAILAND
International Broadcasting Society	IBS · KOREA
International Broadcasting Trust	IBT
International Brotherhood of Electrical Workers	IBEW
International Centre of Films for Children and Young People	ICFCYP
International Channel Network	ICN
International Cinerama Society	ICS · UK
International Communications Industries Association	ICIA
International Conference of Short Animation & Documentary Film Festivals	ICSADFF
International Council for Film, Television & Audio Communications	IFTC
International Council of the National Academy of Television Arts and Sciences	
	ICNATVAS
International Creative Management	ICM
International Development Education Resource Association	IDERA
International Development Media	IDM
International Directory of Electronic Arts	IDEA
International Documentary Association	IDA · USA
International Documentary Filmfestival Amsterdam	IDFA
International Family Entertainment, Inc	IFE
International Federation of Film Archives	IFFA
International Federation of Film Producers' Associations	IFFPA
International Federation of Film Societies	IFFS
International Federation of Television Archives	IFTA
International Federation of the Phonographic Industry	IFPI
International Film and Television Council	IFTC
International Film Conciliation Group	IFCG
International Film Exchange Ltd	IFEX
International Film Festival of India	IFFI
International Film Guide	IFG · UK
International Film Importers and Distributors of America	IFIDA
International Film Marketing	IFM
International Filmographic Reference and Motion-Picture Encyclopedia	INFRAME
International Frequency Radio Board	IFRB
International Institute of Communications	IIC
International Medical Association for Radio and Television	IMART
International Motion Picture and Lecturers Association	IMPALA
International Photographers Guild of the Motion Pictures and Television Industries	
	IPMPI
International Programme for the Development of Communication	IPDC
International Public Television	INPUT
International Quorum of Film and Video Producers	IQ
International Radio and Television Foundation	IRTF
International Radio and Television Organisation	IRTO
International Radio and Television Society	IRTS

International Radio and Television University   IRTU
International Radio Consultative Committee   CCIR
International Scientific Film Association   ISFA
International Secretariat of Arts, Mass Media and Entertainment Trade Unions   ISETU
International Society of Videographers   ISV
International Standards Organisation   ISO
International Tape Association   ITA
International Telecommunications Satellite Organization   INTELSAT
International Telecommunications Union   ITU
International Telephone and Telegraph Consultative Committee   CCITT
International Teleproduction Society   ITS · USA
International Television Association   ITVA · USA
International Television Center   ITC · USA
International Television Committee   ITC · USA
International Television Enterprises London   ITEL
International Television Studies Conference   ITSC
International Television Symposium   ITS · SWITZERLAND
international test signal   *ITS*
International Union of Cinemas   UNIC
International Video Federation   IVF
International Videotex Industry Association   IVIA
International Visual Communication Association   IVCA
Internationale Filmtheaterunion   UNIC
Internationales Institut für Medien und Entwicklung   IMD
Internationales Zentralinstitut für das Jugend- und Bildungsfernsehen   IZI
internegative   *IN / ITN*
interpositive   *IP*
interpositive/internegative   *IP/IN*
interprocessor link   *IPL*
interrupted continuous wave   *ICW*
interrupted feedback   *IFB*
intersymbol interference   *ISI*
interval pulse time modulation   *IPTM*
interval-related carrier   *IRC*
Inuit Broadcasting Corporation   IBC · CANADA
Iranian Cinema Data Bank   ICDB
Iraqi Broadcasting and Television Establishment   IBTE
Irish Film Centre   IFC
Irish Film Institute   IFI
Ishikawa Television Broadcasting Corporation   ITC · JAPAN
Islamic Republic of Iran Broadcasting   IRIB
Islamic States Broadcasting Services Organisation   ISBO
Israel Broadcasting Authority   IBA · ISRAEL
Israel Commercial Television Ltd   ICTV
Israel Educational Television   IETV
Istanbul Film Ajansı   IFA
Istituto per lo Studio e la diffusione del Cinema di Animazione   ISCA
Iwate Broadcasting Co Ltd   IBC · JAPAN
Iwate Menkoi Television Co Ltd   MIT · JAPAN
Iyo Television Inc   ITV · JAPAN

J

Jamaica Broadcasting Corporation	JBC
Japan Media Communication Center	JAMCO
Japan Satellite Broadcasting Inc	JSB
Japan Satellite Television Ltd	JSTV
Japan Sports Vision	JSV
Japanese Victor Corporation	JVC
Jerusalem Communications Centre	JCC · ISRAEL
Jewish Film Festival/Foundation	JFF · UK
joint European submicron silicon	*JESSI*
Joint Industries' Committee for Television Audience Research	JICTAR
Joint Photographics Experts Group	*JPEG*
jolts per minute	*JPM*
Jordan Radio & Television Corporation	JRTV
Journées Cinématographiques de Carthage	JCC · TUNISIA
joystick control panel	*JCP*
Judaica Captioned Film Center	JCFC
Jugoslovenskih Radiotelevizija	JRT · SERBIA
junction field-effect transistor	*JFET*

K

Kabushiki Kaisha Setonaikai Broadcasting	KSB
Kagan World Media Ltd	KWM
Kagoshima Broadcasting Corporation	KKB
Kagoshima Television Station	KTS
Kalaallit Nunaata Radioa	KNR TV
Kallitehniki Etairia Athinon	KEA
Kansai Telecasting Corporation	KTV · JAPAN
Kapisanan ng mga Brodkaster sa Pilipinas	KBP
Katholieke Radio Omroep	KRO
Kathy Fairbairn Media	KFM
Kent Educational Television	KETV
Kentucky Educational Television	KET
Kenya Broadcasting Corporation	KBC · KENYA
Kenya Institute of Mass Communication	KIMC
Kerala State Film Development Corporation Ltd	KSFDC
kilo-voltampere(s)	*KVA*
kilohertz	*KHZ*
kilovolt	*KV*
kilowatts	*KW*
Kinder- und Jugendfilmzentrum	KJF
Kinki Broadcasting System Co Ltd	KBS · JAPAN
Kino Women International	KIWI
Kita-Nihon Broadcasting Co Ltd	KNB
Kobe International Independent Film Festival	KIIFF
Kochi Broadcasting Co Ltd	RKC
Kochi Television Co Ltd	KUTV
Kodak standard	*KS*
Kommunale Kinematografers Landsforbund	KKL
Korean Broadcasting Institute	KBI
Korean Broadcasting System	KBS · KOREA

Krátký Film Ltd	KF
Kring van Nederlandse Filmjournalisten	KNF
Kumamoto Asahi Broadcasting Co	KAB
Kumamoto Broadcasting Co Ltd	RKK
Kumamoto Kenmin Television Corporation	KKT
Kumamoto Telecasting Co Ltd	TKU
Kuwait Television	KTV · KUWAIT
Kyushu Asahi Broadcasting Corporation	KBC · JAPAN

L

Laboratoire d'Etudes sur les Nouvelles Technologies et les Industries Culturelles	LENTIC
laboratory aim density	*LAD*
Lagos Television	LTV · NIGERIA
Lancier Cabling & Monitoring Systems Ltd	LCM
Landmark Entertainment Group	LEG
Laos Central Television	LCTV
large closeup	*LCU*
large optical cavity	*LOC*
large satellite	*L-SAT*
large-scale integration	*LSI*
laser diode	*LD*
laser optical reflection	*LOR*
laser optical transmission	*LOT*
laser video interactive	*LVI*
laserdisc	*LD*
laserdisc player	*LDP*
laserdisc read-only memory	*LD-ROM*
LaserVision	*LV*
LaserVision-Read Only Memory	*LV-ROM*
last frame of action	*LFOA*
last telecast	*LTC*
Latin American Independent Film and Video Association	LAIFA
Latvijas Televizija	LTV · LATVIA
Learning Channel, The	TLC
least objectionable programme	*LOP*
least significant bit	*LSB*
left centre right surround	*LCRS*
left-hand circular polarisation	*LHCP*
Leningradsky Institut Kinoinzhenerov	LIKI
lens-control-system	*LCS*
Lesotho National Broadcasting Service	LNBS
Lesotho Television	LTV · LESOTHO
Liaison of Independent Filmmakers of Toronto	LIFT
library management system	*LMS*
Libyan Arab Jamahiriya Broadcasting	LJB
licensable programme service	*LPS*
licensable sound programme service	*LSPS*
light amplification by the stimulated emission of radiation	*LASER*
light centre length	*LCL*
light-emitting diode	*LED*
light entertainment	*LE*
Light Valve Products Inc	LVPI

lighting director	*LD*
lighting director engineer	*LDE*
lightweight mobile control room	*LMCR*
line of sight	*LOS*
linear predictive coding	*LPC*
linear time-code	*LTC*
liplock	*L/L*
liquid apogee engine	*LAE*
liquid coupling and cooling	*LC²*
liquid-crystal display	*LCD*
liquid crystal light valve	*LCLV*
Literature/Film Quarterly	L/FQ
live action	*LA*
live action camera	*LAC*
local area network	*LAN*
local delivery service	*LDS*
local delivery service (transitional)	*LDT*
local distribution service	*LDS*
local origination	*LO*
local oscillator	*LO*
Lokal-Fernsehen-München	LFM
London Film and Video Development Agency	LFVDA
London Film Festival	LFF
London Film-Makers Cooperative	LFMC
London International Film School	LIFS
London Live Television	LLTV
London Media Workshops	LMW
London Screenwriters' Workshop	LSW
London Video Access	LVA
London Weekend Television plc	LWT
long shot	*LS*
long wave	*LW*
longitudinal difference	*LD*
longitudinal redundancy check	*LRC*
longitudinal time-code	*LTC*
longitudinal videotape recorder/recording	*LVR*
loss of signal	*LOS*
low angle	*LA*
low-colour temperature	*LCT*
low earth orbit	*LEO*
low frequency	*LF*
low light level	*LLL*
low light television	*LLTV*
low mid frequency	*LMF*
low-noise amplifier	*LNA*
low-noise block	*LNB*
low noise block filter	*LNBF*
low-noise convertor	*LNC*
low pass filter	*LPF*
low-power television	*LPTV*
lowband colour	*LBC*
lowband monochrome	*LBM*
lumens per watt	*LPW*
luminance transient improvement/improver	*LTI*

M

machine control system	MCS
Maclean Hunter Television Fund	MHTVF
magnetic tape	MT
magneto-optical	MO
Magyar Mozi és Videófilmagyar	MOVI
Magyar Televízió	MTV · HUNGARY
main switching unit	MSU
Mainichi Broadcasting System Inc	MBS · JAPAN
Mainos-Televisio	MTV · FINLAND
Makedonska Radiotelevizija	MRTV · MACEDONIA
Malta Broadcasting Authority	MBA
Management Information Television GmbH	MITV
Manchester University Television Productions	MUTV
Manitoba Motion Picture Industries Association	MMPIA
manual gain control	MGC
manual volume control	MVC
Marché International des Films et des Programmes pour la TV, la Vidéo, le Câble et le Satellite	MIPCOM
Marché International des Programmes de Télévision	MIP-TV
Marché International du Disque, de l'Edition Musicale et de la Vidéo Musique	MIDEM
Marché International du Film d'Animation pour le Cinéma et la Télévision	MIFA
Mars International Productions	MIP
Mary Tyler Moore Enterprises, Inc	MTM
master antenna television	MATV
master clock	MCL
master control	MC
master control panel	MCP
master control room	MCR
master control unit	MCU
master of ceremonies	MC
master set-up unit	MSU
master shot	MS
masters and dupes	M&D
match dissolve	MD
Matsushita Avionics Development Corporation	MADC
Matsushita Avionics Systems	MAS
Mauritius Broadcasting Corporation	MABC / MBC · MAURITIUS
maximum output level	MOL
maximum usable frequency	MUF
mean time between failures	MTBF
mean time to failure	MTTF
mean time to repair	MTTR
Measures to Encourage the Development of the Industry of Audiovisual Production	MEDIA
Mechanical Copyright Protection Society Ltd	MCPS
Media Access Project	MAP
Media and Communication Services	MCS
media broadband service	MBS
Media Business School	MBS · SPAIN
Media Education Forum for Wales	MEFW
Media Education News Update	MENU

Media Expenditure Analysis Ltd	MEAL
Media Holdings International	MHI
Media Information Australia	MIA
Media International Corporation	MICO
Media Marketing Organisatie	MEMO
Media Technology Centre GmbH	MTC
Media Télévision et Téléspectateurs	MTT
Mediathèque de la Communauté Française de Belgique	MCFB
Medienausbildungszentrum	MAZ
Mediterranean Centre of Audiovisual Communication	MCAC
medium close shot	*MCS*
medium close-up	*MCU*
medium frequency	*MF*
medium long shot	*MLS*
medium scale integration	*MSI*
medium shot	*MS*
medium wave	*MW*
megahertz	*MHZ*
megavolt	*MV*
megawatt	*MW*
Memory-Archives-Programmes TV	MAP TV
Mental Health Film Board	MHFB
Mental Health Media Council	MHMC
Mercato Internazionale Film e Documentario	MIFED
Mesures pour Encourager le Développement de l'Industrie Audiovisuelle	MEDIA
metal-nitride-oxide semiconductor	*MNOS*
metal-oxide chemical vapour deposition	*MOCVD*
metal-oxide field-effect transistor	*MOSFET*
metal-oxide semiconductor/surface	*MOS*
Metro-Goldwyn-Mayer, Inc	MGM
Metropolitan Educational Television Association	META
micro headend	*MHE*
microcell communications simulator	*MCS*
microwave	*MW*
microwave distribution system	*MDS*
microwave integrated circuit	*MIC*
microwave modules and devices	*MMD*
microwave video distribution system	*MVDS*
Mid-Canada Television Funds	MCTV
mid shot	*MS*
Middle East Broadcasting Centre	MBC · UK
Middle East Séquence Couleur à Mémoire	*MESECAM*
Mie Television Broadcasting Co Ltd	MTV · JAPAN
millivolt	*MV*
milliwatt	*MW*
Minaminihon Broadcasting Co Ltd	MBC · JAPAN
mini disc	*MD*
miniature circuit breaker	*MCB*
miniature screw	*MS*
miniature tube	*MT*
minimum discernible signal	*MDS*
minimum focussing distance	*MFD*
minimum operating distance	*MOD*
minimum reporting standards	*MRS*

minimum shift keying	*MSK*
minute of programme	*MOP*
"mit out sound"	*MOS*
Mitteldeutsche Rundfunkwerbung GmbH	MDR
mix/effects	*M/E*
mixed field	*MF*
mixed scan	*MS*
Miyazaki Broadcasting Co Ltd	MRT
mobile control room	*MCR*
Mobile Facilities Basle Ltd	MFB
mobile film unit	*MFU*
mobile production unit	*MPU*
mobile satellite service	*MSS*
mobile videotape recorders	*MVTR*
Modern Satellite Network	MSN
modified frequency modulation	*MFM*
modular transfer function	*MTF*
modulated continuous wave	*MCW*
modulation transfer function	*MTF*
Mogadiscio Pan-African Film Symposium	MOGPAAFIS / MOGPAFIS
molecular beam epitaxy	*MSE*
Mongol Radio and Television	MRTV · MONGOLIA
Moscow Independent Broadcasting Corporation	MIBC
most significant bit	*MSB*
motion analysis camera	*MAC*
motion picture	*MP*
Motion Picture and Television Credit Association	MPTCA
Motion Picture Association of America	MPAA
Motion Picture Export Association of America	MPEAA / MPEA
Motion Picture Foundation of Canada	MPFC
Motion Picture Machine Operators	MPMO
Motion Picture Relief Fund	MPRF
motion picture(s) expert group	*MPEG*
move in	*MI*
move out	*MO*
Movie Acquisition Corporation	MAC
Movie Channel, The	TMC
Movie Makers Guild	MMG
movie of the week	*MOW*
Moving Image Touring & Exhibition Service	MITES
Moving Images and Sound Archives	MISA
Mozgókép Innovációs Társulás & Alapítvány	MIT · HUNGARY
multi-channel microwave/multipoint distribution system/service	*MMDS*
multi-channel television sound	*MTS*
multi emitter coupled logic	*MECL*
multi function	*MF*
multi-linear orientation	*MLO*
multi-network area	*MNA*
multi-role lens	*MRL*
multi-standard television system	*MTS*
multi studio digital system	*MSDS*
multimedia	*MM*
multiple access receiver	*MAR*
multiple (cable) system operator	*MSO*

multiple camera remotes	*MCR*
multiple channel per carrier	*MCPC*
multiple controller interface	*MCI*
multiple frequency shift keying	*MFSK*
multiple quantum well	*MQW*
multiple sub-nyquist sampling encoder/encoding	*MUSE*
multiplex(ed) analogue component	*MAC*
multiplying digital-analogue convertor	*MDAC*
multipoint distribution system/service	*MDS*
Munhwa Broadcasting Corporation	MBC · KOREA
Museo Internazionale del Cinema e dello Spettacolo	MICS
Museum of the Moving Image	MOMI
music and (sound) effects	*M&E*
Music Corporation of America	MCA
Music Film and Video Producers' Association	MFVPA
Music Television	MTV · USA
music television	*MTV*
musical director	*MD*
musical power output	*MPO*
Myanma Television and Radio Department	MTVRD

N

N-channel metal-oxide semiconductor	*NMOS*
Nagano Asahi Broadcasting Co Ltd	ABN · JAPAN
Nagano Broadcasting System	NBS
Nagasaki Broadcasting Co Ltd	NBC · JAPAN
Nagasaki Culture Telecasting Corporation	NCC
Nagasaki International Television Broadcasting Inc	NIB
Nagoya Broadcasting Networks	NBN
Namibian Broadcasting Corporation	NBC · NAMIBIA / NAMBC
Nankai Broadcasting Co Ltd	RNB
nanosecond	*NS*
nanovolt	*NV*
Nara Television Co Ltd	TVN
narration	*NAR*
narrow field acquisition detector	*NFD*
narrowband	*NB*
narrowband frequency modulation	*NBFM*
Nation's Capital Television Incorporated	NCTI · CANADA
Nationaal Radio en Filmtechnisch Instituut	NARAFI
National Academy of Cable Programming	NACP
National Academy of Television Arts and Sciences	NATAS / NATVAS
National Armored Cable Manufacturers Association	NACMA
National Asian American Telecommunications Association	NAATA
National Association for Better Broadcasting	NABB
National Association for Educational Television	NAET
National Association for Higher Education in Film and Video	NAHEFV
National Association of Black Owned Broadcasters	NABOB
National Association of Black Television and Film Producers	NABTFP
National Association of Broadcast Employees and Technicians	NABET
National Association of Broadcast Unions and Guilds	NABUG
National Association of Broadcasters	NAB · USA

National Association of College Broadcasters   NACB
National Association of Commercial Broadcasters in Japan   NAB · JAPAN
National Association of Educational Broadcasters   NAEB
National Association of Farm Broadcasters   NAFB
National Association of Hospital Broadcasting Organisations Ltd   NAHBO
National Association of Independent Television Producers and Distributors   NAITPD
National Association of Media Women   NAMW
National Association of Municipal Cinemas   NAMC
National Association of Performing Artists   NAPA
National Association of Public Television Stations   NAPTS
National Association of Regulatory Utilities Commissioners   NARUC
National Association of State Cable Agencies   NASCA
National Association of Teacher Educators and Advisors in Media Education   TEAME
National Association of Telecommunications Officers   NATOA
National Association of Television and Electronic Servicers of America   NATESA
National Association of Television and Radio Announcers   NATRA
National Association of Television Program Executives   NATPE
National Association of Theatre Owners   NATO
National Association of Video Distributors   NAVD
national audience composition   *NAC*
National Audience Demographics   NAD
National Audio-Visual Centre   NAC
National Audio Visual Library   NAVL
National Black Media Coalition   NBMC
National Broadcasting Company, Inc   NBC · USA
National Cable Antenna Television Association of Canada   NCATA
National Cable Television Association Inc   NCTA
National Cable Television Institute   NCTI · USA
National Captioning Institute   NCI
National Catholic Office for Radio and Television   NCORT
National Center for School and College Television   NCSCT
National Christian Network   NCN
National Citizens Committee for Broadcasting   NCCB
National College Television   NCT
National Committee for the Full Development of Instructional Television Fixed
    Services   NCFDITFS
National Council for Families and Television   NCFT
National Council on Television Violence   NCTV
National Educational Closed-Circuit Television Association   NECCTA
National Educational Film & Video Festival   NEFVF
National Electrical Manufacturers Association   NEMA
National Federation of Local Cable Programmers   NFLCP
National Film and Sound Archive   NFSA
National Film and Television Archive   NFTVA · UK
National Film and Television School   NFTS
National Film Archive   NFA
National Film Board of Canada   NFB / NFBC
National Film Corporation   NFC · SRI LANKA
National Film Development Corporation *(India)*   NFDC
National Film Development Corporation *(Pakistan)*   NAFDEC
National Film Development Fund   NFDF
National Film Finance Corporation   NFFC
National Film Theatre   NFT

National Film Trustee Company	NFTC
National Film Unit	NFU
National Institute of Mass Communication	NIMC / NIMCO
National Instructional Television Association	NITA
National Instructional Television Center	NITC
National Program Production and Acquisition Grant	NPPAG
National Program Service	NPS
National Project for the Improvement of Televised Instruction	NPITI
National Public Affairs Center for Television	NPACT
National Religious Broadcasters	NRB
National Society of Television Producers	NSTP
National Television and Video Association	NTVA
National Television Film Council	NTFC
National Television System Committee	*NTSC*
National Transcommunications Ltd	NTL
National Video and Film Distributors Council	NTFDC
National Video Archive of Stage Performance	NVASP
National Video Corporation	NVC
National Video Resources	NVR
National Viewers' and Listeners' Association	NVALA
near instantaneously companded audio multiplex	*NICAM*
nearly instantaneous companding	*NIC*
Nederlands Instituut voor Audiovisuele Media	NIAM
Nederlandse Bond van Bioscopen	NBB
Nederlandse Christelijke Radio Vereniging	NCRV
Nederlandse Federatie voor de Cinematografie	NFC · THE NETHERLANDS
Nederlandse Film en Televisie Academie	NFTVA · THE NETHERLANDS
Nederlandse Omroepproductie Bedrijf	NOB
Nederlandse Omroepprogramma Stichting	NOS
Nederlandse Vereniging van Producenten en Importeurs van Beeld- en Geluiddragers	
	NVPI
Nelson Holdings International	NHI
net advertising revenue	*NAR*
net rating points	*NRP*
Netherlands Information Service	NIS
network identification	*NI*
Network of Workshops	NOW
network programme analysis	*NPA*
network switching centre	*NSC*
Network Transmission Committee	NTC
neutral density	*ND*
new electronic media	*NEM*
New Media for Europe	NMFE
New Media Markets	NMM
New South Wales Film and Television Office	NSWFTO
New Studio City	NSC · CANADA
new world information order	*NWIO*
New Zealand Film Commission	NZFC
news transmission assistant	*NTA*
Nielsen Cable Activity Report	NCAR
Nielsen Hispanic Television Index	NHTI
Nielsen Station Index	NSI
Nielsen Syndication Service	NSS
Nielsen Television Index	NTI®

Nigerian Television Authority	NTA
Nihon-Kai Telecasting Co Ltd	NKT
Niigata Sogo Television Co Ltd	NST
Niigata Television Network 21 Inc	NT-21
Nippon Hoso Kyokai	NHK
Nippon Television Network Corporation	NTV
Nishi-Nippon Broadcasting Co Ltd	RNC
no baseband processing	*NBP*
no good	*NG*
no sound	*NS*
noise bandwidth	*NB*
noise cancellor	*NC*
noise equivalent power	*NEP*
noise figure	*NF*
noise power ratio	*NPR*
noise reduction	*NR*
noise temperature	*NT*
noiseless camera	*NC*
non-absorbing mirror	*NAM*
non-additive mixing	*NAM*
non-directional	*ND*
non-domestic satellite service	*NDS*
non-drop frame	*NDF*
non-phased colour	*NPC*
non-return to zero	*NRZ*
non-return to zero-level	*NRZ-L*
non-return to zero-mask	*NRZ-M*
non-return to zero-space	*NRZ-S*
non-synchronous switch	*NSS*
non-volatile random-access memory	*NVRAM*
Norddeutscher Filmhersteller Verband	NFV
Norddeutscher Rundfunk	NDR
Nordic Anthropological Film Association	NAFA
normal frequency	*NF*
Norsk Filmforbund	NFF
Norsk Filmklubbforbund	NFK
Norsk Kino- og Filmfond	NKFF
Norsk Rikskringkasting	NRK
Norske Film- og Videoprodusenters Forening	NFVPF
North American National Broadcasters' Association	NANBA
North American Presentation Level Protocol Syntax	NAPLPS
North American Regional Broadcast Agreement	NARBA
North American Releasing	NAR
North East Media Training Centre	NEMTC
North East Television and Film Archive	NETFA
North West Film Archive	NWFA
Northern School of Film and Television	NSFTV
Northern Screen Commission	NSC · UK
nouvel ordre mondial de l'information et de la communication	*NOMIC*
Nouvelles Editions de Films	NEF
Nova Scotia Film Development Corporation	NSFDC
numerical aperture	*NA*

O

Oberoende Filmares Förbund	OFF
octal coded binary	*OCB*
off-screen	*OS*
off-stage	*OS*
Office Audiovisuel de l'Université de Poitiers	AVUP
Office Cinématographique National du Mali	OCINAM
Office de Radio-Télévision du Sénégal	ORTS
Office de Radiodiffusion et de Télévision Sénégalais	ORTS
Office de Radiodiffusion et Télévision de Benin	ORTB
Office de Radiodiffusion et Télévision de Mauritanie	ORTM
Office de Radiodiffusion et Télévision du Niger	ORTN
Office de Radiodiffusion Télévision Camerounaise	CRTV
Office National du Cinéma	ONACI
Office National du Film du Canada	ONF
Office of Cable Signal Theft	OCST
Office of Emergency Communications	OEC
Office Zaïrois de Radiodiffusion et Télévision	OZRT
offset quadrature phase shift keying	*OQPSK*
Oficina de Justificación de la Difusión	OJD
Ogun State Television	OGTV
Oita Broadcasting System	OBS
Okayama Broadcasting Co Ltd	OHK
Okinawa Television Broadcasting Co Ltd	OTV · JAPAN
Omladinska Televizija	OTV · CROATIA
on-air test	*OAT*
on camera	*OC*
on-chip lens	*OCL*
on-off keying	*OOK*
on-screen display	*OSD*
on-screen programming	*OSP*
Onafhankelijke Televisie Producenten	OTP
Onderwijs Media Instituut	OMI
Ondo State Radiovision Corporation	OSRC
Ondo State Television	OSTV / ODTV
one-time only	*OTO*
one-touch (timer) record(ing)	*OTR*
Ontario Film Association	OFA
Ontario Film Development Corporation	OFDC
open architecture receiver	*OAR*
Open University	OU
Open University Production Centre	OUPC
Operation Prime Time	OPT
operational control panel	*OCP*
operational fixed service	*OFS*
operations manager	*OM*
Optical Disc Corporation	ODC
Optical Networks International	ONI
optical receiver	*OR*
optical solar reflector	*OSR*
optical transfer function	*OTF*
optical transmitter	*OT*

optimal pivot point	OPP
orbital test satellite	OBT / OTS
orbital transfer vehicle	OTV
Organisatie van Lokale Omroepen Nederland	OLON
Organisation Catholique Internationale du Cinéma et de l'Audiovisuel	OCIC
Organisation Ibéroamericaine de Télévision	OIT
Organisation Internationale de Radio et de Télévision	OIRT
Organisation Zaïroise des Cinéastes	OZACI
Organismes Français de Radiodiffusion et de Télévision	OFRT
Organización Católica Internacionale del Cine y del Audiovisual	OCIC
Organización de la Televisión Iberoamericana	OTI
original equipment manufacturer	OEM
orthogonal frequency division multiplex(ing)	OFDM
orthogonal mode transducer	OMT
orthomodal transducer	OMT
oscillating colour sequence	OCS
Ostankino Kanal	OK
Österreichische Gesellschaft für Filmwissenschaft, Kommunications- und Medienforschung	OGFKM
Österreichischer Filmförderungsfonds	ÖFF
Österreichischer Rundfunk	ORF
out-of-vision	OOV
output	O/P
output multiplexer	OMUX
outside broadcast	OB
outside rehearsals	OR
over discharge protection	ODP™
over-the-air	OTA
over-the-shoulder shot	OS / OSS
over the top	OTT
Overflow Control Gate	OFCG
owned and operated	O&O
Oxford Independent Video	OIV
Oxford Scientific Films Ltd	OSF
Oxford Television	OXTV

P

p-channel metal-oxide semiconductor	PMOS
Pacific Broadcasting Association	PBA
Pacific Islands Broadcasting Association	PIBA
packet type	PT
Pakistan Film Producers Association	PFPA
Pakistan Television Corporation	PTV
PAL-simple	PAL-S
pan bar imitator system	PBIS
pan bar input system	PBIS
Pan-European Television Audience Research	PETAR
Państwowa Wyższa Szkoła Filmowa Telewizyjna i Teatralna im. Leona Schillera w Łódź	PWSFTVIT
para-social interaction	PSI
parabolic aluminized reflector	PAR
parallel input	PI

parental guidance	*PG*
particle transfer roller	*PTR*
party election broadcast	*PEB*
party line	*PL*
party political broadcast	*PPB*
path distance	*PD*
Paul Kagan Associates, Inc	PKA
pay per channel	*PPC*
pay-per-view	*PPV*
payload	*P/L*
payload assist module	*PAM*
payload assist module-Atlas	*PAM-A*
payload assist module-Delta	*PAM-D*
payload ground support equipment	*PGSE*
peak programme meter	*PPM*
peak to peak	*P-P*
pedigree kick motor	*PKM*
People's Revolutionary Broadcasting Corporation	PRBC
Perbadanan Kemajuan Filem Nasional Malaysia	FINAS
Perfect Vision, The	TPV
Performing Arts Workers Equity	PAWE
peripheral television connector	*PERITEL*
periscope unit and mirror attachment	*PUMA*
Persatuan Pengeluar Filem Malaysia	PPFM
personal computer	*PC*
Persons Tracking Report	PTR
persons using television	*PUT*
persons viewing television	*PVT*
phano-convex	*PC*
phase alternation by line/phase alternate line	*PAL*
phase correlation (motion estimation)	*PHC*
phase-lock(ed) loop	*PLL*
phase modulation	*PM*
phase shift keying	*PSK*
Philadelphia Festival of World Cinema	PFWC
Philips and Du Pont Optical Company	PDO
Philips depressed collector	*PDC*
Philips TV	*PTV*
photo blow-up	*PBU*
pick-up	*PU*
picture clear circuit	*PCC*
picture description instruction	*PDI*
picture in picture	*PIP*
picture line-up generating equipment	*PLUGE*
picture-outside-picture	*POP*
pictures per minute	*PPM*
pictures per second	*PPS*
piezoelectric transducer unit	*PZT*
Plastic Reel Corporation of America	PRC
Point-of-View	POV
point of view	*POV*
Political Action Committee for Cable Television	PACCT
Polskie Radio i Telewizja	PRT
Polskie Stowarzyszenie Filmu Naukowego	PSFN

poly-ethylene	*PE*
polymethyl methacrylate	*PMMA*
polyvinyl acetate	*PVA*
polyvinyl chloride	*PVC*
portable single camera	*PSC*
positive intrinsically negative	*PIN*
positive temperature coefficient	*PTC*
post-deflection acceleration	*PDA*
post-sunset service authorisation	*PSSA*
potential out-take	*POT*
power amplifier	*PA*
power-augmented hydrazine transfer	*PAHT*
power control unit	*PCU*
power flux density	*PFD*
power supply unit	*PSU*
pre-fade listen	*PFL*
pre-sunrise service authorisation	*PSRA*
precision digital decoding system	*PRISM*
precision in line	*PIL*
prediction and retrospective ionospheric modelling over Europe	*PRIME*
prescribed diffusion service	*PDSL*
presentation protocol data unit	*PPDN*
pressure zone microphone	*PZM*
preview	*PV / PVW*
prime time access rule	*PTAR*
printed circuit	*PC*
printed circuit board	*PCB*
private earth station	*PES*
private line	*PL*
probability density function	*PDF*
Producer Services Group, Inc	PSG
producer's net receipts	*PNR*
Producers Alliance for Cinema and Television	PACT · UK
Producers Association, The	TPA · UK
Producers Creative Partnership	PCP
Producers Guild of America	PGA
Producteurs Associés Luxembourgeois	PAL
production assistant	*PA*
production associate	*PA*
production director	*PD*
Production Générale de Films	PROGEFI
production-level video	*PLV*
production manager	*PM*
production services manager	*PSM*
Produzione Atlas Cinematografica	PAC
Produzioni Atlas Consorziate	PAC
Professional Audiovideo Retailers Association	PARA
Professional Casting Report	PCR
professional digital	*PD*
Professional Film and Video Equipment Association	PFVEA
Professional Motion Picture Equipment Association	PMPEA
Professional Systems Network	PSNI
Program for Art on Film	PAF
programmable array logic	*PAL*

programmable logic array	PLA
programmable read-only disc	PROD
programmable read-only memory	PROM
programmable technical equipment control	PROTEC
programme-as-broadcast	P-AS-B
programme-as-completed	P-AS-C
programme as televised	P-AS-T
programme assistant	PA
programme correspondence section	PCS
programme delivery control	PDC
programme director	PD
Programme for the International Launch of Television Series	PILOTS
programme interrupt	PI
programme length commercial	PLC
programme logic device	PLD
programme sequence control	PSC
programme switching centre	PSC
projection television	PJTV
Protective Action for Children's Television	PACT · USA
provisional cut	PC
pseudo-noise	PN
pseudo-random binary sequence	PRBS
public access videotex	PAV
public address	PA
Public Broadcasting Association of Australia	PBAA
Public Broadcasting for a Multicultural Europe	PBME
Public Broadcasting Service	PBS
public domain interface	PDI
Public Interest Video Network	PIVN
public service announcement	PSA
public service broadcaster	PSB
Public Service Satellite Consortium	PSSC
public switched network	PSN
public television	PTV
Public Television International	PTI
Public Television Library	PTL
Public Television Outreach Alliance	PTOA
pulse addition	PA
pulse amplitude modulation	PAM
pulse-code modulation	PCM
pulse distribution amplifier	PDA
pulse duration modulation	PDM
pulse duration width modulation	PDWM
pulse edge modulation	PEM
pulse frequency modulation	PFM
pulse-gated binary modulation	PGBM
pulse internal modulation	PIM
pulse length modulation	PLM
pulse phase modulation	PPM
pulse polarisation binary modulation	PPBM
pulse position modulation	PPM
pulse quaterny modulation	PQM
pulse repetition frequency	PRF
pulse-width modulation	PWM

Q

Qatar Television Service	QTV
quadrature amplitude modulator	*QAM*
quadrature modulation	*QM*
quadrature modulation of the picture carrier	*QUME*
quadrature phase shift keying	*QPSK*
quadruple play	*QP*
quality assurance	*QA*
quality PAL	*Q-PAL*
quarter wave	*QW*
Quarterly Review of Film and Video	QRFV
quartz iodine	*QI*
quasi-direct broadcasting by satellite	*QDBS*
Queen's Film Theatre	QFT
question(s) and answer(s)	*Q&A*
quick kinescope	*QK*

R

Radio and Television Correspondents Association	RTCA
Radio and Television Directors Guild	RTDG
Radio and Television Executives Society	RTES
Radio and Television Research Council	RTRC
Radio Bremen	RB
Radio Caracas Televisión	RCTV
Radio Corporation of America	RCA
radio data system	*RDS*
Radio, Electrical and Television Retailers' Association	RETRA
Radio France Internationale	RFI
radio frequency	*RF*
radio frequency interference	*RFI*
radio-isotope thermo-electric generator	*RTG*
Radio-Keith-Orpheum	RKO
Radio Netherland Training Centrum	RNTC
Radio Netherlands Television	RNTV
radio receive only	*RRO*
Radio Telefís Éireann	RTE
Radio Televisão Portuguesa	RTP · PORTUGAL
Radio-Television Afghanistan	RTA · AFGHANISTAN
Radio-Télévision Animation	RTA · BELGIUM
Radio-Télévision Belge de la Communauté Française	RTBF
Radio Television Brunei	RTB · BRUNEI DARUSSALAM
Radio Televisión de Andalucía	RTVA
Radio-Télévision de la Communauté Française	TVCF
Radio-Télévision (de la) Suisse Romande	RTSR
Radio Télévision Française d'Outre-Mer	RFO
Radio Television Hong Kong	RTHK
Radio-Télévision Ivoirienne	RTI · IVORY COAST
Radio-Télévision Luxembourgeoise	RTL · LUXEMBOURG
Radio Televisión Madrid	RTVM
Radio-Télévision Malagasy	RTM · MADAGASCAR
Radio Television Malaysia	RTM · MALAYSIA

Radio-Television News Directors' Association	RTNDA
Radio Télévision Nouvelle Marche	RTNM
Radio Television Seychelles	RTS · SEYCHELLES
Radio Televiziunea Română Libera	RTVR
Radio Uganda and Uganda Television	RU/UTV
Radiodiffusion et Télévision Nationale du Burundi	RTNB
Radiodiffusion Télévision Algérienne	RTA · ALGERIA
Radiodiffusion-Télévision de Djibouti	RTD
Radiodiffusion-Télévision Gabonaise	RTG · GABON
Radiodiffusion-Télévision Guinéenne	RTG · GUINEA
Radiodiffusion Télévision Marocaine	RTM · MOROCCO
Radiotelevidenie Ostankino	RTO
Radiotelevisão Comercial, LDA	RTC
Radiotelevisión Española	RTVE / TVE · SPAIN
Radiotélévision Tunisienne	RTT
Radiotelevisione della Svizzera Italiana	RTSI
Radiotelevisione Italiana	RAI
Radiotelevizija Beograd	RTB · SERBIA / RTVB
Radiotelevizija Bosnia-Herzegovina	RTV · BOSNIA
Radiotelevizija Crne Gore	RTVCG
Radiotelevizija Ljubljana	RTL · SLOVENIA
Radiotelevizija Novi Sad	RTVNS
Radiotelevizija Priština	RTP · SERBIA / RTVP
Radiotelevizija Sarajevo	RTSA / RTVSA
Radiotelevizija Skopje	TVSK
Radiotelevizioni Shqiptar	RTSH
Radioteleviziunea Română	RTR
Rajawali Citra Televisi Indonesia	RCTI
random-access memory	*RAM*
rapid action cutting equipment	*RACE*
rapid transmission and storage	*RTS*
re-broadcast link	*RBL*
re-broadcast reception	*RBR*
reach and frequency	*R&F*
reaction control system	*RCS*
reaction index	*RI*
read address clock	*RACK*
read after write	*RAW*
read modify write	*RMW*
read-only memory	*ROM*
read out gate	*ROG*
real-time lens error correction	*RLC*
real-time operating system	*RTOS*
real-time video	*RTV*
rear projection	*RP*
receive-only earth satellite	*ROES*
recessed single contact	*RSC*
recordable laser videodisc	*RLV*
red-orange, green, blue-violet	*RGB*
reduced aperture	*RA*
reduced instruction set computer	*RISC*
Régie Media Belge	RMB
regional film theatre	*RFT*
regional operational centre	*ROC*

Regionale Omroep Overleg en Samenwerking	ROOS
Register Media Expenditure Analysis Ltd	Register-MEAL
register transistor logic	*RTL*
Regroupement des Distributeurs Télévision du Québec	RDTVQ
Remote Commercial Television Service	RCTS
remote control	*RC*
remote control degauss	*RCD*
remote control panel	*RCP*
remote control unit	*RCU*
remote detection unit	*RDU*
remote manipulator system	*RMS*
remote pick-up	*RP / RPU*
remote sensor	*RS*
remote subscriber stage	*RSS*
remote switch	*RS*
remote unit	*RU*
René Thévenet et Associés	RTEA
request for proposals	*RFP*
Research and Development in Advanced Communications Technologies in Europe	
	RACE
Research Technology International	RTI · UK
Réseau de Télévision Quatre-Saisons	TQS
Réseau des Sports	RDS
Réseau Interuniversitaire de Recherche et d'Enseignement du Cinéma	RIRECA
residual current circuit breaker	*RCCB*
residual point noise	*RPN*
resistor/capacitor	*RC*
Resources In Training & Education Ltd	RITE
Reti Televisive Italiane	RTI · ITALY
return to bias	*RB*
return to zero	*RZ*
reverberation time	*RT*
reverse shot	*RS*
Revista de Difusión e Investigación Cinematográficas	DICINE
revolutions per minute	*RPM*
rewritable consumer time code	*RCTC*
Richard Price Television Associates	RIPTA / RPTA
right-hand circular polarisation	*RHCP*
Ríkisútvarpið-Sjónvarp	RUV
RKB Mainichi Broadcasting Corporation	RKB
room humidity	*RH*
rooms using television	*RUT*
root mean square(d)	*RMS*
root sum square	*RSS*
Rossijskaja Gosudarstvennaja Teleradioveschateljnaja Kompanija Ostankino	RGTRK
Rossijskaya Moskovskaja Teleradioveschateljnaya Kompanija Moskva	RMTK
Rossijskoje Televidenije	RTV · RUSSIA
rotary-head digital audio tape	*RDAT*
rotating digital audio tape	*RDAT*
rouge vert bleu	*RVB*
Royal Television Society	RTS · UK
run length encoding	*RLE*
run of schedule/station	*ROS*
Rundfunk Anstalt Südtirol	RAS

Scottish Film Archive	SFA · UK
Scottish Film Council	SFC · UK
Scottish Television plc	STV · UK
Screen Actors Guild	SAG
Screen Advertising World Association	SAWA
Screen Cartoonists Guild	SCG
Screen Composers of America	SCA
Screen Directors Guild	SDG
Screen Directors International Guild	SDIG
Screen Extras Guild, Inc	SEG
Screen Production Association of Australia	SPAA
Screen Writers Guild	SWG
screw terminal	*ST*
Seattle International Film Festival	SIFF · USA
second surface mirror	*SSM*
second(ary) audio programme	*SAP*
Secretariado Nacional para o Audiovisual	SNA
Secrétariat International des Syndicats des Arts, des Moyens de Communication et du Spectacle	ISETU
Secrétariat International Spiritain de Communications Sociales par l'Audio Visuel	SISCOMS
Selective Multiple Address Radio and Television Service	SMARTS
Semaine Internationale de Vidéo	SIV
semiconductor laser intersatellite link experiment	*SILEX*
Sender Freies Berlin	SFB
Seoul Broadcasting System Production	SBS · KOREA
separate audio programme	*SAP*
separate magnetic soundtrack	*SEPMAG*
separate optical soundtrack	*SEPOPT*
séquence couleur à/avec mémoire	*SECAM*
sequential thermal anhysteric magnetisation	*STAM*
serial digital interface	*SDI*
serial drag	*SD*
Service Cinématographique du Ministère de l'Information du Mali	SCINFOMA
service module	*SM*
service provider	*SP*
Services Sound and Vision Corporation	SSVC
Servicio Oficial de Difusión de Radiotelevisión y Espectáculos	SODRE
set-up control panel	*SCP*
sets in use	*SIU*
Seychelles Broadcasting Corporation	SBC · SEYCHELLES / SEYBC
shared resource	*SR*
sharp cut	*SB*
Shikoku Broadcasting Co Ltd	JRT · JAPAN
Shin-Etsu Broadcasting Co Ltd	SBC · JAPAN
Shin Hiroshima Telecasting Co Ltd	TSS
Shizuoka Broadcasting System	SBS · JAPAN
Shizuoka Daiichi Television Corporation	SDT
Shizuoka Kenmin Television Co Ltd	SKT
short wave	*SW*
short wave transmitter	*SWT*
shutter control unit	*SCU*
Sianel Pedwar Cymru	S4C
Sierre Leone Broadcasting Service	SLBS

Signal Engineering & Electronics	SEE
signal to noise ratio	*S/N / S/NR*
silent reflex	*SR*
silent videotape recording	*SILVTR*
silicon-controlled rectifier	*SCR*
silicon-intensified/intensifier target	*SIT*
simultaneous broadcast	*SB*
Sindacato Attori Italiani	SAI
Sindacato Nazionale Critici Cinematografici Italiani	SNCCI
Sindacato Nazionale Giornalisti Cinematografici Italiani	SNGCI
Sindacato Colombiano de Trabajadores de Cine	SICOLTRACINE
Sindicato das Artes e Espectaculos	SIARTE
Sindicato de Trabajadores de la Industria Cinematográfica, Similares y Conexos de la R.M.	STIC
Sindicato de Trabajadores Técnicos y Manuales de Estudios y Laboratorios de la Producción Cinematográfica S.I.C. de la R.M.	STPC
Sinema Eserleri Sahlpieri Meslek Birligi	SESAM
Singapore Broadcasting Corporation	SBC · SINGAPORE
Singapore International Film Festival	SIFF · SINGAPORE
single bayonet	*SB*
single channel per carrier	*SCPC*
single contact	*SB*
single lens reflex	*SLR*
single line colour bar	*SLCB*
single perforated	*SP*
single sideband	*SSB*
single sideband suppressed carrier case	*SSBSC*
single system operator	*SSO*
single time code	*STC*
Sistema Brasileiro de TV	SBT
Sistema Nacional de Radio y Televisión Cultural	SINART
Sistema Nacional de Televisión	SNTV
slide-tape	*ST*
Slovenská Požičovna Filmov	SPF
Slovenská Televizia	ST / STV · SLOVAKIA
slow-scan television	*SSTV*
slow wave structure	*SWS*
slung microphone aiming control	*SMAC*
small computer system(s) interface	*SCSI*
Small Countries Improve their Audiovisual Level in Europe	SCALE
small-scale integration	*SSI*
Sociedad Anónima Cinematográfica	SAC
Sociedad Anónima del Video	SAV
Sociedade Independente de Comunicação	SIC
Sociedade Portuguesa de Cinematografia e Video	SPCV
Società Italiana degli Autori ed Editori	SIAE
Società per Azioni Commerciale Iniziative Spettacolo	SACIS
Società Svizzera di Radiotelevisione	SSR
Société Anonyme Tunisienne de Production et d'Expansion Cinématographique	SATPEC
Société Collective de Retransmission du Canada	CRC
Société d'Appareillages Electroniques	SAE
Société d'Edition de Programmes de Télévision	SEPT
Société d'Importation de Distribution et d'Exploitation Cinématographique	SIDEC

Société de Développement de l'Industrie Cinématographique Ontarienne	OFDC
Société de Participations Cinématographiques Africaines	SOPACIA
Société des Réalisateurs de Film	SRF
Société Européenne des Satellites	SES
Société Française d'Etudes et de Réalisations d'Equipements de Radiodiffusion et de Télévision	SOFRATEV
Société Française de Production	SFP · FRANCE
Société Française des Sciences de l'Information et de la Communication	SFSIC
Société Générale des Industries Culturelles Québec	SOGIC
Société Industrielle de Sonorisation	SIS · FRANCE
Société Internationale de l'Image et de Son	SIIS
Société Nationale Antenne 2	A2
Société Nationale de Distribution et d'Exploitation Cinématographique du Burkina	SONACIB
Société Nouvelle de Cinématographie	SNC · FRANCE
Société Nouvelle de Production Cinématographique	SNPC
Société Radio-Canada	SRC
Société Suisse de Radiodiffusion et Télévision	SSR
Société Suisse des Auteurs	SSA
Society for Cinema Studies	SCS
Society for Photo-Optical Instrumentation Engineers	SPIE
Society for the Preservation of Film Music	SPFM
Society of Broadcast Engineers	SBE
Society of Cable Television Engineers *(UK)*	SCTE
Society of Cable Television Engineers *(USA)*	SCTE
Society of Film Distributors Ltd	SFD
Society of Independent Motion Picture Producers	SIMPP
Society of Motion Picture and Television Art Directors	SMPTAD
Society of Motion Picture and Television Engineers	SMPTE
soft focus	*SF*
solar array drive	*SAD*
solar array drive assembly	*SADA*
solar array drive electronics	*SADE*
solar array drive mechanism	*SADM*
solid state	*SS*
Solid State Logic Ltd	SSL
solid state power amplifier	*SSPA*
solid state video recorder	*SSVR*
Solomon Islands Broadcasting Corporation	SIBC
Sony Broadcast & Communications	SBC · UK
Sony digital interface format	*SDIF*
Sony Dynamic Digital Sound™	*SDDS*
Sony Electronic Publishing	SEP
Sony Electronic Publishing Company	SEPC
Sony Music Operations	SMO
sound effects	*FX / SE / SFX*
sound in synch	*SIS*
sound on film	*SOF*
sound on sound	*SOS*
sound on tape	*SOT*
sound on videotape	*SOVT*
sound on vision	*SOV*
sound pressure level	*SPL*
Sources of Women Working In Film, Television and Video	SWIFT

South African Broadcasting Corporation	SABC
South African Film and Television Institute	SAFTI
South African Film and TV Technicians Association	SAFTTA
South African Film and Video Institute	SAFVI
South African Scriptwriters Association	SASWA
South African Society of Cinematographers	SASC
South Australian Film Corporation	SAFC
South West African Broadcasting Corporation	SWABC
Southern Command Network	SCN · PANAMA
space tracking and data network	*STDN*
space transportation system	*STS*
Spanish International Network	SIN
Special Broadcasting Service	SBS · AUSTRALIA
special effects	*FX, SFX, SPEFX, SPFX*
special effects generator	*SEG*
special purpose extra channels for terrestrial radio-communications enhancements	
	SPECTRE
special temporary authorisation	*STA*
specialised common carrier	*SCC*
Specialised Telecommunication Service	STS · USA
spectral power distribution	*SPD*
spectral recording	*SR*
spectrally shaped quadrature amplitude modulator	*SSQAM*
spectrum management	*SM*
split-luminance/split chrominance	*SLSC*
sponsor identification	*SI*
sponsor identification index	*SII*
Sports Network, The	TSN
Sri Lanka Broadcasting Corporation	SLBC
Sri Lanka Rupavahini Corporation (Television)	SLRC
stage manager	*SM*
standard long play	*SLP*
standard play	*SP*
standing wave ratio	*SWR*
start of active video	*SAV*
State Audio Visual Centre	SAVC
Statens Audiovisuella Central	SAVC
Statens Filmcentral	SFC · DENMARK
Statens Studiesenter for Film	SSFF
station identification	*SI*
station independence programme	*SIP*
station manager	*SM*
station programme cooperative	*SPC*
Station Research Group	SRG · USA
Stedelijk Hoger Instituut voor Visuele Kommunikatie en Vormgeving	SHIVKV
Steering Committee for/on the Mass Media	CDMM
stereo generator	*SG*
Stichting Audiovisuele Manifestaties	SAM
Stichting Audiovisuele Vorming	SAVE
Stichting Ether Reclame	STER
Stichting Film en Wetenschap-Audio Visueel Archief	SFW-AVA
Stichting Migranten Media Onderwijs	SMMO
Stichting Nederlandse Onderwijs-Televisie	NOT

Stichting ter Bevordering van het Wetenschappelijk Onderwijs in de Mediakunde	SWOM
Stichting ter Exploitatie van Kabeltelevisierechten	SEKAM
Stichting Vlaamse Filmproductie	SVF
still frame audio	*SFA*
Stimulating Outstanding Resources for Creative European Screenwriting	SOURCES
stock shot	*SS*
storage instantaneous audimeter	*SIA*
strokes interpreted animated sequences	*SIAS*
studio address	*SA*
studio to headend link	*SHL*
studio-transmitter link	*STL*
Stuntmen's Association of Motion Pictures	SAMP
sub-carrier	*SC*
sub-carrier distribution amplifier	*SCDA*
subject to non-renewal	*SNR*
Subscriber Management Systems	SMS
subscriber service amplifier	*SSA*
subscription television	*STV*
Subscription Television Association	STA
subsidiary communications authorisation	*SCA*
Südwestfunk	SWF
Suid-Afrikaanse Uitsaaikorporasie	SAUK
Summary of Information on Film and Television	SIFT
Summary of World Broadcasts	SWB
Sun Television Co Ltd	SUN
Suomen Elokuvasäätiö	FFF
Suomen Elokuvatuottajien Keskusliitto	COFFP
super high-band	*SHB*
super high-band aperture	*SHBA*
super high frequency	*SHF*
super quality playback	*SQPB*
Super VHS quasi playback	*SQPB*
super video graphics array	*SVGA*
Super-Video Home System	*S-VHS / SVHS*
super wide	*SW*
superimpose	*S/I*
superior performance	*SP*
superior tape	*ST*
supervising producer	*SP*
surface-acoustic-wave	*SAW*
surface mount technology	*SMT*
Surinaamse Televisie Stichting	STVS
Surya Citra Televisi	SCTV
Svensk Filmindustri, AB	SF
Svenska Filminstitutet	SFI
Svenska Institutet	SI
Sveriges Film och Videoproducenters Förening	SVIP
Sveriges Television AB	SVT
Swaziland Television Authority	STVA
Swedish Broadcasting Corporation	SBC · SWEDEN
Swedish Film Institute	SFI
Swedish Institute	SI
swift servo system	*SSS*

Swiss Broadcasting Corporation	SBC · SWITZERLAND
switched mode power supply	*SMPS*
synch generator	*SG*
synch signal generator	*SSG*
synchronised power pack	*SPP*
synchronising pulse generator	*SPG*
Syndicat Cinémas d'Art, de Répertoire et d'Essai	SCARE
Syndicat des Constructeurs d'Appareils Radio Récepteurs et Téléviseurs	*SCART*
Syndicat des Industries de Matériels Audiovisuels Electroniques	SIMAVELEC
Syndicat des Producteurs de Films Publicitaires	SPFP
Syndicat des Producteurs de Programmes Audiovisuels	S2PA / SPPA
Syndicat des Réalisateurs et Créateurs du Cinéma, de la Télévision et de l'Audiovisuel	SRCTA
Syndicat des Techniciennes et Techniciens du Cinéma et Vidéo du Québec	STCVQ
Syndicat Français des Artistes Interprètes	SFA · FRANCE
Syndicat National des Techniciens et Réalisateurs de la Production Cinématographique et Télévisuelle	SNTR
Syndicat National des Techniciens et Travailleurs de la Production Cinématographique et de Télévision (Audio-Visuel)	SNTPCAT
Syndicat National des Travailleurs et Travailleuses en Communication	SNTC
system remote	*SR*
Színházi Dolgozók Szakszervezete	SZDSZ

T

table of pages	*TOP*
Taiheiyo Hoso Kyokai	THK
Taiwan Television Enterprise	TTV · TAIWAN
Tampereen Tietoverkko	TTV · FINLAND
tape control unit	*TCU*
tape management and scheduling system	*TMS*
tape stabilising	*TS*
tape unit	*TU*
Te Tumu Whakaata Tonga	NZFC
technical apparatus for the rectification of indifferent film	*TARIF*
technical coordinator	*TC*
technical difficulties	*TD*
technical director	*TD*
technical manager	*TM*
Technical Panel for International Broadcast	TPIB
Technologie Elettroniche Milanesi	TEM
Tele-Aerials Satellite Ltd	TAS
Télé-Liban	TL
Télé Lyon Métropole	TLM
Télé Toulouse	TLT
telecine	*TC*
telecine analysis film	*TAF*
telecommand	*TC*
Telecommunications, Inc	TCI
Télédiffusion de France	TDF
Teledifusão de Macau	TDM
Teledwyr Annibynnol Cymru	TAC
telejector	*TJ*

telemetry	*TM*
telemetry, command and ranging	*TCR*
telemetry, tracking and command	*TTC*
teleplay	*TP*
teletext read-only memory	*TROM*
teletype	*TT*
Televidenie Peterburg	TVP
Televisão Experimental	TVE · MOZAMBIQUE
Televisão Independente	TVI · PORTUGAL
Televisão Nacional de Cabo Verde	TNCV
Televisão Popular de Angola	TPA · ANGOLA
Televisi Pendidikan Indonesia	TPI
Televisie- en Radio- Omroepstichting	TROS
Televisió de Catalunya	TVC · SPAIN
Televisió Valenciana	TVV
television	*TV*
télévision à haute définition	*TVHD*
Television Accessory Manufacturers Institute	TAMI
Television Advisory Committee for Educational Television	TACET
Television Advisory Committee of Mexican Americans	TACOMA
Television Aichi Corporation	TVA
Television Allocations Study Organisation	TASO
Television and Radio Industries Club	TRIC
Television and Radio Political Action Committee	TARPAC
Television and Screen Writers' Guild	T&SG
television audience measurement	*TAM*
television audience programme evaluation	*TAPE*
television automatic sequence control	*TASCON*
television broadcast satellite	*TVBS*
Television Broadcasts Ltd	TVB · HONG KONG
Television Bureau of Advertising	TBA / TVB · USA
Television Business International	TBI
Television Channel Nine Pty Ltd	TCN
Television Critics Association	TCA
Televisión de Galicia	TVG · SPAIN
Télévision (de la) Suisse Romande	TSR
television disc	*TED*
Television Entertainment Group	TEG
Televisión Federal SA	TELEFE
television film exhibit	*TFE*
Television Française 1	TF1
television graphics adaptor	*TVGA*
Television Hokkaido Co Ltd	TVH
television households	*TVHH*
Télévision Indépendante	TVI · BELGIUM
Television Information Centre	TVIC
Television Information Office	TIO
television infrared observing satellite	*TIROS*
television interference	*TVI*
Television Iwate Corporation	TVI · JAPAN
Television Kanagawa Co Ltd	TVK · JAPAN
television lines	*TVL*
Television Miyazaki Co Ltd	UMK
Télé(vision) Monte Carlo	TMC

Televisión Nacional de Chile	TNC · CHILE
Television Nagasaki Co Ltd	KTN
Television New Zealand Ltd	TVNZ
Television Niigata Networks Co Ltd	TNN
Television Nishi Nippon Corporation	TNC · JAPAN
Television Northern Canada	TVNC
Television of Thailand	TVT · THAILAND
Television Oita System Co Ltd	TOS
Television Ontario	TVO · CANADA
television operating centre	*TOC*
Television Osaka Inc	TVO · JAPAN
television pick-up	*TP*
Television Program Export Association	TPEA
television receive-only (terminal)	*TVRO*
tele(vision) recording	*TVR*
television relay using small terminals	*TRUST*
Television Saitama Co Ltd	TVS · JAPAN
Television Systems Ltd	TSL
Television Technology Corporation	TTC
television terminal	*TVT*
Télévision Togolaise	TVT · TOGO
television translator relay	*TTR*
Television Trust for the Environment	TVE · UK
television typewriter	*TVT*
Television Users' Group	TUG
Television Writers' Guild	TWG
Television Yamaguchi Co Ltd	TYS
Televisione della Svizzera Italiana	TSI
Televisora Andina de Mérida	TAM
Televizija Beograd	TVB · SERBIA
Televizija Slovenija	TVS · SLOVENIA
Televiziunea Română Libera	RTV · ROMANIA
temperature-compensated crystal oscillator	*TCXO*
terrestrial interference	*TI*
test equipment	*TE*
Thai Sky TV	TST
Theatre Alignment Program	*TAP*
thermal magnetic duplication	*TMD*
thermo magnetic video highspeed duplication	*TMD*
thin film technology	*TFT*
Thorson Digital Image	TDI
through the lens	*TTL*
tight close-up	*TCU*
till forbid	*TF*
till further notice	*TFN*
time base corrector/correction	*TBC*
time-base error	*TBE*
time code	*TC*
time code in picture	*TCIP*
time compressed integration of line colour signals	*TCI-LI*
time compressed integration of luminance and line-sequential colour signals	*TCI-LSI*
time delay spectrometry	*TDS*
time division multiple access	*TDMA*
time division multiplex	*TDM*

time random multiple access	*TRMA*
time-shared, interactive computer-controlled information television	*TICCIT*
time spent viewing	*TSV*
timed frequency modulation	*TFM*
timing chain	*TIC*
timing control unit	*TCU*
timing reference signal and line identification	*TRS-ID*
timing unit	*TU*
title card	*TC*
to be announced	*TBA*
to be determined	*TBD*
Tohoku Broadcasting Co Ltd	TBC
Tokyo Broadcasting System Inc	TBS · JAPAN
Tomiuri Telecasting Corporation	YTV · JAPAN
Toronto Women in Film and Television	TWIFT
torque-motor-driven beam steerer	*TMBS*
total audience	*TA*
total harmonic distortion	*THD*
total prime time	*TPT*
total running tape/time	*TRT*
total story tape	*TST*
total survey area	*TSA*
Totale Cine Video	TCV
tracking and data relay satellite (system)	*TDRS(S)*
Training Film & Video Association	TFVA
Trans World International	TWI
transfer of control	*TC*
transfer orbit stage	*TOS*
transient intermodulation distortion	*TIM*
transient recovery circuit	*TRC*
transistor power amplifier	*TPA*
transistor-transistor logic	*TTL*
transmission control unit	*TCU*
transmitter power output	*TPO*
transverse electromagnetic wave	*TEM*
transverse-junction stripe	*TJS*
Transworld Entertainment	TWE
travelling wave amplifier	*TWA*
travelling wave tube	*TWT*
travelling wave tube amplifier	*TWTA*
Tres Américas Video Home	TVAH
Trinidad & Tobago Television Company	TTT
Trinity Broadcasting Network *(St Kitts)*	TBN
Trinity Broadcasting Network *(USA)*	TBN
triple play	*TP*
trufocus	*TF*
Tulip-TV Inc	TUT
Tun Abdul Razak Broadcasting Training Institute	IPTAR
tuned port infinite baffle	*TPIB*
tuner/demodulator	*TDM*
Turkish Radio and Television Corporation	TRT
Türkiye Radyo Televizyon Kurumu	TRT
Turner Broadcasting System, Inc	TBS · USA
Turner Educational Services	TES

Turner Entertainment Company	TEC
Turner Home Entertainment	THE
Turner Network Television	TNT
Turner Program Services	TPS
tutored video instruction	*TVI*
TV Cartoons	TVC · UK
TV Globo Ltda	TVG · BRAZIL
TV Kampuchean	TVK · CAMBODIA
TV movie	*TVM*
TV Setouchi Broadcasting Co Ltd	TSC
TV Shinshu Broadcasting Co Ltd	TSB
TV-U Fukushima Inc	TUF
TV-U Yamagata Inc	TUY
Twentieth Century Fox Film Corporation	TCF
two pin	*TP*
TXN Kyusyu Co Ltd	TVQ
Tyne Tees Television	TTTV

U

Ukrajinska Telebačennja	UT
Ulster Television plc	UTV
ultra dispersion and durability	*UDD*
ultra high definition television	*UDTV*
ultra high frequency	*UHF*
ultra large-scale integration	*ULSI*
ultra-violet	*UV*
unavailable, on order	*UOO*
uncommitted logic array	*ULA*
unfit for broadcast	*UFB*
uni-junction transistor	*UJ*
Union Cinématographique Africaine	UCINA
Union Circoli Cinematografici Arci Nova	UCCA
Unión de Productores de Cine y Televisión	UPCT
Union des Auteurs, Réalisateurs et Techniciens du Cinéma et de la Télévision	UART
Union des Cinéastes Amateurs Huitistes Mondiaux	UCAHM
Union des Producteurs de Films	UPF
Union des Producteurs de Programmes de Télévision	UPPT
Union des Radiodiffusion Télévisions Nationales d'Afrique	URTNA
Union Européenne de Radio-Télévision	UER
Union Européenne du Spectacle Cinématographique	UESC
Union Fédérale des Associations de Téléspectateurs	UFAT
Union Française des Œuvres Laïques d'Education par l'Image et par le Son	UFOLEIS
Union Française du Film pour l'Enfance et la Jeunesse	UFFEJ
Union Générale Cinématographique	UGC
Unión Internacional de Telecomunicaciones	UIT
Union Internationale des Associations Techniques Cinématographiques	UNIATEC
Union Internationale des Cinémas	UNIC
Union Internationale des Télécommunications	UIT
Union Luxembourgeoise des Producteurs Audiovisuels	ULPA
Union National Syndicale des Cinémas Familiaux	UNSCF
Union Nationale des Cinéastes Burkinabés	UNCB
Union Nationale Inter Ciné-Clubs	UNICC

Union pour le Financement du Cinéma et de l'Audiovisuel	UFCA
Union Syndicale de la Production Audiovisuelle	USPA
Unione Europea dello Spettacolo Cinematografico	UESC
Unione Internazionale dei Cinema	UNIC
Unione Italiana Circolo del Cinema	UICC
Unione Nazionale Autori e Cinetecnici	UNAC
Unione Nazionale Distributori Film	UNDF
Unione Nazionale Esportatori Film e Audiovisivi	UNEFA
Unione Nazionale Industrie Cinetelevisive Specializzate	UNICS
Unione Nazionale Industrie Tecniche Cinetelevisive	UNITC
Unione Nazionale Produttori Film	UNPF
Unione Nazionale Unitaria Professionale Autori Drammatici e Cinematografici	
	UNUPADEC
Unité Fonctionnelle Cinéma Communication Information	UFCCI
United Cable Programmes	UCP
United Cinemas International	UCI
United International Holdings	UIH
United International Pictures	UIP
United Nations Television	UNTV
United Scenic Artists	USA
universal asynchronous receiver	*UAR*
universal asynchronous receiver-transmitter	*UART*
universal decimal classification	*UDC*
universal synchronous/asynchronous receiver-transmitter	*USART*
Universidad Radiofonica y Televisual Internacional	URTI
Universidade Radiofonica e Televisiva Internacional	URTI
Université Radiophonique et Télévisuelle Internationale	URTI
University Film and Video Association	UFVA
University Film and Video Foundation	UFVF
University of California Los Angeles	UCLA
University of Southern California	USC
Up-Front Buying Guide	UFBG
US Environment Film Festival	USEFF
user communications manager	*UCM*

V

V-groove substrate inner stripe	*VSIS*
Valtion audiovisuaalinen keskus	VAVK
variable conductance heat pipe	*VCHP*
variable focal length/lens	*VFL*
variable speed unit	*VSU*
Verband der Filmverleiher	VDF
Verband der Szenenbildner, Filmarchitekten und Kostümbildner	SFK
Verband Deutscher Spielfilmproduzenten	VDS
Verband Schweizerischer Filmgestalter/innen	VSFG
Vereinigung der Rundfunk-, Film- und Fernsehschaffenden	VRFF
Verenigde Audiovisuele Produktiebedrijven	VAP
Verenigde Commercial Producenten	VCP
Vereniging Geschiedenis, Beeld en Geluid	GBG
Vereniging ter Exploitatie van Vertoningsrechten op Audiovisueel Materiaal	VEVAM
Vereniging van Arbeiders-Radio-Amateurs	VARA
Vereniging van Audiovisuele Medewerkers in de Gezondheidszorg	VAMG

Vereniging van Leveranciers van Audio-Visuele Media	VLAM
Veronica Omroep Organisatie	VOO
vertical blanking interval	*VBI*
vertical drive	*VDR*
vertical interface reference signal	*VIRS*
vertical interval cub-carrier	*VISC*
vertical interval/information time code	*VITC*
vertical interval multi-channel audio system	*VIMCAS*
vertical interval reference	*VIR*
vertical interval test signal	*VITS*
vertical metal-oxide-silicon	*VMOS*
vertical radiation pattern	*VRP*
Verwertungsgesellschaft der Film- und Fernsehproduzenten	VFF
Verwertungsgesellschaft Filmschaffende	VFS
Verwertungsgesellschaft für Audiovisuelle Medien	VAM
Verwertungsgesellschaft für Nutzungsrechte an Filmwerken MbH	VGF
very close-up	*VCU*
very high density	*VHD*
very high frequency	*VHF*
very large-scale integration	*VLSI*
very long play	*VLP*
very long shot	*VLS*
very low-angle dolly	*VLAD*
very low frequency	*VLF*
very small aperture terminal	*VSAT*
vestigial sideband	*VSB*
Victor Company of Japan	JVC
Victorian Council for Children's Films and Television Ltd	VCCFT
Videfilm Producers International Ltd	VPI
video-assisted instruction	*VAI*
video-black-video	*VBV*
video, blanking and synchs	*VBS*
video cassette/cartridge recorder	*VCR*
Video Collection International	VCI
Video Copyright Protection Society	VCPS
Video Courses in Industry Unit	VCIU
video data sequence	*VDSQ*
video disc recorder	*VDR*
video display processor	*VDP*
video display terminal	*VDT*
video display unit	*VDU*
video distribution amplifier	*VDA*
video editing terminal	*VET*
Video Editora República	VER
Video Education Centre	VEC
Video Free America	VFA
video frequency	*VF*
video graphics array	*VGA*
video high density	*VHD*
Video Home System	VHS
video index search system	*VISS*
Video Industries Distributors Association	VIDA
video layout terminal	*VLT*
video noise analyzer	*VNA*

video noise reduction	*VNR*
video operator	*VO*
Video Performance Ltd	VPL
Video Professional	VP
video programming by teletext	*VPT*
video recording camera	*VRC*
video signal	*VS*
Video Software Dealers Association	VSDA
video status memory	*VSM*
video tape on line	*VTOL*
video terminal	*VT*
Video Trade Association	VTA
Video Transmission Engineering Advisory Committee	VITEAC
video tuning system	*VTS*
video-video-video	*VVV*
videocassette	*VCS*
videodisc long player	*VLP*
videotape	*VT*
videotape electronic recording apparatus	*VERA*
videotape player	*VTP / VTR*
videotape recorder	*VTR*
videotape recording	*VTR*
videotape recording system	*VTRS*
Vidéotransmission Internationale	VTI
Vietnam Radio and Television	VNRT
Viewers for Quality Television	VQT
viewers per household	*VPH*
viewers per set	*VPS*
Viewers-Per-1000 Viewing Households	VPVH
viewers per viewing household	*V/VH / VPVH*
viewers' consultative council	*VCC*
viewfinder	*VF*
viewfinder information display extension	*VIDEX*
violet, indigo, blue, green, yellow, orange, red	*VIBGYOR*
virtual hardware monitor	*VHM*
virtual reality	*VR*
vision electronic recording apparatus	*VERA*
vision operator	*VO*
vision supervisor	*VS*
Visual Broadcast Services	VBS
visual display unit	*VDU*
visual effects	*VFX*
visual graphics adaptor	*VGA*
visual index search system	*VISS*
visual information processing system	*VIPS*
visual station identification	*VSI*
visual system transmission algorithm	*VISTA*
visually integrated edit workstation	*VIEW*
Vlaamse Audiovisuele Regie	VAR
Vlaamse Televisie Maatschappij	VTM
voice frequency	*VF*
Voice of the Listener and Viewer	VLV
voice-over	*VO*
voice-over credits	*VOC*

volatile random-access memory	VRAM
voltage-controlled amplifier/attenuator	VCA
voltage-controlled oscillator	VCO
voltage-dependent resistor	VDR
voltage standing wave ratio	VSWR
voltage synthesis tuning	VST
voltage-tuned oscillator	VTO
voltampere(s)	VA
volume indicator	VI
volume unit	VU
Vrijzinnig Protestantsche Radio-Omroep	VPRO
Vserossijskaja Gosudarstvennaja Televizionnaja i Radioveschateljnaja Kompanija	VGTRK
Vsesoiuznyi Gosudarstvennyi Institut Kinematografii	VGIK
Vsesojuzny Nauchno-Issledovateljsky Institut Isskusstvoznanija	VNII
Vsesojuzny Nauchno-Issledovateljsky Kinophotoinstitut	NIKFI
Vsesojuzny Nauchnoissledovateljsky Institut Kinoiskusstva	VNIIK
Vsesojuzny Nauchnoissledovateljsky Institut Televidenija i Radioveschanija	VNIITR

W

Wakayama Telecasting Corporation	WTV
Wallonie-Bruxelles Images	WBI · BELGIUM
Wallonie Image Production	WIP
Warner Amex Satellite Entertainment Company	WASEC
Warner Brothers Inc	WB
wave band	WB
wave form monitor	WFM
waveguide	W/G
wavelength	WL
Welzijn, Volksgezondheid en Cultuur	WVC
Werbefunk Saar GmbH	WFS
Werbung in Südwestfunk GmbH	WIS
Westdeutscher Rundfunk Köln	WDR
Westdeutsches Werbfernsehen GmbH	WWF
Western Instructional Television, Inc	WIT
Western International Communications Ltd	WIC · CANADA
white balance	WB
wide angle	WA
wide field acquisition detector	WFD
wide shot	WS
wideband FM	WBFM
wideband videotape recorder	WBVTR
Women Against Media Myths	WAMM
Women in Cable	WIC · USA
Women in Film and Television Inc	WIFT
Women in the Motion Picture Industry	WMPI
Women Make Movies	WMM
Women of the Motion Picture Industry International	WOMPI
Women's Audio Visual Education Scheme	WAVES
Women's Film, Television and Video Network	WFTVN
Women's Media Project	WMP
Women's Media Resource Project	WMRP

Workers Film Association	WFA
workprint	*WP*
World Association for Christian Broadcasting	WACB
World Association for Christian Communication	WACC
World Broadcasting Information	WBI · UK
World Broadcasting Syndication Distribution	WSBD
World International Network	WIN
World Radio and Television Handbook	WRTH
world system teletext	*WST*
World Wide Video Festival	WWVF
Worldwide Entertainment News	WWEN
Worldwide Television-FM DX Association	WTFDA
Worldwide Television News	WTN
write address clock	*WACK*
write OK	*WOK*
write once, read many	*WORM*
Writers' Guild of America East, Inc	WGAE
Writers' Guild of America West, Inc	WGAW
Writers' Guild of Canada	WGC

X

X-carved tablet	*XT*

Y

Yamagata Broadcasting Co Ltd	YBC
Yamagata Television Station	YTS
Yamaguchi Broadcasting Co Ltd	KRY
Yamanashi Broadcasting System	YBS
Yamashita Engineering Manufacture Inc	YEM
Yayasan Televisi Republik Indonesia	TVRI
yellow cyan magenta	*YCM*
Yorkshire Television	YTV · UK

Z

Zambia National Broadcasting Corporation	ZNBC
Zentraleinrichtung für AV-Medien	ZEAM
Zentrum für Neue Medien	ZNM
zero insertion force	*ZIF*
Zimbabwe Broadcasting Corporation	ZBC
Zimbabwe Film and Video Association	ZFVA
Zimbabwe Film, Television and Allied Workers Union	ZIFTAWU
Ziz Radio and Television (St Kitts and Nevis)	RTZIZ / ZIZRT
zoom back	*ZB*
zoom in	*ZI*
zoom out	*ZO*
Zweites Deutsches Fernsehen	ZDF

Country Index

This index lists all acronyms, excluding technical terms, by their country of origin. In many cases identical acronyms originate from different countries; in rare cases identical acronyms originate from one country.

Afghanistan
RTA

African continent
AWIFAV
see separate countries

Albania
RTSH

Algeria
CSA
ENTV
RTA

Angola
EDECINE
IAC
TPA

Antigua and Barbuda
ABBS
ABS

Argentina
ATA
ATC
AVH
AVIA
CERC
IAC
SAC
TELEFE
TVAH
VER

Australia
ABA
ABC
ABCB
ABT
ACCFT

ACTAC
ACTF
AFC
AFCBS
AFFC
AFFC
AFFM
AFI
AFTRS
AFTS
ANTC
ASDA
ATOM
AVDAA
CAAMA
FAACS
FACB
FACTS
FFC
HACBSS
HACBUS
MIA
NFSA
NSWFTO
PBAA
RCTS
SAFC
SBS
SPAA
SWIFT
TCN
VCCFT
WIFT

Austria
HFMDK
OGFKM
ÖFF
ORF
VAM
VFS

Bahamas
BCB

Bangladesh
BNBA
BTV
NBA
NBAB
NIMC
NIMCO

Barbados
CABC
CBC
CBU

Belgium
AAV
AEEMA
AEFA
AGFA-
  Gevaert
AID
AIDAA
AMC
APEC
BRT
BRTN
CARTOON
CBA
CIAVER
CIDC
CILECT
CIRTEF
CLAV
CNC
COST
CPBC
CRAC
DAVID
DELTA
EAFF
EAVE
ECCA
EGTA
ENSAV
ESPRIT
ESTA

EUREKA
EUROAIM
EUROVIP
EVA
FACINEB
FEMI
FERA
FET
FIAF
GRAD
HITCS
HRITCS
IAD
IAVS
IEE
IFFA
IHECS
IMART
INRACI
INSAS
LENTIC
MCFB
MCS
MEDIA
NARAFI
OCIC
RACE
RIRECA
RITCS
RMB
RTA
RTBF
SEE
SHIVKV
SVF
TVCF
TVI
UESC
UPPT
VAR
VTM
WBI
WIP

Belize
BCB

Benin
BTV
ORTB

Bosnia-Hercegovina
RTSA
RTV
RTVSA

Brazil
ABERT
ABEVC
FCB
FLAPF
SBT
TVG

Brunei Darussalam
RTB

Bulgaria
BT
BTV

Burkina Faso
CERAV
CNCB
DIPROCI
FEPACI
FESPACO
SONACIB
UNCB

Burundi
RTNB

Cambodia
CTV
TVK

Cameroon
CRTV
FODIC

Canada
ACFC
ACPFT
ACTC
ACTRA
ACTRF
ADISQ
ADRC
AIFVA
AMPDC
AMPIA
APCQ
APFTQ
APFVQ
APVQ
AQCC
AQEC
AQRRCT
ATEC
BBC
BCMPA
CAB
CAMPP
CAVCO
CBC
CBRA
CCA
CCAVT
CCC
CCTA
CFDC
CFMDC
CFMT
CFTPA
CIFC
CIS
CMPDA
CRC
CRRA
CRTC
CSC
CTQC
CTSDF
CTV
CWRT
DGC
EPS
FAVA
FSAC
FUND
FVSO
IBC
IDERA (Film
  & Video)

IFAVA
IFCO
LIFT
MCTV
MHTVF
MISA
MMPIA
MPFC
NANBA
NCATA
NCTI
NFB
NFBC
NSC
NSFDC
OFA
OFDC
ONF
POV
RDS
RDTVQ
SCN
SMPIA
SNTC
SOGIC
SRC
STCVQ
TQS
TSN
TVNC
TVO
TWIFT
WGC
WIC

Cape Verde
TNCV

Chile
TNC

China
BBI
CCTV

Colombia
ACCO
ACOCINE
ANALTRA-
  RADIO
FOCINE
INRAVISION
SICOLTRA-
  CINE

Congo
ONACI

Cook Islands
CIBC

Costa Rica
CANAMECC
SINART

Croatia
HRT
HRTV
HTV
OTV

Cuba
CIC
EICTV
ICAIC

Cyprus
BRTK
CBC
CYBC

**Czech
Republic**
ČST
ČSTV
FAMU
FITES
IBTO
IRTO
KF
OIRT
SPF

Denmark
AVM
DFI
DMC
DR
FDA
FDS
IVENS
NAFA
SFC
SMID

Djibouti
RTD

Ecuador
IETEL

Egypt
ASBU
ERTU

El Salvador
ANTEL

Finland
COFFP
FFF
MTV
SAVC
TTV
VAVK

France
A2
AAVS
ACA
ACFEA
ACIC
ACPCA
ACRIF
ADACOM
ADETE
ADICIEL
ADRC
AFC
AFCA
AFCAB
AFCAE
AFDAS
AFICCA
AFIFF
AFIT
AFNOR
AFOMAV
AFPF
AFRHC
AITV
ALAI
ALPA
AMI
ANADET
ANGOA
ANTEA
ANTEA
APCEIS
APDS
API
APRAC

APRICA
ARAS
ARAV
ARP
ARTE
ARTER
ASE
ATM
AUDECAM
AVCP
AVUP
BILIFA
BLEC
BLIC
CAPAC
CAPRICAS
CARCICAS
CCETT
CDMM
CEIS
CEPI
CERIS
CFEJ
CFG
CFI
CGVT
CIAVU
CIC
CICA
CICAE
CICCE
CICT
CICV
CIDALC
CIDECCA
CIE
CIFEJ
CIITC
CIOAPDS
CIRCA
CIRCAV
CLCF
CMCA
CNAP
CNC
CNCL
CNPA
CNSAD
COFECIC
COSIP
CRCC
CREATIS
CRECA
CRETE

CRMC
CSA
CSEA
CSI
CSPEFF
CST
ECPA
ECTO
ECTVY
EFET
EMG
ENLL
ENSAD
ESA
ESCA
ESCO
ESCOMA
ESEC
ESRA
ESTCA
ETPA
EUTELSAT
EVS
FCFC
FCR
FEITIS
FEMIS
FIAD
FIAPF
FIDES
FIFA
FIFARC
FIFEJ
FIFI
FIFREC
FIPA
FIPFI
FISTAV
FITCA
FLEC
FMI
FNDF
FNITCA
FPF
FR3
FRC
GACSO
GEECT
GEEMAC
GEFCA
GEHRA
GIA
GPSMVAV
GREC

GREC
GRESEC
GRISS
HA
HACA
HDTP
IBF
IBFG
ICAF
ICFCYP
ICS
IDA
IDATE
IDEA
IDHECOM
IDM
IFCA
IFCG
IFCIC
IFFPA
IFPIA
IFTC
IIIS
IMAC
INA
IPDC
IPG
IRCAV
IRTU
ISEC
ISFA
ISIC
MAP TV
MCAC
MIDEM
MIFA
MIP
MIP-TV
MIPCOM
MTT
NEF
OFRT
PROGEFI
RFI
RFO
RTEA
S2PA
SAE
SATIS
SCARE
SEPT
SFA
SFP
SFSIC

SIIS
SIMAVELEC
SIS
SISCOMS
SITI
SNC
SNTPCAT
SNTPCT
SNTR
SOFRATEV
SOPACIA
SPFP
SPPA
SRCTA
SRF
TDF
TDI
TF1
TLM
TLT
UART
UCAHM
UFAT
UFCA
UFCCI
UFFEJ
UFOLEIS
UGC
UNIATEC
UNIC
UNICC
UNSCF
UPF
URTI
USPA
VTI

Fuji
FNVC

Gabon
ACG
CAC
CENACI
RTG

Germany
AFF
AGFA-
  Gevaert
AKM
ARD
ARRI
AVMZ

AWF
BDF
BDFA
BFF
BFS
BHDTV
BJF
BKS
BR
BRW
BTS
BVDFP
CAMECO
CDFM
DFA
DFFB
DGMG
DIFF
DIN
DIZ
DSF
DW
ECA
ECCO
EDI
EFA
EFDO
EIM
EZEF
FBW
FES
FFA
FIPRESCI
FKTG
FSK
FWU
GRECO
GÜFA
GWFF
HBI
HDF
HFF
HFF
HR
IMD
IMM
INM
IRT
IWF
IZI
JFF
KJF
LFM
MDR

MITV
MTC
NDR
NFV
RB
RTM
SFB
SFK
SR
SWF
UFITA
VDF
VDS
VFF
VGF
VRFF
WBF
WDR
WFS
WIS
WWF
ZDF
ZEAM

Ghana
GBC

Gibraltar
GIBBC

Greece
ERT
ET
GFC
KEA

Greenland
KNR TV

Guinea
RTG

Guyana
GBC
GUYBC

Haiti
CONATEL

Hong Kong
ATV
EFS
RTHK
STAR TV

TVB

Hungary
MIT
MOVI
MTV
SZDSZ

Iceland
IFF
RÚV
SÍK

India
ATN
BIFF
DDI
FTII
FTTI
IFFI
KSFDC
NFDC

Indonesia
AMPPA
IKJ
RCTI
SCTV
TPI
TVRI

Iran
FCF
ICDB
IRIB

Iraq
IBTE

Ireland
EVE
FIFS
FII
IFC
IFI
IRTC
RTE

Israel
IBA
ICTV
IETV
JCC

Italy
ABE
ABS
ACEC
ACT
ACTA
AGIS
AIACE
AIC
AICC
AICCA
AICP
AIDAC
AILS
AIMC
AISCA
AITC
AITS
ANCCI
ANDTA
ANEC
ANICA
ANIPA
ANSEOC
ANTI
AOCI
APD
APICE
ATIC
CCC
CCC
CCR
CCTV
CDA
CDI
CECS
CGS
CIAC
CICT
CINIT
CISAS
CLCT
CRC
CSC
CSC
CSCTV
CTA
CTC
CTV
DARC
DIFI
DPT
EAGC
FAC

FAPAV
FAVAV
FEDIC
FIAIS
FIC
FICC
FICE
FICTS
FILIS
FNC
FRT
ICEC
ISCA
MICS
MIFED
PAC
PAC
RAI
RAS
RTI
SACIS
SAI
SIAE
SNCCI
SNGCI
TCV
TEM
UCCA
UICC
UNAC
UNDF
UNEFA
UNICS
UNITC
UNPF
UNUPADEC
WSBD

Ivory Coast
CNC
INSET
RTI

Jamaica
CARIMAC
JBC

Japan
AAB
ABA
ABC
ABN
ABS
AKT

ANB
ATV
BBC
BPCJ
BSN
BSS
CBC
CTC
CTV
EBC
EIAJ
FBC
FBS
FCT
FICCS
FTB
FTV
GBS
GTV
HAB
HBC
HBF
HTB
HTV
IBC
ITC
ITV
JAMCO
JRT
JSB
JSV
JVC
KAB
KBC
KBS
KIIFF
KKB
KKT
KNB
KRY
KSB
KTN
KTS
KTV
KUTV
MBC
MBS
MICO
MIT
MRT
MTV
NAB
NBC
NBN

NBS
NCC
NHK
NIB
NKT
NST
NT-21
NTV
OBS
OHK
OTV
PBA
RBC
RCC
RKB
RKC
RKK
RNB
RNC
RSK
SBC
SBS
SDT
SKT
STS
STV
SUN
TBC
TBS
THK
TKU
TNC
TNN
TOS
TSB
TSC
TSK
TSS
TUF
TUT
TUY
TVA
TVH
TVI
TVK
TVN
TVO
TVQ
TVS
TYS
UMK
WTV
YBC
YBS

YEM	**Madagascar**	**Mozambique**	SMMO	NAFDEC
YTS	RTM	INC	SOURCES	PFPA
YTV		TVE	STER	PTV
	Malaysia		SWOM	
Jordan	ABU	**Myanmar**	TROS	**Panama**
JRTV	AIBD	MTVRD	VAMG	SCN
	FINAS		VAP	
Kenya	IPTAR	**Namibia**	VARA	**Peru**
KBC	PPFM	NAMBC	VCP	CLACPI
KIMC	RTM	NBC	VEC	RTP
URTNA		SWABC	VEVAM	
	Mali		VLAM	**The**
Korea	CNPC	**The**	VOO	**Philippines**
CBSK	OCINAM	**Netherlands**	VPRO	KBP
IBS	SCINFOMA	AFN	WRTH	
KBI		AIERI	WVC	**Poland**
KBS	**Malta**	AVRO	WWVF	PRT
MBC	MBA	BOOS		PSFN
SBS		CAWO	**New Zealand**	PWSFTVIT
	Martinique	COBO	CTV	
Kuwait	CFVF	COM	IAFF	**Portugal**
KTV		DIFA	NFU	ACTING
	Mauritania	EAFA	NZFC	APRFP
Laos	ORTM	EO	TVNZ	COL
LCTV		GBG		ETC
	Mauritius	GNS	**Nicaragua**	FPCA
Latvia	MABC	IAMCR	SNTV	GER
LTV	MBC	IAMS		IPC
		IDFA	**Niger**	RTC
Lebanon	**Mexico**	IKON	ORTN	RTP
TL	AMFI	IVF		SCALE
	ASTISA	KNF	**Nigeria**	SIARTE
Lesotho	CCC	KRO	ABS-TV	SIC
LNBS	COTSA	MEMO	BCOS	SNA
LTV	CUEC	NBB	BRTV	SPCV
	DICINE	NBF	LTV	SPSS
Libya	IMCINE	NCRV	NTA	TVI
LJB	IMEVISION	NFC	ODTV	
PRBC	OIT	NFTVA	OGTV	**Qatar**
	OTI	NIAM	OSRC	QTV
Luxembourg	STIC	NIS	OSTV	
CLT	STPC	NOB		**Romania**
CNA		NOS	**Norway**	RTR
IVIA	**Monaco**	NOT	ASIFA	RTV
PAL	TMC	NVPI	KKL	RTVR
RTL		OLON	NAMC	
SES	**Mongolia**	OMI	NFF	**Russia**
ULPA	MRTV	OTP	NFK	CT
		RNTC	NFVPF	KIWI
Macao	**Montenegro**	RNTV	NKFF	LIKI
TDM	RTVCG	ROOS	NRK	MIBC
		SAM	SSFF	NIKFI
Macedonia	**Morocco**	SAVE		OK
MRTV	CCM	SEKAM	**Pakistan**	RGTRK
TVSK	RTM	SFW-AVA	CBFC	RMTK

- 324 -

RTO
RTV
SPTV
TVP
VGIK
VGTRK
VNII
VNIIK
VNIITR

**São Tomé
and Principe**
CST

Saudi Arabia
ISBO

Senegal
ACS
ASSECCI
CCA
CESTI
CIDC
CINESEAS
CNA
FAMW
ORTS
SIDEC
SNPC
UCINA

Serbia
BONAC
JRT
RTB
RTP
RTVB
RTVNS
RTVP
TVB

Seychelles
RTS
SBC
SEYBC

Sierra Leone
SLBS

Singapore
SBC
SIFF

Slovakia
ST

STV

Slovenia
RTL
TVS

**Solomon
Islands**
SIBC

Somalia
MOGPAAFIS
MOGPAFIS

South Africa
AFTC
CFVF
CIFF
CPA
CVS
FAWO
FMA
NTVA
PAWE
SABC
SAFTI
SAFTTA
SAFVI
SASC
SASWA
SAUK

Spain
ACPC
ADICAN
ADIVAN
AFYVE
AIPV
ANDICCA
ANEPA
AVE
CCRTV
CEV
CRTG
CRTVG
EFFAM
EITB
ETB
FAP
FIAT
FORTA
IBFPA
ICAA
IFTA
IORTV

MBS
OJD
PILOTS
RTVA
RTVE
RTVM
SAV
TVC
TVE
TVG
TVV
UPCT
VP

Sri Lanka
NFC
SLBC
SLRC

St Kitts
RTZIZ
TBN
ZIZRT

St Lucia
HTS

**St Vincent
and the
Grenadines**
SVG TV

Suriname
ATN
ATV
STVS

Swaziland
STVA

Sweden
BUFF
IAWRT
OFF
SBC
SF
SFI
SFP
SI
SVIP
SVT

Switzerland
AAV
ACRIRA

ACS
ACSR
AETC
AGICOA
AIVAC
ARC
ASDF
ASED
ASJC
ASRF
ASTF
BABEL
BDT
BECT
CCIR
CCITT
CISA
CTD
DRS
EBC
EBU
EGAKU
ESAV
FCA
FFD
FICC
FIFAL
FIFART
FIFEL
FOCAL
FTB
GSFA
IFFS
IFRB
ISETU
ISO
ITC
ITS
ITU
MAZ
MFB
RTSI
RTSR
SBC
SDF
SFTV
SFV
SIV
SKV
SRG
SSA
SSR
SSR
STFG
SVFJ

SVKF
TSI
TSR
UER
UIT
VSFG
ZNM

Taiwan
BCC
CMPC
CTS
CTV
TTV

Thailand
BBTV
IBC
TST
TVIC
TVT

Togo
RTNM
TVT

**Trinidad and
Tobago**
TTT

Tunisia
JCC
RTT
SATPEC

Turkey
ART
IFA
SESAM
TRT

Uganda
RU/UTV

Ukraine
UT

**United
Kingdom**
ABW
ACLB
ACTT
ADAPT
AEEU-EETPU
AFVM

AFVPA	CAA	FACT	JSTV	PBME
AIC	CACLB	FAME	KETV	PCP
AIM	CADA	FBU	KFM	PCR
ALTO	CARM	FEU	KWM	PDO
AME	CAVIAR	FFD	LAIFA	PETAR
AMES	CBA	FFI	LCM	QFT
AMFIT	CBP	FIA	LFF	Register-
APRS	CC	FOCAL	LFMC	MEAL
ART	CEA	FSU	LFVDA	RETRA
ATM	CED	FTT	LIFS	RIPTA
AVA	CES	FTTV	LLTV	RITE
AVA	CET	GBA	LMW	RPTA
AVLS	CEVMA	GBCT	LSW	RTI
BAC TV	CFL	GBFE	LVA	RTS
BAFC	CFTC	GFPAFA	LWT	S4C
BAFTA	CFTF	GFPE	MAC	SAWA
BARB	CFU	GFVL	MBC	SBC
BATC	CGGB	GLT	MCPS	SCET
BAVA	CMCR	GMTV	MEAL	SCTE
BBC	COLT	GOLT	MEFW	SFA
BBC-WSTV	CPBF	GSE	MENU	SFC
BBFC	CT	GTC	MFVPA	SFD
BBFC	CTA	GVG	MHMC	SIFT
BCC	CTA	HEFVL	MITES	SIS
BCTV	CTBF	HVC	MOMI	SMO
BECTU	CTE	IABM	MUTV	SOBA
BETA	CTG	IAC	NAHBO	SSL
BFB	CTV	IAC	NAHEFV	SSVC
BFC	CTVC	IBA	NAVL	STV
BFDG	CV	IBC	NEMTC	SWB
BFFS	D&AD	IBE	NETFA	TAC
BFI	DBA	IBS	NFA	TAS
BFTPA	Television	IBT	NFDF	TBI
BIMA	DBC	ICS	NFFC	TEAME
BISFA	DC	ICSADFF	NFT	TFVA
BKSTS	DGGB	IEE	NFTC	TPA
BMTT	EAFA	IFDA	NFTS	TRIC
BPG	EBC(NI)	IFG	NFTVA	TSL
BREMA	EBC(UK)	IFPA	NMFE	TTTV
BRU	EBCS	IFPI	NMM	TUG
BSAC	ECC	IIC	NOW	TVC
BSB	ECF	INFRAME	NSC	TVE
BSC	EETPU	IPPA	NSFTV	TWI
BSC	EFTSC	ISBA	NTL	UCI
BSD	EIEM	ITC	NVALA	UIP
BSF	EIFF	ITEL	NVASP	UTV
BSKYB	EITF	ITN	NVLA	VBS
BSS	ELT	ITSC	NWFA	VCI
BUFVC	EMFV	ITV	OIV	VCIU
BVA	EMMA	ITVA	ONI	VCPS
BVE	EPPG	IUHFC	OSF	VLV
BVHT	ERA	IVCA	OU	VPL
BVTV	ETA	IWM	OUPC	VTA
C4	ETV	JFF	OXTV	WACC
CA	FAA	JICTAR	PACT	WAMM

WAVES	AIMS	BFC/NCC	CSL	IAIP
WBI	AIR	BFI	CTAB	IAMHIST
WFA	AIT	BIB	CTAC	IAS
WMRP	AITS	BINA	CTAM	IASUS
WTN	AIVF	BMI	CTIC	IATSE
WWEN	AMC	BP	CTM	IAV
YTV	AMC	BP	CTW	IBEW
	AMIA	BPEF	CUFC	IBFM
United States	AMOL	BPL	CVCCC	IBS
of America	AMPAS	BPME	CWA	ICEA
A&E	AMPEC	BRC	DBSA	ICIA
AAAA	AMPTP	BTRE	DFA	ICM
AACTO	AMST	BTS	DGA	ICN
AAPTS	AMST	BTSC	DIFF	ICNATVAS
ABC	ANSI	C-SPAN	DWW	IDA
ABMPTP	APB	CAA	EBS	IEEE
ACATS	APTPA	CAB	EBS	IERT
ACBB	APTS	CAF	EDI	IFE
ACE	AR&D	CARA	EEN	IFEX
ACE	ART	CARTA	EFLA	IFFM
ACN	ARTNA	CATA	EIA	IFIDA
ACN	ARTS	CBA	EIC	IFM
ACN	ASA	CBC	EMRC	IFP
ACSN	ASC	CBI	ERI	IFP/West
ACSN	ASFA	CBN	ESPN	IFPA
ACT	ASFFHF	CBS	ETRAC	IFPA
ACT	ASI	CCA	ETS	IMPALA
ACT	ASTA	CCC/UN	EVN	INPUT
ACTRS	ASTVC	CCFC	EWTN	INTELSAT
ACTS	AT&T	CCT	F/VA	INTV
ACTS	ATAS	CCTI	FACS	IPMPI
ACTS	ATC	CCTM	FCC	IQ
ACUBS	ATFP	CCTMA	FCI	IRTF
ACVL	ATS	CEDIA	FIM	IRTS
AEA	ATS	CFC	FIT	ISV
AEG	ATSC	CFDA	FIVF	ITA
AEJMC	ATTC	CFI	FMPP	ITBC
AERT	AVA	CFTCA	FNN	ITC
AES	AVA	CHN	FNN	ITC
AFA	AVS	CIC	GACC	ITNA
AFBA	AWRT	CICFF	GPNITL	ITO
AFCF	BAPSA	CINE	HAU	ITS
AFI	BAR	CLEARTV	HBO	ITVA
AFM	BAVC	CMT	HFFS	ITVS
AFMA	BBB	CNAD	HFFS	JCFC
AFN	BBM	CNBC	HJT	KET
AFRTS	BCCA	CNN	HRTS	L/FQ
AFTRA	BCFM	COLTAM	HSN	LEG
AFTS	BCFMA	COMPACT	HTN	LVPI
AFVA	BDA	COMPO	HTR	MADC
AGMA	BEA	CONTAM	HUT	MAP
AGVA	BERC	COST	IA	MAS
AICE	BEST	CPB	IAAB	MCA
AICP	BET	CPT	IABM	META
AIM	BFA	CSCC	IAFS	MGM

MHFB	NCT	RTRC	TPEA	VNRT
MHI	NCTA	SAG	TPIB	
MMG	NCTI	SAMP	TPS	**Zaïre**
MPAA	NCTV	SBCA	TPV	OZACI
MPEA	NEFVF	SBE	TTC	OZRT
MPEAA	NEMA	SBS	TVB	
MPMO	NFLCP	SCA	TWE	**Zambia**
MPRF	NHI	SCG	TWG	ZNBC
MPTCA	NHTI	SCS	UCLA	
MSN	NITA	SCTE	UCP	**Zimbabwe**
MST	NITC	SDG	UFBG	ZBC
MTM	NPACT	SDIG	UFVA	ZFVA
MTV	NPITI	SEG	UFVF	ZIFTAWU
NAATA	NPPAG	SEP	UIH	
NAB	NPS	SEPC	UNTV	
NABB	NRB	SIFF	USA	
NABET	NSI	SIMPP	USC	
NABOB	NSS	SIN	USEFF	
NABTFP	NSTP	SMARTS	VFA	
NABUG	NTC	SMPTAD	VIDA	
NAC	NTFC	SMPTE	VITEAC	
NACB	NTFDC	SMS	VPI	
NACMA	NTI®	SNC	VPVH	
NACP	NVC	SPFM	VQT	
NAD	NVR	SPIE	VSDA	
NAEB	OCST	SPN	WACB	
NAET	ODC	SRG	WASEC	
NAFB	OEC	STA	WB	
NAITPD	OPT	STIA	WGAE	
NAMW	PACCT	STOC-TV	WGAW	
NAPA	PACT	STS	WIC	
NAPLPS	PAF	STVRC	WIN	
NAPTS	PARA	SWG	WIT	
NAR	PBS	T&SG	WMM	
NARBA	PFVEA	TACET	WMP	
NARUC	PFWC	TACOMA	WMPI	
NASCA	PGA	TAMI	WOMPI	
NATAS	PIVN	TARPAC	WTFDA	
NATESA	PKA	TASO		
NATO	PMPEA	TBA	**Uruguay**	
NATOA	PRC	TBN	AIR	
NATPE	PSG	TBS	ANDEBU	
NATRA	PSNI	TCA	IAB	
NATVAS	PSSC	TCF	SODRE	
NAVD	PTI	TCI		
NBC	PTL	TEC	**Vanuatu**	
NBMC	PTOA	TEC	PIBA	
NCAR	PTR	TEG		
NCCB	QRFV	TES	**Venezuela**	
NCFDITFS	RCA	THE	CACI	
NCFT	RKO	THR	FONCINE	
NCI	RTCA	TIO	RCTV	
NCN	RTDG	TLC	TAM	
NCORT	RTES	TMC		
NCSCT	RTNDA	TNT	**Vietnam**	

Subject/Theme Index

This is a *selective* index by subject and theme. It does not include entries for "film", "broadcasting", "documentary", "television" etc., since this would have created unnecessarily large and unmanageable entries. Technical terms have not been included in this index.

COLTAM
CONTAM
GEAR
HTR
JICTAR
NAD
NCAR
NSI
NSS
NTI
PBS
PETAR
PTR
UFBG

avant-garde
see experimental

black issues
racism
ABMPTP
ABW
AFTC
BAFC
BCFM
BEST
BET
BFB
BMTT
BVTV
CARM
CPBF
CVS
NABOB
NABTFP
NBMC

captioning
see dubbing

Catholicism
ACEC
ACTRS
CAMECO
CARTA
CCC · ITALY
CCTV · ITALY
CTV · ITALY
KRO
NCORT
OCIC

censorship
BBFC
CBFC
CPBF

children
youth
ACCFT
ACT · USA
ACTAC
ACTF
AME
BAC TV
BOOS
BUFF
CC
CCFC
CCR
CCTI
CCTM
CFTCA
CFTF
CFU
CICFF
CIFEJ
CTW
DFI
DIFF · USA
FIFEJ
ICFCYP
IZI
JFF · GERMANY
KETV
KJF
LMW
MPFC
NKFF
NPS
PACT · USA
PBS
VCCFT

Christianity
ACLB
ACTS
BBB
BFC/NCC
CACLB
CAMECO
CBN
CBSK
CEVMA
CFDA

CLEARTV
CTM
EO
EZEF
NCN
NCRV
THK
VPRO
WACB
WACC

cinematography
ACCO
AFVM
AIC · ITALY
ASC
ASTVC
BSC
CSC · CANADA
IAC · UK
SASC
VFS

complaints
BCC
BSC

conferences
meetings
seminars
AME
CACI
CICA
CICFF
ECC
ECCO
EFFAM
EFTSC
EIEM
FIFREC
FOCAL ·
    SWITZERLAND
GEHRA
IBC · UK
ICSADFF
IDFA
IEEE
ITSC
IUHFC
MBS · SPAIN
MITES
NATO
NEFVF

PBME
SSFF

conventions
see conferences

copyright
intellectual
    property
piracy
royalties
ADRC · CANADA
AFVPA
AFYVE
AGICOA
ALPA
ANICA
BMI
CBRA
CCAVT
CCC · CANADA
CRC · CANADA
CRRA
FACT
FAP
FAPAV
FAVAV
FVSO
GÜFA
GWFF
IFPI
MCPS
MFVPA
NFDC
SCA
SIAE
TFVA
VCPS
VEVAM
VFF
VGF

critics
journalists
ACTRA
APB
AQCC
ASJC
ASSECCI
BPG
CCC/UN
CESTI
CISAS

USC
VAVK
VCIU
VEC
VGIK
WAVES
WBF
WFA
ZEAM
ZNM

electronic art
EVS
HBI
IDEA
WWVF

engineering
AAVS
AES
AEEU-EETPU
BTRE
BTS
IBE
IEE
IEEE
IRT
IWF
PBS
SBE
SCTE · UK
SCTE · USA
SEE
SMPTE
SPIE
VCIU
YEM

environment
nature
wildlife
BSS
CLCT
FIFARC
IWF
OSF
MAP
NPS
PBS
PTI
TVE · UK
USEFF
WTN

exhibitions
see conferences

experimental
avant-garde
AIACE
ARTE
BAFTA
C4
CERC
FIFREC
LFMC
MOMI
TVE ·
    MOZAMBIQUE

feminism
see women's
issues

festivals
AFCAB
AFIFF
BIFF
BUFF
CICA
CICFF
CLACPI
DIFF · USA
EIFF
EITF
FESPACO
FICCS
FIFA
FIFI
FIFAL
FIFARC
FIFART
FIFEJ
FIFEL
FIFREC
FIPA
FNC
IAFF
ICSADFF
IDFA
IFFI
JCC · TUNISIA
JFF · UK
KIIFF
LFF
MOGPAAFIS
NEFVF

PFWC
SIFF · SINGAPORE
SIFF · USA
USEFF
WWVF

film schools
see education

film societies
BFFS
FICC ·
    SWITZERLAND
FIFS
FSU
GACSO
IFFS
NFK
WFA

HDTV
ACATS
ATM · UK
BHDTV
EUREKA
HDTP

health
medical
AWF
BSS
CHN
CNN
EMFV
IAMS
IMART
IWF
MHFB
MHMC
NAHBO
VAMG
WTN

history
AFRHC
AIC · ITALY
BVHT
CTA · UK
DGMG
FIAF
FIFA
GBG
GEHRA

IAMHIST
IUHFC
IWM
MOMI
NFTVA · UK
NIS
SFC · UK
SFW-AVA
URTI
WBF
WIT

independent
film-making
ACPFT
AFMA
AICP · USA
AIFVA
AIPV
AIVF
AMPIA
ANICA
APICE
AVA · UK
BAVC
BDF
CCAVT
CFMDC
CFTPA
CIFC
CIFC
CIFF
CRC · CANADA
DIFA
DIFF
EAVE
EMG
EUROAIM
EUROVIP
FAVA
FIPFI
FIVF
FORTA
GRECO
IAIP
IFAVA
IFCO
IFDA
IFEX
IFFM
IFP
IFP/West
IFPA · USA

L/FQ
LMW
LSW
MEDIA
NSFTV
PILOTS
SASWA
SOURCES
SSA
SVF
SWG
T&SG
TWG
UART
UCCA
UFITA
UNAC
UNUPADEC
USPA
WGAE
WGAW
WGC

sculpture
see art

seminars
see conferences

sound
AES
AISCA
AITS · ITALY
APRS
BKSTS
CCIR
CCITT
CTA · ITALY
EFET
ESRA
ESTCA
ETPA
FIAIS
GBC · GHANA
GBFE
IABM · UK
IAD
IBS · UK
IFPI
IIIS
INA
MISA
NFSA

SATIS
SFW-AVA
SIIS

sport
BET
CNN
CSL
DSF
ESPN
FICTS
JSV
KWM
ORF
RDS
TNT
TSN
TWI
WTN

subtitling
see dubbing

symposia
see workshops

wildlife
see environment

women's issues
feminism
AFIFF
AWIFAV
AWRT
CISAS
CWRT
DWW
FAMW
IAWRT
KIWI
MHMC
NAMW
SWIFT
TWIFT
WAMM
WAVES
WFTVN
WIC · USA
WIFT
WMM
WMP
WMPI
WMRP

WOMPI

workshops
symposia
ABW
ASIFA
CICA
DWW
IDFA
IFCO
ITS · SWITZERLAND
KETV
LMW
LSW
MOGPAAFIS
NEFVF
NOW
SASWA
SOURCES
SSFF

writing
see scriptwriting

youth
see children

Bibliography

The following bibliography represents a list of the most useful publications consulted for the research for this book. In addition, numerous technical brochures, leaflets and booklets from manufacturers and suppliers, as well as some 100 trade magazines, journals and newsletters, were scanned.

Annuaire des Membres de 1992 /
Membership Directory 1992
Ontario: Film Studies Association of
Canada/Association Québécoise des
Etudes Cinématographiques, 1992.

Annuaire du Cinéma Télévision Vidéo
1992
44th edition
Paris: Editions Bellefaye, 1992.

Annuario del Cinema Italiano 1989-90
Edited by Alessandro Ferraù
Rome: Centro studi di cultura
promozione e diffusione del cinema,
1989.

Aries, S J
Dictionary of Telecommunications
London; Boston: Butterworths, 1981.

L'Association des Trois Mondes
Dictionnaire du Cinéma Africain
Paris: Editions Karthala, 1991.

Barnouw, Erik
Tube of Plenty: The Evolution of
American Television
2nd revised edition
New York; Oxford: Oxford University
Press, 1990.

Bayard-White, Claire and Signe Hoffos
Interactive Video: Introduction and
Handbook
London: National Interactive Video
Centre, 1988.

Beaver, Frank E
Dictionary of Film Terms
New York: McGraw-Hill, 1983.

Benn's Media 1993
Tonbridge, Kent: Benn Business
Information Services, 1993.

Benson, K Blair and Jerry Whitaker
Television and Audio Handbook: for
Technicians and Engineers
New York: McGraw-Hill Publishing
Company, 1990.

Both, C J
The World's Radio Broadcasting
Stations and European FM/TV
Weesp: De Muiderkring, 1989.

The British Council
Directory of International Film and
Video Festivals 1993 and 1994
London: The British Council, 1993.

British Film Institute Yearbook 1993
Edited by David Leafe
London: British Film Institute, 1992.

British National Space Centre
Space News Bulletin
London: BNSC, Winter/Spring 1993.

The Broadcast Communications
Dictionary
Edited by Lincoln Diamant
New York: Hastings House Publishers,
1974.

Broadcasting Terms and Abbreviations
2nd edition
Basingstoke: Sony Broadcast &
Communications (Training and
Engineering Information Department),
1991.

Brown, Les
Les Brown's Encyclopedia of Television
3rd edition
Detroit; London: Gale Research, 1992.

Browne, Steven E
Film, Video: Terms and Concepts
Boston; London: Focal Press, 1992.

Browne, Steven E
Videotape Editing: A Postproduction
Primer
Boston; London: Focal Press, 1989.

The BUFVC Handbook for Film &
Television in Education 1991/92
London: British Universities Film and
Video Council, 1991.

Buttress, F A
World Guide to Abbreviations of
Organizations
9th edition; revised by H J Heaney
Glasgow; London: Blackie, 1991.

Cable and Satellite Yearbook 1992
London: 21st Century Publishing, 1992.

The CFTPA/ACPFT Guide 1993
Toronto: Canadian Film and Television
Production Association/Association
Canadienne de Production de Film et
Télévision, 1993.

CinémAction
L'enseignement du cinéma et de
l'audiovisuel dans l'Europe des douze
Paris: INRP-Corlet-Télérama-CEE, 1991.

Commonwealth Broadcasting
Association Handbook 1993/94
London: Commonwealth Broadcasting
Association, 1993.

Corporation for Public Broadcasting
Annual Report 1992
Washington: CPB, 1993.

Council of Europe activities in the
media field [DH-MM (91) 3]

Strasbourg: Conseil de l'Europe/Council
of Europe, 1991.

Councils, Committees & Boards: A
handbook of advisory, consultative,
executive and similar bodies in British
public life
7th edition
Edited by Lindsay Sellar
Beckenham, Kent: CBD Research,
1989.

Delson, Dann and Edwin Michalove
Delson's Dictionary of Cable, Video
and Satellite Terms
Thousand Oaks, CA: Bradson Press,
1983.

Department of Trade and Industry
High Definition Television (HDTV): The
Potential for Non-Broadcast
Applications
London: HMSO, 1990.

Dictionary of Image Technology
Edited by Bernard Happé
2nd edition
London; Boston: Focal Press, 1988.

Directory of African Film-Makers and
Films
Compiled and edited by Keith Shiri
Trowbridge, Wiltshire: Flicks Books,
1992.

Directory of British Associations &
Associations in Ireland
11th edition
Edited by G P Henderson and S P A
Henderson
Beckenham, Kent: CBD Research,
1992.

Directory of European Community
Trade and Professional Associations
5th edition
Luxembourg; Brussels: CEC/Editions
Delta, 1992.

Directory of European Industrial &
Trade Associations
5th edition
Edited by Robert W Adams
Beckenham, Kent: CBD Research,
1991.

Directory of European Professional &
Learned Societies
4th edition
Edited by Robert W Adams
Beckenham, Kent: CBD Research,
1989.

Directory of the Canadian Film,
Television and Video Industry 1992
Montreal: Telefilm Canada, 1992.

Dunnett, Peter J S
The World Television Industry: An
Economic Analysis
London; New York: Routledge, 1990.

Dutch Film Guide 1993
Amsterdam: Holland Film Promotion,
1993.

EOS Data and Information System
(EOSDIS) booklet
Washington: National Aeronautics and
Space Administration, 1992.

European Group of Television
Advertising (EGTA)
Television Advertising in Europe: An
Introduction to EGTA
Brussels: EGTA, 1992.

El ½: Directorio de Produccion Cine-
Video 1992
Mexico: Producciones Imaginarte,
1992.

Ellmore, R Terry
NTC's Mass Media Dictionary
Lincolnwood, Chicago: National
Textbook Company, 1991.

Encyclopedia of Associations
27th edition, 1993 (3 volumes)

Edited by Deborah M Burek
Detroit; London: Gale Research, 1992.

Ensign, Lynne Naylor and Robyn Eileen
Knapton
The Complete Dictionary of Television
and Film
New York: Stein and Day, 1985.

Eurocréation Production/IDATE
Guide du Cinéma et de l'Audiovisuel
en Europe Centrale et Orientale
Paris: Institut d'Etudes Slaves, 1992.

Euromonitor
The European Directory of Trade and
Business Associations
London: Euromonitor Publications,
1990.

The Europa World Year Book 1992
33rd edition, volume II
London: Europa Publications: 1992.

The Europa World Year Book 1993
34th edition, volume I
London: Europa Publications: 1993.

European Cable Communications 1992
Technical Programme and Exhibition
Catalogue
London: Cable Television Association,
1992.

The European Television Directory
1992
Henley-on-Thames: NTC Publications,
1992

The Evolution of CCD Imagers
Basingstoke: Sony Broadcast &
Communications, 1992.

Factfile '93
London: Independent Television
Commission, 1992.

Film + Video: Ausbildung an Schulen
für Gestaltung in der
Schweiz/Formation dans les écoles d'art

en Suisse
Lausanne: FOCAL, 1993.

Foster, Robin and Stuart Holder
Europe's Television in the 1990s:
Growth, Opportunities or Regulation?
Special Report no. 2041
London; New York: The Economist
Intelligence Unit, July 1990.

Glossary of Filmographic Terms
Brussels: FIAF, 1985.

Gordon, M, A Singleton and C Rickards
Dictionary of New Information
Technology Acronyms
2nd edition
London: Kogan Page; Detroit: Gale
Research Company, 1984.

Le Guide de l'Audiovisuel Européen
2nd edition
Brussels: Edimedia, 1991.

Hartwig, Robert L
Basic TV Technology
London; Boston: Focal Press, 1990.

Head, Sydney W
World Broadcasting Systems: A
Comparative Analysis
Belmont, California: Wadsworth
Publishing Company, 1985.

Howell, W J Jr
World Broadcasting in the Age of
Satellite: Comparative Systems, Policies,
and Issues in Mass Telecommunications
Norwood, New Jersey: Ablex
Publishing Corporation, 1986.

Howkins, John and Michael Foster
Television in 1992: a guide to Europe's
new television, film and video business
London: Coopers & Lybrand, 1989.

Hutson, Geoffrey H, Peter J Shepherd
and W S James Brice
Colour Television: System Principles,
Engineering Practice and Applied

Technology
New York: McGraw-Hill Book
Company, 1990.

IBC - International Broadcasting
Convention 1992
Technical Programme and Exhibition
Catalogue
London: IBC, 1992.

International Handbook of Broadcasting
Systems
Edited by Philip T Rosen
Westport, CT: Greenwood Press, 1988.

International Organisations
26th edition, 1992 (2 volumes)
Edited by Linda Irvin
Detroit; London: Gale Research, 1992.

International Television and Video
Almanac 1992
Edited by Barry Monush
New York: Quigley Publishing Co.,
1992.

Isailović, Jordan
Videodisc Systems: Theory &
Applications
Englewood Cliffs, New Jersey: Prentice-
Hall, 1987.

ITC Annual Report & Accounts 1992
London: Independent Television
Commission, 1993.

Japan NAB Handbook 1992/93
Tokyo: National Association of
Commercial Broadcasters in Japan,
1992.

James Capel
The James Capel Television Book
London: James Capel, 1991.

Jordan & Sons
Britain's TV and Radio Industry
Bristol: Jordan & Sons, 1991.

Jung, U O H
Elsevier's Foreign-Language Teacher's
Dictionary of Acronyms and
Abbreviations
Amsterdam: Elsevier, 1985.

Kagan World Media
European Cable Program Networks
London: Kagan World Media, 1992.

Katz, Ephraim
The Film Encyclopedia
New York: Thomas Y Crowell, 1979.

Lange, André and Jean-Luc Renaud
The Future of the European Audiovisual
Industry
Manchester: European Institute for the
Media, 1989.

Laser Satellite Communications
Edited by Morris Katzman
Englewood Cliffs, New Jersey: Prentice-
Hall, 1987.

Locksley, Professor Gareth
Television Broadcasting in Europe and
the New Technologies
Luxembourg: Office for Official
Publications of the EC, 1988.

Logica Consultancy
Television Broadcasting in Europe:
Towards the 1990s
London: Logica Consultancy, 1987.

NAB 93
Program & Buyer's Guide
Washington: National Association of
Broadcasters, 1993.

Negrine, Ralph and Stylianos
Papathanassopoulos
The Internationalisation of Television
London: Pinter Publishers, 1990.

Nielsen National Reports/Services
Directory 1992-1993
New York: Nielsen Media Research,
1992.

Noam, Eli
Television in Europe
New York; Oxford: Oxford University
Press, 1991.

MacDonald, Barrie
Broadcasting in the UK: a guide to
information sources
London; New York: Mansell Publishing,
1988.

Maggiore, Matteo
Audiovisual production in the single
market
Luxembourg: Office for Official
Publications of the European
Communities, 1990.

Maral, G and M Bousquet
Satellite Communications Systems
Translated by S David
Chichester: John Wiley & Sons, 1986.

Maybury, Richard
The Beginner's Guide to Satellite TV
Harmondsworth, Middlesex: Penguin
Books, 1987.

The Media in Western Europe: The
Euromedia Handbook
Edited by Bernt Stubbe Østergaard
London; Newbury Park; New Delhi:
Sage Publications, 1992.

The Media Map 1992
London: CIT Publications, 1992.

MEDIA: Guide for the Audiovisual
Industry
9th edition
Brussels: Commission of the European
Communities, 1993.

MEDIA Programme
Brussels: Commission of the European
Communities, 1993.

MediaNet 93
Technical Programme and Exhibition
Catalogue

Munich: MediaNet, 1993.

Millerson, Gerald
The Technique of Television Production
11th edition
Boston; London: Focal Press, 1985.

MIPCOM Guide 1992
Technical Programme and Exhibition
Catalogue
Paris: Midem Organisation, 1992.

Motion Picture Almanac 1992
Edited by Barry Monush
New York: Quigley Publishing Co.,
1992.

Multimedia 93
Event Guide
London: EMAP Maclaren, 1993.

Murith, Jean
Dictionnaire des Sigles & Abréviations
Techniques & Scientifiques
Paris: Technique & Documentation-
Lavoisier, 1982.

The National Directory of Addresses
and Telephone Numbers®
1993 edition
Detroit: Omnigraphics, 1992.

NFTU's Film and TV technical terms in
English and five Nordic languages
Stockholm: Proprius, 1983.

Oakey, Virginia
A Dictionary of Film and Television
Terms
New York: Barnes and Noble Books,
1983.

Osmańczyk, Edmund Jan
Encyclopedia of the United Nations and
International Agreements
Philadelphia; London: Taylor and
Francis, 1985.

Pan-European Associations: a directory
of multi-national organisations of

Europe
2nd edition
Researched and edited by C A P
Henderson
Beckenham, Kent: CBD Research,
1991.

Penney, Edmund F
The Facts on File Dictionary of Film
and Broadcast Terms
New York; Oxford: Facts on File, 1991.

Pim, Dennis N
Television and Teletext
Basingstoke: Macmillan Education,
1988.

Porter, Vincent
Beyond the Berne Convention:
Copyright, Broadcasting and the Single
European Market
London: John Libbey & Company,
1991.

Pritchard, Wilbur L and Joseph A Sciulli
Satellite Communication Systems
Engineering
Englewood Cliffs, New Jersey: Prentice-
Hall, 1986.

Public Broadcasting Directory 1991-
1992
Washington: Corporation for Public
Broadcasting, 1991.

Researcher's Guide to British Film &
Television Collections
4th revised edition
Edited by James Ballantye
London: British Universities Film and
Video Council, 1993.

Rumsey, Francis
Stereo Sound for Television
Boston; London: Focal Press, 1989.

Satellite Communications Systems
2nd edition
Edited by B G Evans
London: Peter Peregrinus, 1987.

SATIS Exhibition Catalogue 1993
Paris: Le Salon Européen des
Techniques de l'Image et du Son, 1993.

Scholz, Bernhard and Larin Scholz
Das Scholz Film Fernseh ABC
Hamburg: BERO-Traders SCHOLZ
Fachverlag GmbH, 1992.

Screen International Film and
Television Yearbook 1992/93
Edited by Peter Noble
London: Screen International, 1992.

Slater, James N
Cable Television Technology
Chichester: Ellis Horwood, 1988.

Slater, Jim
Modern Television Systems to HDTV
and beyond
London: Pitman Publishing, 1991.

Slater, J N and L A Trinogga
Satellite Broadcasting Systems: Planning
and Design
Chichester: Ellis Horwood, 1985.

Slide, Anthony
The International Film Industry: a
historical dictionary
Westport, Connecticut; London:
Greenwood Press, 1989.

Slide, Anthony
The International Television Industry: a
historical dictionary
Westport, Connecticut; London:
Greenwood Press, 1986.

St Maur, Suzan
The A-Z of Video and Audio-Visual
Jargon
London; New York: Routledge & Kegan
Paul, 1986.

Stephenson, D J
Newnes Guide to Satellite TV:
Installation, Reception and Repair
2nd edition

Oxford: Newnes, 1991.

Sterling, Christopher H and John M
Kittross
Stay Tuned: A Concise History of
American Broadcasting
Belmont, California: Wadsworth
Publishing Company, 1978.

Swiss Films 1993
Zürich: Swiss Film Center, 1993.

Tavenas, Stéphane and François Volard
with the collaboration of David
Laloum; translated by David Clougher
Guide of European Cinema. Production,
Financing Sources, Producers,
Distributors.
Paris: Editions Ramsay/Eurocinéma,
1989.

Teletalk: A Dictionary of Broadcasting
Terms
Compiled by Peter Jarvis
London: BBC Television Training, 1991.

Television Engineering: Broadcast,
Cable and Satellite
Edited by R S Roberts
London: Pentech Press, 1985.

Trade Associations and Professional
Bodies of the United Kingdom
10th edition
Edited by Patrica Millard
London: Gale Research International:
1991.

Trundle, Eugene
Newnes Guide to TV & Video
Technology
Oxford: Heinemann Newnes, 1988.

Union International des
Télécommunications
Répertoire Général de l'UIT / ITU
Global Directory
6th edition
Geneva: Union International des
Télécommunications (UIT), 1993.

Union of International Associations
Yearbook of International Organizations
1990/91
8th edition
Munich; New York; London; Paris: K G
Saur, 1990.

Variety International Film Guide
Edited by Peter Cowie
London: André Deutsch, 1991, 1992,
1993.

Watson, James and Anne Hill
A Dictionary of Communication and
Media Studies
London; New York; Melbourne;
Auckland: Edward Arnold, 1989.

The WBI Directory: A Guide to
International Broadcasters
Edited by Richard Measham
London: BBC Monitoring, 1992.

Weiner, Richard
Webster's New World Dictionary of
Media and Communications
New York: Webster New World: 1990.

Who Does What in Europe?: An
introduction to the cultural role and
policies of the European Community,
Council of Europe, UNESCO and other
pan-European institutions, and the
scope they provide as sources of
finance
Compiled by Rod Fisher
London: Arts Council of Great Britain,
1990.

Who's Who in Commonwealth
Broadcasting 1993
London: Commonwealth Broadcasting
Association, 1993.

Williamson, Mark
The Communications Satellite
Bristol; New York: Adam Hilger, 1990.

The World Media Handbook 1992-94
New York: United Nations, 1992.

The World of Learning 1993
43rd edition
London: Europa Publications: 1992.

World Radio and Television Handbook
1993
London: Billboard, 1992.

Wurtzel, Alan
Television Production
2nd edition
New York: McGraw-Hill Book
Company, 1985.